Mexican Democracy

Mexican Democracy

A Critical View

THIRD EDITION

Kenneth F. Johnson

Epilogue by
Robert R. Bezdek

PRAEGER

PRAEGER SPECIAL STUDIES • PRAEGER SCIENTIFIC

New York • Philadelphia • Eastbourne, UK
Toronto • Hong Kong • Tokyo • Sydney

Library of Congress Cataloging in Publication Data

Johnson, Kenneth F.
Mexican democracy.

Bibliography: p.
Includes index.
1. Mexico — Politics and government — 1970-
I. Title.
JL1231.J63 1984   972.08'3   84-11614
ISBN 0-03-064048-2
ISBN 0-03-064049-0 (pbk.)

Published in 1984 by Praeger Publisher
CBS Educational and Professional Publishing,
a Division of CBS Inc.
521 Fifth Avenue, New York, NY 10175 USA

Printed in the United States of America
on acid-free paper

Dedicated to the following persons
for their faith, encouragement, fortitude, and love:
Oscar and Elena Monroy,
Nina M. Johnson,
Andrea Louise Johnson, and
Estela Marie Johnson.

Preface and Acknowledgments

In the early days of 1984 several Mexican colleagues and I pondered Mexico's most critical needs for the 1980s. We agreed that food and overpopulation were among the greatest shortcomings, part of a worldwide crisis that is growing. With its 3.5 percent annual population growth rate, Mexico contributes mightily to the hemisphere's overpopulation problem. This is evidenced by the continuous stream of socioeconomic refugees traveling north across the border. Mexico is one of many Third World countries whose population strains the planet's food production capacity to sustain life. The earth's estimated population of 4.4 billion in 1980 should crowd 6 billion at this century's end, and Mexico could double its population in that period. Without ecological protection and expanded food supplies, life could become unlivable in Mexico and elsewhere, a situation that inevitably would spill over into the United States. Some argue that it already has and that as much as 10 percent of Mexico's 70 million plus population now lives clandestinely north of the border. Thus, the interface between Mexico and the United States is profound and likely to be permanent.

Later in 1984 other Mexican friends joined me. They were a younger group and saw birth control as vital to Mexico's national survival. We made a list of challenges that the Mexican political system must confront, vital challenges. Among them were provision of expanded secondary education, finding ways to keep Mexicans employed at home without the need for clandestine emigration, controlling inflation, ending political violence both by official and opposition groups, expanded press and political freedoms, control of the balance of payments, a war against governmental and private corruption, decentralization of industry, ending air and water pollution, improving the quality of life for peasants and the urban poor, and inevitably the shortage of food!

Many rich hours were spent with the poet-philosopher Oscar Monroy Rivera, who shared with me his impressions of a recent study trip to the Federal District, Mexico's capital, from which he returned deeply moved by the hunger prevalent in its streets, the contamination of the air, the unhealthy crush of humanity into subway tunnels and crawl-space dwellings.[1] We noted that Mexico's human crush extended north to the Texas border area with greater desperation than either of us could remember; in particular, begging had gotten much worse along the border during the last five years.[2] That time frame included a major economic boom and then a bust in Mexico, a tragic cycle tied to false hopes for petroleum-based wealth. In its aftermath thousands of businesses had collapsed, unemployment mushroomed, the peso suffered a number of severe devaluations (it was worth less than half what it had been ten years ago), and Mexico traversed its worst times since World War II. In this atmosphere the food needs of the people were not being met, and there were reasons why not.

Austerity in agricultural policy favored Mexico's landed elites, who were thriving by raising food to export to the United States. The food needs of the common people were neglected. According to an American scholar who wrote to me from Guanajuato, the peasants were in a "relentless squeeze" leading to accelerated displacement of helpless poor out of the countryside and into the larger cities where concerned social critics would recoil in shame at what was happening to their people.[3] The same American wrote me of daily local reports of land invasions, peasant seizures of government facilities, violent demonstrations, and deliberate withholding or burning of crops "by those squeezed between inflation and low guarantee prices," that is, those who had not already been driven from their land by government-protected gunmen employed by wealthy landed gentry.[4] It sounded like the inhumane conditions Emiliano Zapata had fought against during and after the Great Revolution of 1910-17. The promises of land reform and food remained a Mexican enigma.

A capital city daily appropriately lamented that in 1984 "30 million persons will be in the situation of being unable to provide themselves with a satisfactory level of food."[5] The figure 30 million is shocking compared with Mexico's estimated 70 million total population in 1984; this includes the alleged 3 to 10 million residing clandestinely in the United States. But even that figure would be eroded away. The U.S. Immigration Service, called *La Migra* in Mexico, was deporting in excess of one million illegal aliens annually. Most of these were Mexican citizens. They needed money not just for themselves but to send to dependents in Mexico. Some also came to avail themselves of medical and social services in the United States.[6] And a backlash was growing against the clandestine immigrants on the U.S. side. Stiff legislation to end such migration continued to be debated in Congress.

Our conversations drifted to the emerging phenomenon of a Fourth World—refugees, disadvantaged and persecuted ethnic groups, economic and political victims displaced from Third World countries like Mexico. We were subsequently joined by the novelist Marco Antonio Jerez and the historian Kieran McCarty who shared our concerns for the disadvantaged. It seemed that American foreign policy in Central America was creating hungry refugees swarming through Mexico and into the United States. The Border Patrol noted a sharp increase in the numbers of Central American refugees being apprehended at the border. Might not the billions being spent to fight communism in Central America be more wisely invested in combating hunger throughout the entire region? Did not the channeling of this money through the hands of repressive military governments in Central America merely create an atmosphere of desperation favorable to the growth of communism? And was there not reason to fear that Mexico's own military establishment might come out of the barracks and enter the political arena should the Central American conflict spread to Mexico's southern border?

As these talks among old friends and colleagues wore on, and we took stock of our own trials and setbacks, it seemed that all of us were somewhat better off now than five years before. But this was not true of the people of Mexico and their displaced neighbors to the south. As we shared many sobering doubts and fears, I grew perplexed by my own feeling of inadequacy to help these displaced Mexicans and Central Americans. But there were those who were trying to do so in concrete terms. Prominent among them was the Reverend John Fife and his Tucson, Arizona, refugee center, then helping to spread the ethic of a new religious sanctuary movement in open defiance of the U.S. government. Rev. Fife believed that the Christian ecumenical revolutionary movement was the one force destined to undermine and replace both repressive communism and capitalism in Latin America, a long-term apocalyptic view with deep moral and political elements. Meanwhile, more concretely, American immigration and refugee laws were being challenged; the work of God was on a collision course with officialdom. This was a grass roots movement for policy change. Could not similar forces be evoked in Mexico? Perhaps, indeed, they had been!

Such a possibility is really what this third edition of *Mexican Democracy* has been revised to show: that forces for political change have emerged in Mexico, despite the severe distress into which its social and economic systems have plunged.[7] This is also a somewhat more optimistic view of Mexican socioeconomic and political development than I expressed in the previous two editions. Although in socioeconomic terms things have undoubtedly gotten much worse in Mexico since the last edition, it seems that advances have been made toward political pluralism and toward popular redress of grievances. I assume that any steps toward incorporating more people into the political process and toward solving their perceived socioeconomic problems are positive ones. But there is a long and difficult road ahead. The major challenges along that way are treated in the pages to follow; and although Oscar Monroy and I may wax hopeful, it is at best a shaky hope and full of caveats.

A number of persons contributed importantly to this revised work but they are exempt from liability for its errors and shortcomings. Valuable criticism came from political scientists Roderic Camp and Stephen Mumme, historian Don Mabry, and economist John Barchfield. The writing progressed during a difficult period of health for the author and the revision would not have been completed without the support of my wife, Nina M. Johnson, whose contribution to my health, the research, and the manuscript preparation was of major proportions. The splendid Ozark countryside around Hermann, Missouri, provided a background for much of the writing; there I benefitted from the Third World–related wisdom and insight of a unique folk artist, Charles R. Skelton, whose friendship and encouragement will not be forgotten.

In New York, Dorothy Breitbart and Karen Louise Hansen provided highly valued encouragement and criticism. A trip into northern Mexico, along the border area, and especially to Arizona provided me with additional bibliographic resources and human testimony. Since the last edition an assortment of material has reached me from the Mexican capital via Oscar Monroy, Raúl González Schmal, and several friends in the Mexican government who asked to remain anonymous. The overall effort has resulted in a book of which some 60 percent is new or updated.

Special gratitude is owed to Robert Bezdek who wrote the epilogue based on his ongoing research in San Luis Potosí, the scene of one of Mexico's most notable contemporary locally based drives toward political pluralism. Some of the optimism contained in this edition is inspired by Bezdek's work and by the promise of those important recent events. I benefitted also from the critical insights of Sergio Tristán, Ricardo Flores, and Mizrahim Borboa. The final writing was done on the Great Plains while the author worked during 1984 on a study of Spanish-speaking migrants. My warmest thanks go to James McKenney, John Hartman, David Farnsworth, Sherri Bayouth, and other fine colleagues at Wichita State University for sharing their ideas and resources with me.

Some day I shall be able to thank individually a considerable group of illegal Mexican aliens whose friendship I have cultivated in order to study the phenomenon in which they find their lives enmeshed. Several of these IMAs brought me their favorite protective amulet from the Virgin of San Juan de Los Lagos along with personal blessings, an honor I can best reciprocate by not directly naming these dignified sojourners who till America's soil and harvest her crops. Nonetheless, they provide a living interface between our two nations that should be recognized, even honored.

Kenneth F. Johnson
Wichita State University

NOTES

1. The previous edition of *Mexican Democracy* devoted the better part of a chapter to the life and works of Oscar Monroy Rivera. In recent years he has had the satisfaction of seeing his campaign for public decency in Nogales, Sonora achieve some fruition. Also, Monroy has been recognized prominently at the national level in Mexico for his civic work, his social criticism, and for his writing. See *Diorama Excelsior*, May 23, 1982, and the longer interview concerning Monroy's bilingual poetry venture "New Kauri" by Ricardo Castillo Mireles in *Excelsior*, June 15, 1982. I now have in progress a translation of his *El profeta del silencio* that will appear along with a biography of Monroy and a sociopolitical analysis of the community environment in which he lives and works.
2. *El Fronterizo* (Chihuahua), January 9, 1984.
3. John W. Barchfield to Kenneth F. Johnson, January 6, 1984.
4. John W. Barchfield, "The Continuity of Injustice: Agrarian and Alimentary Policies of the New Mexican Administration," typescript, p. 9, publication forthcoming in *Journal of Economic Issues,* courtesy of J.W. Barchfield.
5. An editorial in *Uno Mas Uno,* January 8, 1984.
6. See Marvin Alisky, "Migration and Unemployment in Mexico," *Current History*, 82 (1983): 430.
7. A Mexican skeptic believes that his people are hopelessly "trained" to accept corruption in the political system and to sell themselves to power rather than compete for its control. The system of opposition parties is a pantomime without substance. But things in Mexico have worsened to the point that voting for the PAN (National Action Party) opposition in northern Mexico has become a convenient way for people to register their disapproval of the status quo monopoly of power by the single dominant party PRI (Institutional Revolutionary Party). However, if the concept of people's solidarity gains ground from the various recent opposition wins then a truly unique solution may emerge in Mexico. People's solidarity, the marginal people as a mass organization, holds the only potential force capable of countervailing established regime control. This dim skeptical hope is increasingly heard in Mexico today. See Rodrigo Saldaña Guerrero, "Alternativas para un pueblo indefenso," *Solidarismo,* No. 11, October, 1983, pp. 9–13.

Contents

List of Abbreviations

ABM	Mexican Bankers Association
ACM	Mexican Catholic Action
AMS	Mexican Insurance Association
Banrural	Rural Bank
CAMCO	American Chamber of Commerce (in Mexico)
CANACINTRA	National Chamber for Industrial Transformation
CARG	Assistance Coordinator for Guatemalan Refugees in Mexico
CCE	Business Coordinating Council
CCI	Independent Peasant Central (syndicate)
CCM	Mexican Peasants Confederation
CEIMSA	Mexican National Import–Export Company
CEN	National Executive Committee (PRI)
CIANO	Northwest Center for Agricultural Research
CMHN	Mexican Businessmen's Council
CNA	National Agrarian Commission
CNAC	National Committee for Hearings and Consultation
CNC	National Peasants Confederation (PRI)
CNED	National Confederation of Democratic Students
CNG	National Cattlemens' Association
CNH	National Strike Committee
CNOP	National Confederation of Popular Organizations (PRI)
CNPA	National Coordinator for the Plan of Ayala

CNPP	National Confederation of Small Property Owners
COCEI	Coalition of Workers, Peasants, and Students of the Isthmus
COM	World Labor House
CONAMUP	National Coordinator of Popular Urban Movements
CONASUPO	National Staple Foodstuffs Company
CONCAMIN	Confederation of Industrial Chambers of Commerce
CONCANACO	Confederation of National Chambers of Commerce
COPARMEX	Confederation of Mexican Employers
CROM	Regional Confederation of Mexican Workers
CTM	Mexican Workers Confederation (PRI)
DAAC	Department of Agrarian Affairs and Colonization
DINA	National Diesel Industries of Mexico
FAIR	Federation for American Immigration Reform
FCI	Independent Peasant Front
FCP	Potosinan Civic Front
FEP	Popular Electoral Front
FITIM	International Industrial Metalworkers Federation
FNET	National Federation of Technical Students
FONAFE	National Fund for Ejido Development
FSI	Independent Syndicate Front
FSTSE	Federation of Syndicates of Workers in the Service of the State
IMA(s)	illegal Mexican aliens
IMF	International Monetary Fund
IMSS	Mexican Social Security Institute
INEA	National Adult Education Institute
INFONAVIT	Institute for the National Housing Fund for Workers

INS	Immigration and Naturalization Service (U.S.)
IPN	National Polytechnic Institute
ISSSTE	Social Service Institute for State Employees
LEA	Luis Echeverría Alvarez
LNC	National Peasant League
LULAC	League of United Latin American Citizens (U.S.)
Nacional Financiera	National Development Bank
OIPUH	Independent Organization of United Huasteca Peoples
OPEC	Organization of Petroleum Exporting Countries
PAN	National Action Party
PCM	Mexican Communist Party
PDM	Mexican Democratic Party
PDP	Democratic Potosinan Party
PEMEX	Mexican Petroleum Company (state-owned)
PGR	Attorney General of the Republic
PLM	Mexican Labor Party
PMT	Mexican Workers Party
PNA	National Agrarian Party
PND	National Democratic Party
PNR	National Revolutionary Party (predecessor to PRI)
PPS	Popular Socialist Party
PRI	Institutional Revolutionary Party (the dominant governing party and institution in Mexico since 1929, previously known as PNR and PRM)
PRM	Revolutionary Mexican Party (predecessor to PRI)
PSR	Socialist Revolutionary Party
PST	Socialist Workers Party
PSUM	Unified Mexican Socialist Party
SAM	Mexican Nutritional System
SARH	Secretariat of Agriculture and Hydraulic (WATER) Resources
SCGF	Ministry of the Federal Controller General

SEP	Secretariat of Public Education
SICARTSA	The Lázaro Cárdenas Steel Complex
SNDE	National Syndicate of Educational Workers
SNTE	National Syndicate of Educational Employees
SRA	Secretariat of Agrarian Reform
SSA	Secretariat of Health and Assistance
STPRM	Petroleum Workers Syndicate of the Mexican Republic
STUNAM	Employees Syndicate of the National University of Mexico
SUTERM	Electric Workers United Syndicate of the Mexican Republic
UCP	Potosinan Civic Union
UGOCM	General Union of Mexican Workers and Peasants
UNAM	National Autonomous University of Mexico
UNS	National Sinarquisa Union
WHO	World Health Organization

Glossary

agraristas   those with agrarian political interests and allegiances
aguardiente   a strong popular alcoholic drink
alcaldía   a municipal subdivision of the audiencia (similar to *corregimientos*)
altiplano   highlands
amparo   Mexican legal remedy (writ, injunction, habeas corpus, etc.)
apertura democrática   democratic openness
arriba y adelante   campaign slogan of Luis Echeverría Alvarez
asentamientos ilegales   illegal or squatter settlements
audiencias   an administrative subdivision of New Spain to facilitate control by the crown
autocrítica   self-criticism
aviador(es)   phantom bureaucrats receiving a contrived salary for little or no work
aviadura   a fake job and/or wage
baldíos   idle nationally owned lands
Banco Agrícola'   Agriculture Bank
Banco Ejidal   Ejido Bank
barrio   neighborhood
cacique   political boss
camarillas   power cliques
campesino   peasant-farmer
caudillo   military leader or head of state
Central de Abastos   food distribution center of CONASUPO
charros   official PRI-sponsored labor syndicates
corregimiento   a local jurisdiction in New Spain with primary control by the crown
cristeros   soldiers of Christ in the 1920s and thereafter, restorationists and fundamentalists
curandero   faith healer, sometimes called sorcerer
dedazo   authoritarian designation of one's successor (or of a person to fill a given position)
desaforado   stripped of congressional immunity
desmayada   faltering
despojo   forced seizure of land
destape   the unveiling of a presidential candidate
diputados de partido   at-large congressional representatives

ejido   a system of communal farms and/or individual farms with titles granted, controlled, and (nominally) supported by the state

el corcholatazo   the unveiling of José López Portillo as candidate

embute   bribe paid to journalists for favorable reporting

enanismo   dwarfishness

encomienda   a land grant system in New Spain carrying rights to exploit Indians as laborers

engranaje propio   popular grass roots support

estanquillo   open-air vending booth

gachupines   European-born Spaniards holding political power in Mexico

Gobernación   an executive branch of government (roughly Interior and Justice plus CIA combined in U.S. comparison)

guayabera   Luis Echeverría's shirt sleeve informal political style, named for the tropical shirt *guayabera*

hacendado   large-scale land owner

hazaña   exploit, feat

jacquerie   a popular (peasant) uprising

latifundio   large land holding

levantadedos   finger-raising yes-men

los intocables   the untouchables

los penecilinos   an elite management crew within the military

machismo   political intransigence (male domination) refusal to compromise

malinchismo   collaboration with foreign influences

maquiladora (maquila)   the Mexican part of twin plant border industries

Maximato   the period of Calles' political domination in the 1920s

mordida   bribe (bite)

municipio   municipality (city-county combined in U.S. comparison)

Nacional Financiera   National Development Bank

navista   followers of Dr. Salvador Nava

Opus Dei   God's Work, a right-wing Catholic socioeconomic and political organization with international scope

panista   member-follower of the PAN

paracaidismo   squatting, illegal land invasion

paraestatal(es)   state-run economic enterprises

peninsulares   Spaniards born in Spain who migrated to early Mexico

pepenador   trash scavenger

plazas   real jobs or positions

porros   organized student paramilitary squads

presidentes de dedo   imposed presidents

presidio   frontier garrison used to protect colonists in New Spain

prestanombres   those loaning their names to foreigners

priista   member-follower of the PRI
Procuraduría   Attorney General's office
pulque   a strong popular (often illegal) alcoholic drink
regente   mayor of Mexico's Federal District
repartimiento   a system of forced labor assignment in New Spain
rurales   mercenary rural police employed by the dictator Porfirio Díaz
sacadólares   those who sneak their dollars out of Mexico
sexenio   six-year presidential term
sinarquistas   members of the UNS
soberbia   haughtiness
tapadismo   the practice of using tapados in the nomination-electoral practice
tapado   the veiled one(s) or candidate
Televisa   a television chain of major economic importance often serving official PRI interests
tlatoani   Aztec sacrificial priest
vendepatria   selling out one's country
verdadero tapado   the true veiled candidate
Zócalo   the central plaza of a Mexican town, especially the capital city

One

Mexican Political Life:
A Contemporary Profile

POLITICAL ENIGMAS AND QUALITY OF LIFE
REALITIES IN THE 1980S

Since the Spaniards conquered Mexico in the early sixteenth century successive stewards of power have struggled and floundered at the task of nation building. It is difficult for a nation to emerge without leaders to mold a popular consensus. A benevolent monarch, or benevolent and caring colonial administrators, might have legitimized the state through popularly held supportive feelings, attitudes, and civic participation. There have been periods in Mexican history when important steps were made toward the building of such a popular consensus, as during the Reform Era of the mid-nineteenth century. But always there emerged from the Mexican populace conniving figures like Antonio López de Santa Anna, Porfirio Díaz, and Plutarco Elías Calles, whose allegiance was owed primarily to themselves and their supporting cliques or *camarillas* rather than to the citizenry as a whole. Among Mexican leaders, personal goals came to rival public morality and often replaced it. Law as the basis for an ordered society was often usurped by greed and violent force. It is an open question for historians whether Mexicans have died more often in their allegiance to the personal ambitions of short-sighted leaders or through pursuit of broad ideas in quest of the ever fleeting "good life." The political enigmas and quality of life realities of Mexico in the 1980s are inextricably wed to this historical drama. It is Mexico's continuing, difficult story.

Part of that story takes form in the role intellectuals have come to play in today's Mexico. One contemporary scholar-critic, Enrique Krauze, finds that his nation's writers, poets, philosophers, and educated civic leaders have not shaped currents of change as has been the case in other societies, including some other Latin American countries. He finds that most of the Mexican intellectual left now depends on the state's budget, that their political parties lack genuine popular support, and they are distant from the poignant concrete realities of misery and suffering in Mexico's daily life. Further, he contends, Mexico has failed to develop a populist intellectual tradition, which is surprising given Mexico's predominantly agrarian peasant population throughout history. "Many of today's social problems are rooted in the failure of . . . [Mexico's] intellectuals to recognize the country's rural culture as something valuable in its own right."[1] Instead the Mexican countryside has been pillaged, despoiled, and the best of it appropriated by oligopolists with selfish ends. The public good has too often been identified with the comfort of elites, and intellectuals themselves have become largely a privileged elite.

Another way of putting this might be to say that since Mexico's intellectuals have for the most part become appendages of the state, they have been unable to insist independently that law and morality be incorporated into the state's guiding norms. The essay by Krauze argues that the Mexican state helps proliferate intellectuals, often in the form of technocrats, via subsidized educational programs both domestically and abroad. The state then tries to absorb these progeny, almost incestuously, and "in a Kafkaesque net of loyalties, it is unlikely they will be able to introduce real or substantial changes, no matter what the amount of money spent on their training."[2] Those who depend economically and socially on the state have a natural tendency to revere it. To question this reverence, or openly disparage it, becomes ipso facto sedition. But there is much more than just the cooptation of intellectual energies and skills underlying Mexico's present condition as a pariah nation, resting nervously while the sprouts of major social upheaval emerge. There is also a basic, perhaps noncognitive, human psychological factor.

For many years I have felt that something deeply ingrained in the Mexican psyche impedes the functioning of law and morality as bases of a political system designed to bring about socioeconomic justice. That belief was reinforced when one of Mexico's greatest living thinkers, the novelist Carlos Fuentes, told a Kansas audience in the spring of 1984 that "intelligence in the United States is equated with industriousness, but intelligence in Mexico is equated with maliciousness," to paraphrase his comment. Although it is a poor omen for Mexico, I take some reassurance when a 74-year-old Mexican jurisconsult, born at the onset of the great revolution of 1910-17, independently volunteers a further corroborating view. He is Raúl F. Cárdenas and the term he chooses to capture this feeling is "Machiavellianism," which defines the reason, he says, why Mexican politics have been perverted so as to keep law and morals at the very margin of public life.[3] Why should Mexicans be more Machiavellian than other nations? Cárdenas has not said that Mexicans are intrinsically Machiavellian; he said that Machiavellianism has permeated Mexico and has kept the political system from developing on the basis of law and morality. I suspect that the psychic baggage of Mexicans harbors the causal factor. Carlos Fuentes seems to agree.

This cannot be demonstrated without the extensive collaboration of humanistic philosophers, poets, and scholar-writers. Nor would that collaboration be complete without a substantial input from clinical psychology and psychiatric medicine. Proof, thus, will be long in coming; but that fact makes the basic suspicion no less worthy of contemplation. There is obviously something quite fundamentally and painfully wrong in Mexico today if we are to believe the protestations, and the suffering, of the Mexicans themselves. There is surely nothing ethnocentric about the observation that Mexico's quest for the good life has been stymied.

A noted American scholar wrote to me that grounds exist for believing that in the colonial period of Mexican history there was less corruption and more respect for civil liberties than in present-day Mexico.[4] That issue is more correctly left to the province of historians, yet it tends to support the contentions of Raúl Cárdenas as to long-range trends toward socioeconomic and political atrophy in Mexico. Cárdenas alleges that "hatreds have been created, not class but personal hatreds, and the economic, social, and political crises of Mexico have turned them against solidarity and toward individualistic, egoistic, and apathetic behavior" that leaves humans with little but desperation.[5] Thus, he contends, people in Mexico today accept fraud, terrorism, even bodies lying in the street with no public show of pity, as facts of life. This sounds very much like a war of all against all, in which almost everyone is certain to lose. If we had a true democracy, says Cárdenas, the pressure of public conscience would be enough to change governments or bring about reform without spilling blood. But in Mexico, he adds, those who govern lead us about like a flock of sheep. And speaking of the recently departed presidential regime he states categorically "never, as under the government of José López Portillo was there a situation of such lawlessness."[6] Where, we ask, are Mexico's intellectuals? Are they all government dependents as Krauze alleges? Do any of them care for the poor masses?

There is abundant evidence pointing to political alienation and social despair as constants in contemporary Mexican life. Some intellectuals have taken up that theme. In the mid-1950s, the Mexican essayist Juan Rulfo published a collection of short stories which hammered out the bitterly pathetic theme of utter despair pervading the lives of rural Mexicans, a curse from which seemingly there was no escape. Thirty years later, in 1983, it is hard to see that the quality of life has changed much for most Mexicans, perhaps even for as many as 80 percent of them. That is not an ethnocentric American view but a widely shared Mexican conviction both within and outside that nation's governing circles. Rulfo's vision was that too much of Mexico was an inhospitable burning plain from which people had to migrate. Often they went to Mexico City, the locus of power, in the hope that some largesse of that center would trickle outward and downward. Land was given to the peasants to keep them happy, but nobody said anything about guaranteed irrigation, or fertilizer, or credit. The countryside was threatening, the earth was hard and washed away: "we don't think the plow will cut into the earth of the Plain that's like a rock quarry. . . ." But when the people complained, they heard "you can state that in writing. And now you can go. You should be attacking the large-estate owners and not the government that is giving you the land. Wait, Sir! We haven't said anything against the Center. It's all against the Plain. You can't do anything when there's nothing to work with."[7]

At times Rulfo's Mexicans look beyond the horrors of the plain. It symbolizes life's orbit for most of them. Life is not entirely without beauty; there are "colors running serpentine through the sky . . . [then] the sun bursts forth, making the blades of grass glisten."[8] Nature's inspiration is there to give the Mexicans a fleeting hope, as is the superstitious faith that keeps them going, travelling on to their guilt, toward knowing death.[9] The Mexicans must fight for recognition, for a cause, "and even if we don't have any flag right now to fight for, we must hurry and pile up money, so when the government troops come they'll see that we're powerful."[10] Thus the struggle is confessed to be for the support of mankind more than for ideas. But whatever the horizon, its refuge is dimmed or interdicted by that power emanating from the center, Mexico City, the all powerful seat of government, whose decrees are usually final for that impoverished peasant mass of the population. For them Mexico City sends out few or no streams of satisfactions, as social scientists are wont to call them. Few happiness decrees come from the troubled center, a city today of monstrous proportions that is largely cold and insensitive, or to borrow Rulfo's words once again and juxtapose them, a city "wrapped in ashy smog . . . the place where sorrow nests."[11]

If Mexico lacks an intelligentsia that works as a force for real change, and if the nation is ruled by a center that shows no pity and welcomes no criticism, then the capital city itself may become a kind of barometer for the quality of life and for political volatility. Contemporary Mexican critics write of the anarchy of Mexico City.[12] The capital is an appropriate place to begin in explaining why the way to the good life in Mexico is still an enigma, probably a permanent one, especially now some 30 years after Juan Rulfo's brooding assessment appeared. The seat of government is still called "the Center" by contemporary analysts. Political power begins in the capital. Mexico City dictates major official candidacies in even the most distant states and for most contests being named a candidate is the same as winning, although there are signs that this traditional pattern might be giving way. Resentment is widely expressed over political impositions from the center. A controversial federal senator from Sonora, at the very time he was the focus of a national corruption scandal in 1981, was easily imposed by Mexico City on that distant northern state. Although the senator may have been born in Sonora, "he never lived there, no one knows him as a friend nor if he owns property there . . . in short he is a Sonoran from '*allá*,' from there, the distant center, from where he was sent to conduct his political campaign."[13] It is from the center that all major administrative posts are filled as well. State and local governments do have powers of appointment, at least on paper, but they can be and are usurped regularly by the national government. The president of Mexico can and does intervene in states to depose an elected governor if he chooses. Governors can ruin and/or depose local mayors.

The center is also a gigantic magnet attracting the dispossessed and unfortunate from throughout the Mexican countryside. Competing regional magnets are Guadalajara and Monterrey. The northern border area also attracts Mexico's economic refugees by the millions. Mexico is fast becoming an urban country. At the beginning of the twentieth century Mexico's rural population, living in towns of 2000 or less, accounted for some 80 percent of the national total. By 1975 over 60 percent of the national population lived in those larger population centers that the Mexican government considered urban.[14] Clearly the rural cultural tradition of Mexico is being lost. It is foreseen that with present migratory tendencies continuing, by the year 2000 only 20 percent of Mexico's population will be considered rural. That 20 percent may also be the only ones breathing relatively clean air. As any recent visitor to Mexico City can readily vouch, the capital city's air is horrendously polluted from unplanned industrial growth and the absence of smog control measures that in other parts of the world have been successfully imposed on automobiles. There are numerous claims that Mexico City has the dirtiest air in the entire world, a major quality of life factor in itself.

The capital city presents great contrasts of conspicuous affluence and poverty. The majority of its inhabitants live in squalor. Some 30 percent of the capital's population consists of immigrants from other parts of the country drawn by the cruel illusion of opportunity. Some 20 percent of all Mexicans (including Mexico City) live in Mexico City. Around 60 percent of all Mexicans live on the high plateau or *altiplano* surrounding Mexico City and about 80 percent of the nation's industrial activity goes on there as well. The ingredients for pollution, for human contamination, overcrowding, interpersonal conflict, and societal neuroses are all present in great abundance.

Mexico's 1983-4 estimated national population is around 70 million with a 3.5 percent annual increase. The total national population is expected to double in 20 years providing there are no drastic changes in the rate of population growth or in the extent of Mexican emigration, principally to North America. Mexican emigration is the topic of a separate chapter in this book. Less is known quantitatively about immigration into Mexico, especially from Central America. This, as will be noted presently, could affect Mexico's future population statistics.

Mexico City had an estimated 17 million inhabitants in 1983. This included both the Federal District and the immediate environs that constitute the larger metropolitan area. Admittedly there is some arbitrary judgment involved in arriving at that population figure. If one were to include the entire altiplano surrounding the Mexican capital the figure would be much higher. This population constellation consumes 35 percent of the national food production and 25 percent of Mexico's estimated total urban water supply.[15]

From the time of the Spanish conquest in the early 1500s until the middle of the present century the inhabited part of Mexico City grew to 24,000 hectares. Then, from 1953 to 1980, it more than doubled to 67,000 hectares.[16] Preliminary figures from the 1980 census indicated that since 1971 the center area grew by 84,541 inhabitants from rural-to-urban migration alone. Some 62 percent of the economically active population in the Mexico City area is either unemployed or underemployed. This represents 22 percent of the national work force and 43 percent of the work force population of major urban centers. Some of the unemployed could be hired to perform public sanitation chores, for it is estimated that 75 percent of Mexico City's trash and garbage is dumped in exposed open areas and that 25 percent of it is left to rot in the public street.[17]

The Federal District metropolitan area has only 13,000 hectares left of its original green forest and oxygen-producing areas, meaning that just 3.3 percent of the present urban area can be considered "green."[18] Air pollution damages both vegetation and humans, and some 600 tons of contaminants are sent airborne daily. As Mexico City has spilled over into the adjacent state of Mexico most ejidal properties (rural cooperative and collective farms) that might have been used for multifamily dwellings have been acquired largely for luxury homes, businesses, and industries. This leaves at least 50 percent of the total population of 17 million living in marginal areas that are considered slums by Mexican standards; people residing in those areas constitute what has been called *poblaciones manicomaniales,* madhouse societies, in which criminal behavior, child abuse, and diverse psychiatric illnesses are rife.[19] Nor are conditions expected to improve during the remainder of the twentieth century. According to one source:

Mexico City is not a unique case (among Third World nations) but it is an extreme one. According to United Nations predictions it will become the world's most populated city by the year 2000. Although local urban specialists are hoping that the figure will be less than predicted, it is expected that Mexico City will then have 31 million inhabitants.[20]

In such an environment the doomsday visions of Juan Rulfo are firmly anchored in contemporary urban reality. It is therefore amazing that Mexicans in such great numbers continue to migrate into the capital.

But quality of life realities in the countryside explain why so many Mexicans do in fact migrate desperately into the Mexico City conglomerate. In the nearby state of Hidalgo peasants have organized into a rural protective association known as OIPUH (*Organización Independiente de Pueblos Unidos de las Huastecas*) which defends local villagers against the rural bosses or *caciques* in the Huasteca region. The leaders of OIPUH claimed in 1983 to have recaptured by invasion 23,000 hectares of land taken illegally from them by the caciques. That would have been nearly the size of the Mexico City area for 1953. Héctor Martínez, a spokesman for OIPUH, claims that the proof of his organization's success lies in the de facto militarization of the region which the caciques have persuaded the government to carry out without formally declaring a state of seige.[21] Publications and notices of OIPUH have been confiscated and burned, members of the group have been tortured. Promised irrigation and food storage projects started by the government have been cut short because funds ran out or "disappeared," schools that were started remain unfinished, promised drinking water never arrived and people drank from ditches; finally a drought forced the Hidalgo peasants to look for their own solution by forming the OIPUH organization, which celebrated the sixth anniversary of its founding in May of 1983.[22]

The organization says it has been forced by the Mexican government to become clandestine. Extreme precautions were taken in permitting a reporter to visit their annual assembly. Some of the old ones said they remembered how the caciques treated the Indians around the time of the revolution: "they got us drunk with *aguardiente* only to kill whomever they could later on and take their lands."[23] They related having passed years of peonage at no more pay than 80 centavos per day while beseeching the center for relief through the agrarian reform program. No one in the government responded, not even into the 1980s when hunger moved the Indian peasants to collective forceful action. The governor of Hidalgo has two options, according to the militants of Huasteca: "destroy OIPUH or respect us."[24] That would imply respect from the federal administration as well.

One of their leaders is Alejandro Hernández Dolores who allegedly deserted from the Mexican army. But the Indians say he is not a guerrilla as the government claims, he is just one of them, he represents their interests, and he, like OIPUH, is not just a regional happening but is part of an uprising that spreads out across the country via the CNPA (*Coordinadora Nacional Plan de Ayala*) or National Coordinator of the Plan of Ayala. Symbolically the Indians have tied their movement to the historical promise of freedom and justice embodied in Emiliano Zapata's original Plan de Ayala of 1911. In that year Zapata, the symbolic father of armed agrarian liberation, published a declaration saying that Mexico's lands and water were monopolized by a very few Mexicans, and that these would be expropriated by his agrarian rebels to create farms, *ejidos,* colonies, townsites, and tillable lands. He also declared that all those opposing the *Plan de Ayala* would have their properties seized.[25] Thus a precedent for land seizure by dispossessed peasants was well rooted in Mexico's revolutionary tradition. No wise Mexican official today would take the name of Zapata in vain, so powerful and revered is that symbol, yet many would strenuously object to contemporary actions carried out in his name.

That was the Mexican government's dilemma in 1983 as peasants in Hidalgo and elsewhere rose up in the name of Zapata. In Hidalgo the government, both state and federal, offered the peasants token land and medical treatment in efforts to quell their resistance, but these offers were refused. Troops were also sent to protect federal officials who made other offers including schools, corn, clinics, and safe drinking water. The uprising caused concern. An armed clash took place between armed government agents and peasants in which one peasant died and members of the PDM, the Mexican Democratic Party, were expelled from one town. Their homes were subsequently ordered destroyed by the government. Many peasants were pressed into forced labor for the caciques and their women allegedly violated by soldiers. One peasant leader, Domingo Hernández, was taken up in a government helicopter and told he must promise to give up the resistance or be dropped out in mid-air.[26] The rural loan bank known as *Banrural* pressured the peasants for money loaned for the purchase of cattle; but there was no legal recourse against any of these abuses. There was no political party to represent their interests. The governor, Rossell de la Llama, had, through his persecution, turned the Indians of the Huasteca into guerrillas despite themselves: "each one of us is now an Alejandro Hernández Dolores."[27] Sadly, there is still poverty, disease, and desperate want in the Mexican countryside despite all the utopian promises made since the Revolution of 1910 swept across the Mexican landscape.

Mexico's urban areas are also scenes of human crisis as Mexico City amply testifies. The urban needy have also organized for self-defense outside the official power structure. This can most readily be seen in the CONAMUP (*Coordinadora Nacional del Movimiento Urbano Popular*) which also celebrated its fourth national meeting in the Federal District in May of 1983. This was an assembly of persons representing the small businessmen, housewives, artisans, and slum residents of Mexico's many urban areas whose common cause was the alarming lack of public services, uncertainty of land tenure, protection of renters, underemployment, inflation, the allegedly deliberately caused scarcity of basic staple goods, and the indifference of governing bureaucracies in meeting the needs of the urban masses.[28] These poor people are also disillusioned with promises from political parties, including those on the left, and have found limited satisfaction only in forming small pressure and protective organizations of their own. They have varied names ranging from the Popular Front for Land and Liberty of Monterrey, the Popular Defense Committee of Durango, the Popular Front of Zacatecas, and the Union of Peoples' Colonies of the Valley of Mexico. Under the aegis of CONAMUP these groups held their first national reunion in Monterrey in 1980 and have met annually since then. They believe that the government, tied to servicing the foreign debt and wasting the remainder of its revenue through corruption, can offer only ideological palliatives and repression.[29] These urban movements are not yet clandestine as has occurred in the countryside.

Everywhere urban Mexicans feel they are being strangled as the quality of life worsens. They are extorted by urban transit systems and by the police, medical care is either inadequate or nonexistent, in many proletarian suburbs the running water works only from one to three o'clock in the morning while in the wealthy communities like Pedregal in Mexico City it runs all the time. The ex-mayor of the Federal District, Carlos Hank González, is believed to have enriched himself by creating false water shortages, then selling water, and by forcing poor *colonos* off their land to build housing complexes for the wealthy. Repression for these people is not just something accomplished by force. Repression means the absence of basic human services. It also appears in the form of judicial corruption. When annual rent increases inevitably result in delinquency of payment, lawyers and judges arrange to have civil proceedings turned into criminal charges of *despojo* or forced seizure of land. Inevitably the police are sent to force the renters out of their miserable shelters. When Sergio Alcazar, a member of the political party PSUM (Unified Socialist Party of Mexico), defended the protective actions of CONAMUP he was jailed, leading to speculation that the urban defense organization had ties with that party. This CONAMUP denies, but it has no confidence in the new urban officials of the ruling PRI who have not bettered the quality of life any more than did their predecessors[30] (under one name or other the

PRI, Institutional Revolutionary Party, has governed Mexico since 1929).

Inevitably, perhaps, groups like CONAMUP are targets for infiltration by the more extremist elements of the Marxist left. Examination of the publication *Pueblo,* which appears in the Federal District, supports this. A special edition appearing in 1983 and circulated about Mexico carried Marxist symbols and rhetoric while supporting CONAMUP and other citizens' protective groups, by name. The publication purports to offer only "information" to the reader and describes the ways the "bourgeois press" confuses the public by "mixing up the news." It offers instruction on how to report information affecting worker solidarity including disappearances, strikes, contamination, etc. It contains poetry (from the *Pueblos del Sur de Veracruz*—Villages of Southern Veracruz) decrying repression against the working class without stating exactly who is to blame. All the content is oriented toward worker solidarity and the class struggle. Letters from revolutionary groups in Guatemala and Peru are reprinted. Mexican revolutionary symbolism (pictures of Emiliano Zapata) is used; but the hammer and sickle are also there, almost subliminally.[31] Perhaps the question of CONAMUP's affiliation with the far left should be left open as of this writing; the issue may, of course, invite future hostility from the Mexican regime.

Here it is well to summarize the political realities that allow Mexico's quality of life to continue at its depressed level well into the 1980s. In closing one chapter of the previous edition of *Mexican Democracy* I saw a potential ray of hope in the presidential succession of 1976 which brought José López Portillo to power in Mexico City. He was the first Mexican president to have come directly to power from a cabinet position as finance minister and who had little or no previous political experience via electoral channels. There was reason to expect that López Portillo might bring sound fiscal management to Mexico and promote humane social goals. I hoped then that the new president would have the genius to bring Mexico out of its economic malaise. Perhaps the then newly projected oil revenues would do the trick. But I also stipulated that the economic malaise was "intimately linked with corruption, a social and political malaise. If Mexico's suffering millions are to have a glimpse of hope within the next decade, the politics of plunder and poverty will have to undergo radical and lasting changes in their operating norms."[32] But those norms did not change under López Portillo and my expressed glimmer of hope for political reform in Mexico died out.

As these lines are written, former president López Portillo has become the target of a general public repudiation which is national in scope. It includes even members of his own party. The former president, his family, his former director of the state-owned oil monopoly, and numerous former officials, are being criticized by the official press and condemned by the opposition, and by the public and their parliamentary representatives. In some cases formal criminal charges of corrupt enrichment have been brought by the *Procuradería General de la República,* the Mexican federal justice department. One of the worse cases is that of the former director of PEMEX, the state-run oil monopoly, which will be treated in detail in Chapter Six. Mexicans have awakened to the fact that their great oil wealth has been lost to internal corruption and weakened further by the vicissitudes of the international petroleum market. López Portillo and his entourage are being blamed for most of the oil disaster.

In recent years it has been increasingly fashionable to criticize Mexican presidents once they are out of office. This was especially true following the government's massacre of protesting students at Tlatelolco in 1968, an event that will be dealt with in Chapter Four. But in this observer's memory it has not been fashionable for an incumbent president to ask his predecessor to leave Mexico for the latter's own sake, at least not since the Lázaro Cárdenas era of the 1930s. In the words of a Brazilian journalist closely acquainted with the Mexican political scene:

Last April President Miguel de la Madrid, in office barely four months, asked his predecessor López Portillo to leave the country for his personal safety. Hours later López Portillo and his wife flew to New York and Paris in a private Boeing jet owned by Carlos Hank González, former mayor of Mexico City. Meanwhile, in the blue waters off Acapulco, the transoceanic yachts of the former president and the former mayor received orders to sail to the French Riviera.[33]

The former president and former mayor are not the only public officers who stand in glaring affluent contrast to the material status of most Mexicans. It is believed that thousands of other government officials regularly become obscenely wealthy via illicit dealings during each *sexenio.* The former director of PEMEX, Jorge Díaz Serrano, is formally accused of illegal enrichment accounting to 34 million dollars. The former police chief of the Federal District, Arturo Durazo Moreno is accused of illicit enrichment including smuggling and the acquisition of peasant-owned ejidal lands in the state of Guerrero to build himself a 15 hectare weekend residence. Apparently Durazo Moreno did not pay for the lands which, now walled in, contain several homes, a castle, a dog-racing track, several lakes, and heliports; an incredible display of ostentatious wealth in a poor country. It was estimated that using the standards for subsidized worker housing under Mexico's program run by INFONAVIT (Institute for the National Housing Fund for Workers) some 10,000 persons could be adequately lodged in Durazo Moreno's country residence near Zihuatanejo, Guerrero, alone.[34] It is no wonder, then, that Mexicans who are crushed into the city slums, lacking public services, or scratching a living out of inhospitable rural areas, fighting "the Plain," would be organizing themselves into protective groups and ready to rebel.

Here we see cases of high Mexican officials who, departing public office, have left behind them enormous misery unmitigated by the promises their party made but never came close to keeping; and they are owners of expensive estates, airplanes, and yachts. Their legacy to the new president, Miguel de la Madrid, is hardly enviable. To him falls the task of honoring his major campaign theme, "moral renovation," and certainly Mexico needs that. But, as I have pointed out, Mexico needed the same when López Portillo came to the presidency in 1976 and serious observers thought he just might try. To the contrary, unemployment, scarcity, and want increased. So did corruption, a fact of life not lost on the poor. Now however, more of the poor are organized in both rural and urban areas. The cause of poverty has become a tangible and visible threat to the regime, one consequence of Mexico's governmental style.

Yet, one may inquire, has there been no political reform of any sort in Mexico? It is true that in 1977 the parliament enacted some major political reforms focusing on the electoral system. This allowed new opportunities for opposition parties to participate. It enhanced the powers of the Chamber of Deputies, which was already more powerful than the Senate. Some political critics today, as will be seen, advocate abolishing the Senate altogether. Its 64 members have fixed terms of six years. The Chamber of Deputies, on the other hand, has 300 seats corresponding to specific electoral districts plus 100 additional seats at-large (divided among the various states) that are awarded on the basis of proportional representation, giving the Chamber a total of 400 seats. The single-member district seats are awarded on a majority vote basis and the term is a fixed three years. If a given party wins fewer than 60 seats by majority vote districts, and if that same party has entered electoral contests in at least one-third of the total 300 electoral districts into which the nation is divided, then there is a formula for giving it a share of the 100 at-large seats. As of this writing, this proportional representation formula has given increased membership in the Chamber to several new opposition parties of the left and to one of the center-right. Principal beneficiaries of this reform today are the centrist PAN (National Action Party) and the leftist PSUM (Unified Socialist Party of Mexico). These and the entire political party spectrum are treated in Chapter Five.

But opposition members of the Chamber of Deputies are a tiny minority. There are no true opposition members at all in the Senate and there never have been since the PRI adopted that name in the 1940s. The principal legislative voice is the Chamber, and under the hegemony of the PRI it is difficult to promulgate concrete change in that forum. Even though the government itself indicted the former director of PEMEX for fraud during the López Portillo sexenio, it was difficult for the Chamber of Deputies to use its power in 1983 to lift that man's legislative immunity as a member of the Senate so that he could be prosecuted. The PEMEX scandal was both a national and international issue. Even as glaring a case of probable guilt as that being considered by the Chamber passed only after great institutional resistance. Thus, it is hard to imagine concrete action being directed toward the governor of Hidalgo for the "minor" local crime of ordering terrorism against the peasants, or toward the governor of Sinaloa for the same well-documented charge. This is not to prejudge anyone's guilt. But the trappings of political democracy in Mexico do not provide the public a justice system wherein a meaningful redress of grievances is possible. It is as if the Mexican parliament were a debating club for an elite that ignores mass suffering; it is all part of a planned system, a pantomime. When elites belonging to the state are to be accused and tried, justice grows elusive.

But all is not negative. There are those who believe that Mexico has the potential for internal reform. One Mexican political analyst, Mauricio González, who was admittedly an admirer of President José López Portillo, felt that Mexicans are more expert in creating mirages than in transforming reality. The mirage, he asserts, is a sense of order rooted in the PRI as an omnipotent finger-pointer constantly indicating who belongs in which place and how each person ought to act. The presidential candidate of the PRI visits a prefabricated audience, a special stage that guarantees victory.[35] The reason for the campaign is quite simply so that the people will at least know the name and picture of the person who is to be their next president.[36] That candidate must fit into an established mosaic which is the political system. López Portillo could not have been chosen as the PRI's presidential candidate in an open and competitive convention; he lacked the qualifications to run for elective office. Instead he was picked by the outgoing president, Luis Echeverría, as a trusted friend. The fear of Mauricio González is that such a political system permits enormous authority to lodge in the hands of one man; and if the system becomes vice-ridden then only a uniquely Mexican solidarity can save it. But that solidarity may spawn self-defeating violence, and the dictatorship–revolt cycle could follow as elsewhere in Latin America. He asks, why not open up the system's trenches peacefully to irrigate the country voluntarily, with the waters of true democracy?[37] Yet to expect someone like López Portillo to do that alone is unrealistic; his calling was essentially that of a poet, and his sense of order would not let him disturb the system mosaic then in place, which he inherited along with the presidency.

The Mexican analyst finally gives us insight into an intriguing component of the Mexican leadership character that one dares not ignore. Referring to the former president fondly as Don Pepe he explains (not excuses) López Portillo's flagrant nepotism while in office: "Often Don Pepe does not think in political terms but in those of personal intimacy. For him there are no borders separating that which is personal and that which is political. He perceives no thresholds. In good faith he thinks that what is good for his family is good for the country."[38] North American scholars might well ponder the assertion that a Mexican leader truly may not distinguish between family welfare and national welfare. One wonders if that proposition can be advanced generically about all post-revolutionary presidents in Mexico. When incumbent President Cárdenas ordered his predecessor, Calles, out of the country in the 1930s did Calles not make the distinction? Did not López Portillo do so when advised by his successor to take an indefinite foreign vacation in 1983? Again this notion returns to perplex and confound us in the words of a contemporary Mexican intellectual, Octavio Paz, who enjoys world acclaim: speaking of all Latin America, and in a broad historical context, he writes:

> The patrimonialist system has been the central reality in our countries, as it had been in Spain. In this system the head of government—prince or viceroy, tyrant or president—directs the state and the nation like an extension of his own patrimony, in other words, like his own family.[39]

In the pages to follow let us keep the matter of personalism in mind, especially as it relates to the requisites of stable leadership, questions of power-sharing and succession, and especially in the handling of political dissent. The dilemmas of Mexico are many; so are her resources. One of the strongest of these is her rural folk, a downtrodden people but with fine instincts and impressive creative skills. They could probably feed all the Americas if given a fair and reasonable chance. Many of them exhibit the high moral character that is needed for progressive leadership from the center as well.

RICHES OR CURSES: AGRICULTURE, MIGRANT WORKERS, AND OIL

The Food Problem and Agriculture

Mexico's Revolution and the nation-building process emerging from this period left a Mexican state that acknowledged formal commitments to land reform in favor of peasant and small-scale family agricultural producers. The times were rich in populist rhetoric that would not be easily put aside. By the early 1930s Mexico seemed to be run by a *caudillo* and his clique who were dedicated to protecting the institution of *latifundio* (large landholding) agriculture. Then, in the mid 1930s, President Lázaro Cárdenas changed course and sought to honor the Revolution's commitments to the peasants by distributing agricultural lands in more than a token manner. He brought the small landholders under the tutelage of an ostensibly populist state. Cárdenas is remembered today as a great socialist reformer. He also, however, created a dependency relationship of the peasants to the state that could be twisted and exploited by successive regimes. Nor did Cárdenas wipe out the basic process of capital accumulation that allowed bourgeois agricultural interests to increase their power relative to the common people. Thus the Cárdenas era (1934-40) laid the basis for one of Mexico's most fundamental contemporary agrarian problems, the difficult coexistence of a large estate–owning capitalist elite with a neglected, and often dispossessed, rural agrarian mass.[40] The capital accumulation goals of the elite do not supply Mexico's basic food need; the institutionalized neglect of the peasants prevents them from doing it either, and the shortage of basic staple foods is one of Mexico's great problems today.

At the close of the Cárdenas presidency the state and national governments in Mexico were operating with more singularity of purpose insofar as agrarian policy was concerned. This meant decreasing attention to peasants seeking continued openings to land ownership. The Cárdenas years had seen *campesino* (peasant) benefits as the primary goal of agrarian policy. By 1940, with the coming of President Avila Camacho, the goal of the Mexican government was to increase agricultural production. Large landowners got the nod and export production was favored. By 1945 agriculture, manufacturing, and cattle-raising constituted over 40 percent of the national income.[41] Principal agricultural export crops were rice, wheat, sugar, coffee, barley, and cotton. The export agricultural sector was one of Mexico's principal sources of the vital foreign exchange needed to promote Mexico's development goal of import substitution through domestic industrialization.

New amendments to the agrarian code during the 1940s and 1950s gave further preference to large landholders over peasants; examples were provisions exempting plantations of key export items like rubber, olives, etc., from earlier land limitations. Many cattle ranches were similarly exempted. Organizations like the UGOCM (General Union of Mexican Workers and Peasants) under Jacinto López clashed with post-Cárdenas governments. The government of President Miguel Alemán (1946–52) diverted money from the peasant land reform programs and invested it in irrigation projects designed to help the large-scale private agricultural sector to export more. Neglect of the ejido in favor of large-scale private agriculture meant investment in export agriculture at the expense of domestically consumed foodstuffs, a policy that has characterized Mexican national governments to the present day. By the late 1960s Mexican agriculture was being decapitalized, contributing more income to banks and more foreign exchange to the government than was reinvested in the agricultural sector overall.

Heberto Castillo, a Mexican critic of his nation's agricultural malaise, contends that 1972 was the critical year when Mexico stopped being an exporter of grains and started importing them.[42] This initiated what may have been Mexico's worst food supply problem since the Cárdenas era. "In 1980 we bought 11 million tons of grain from abroad, principally in the United States. This year [1983] the grain importation has been estimated at over 8 million tons. But the dollars cost us six times more today than in 1980."[43] That is one way of sketching Mexico's contemporary agricultural crisis. It can be laid in some measure on the exceptions to the agrarian code instituted under President Alemán. These, in effect, allow so-called small property owners to become relatively large, for instance to have up to 300 hectares of irrigated fruit production, while the ejido owners (ejidatarios) could have no more than 10 hectares. By recourse to the *amparo agrario* (agrarian refuge injunction) large-property owners can now prevent their idle lands from being turned over to peasant petitioners by simply tying up the land grants in litigation for years. With justice often for sale in the Mexican judicial system, the *latifundista* (large landholder) keeps the lands indefinitely in litigation leaving the peasants with a scrap of paper containing only the empty promise of land.[44]

According to information released by the Center for Agrarian Studies in Mexico, some 30 million hectares of land for which peasants have petitioned have not been parceled out due to amparo proceedings against them. There is a backlog of at least 60,000 legal actions filed concerning land grant petitions. This source contends that more than half the national territory is in the hands of ranchers, that 17 million hectares of arable land remain idle, and that 9,000 so-called small property owners constitute a de facto elite that possesses the best of the nation's lands.[45] Despair over this state of affairs motivates much of the rural-to-urban migration that today fills Mexico's urban slum zones. Staple food production is restrained.

Research has established the existence of rural agricultural elites in Mexico. The case of Sinaloa is especially noteworthy as many of the tomatoes enjoyed in the United States are imported from that state. Capital accumulation and U.S. technology flowed southward into Sinaloa to produce vegetables for export north during winter months. Mexican producers had an economic interest in becoming part of existing international agribusiness systems. The Mexican government helped with infrastructure investment, specifically roads, irrigation, and railroads. The Mexican rural elite subverted farmworker protective movements in the state and obtained use of ejido lands both legally and illegally. Water access preference for the Mexican tomato exporters was secured by bribes and other illegal means, much to the despair of ejidatarios and peasant landowners.[46]

Because of the foregoing much of Mexico's food production potential has been set back since the best lands are held by large export-oriented agribusinesses, often in collaboration with foreign interests. Domestic production is neglected. Absentee landlords keep idle lands out of domestic food production. The cost of staple goods to the popular classes is elevated artificially, despite such government subsidy programs such as CONASUPO (which will be taken up in Chapter Six). "The social tension in the countryside is inescapable and forewarns explosions of violence."[47] In Mexico the goal of "land to those who will till it" has yet to be realized.

The foregoing is, to be sure, an extremely negative view. Let us therefore sketch briefly the efforts made by a recent Mexican government to solve Mexico's agriculture/food problem or "ag-lag." In early 1980 President José López Portillo announced creation of a Mexican food system to be called SAM that was accompanied by a new agricultural production statute. It attacked the basic problem, that production of staple food goods had remained rather fixed over the previous ten years. Given population increase and urban growth the net result was a decline in the per capita food supply. Petroleum-related inflation in the economy generally had increased food prices thereby aggravating the problem of malnutrition in Mexico. The SAM program had the goal of achieving self-sufficiency in corn and beans by 1982 and in a variety of other staples by 1985. Government investment would help bring abandoned or under-utilized lands into production by small-scale growers. Increased price guarantees would stimulate production by both large and small producers. The government's food distribution agency CONASUPO would be utilized to deliver subsistence food "baskets" to needy Mexicans.[48]

The Secretariat of Agriculture and Hydraulic (Water) Resources (SARH) was charged with setting new production goals for Mexico at both the small scale and agribusiness levels. The new law also provided for creating special production units of small-scale growers and/or ejidatarios who would join cooperatively to grow basic staple crops. These newly created units would be eligible for subsidized credit and other government-sponsored incentives. The agricultural program proposed by López Portillo purported to end corrupt administration of Mexican agriculture. There were allusions to a new alliance of government and peasants through the technique of subsidized production, processing, consumption, and credit.

But the financing of this ambitious program depended on oil revenues which, as we have seen, collapsed in 1981 and 1982. When President Miguel de la Madrid announced his own national development plan in 1983, the SAM experiment had all but disappeared, having failed to achieve its goals. Hope that PND would succeed where SAM had failed was clouded by Mexico's ongoing political and economic disorder. Thus Mexico continued exporting food to earn foreign exchange and importing basic staples to feed its people.

It will be asked by the reader why, then, would Mexico export food and then import to satisfy its domestic needs. Mexico, of course, hopes to export more than it imports so as to earn a dollar surplus. The national government needs to bring in dollars, or hard currency, to pay its bills and maintain the value of its own peso. That has often meant that foreign exchange from agricultural exports was used to underwrite public domain infrastructure projects, such as irrigation systems, purchase of oil production equipment, support for the automotive industry, and the building of transportation systems. When foreign exchange became inadequate for these purposes the Mexican government resorted to foreign credits and borrowing. That was the picture during most of the 1970s. The foreign debt grew and servicing this enormous foreign debt (estimated at above 80 billion dollars in 1983) provides another reason to export more food to gain more foreign exchange since the foreign debt cannot usually be paid off in pesos.

Another reason for neglecting the domestic market is that Mexico's poverty is so extensive as to limit that market's attractiveness to large-scale producers. Wheat and corn for tortillas are not as lucrative as tomatoes for export. This, of course, is no excuse for not allowing the peasants to produce wheat and corn on their own plots and thereby satisfy some of the domestic need. Guaranteed prices for agricultural products are often set too low by the Mexican government with the result that peasants cannot pay their debts from planting and they become hopelessly indebted to Banrural. That threat inspires many small producers of grain and beans, basic Mexican staples, to reduce their planting which further aggravates the food shortage. In regions like the Huasteca in the state of Hidalgo, and in Guerrero, the problems of indebtedness and drought have obligated producers to plant only for their own consumption with nothing for the market. At midyear 1983 Mexico's inflation rate was officially listed at 48 percent with the most severe price increases occurring in bread, tortillas, beef, canned fish, and powdered milk.[49] This trend would hit hardest at that 60 to 80 percent of the population who are already undernourished and/or on subsistence budgets.

In the 1980s Mexico's agricultural challenge has been complicated by its overall economic crisis. Natural phenomena have also been unkind, such as severe drought conditions in 1982, and a 3.4 percent plus annual rate of demographic increase which seems always to keep staple food demand ahead of its supply. Mexico continues to be tied to food purchases in the United States. In 1983 Mexico signed a food-buying credit agreement with Canada. All of this increases the foreign debt. Observers believe that agriculture-related foreign indebtedness and foreign penetration of Mexican agribusiness all threaten the nation's future ability to control its own food supply. Mexico cannot be a truly independent nation without solving this basic food problem. As the need continues, evidence of social injustice becomes more inescapable. It is a tangible and easily understood theme for opposition political groups that would radically alter the stability of Mexico's contemporary life.

Clandestine Migration

The emigration of Mexican workers north into the United States follows directly from Mexico's agricultural dilemma as part of the broader national economic problem. Worker migration, both legal and clandestine, is treated more thoroughly in Chapter Seven. The phenomenon itself has distinct historical roots. About half of Mexico was lost to the United States in a war which ended in 1848 (see Chapter Two). Thus, migratory patterns northward into what is now California, Arizona, New Mexico, Texas, and some areas beyond were already established at that time. American railroads traditionally carried Mexican political exiles throughout the United States and some cities like St. Louis, Missouri, were sites where major decisions were made affecting the Revolution. Mexican migration into the United States has been continued on the basis of established, legal patterns. But during the twentieth century a number of quota and other restrictive laws appeared in the United States which made such migration illegal and forced it to become clandestine.

Maldistribution of wealth, land tenure patterns that force peasants off agricultural land, governmental corruption in the sharing of social and infrastructure benefits, social and political violence, and overpopulation, all interact to make Mexico a place for people to leave. Mexico, it should be remembered, had approximately 70 million people in 1983. About half of them are under 21 with little or no chance for employment in a country whose available work force is chronically unemployed or underemployed by nearly 50 percent by Mexican standards. Current research reported in Chapter Seven documents the impetus that drives Mexicans to come surreptitiously to the United States to seek work. Some feel it is worthwhile even deliberately to get caught, so desperate is their socioeconomic condition. There is, to be sure, an invitation for Mexicans to emigrate into the United States in the desire of U.S. businesses, both urban and rural, for a dependable supply of workers to do menial and often unpleasant tasks which U.S. workers generally will not accept.

In the 1980s an emotional debate formed in the United States (and to some degree in Canada) as to the impact and significance of illegal Mexican aliens. The organization FAIR (Federation for American Immigration Reform) published results of a 1983 poll indicating not only that Americans generally favored controlling the illegal entry of Mexican and other immigrants but that blacks and Hispanics also concurred.[50] The issue arose over continued federal legislative efforts to punish employers of illegal aliens in the United States. One quirk in the legal structure favoring clandestine migration has been that it was not illegal for U.S. employers to hire illegal aliens (but such hiring in Canada was illegal).

Because it is impossible to take an accurate census of an illegal or clandestine population we do not know how many illegal Mexican aliens currently reside in the United States, although in 1980 there was a basis for alleging that 3 million Mexicans were here illegally.[51] But there is no way to prove that estimate. Into the mid-1980s other estimates approach 5 million but with similar scientific weaknesses. Based on the present writer's research in the field, as reported in Chapter Seven, there are certainly millions of illegal Mexican aliens living and working here. Determining what impact they have can be just as difficult as verifying their number. A survey commissioned by the U.S. Congress in 1980[52] stated that there were some 6 million illegal aliens in the United States counting all ethnic groups. It acknowledged the widespread belief in America that illegal aliens damage both society and the economy, that the aliens are vulnerable to economic exploitation, that they are preyed upon by criminals, that they fail to report health problems thus spreading contagions, that they fail to educate their children or do so wrongfully at U.S. public expense, and that their continued presence damages U.S. government credibility vis a vis domestic law enforcement.[53]

The United States could put up a "cactus curtain" along the southern border and a "prairie curtain" to the north but this would surely damage our relationships with both Canada and Mexico. In the latter case a rapid and radical closing of the border could provoke social revolution. That probably would not benefit the United States politically or economically; but it might solve part of the alien migration problem if a new and presumably socialist state on the Cuban or Nicaraguan model were implanted in Mexico (it could also overburden the Soviet Union should it acquire another dependent/client state). Or the United States could open its borders and try to absorb all of Mexico. That possibility is remote. Yet Mexican scholars often joke that what their nation lost to the United States by war in 1848 they will gradually retake via clandestine migration. Retaking lost territory and swelling the political clout of the Hispanic population in the American southwest are not, of course, exactly the same thing.

Given Mexico's chronic unemployment problem and its rate of population increase, that nation will need to make its existing birth control program more effective since there seems little likelihood that these new people will ever be absorbed in the work force through economic growth during the remainder of the twentieth century.

The traditional worker and peasant sectors in Mexico contribute most to the overpopulation and overurbanization problem. Therein originates pressure to emigrate northward. Mexican economic development in recent years has been dominated by petroleum and steel production, which are capital intensive industries not labor intensive. Setbacks in both these industries (owing to international market factors as well as to domestic political corruption) during the early 1980s cast serious doubt as to when they will be able to have meaningful impact on Mexico's unemployment problem. Economic development on the northern border has absorbed many workers but has attracted many more than can be employed. Government officials in Mexico who would rather not tackle this difficult and complex problem can acquiesce, indefinitely they hope, in continued emigration northward and continued U.S. neglect in controlling the phenomenon. Thus Mexico has an outward human thrust that cannot be ignored either by the United States or Canada. Indeed, the latter nation is increasingly used as a vehicle for the illegal aliens of various nations to gain surreptitious entry into the United States.

Even if the United States were prepared to absorb Mexico's excess population indefinitely it would not spare the inevitable upheaval that must come someday over this problem of displaced humanity. U.S. immigration policy, or the absence thereof, shares some of the guilt for their predicament. The inescapable paradox of American immigration policy up until the early 1980s was hardly encouraging. Two scholars cited it as "The Wink," meaning that restrictive legislation was combined with administrative winking at massive violations. Cheap labor from Mexico was desired by many American citizens for their enterprises.[54]

Management and investor elites in Mexico have little motive to share more of their profits to keep Mexicans at home. Should the Mexican government force such profit sharing at meaningful levels it would cause major upheavals in Mexico's economic system. The inescapable fact is that much of Mexico's political economy has been erected on a shaky foundation of social injustice and human neglect. The Mexican oil riches, upon which such great hopes were based in the late 1970s, created an economic crisis in the early 1980s as will be seen presently. Mexico could, of course, stimulate new internal cottage industries and subsidize small-scale agricultural production as ways of putting its people to work and feeding them. It could seek to develop major exporting capabilities as Japan, Taiwan, and Hong Kong have done. But that would require some drastic reform in the governing and planning mentality that prevails in Mexico. The likelihood of such reform is one of the central themes of this book.

Petroleum Reserves and Riches

A third and final aspect of this survey of Mexico's political economy is the role of oil. At the turn of this century Mexico's annual oil production was minimal. But by the time of the Revolution in 1911 the nation produced about 12 million barrels per year. Most of this production was in the hands of foreign developers, many of them American and British. By 1921 Mexico was producing 193 million barrels annually making it the world's second largest producer following the United States.[55] In 1938, under President Cárdenas, Mexico's oil reserves became the exclusive province of a new state enterprise, *Petroleos Mexicanos,* or PEMEX. This action against foreign capitalists coupled with Cárdenas's promotion of radical agrarian reform served to convince many critics that the president was indeed a socialist if not worse.

In successive years the growth of PEMEX into a giant state monopoly gave the Mexican government a new measure of control over its population and over the commercial and industrial sectors as well. By keeping gas prices low, transportation fares were also kept within reach of the popular classes. Since businesses depended on PEMEX for fuel they had a built-in motive to tolerate the political system's norms and output. By 1973 Mexico was approaching the 1 million barrel per day mark in oil production. That was during the sexenio of Luis Echeverría Alvarez. At this time also the Arab-inspired Third World oil cartel known as OPEC was created and the world price of oil was shortly multiplied by four. Mexico, at the time, was not self-sufficient in oil and depended on imports to supplement what PEMEX generated. "Mexico paid $124 million for oil imports in 1972, but $382 million in 1974 under OPEC".[56] This motivated the Echeverría administration to undertake major capital investments in oil equipment to enable PEMEX to make Mexico self-sufficient and free it from the clutches of OPEC. The consequence of this spending was that Mexico's foreign debt rose from $9.5 billion in 1974 to $20 billion in 1976, Echeverría's last year in office.[57] In August of that year he took the controversial but necessary step of devaluing Mexico's peso, the first time that had been done since 1954. The president also took the unpopular step of freeing gas prices charged by PEMEX thus raising public transportation costs but immediately generating more development capital for PEMEX.

When President José López Portillo took office at the end of 1976, Mexico's known petroleum and natural gas reserves were in the neighborhood of 12 billion barrels. In 1978 the explorations of PEMEX yielded a 40 billion barrel global expectation. By 1981 Mexico was pumping nearly

3 million barrels per day compared with fewer than 1 million daily in 1973. By that time Mexico had become a major world exporter of petroleum and could easily satisfy its own internal demands. Subsequently, in 1982, Mexico's combined oil and gas (hydrocarbon) reserves were being estimated at more than 75 billion barrels.

The strength of oil as the basis for economic salvation for Mexico was undercut by at least two major events in 1981 that were both domestic and international in scope. The first was a glut in the world supply of oil that occurred partly because of conservation measures in Europe and America and partly because OPEC had lost some control over the production of its members. The second was a major scandal that erupted in the management of PEMEX, forcing its director Jorge Díaz Serrano to resign and linking him to corrupt spending practices in connection with foreign purchases of oil tankers and oil production equipment. It also implicated the incumbent president and threatened Mexico's internal political stability. The outcome of these events, in the short term, was disastrous for Mexico.

Cracks began to appear in the Mexican economy, which had been touted to the world as healthy during the entire sexenio of President López Portillo. In February and August of 1982 López Portillo was forced to devalue the peso, this in his last year in office, just as his predecessor had also been forced to do. Mexico needed to export more in order to earn hard money to pay its foreign debt and to underwrite its own currency. Devaluation made Mexican goods (such as oil) temporarily cheaper for foreigners to acquire. It also acknowledged that Mexico had severe internal financial management difficulties. Money started to leave the country clandestinely and President López Portillo took the strong measure of nationalizing the banks, followed by a third peso devaluation in December 1982. This left the peso at approximately 82 percent below its value at the beginning of that same year. Mexico had borrowed heavily from U.S. and other foreign banks to finance its oil explorations, to be paid off by the assumed unlimited oil proceeds. The foreign debt rose from $34 billion in 1978 to $50 billion in 1980 and passed $80 billion in 1982. The Mexican government's deficit, expressed as a percent of gross domestic product, rose from under 6 percent in 1978 to 18 percent in 1982. Inflation in the United States forced the cost of servicing the foreign part of the debt steadily higher. In 1982 the inflation rate in Mexico approached 100 percent (from 30 percent in 1981) and this also influenced the decision to devalue the peso. Also in 1982, a critical year, the prolonged world oil glut forced international prices down. Mexico's dollar earnings thus dropped; there simply were not enough dollar reserves to support the peso. Mexico's economy started to collapse.

When President Miguel de la Madrid began his sexenio at the end of 1982 the Mexican government was responsible for about 75 percent of the total national foreign debt of some $80 billion and the remainder was in private obligations. The government would be expected to pay some $20 billion of that by 1984. It seemed incapable of raising such a figure, at least on the basis of oil revenues. To avoid default Mexico borrowed some $5 billion to pay its interest obligations in 1983, but this constituted another debt owed to foreign banks. The flood of oil dollars pumped into Mexico during the López Portillo years raised Mexico's inflation rate, which peaked in 1982 just as dollar earnings from the international sale of oil were being drastically reduced. Add to this the petroleum management scandal revealing that millions of dollars had been stolen from the national patrimony, and the accompanying loss of prestige faced by the government internationally, and you had a basis for doubting that oil in Mexico had been a blessing. With its money in collapse and unemployment rampant, Mexico will not easily remove the stigma of failure it held in the early 1980s even in the eyes of its neighbors in the Third World: "... the Mexican people have lost their confidence. Its economy strangled by the fall in oil prices, Mexico has little else to sell to the world except coffee, vegetables, and a few manufactured items."[58]

INTERNATIONAL FORCES AND CONSTRAINTS

Mexico's internal fortunes are intimately linked to the economy of the United States. But usually, except when the Mexican government is nearing default on its debts to the United States, its economic ties and obligations are often played down in favor of other areas of international affairs where Mexico is relatively free to follow an independent course. Most notable during the 1980s has been Mexico's approach to the growth of international conflict and outright war in Central America. Mexican President Miguel de la Madrid met with President Ronald Reagan in La Paz, Mexico, in August of 1983. The latter sought to justify U.S. intervention in El Salvador and Nicaragua, and the U.S. troop buildup in Honduras, on the grounds of America's moral obligation to help free the Central American peoples of communist oppression and to alleviate economic distress in the region. Besides, Reagan asserted, the United States was asked by Honduras and El Salvador to send its aid and military advisers to combat leftist insurgents. Reagan implied that since Cuba and the Soviet Union were behind the insurgency, and were also supporting the leftist government of Nicaragua, that a generalized threat to the hemisphere existed. It should be noted that the Rio Treaty of 1947 stipulated that if one signatory nation of the hemisphere should be attacked by an outside force, all members of that pact would be obliged to help defend against a common enemy. President Reagan's pronouncement did not invoke the Rio Treaty as such but stressed that a communist threat to the hemisphere existed.

Speaking for Mexico, President de la Madrid rejected the notion that revolution in Central America was being fostered directly by Cuba and the Soviet Union, even though those countries did have aid missions there. De la Madrid also asked the U.S. president to help end confrontational politics in Central America, referring to the U.S. war games in Honduras and the sending of warships to patrol waters off the coasts of Nicaragua. The U.S. position stated by Reagan and echoed by Secretary of State George Shultz was that the U.S. military exercises in the region were necessary to discourage further communist aggression. But de la Madrid urged his belief that Salvadoran rebel arms were not being smuggled in by Cuba or the Soviet Union but rather were purchased on the open black market or captured from the Salvadoran government's own forces. During the previous administration of José López Portillo, Mexico and France had issued a joint declaration recognizing the Salvadoran rebel movement as a bona fide political force to be dealt with in that war-torn nation. The essential difference between the U.S. and Mexican positions is capsulized in the latter's contention that the Central American states should be treated as responsible sovereign bodies which can be expected to act in the best interest of the regional community of nations. The U.S. position harkened back to the Big Stick diplomacy of Theodore Roosevelt, reserving for the United States a role as hemispheric policeman.

Both nations expressed support for the initiative of the Contadora Group (Mexico, Venezuela, Colombia, and Panama) which met several times during 1983 to work out a peace initiative in Central America through their own good offices. Mexico, of course, would have preferred to see the region's troubles left entirely in the lap of the Contadora initiative with no independent U.S. intervention of any sort. Mexico has a tradition of going it alone in its Latin American relations without regard to the preferences of the United States. Since Fidel Castro's revolution triumphed in Cuba in 1959, Mexico has kept its diplomatic doors open to Cuba despite various anti-Castro embargoes and diplomatic pressures instituted by the United States. Many observers believe Mexico contributed importantly to maintaining hemispheric peace by keeping an open dialogue with Cuba. In the case of Chile, following the bloody coup there in 1973, Mexico again departed from the U.S. lead by breaking ties and condemning the Pinochet regime and by welcoming Chilean exiles and former officials of the fallen Allende government. During the government of President Echeverría (1970–76) Mexico made no secret of its disapproval of U.S. support for the Pinochet dictatorship in Chile. Echeverría had hosted President Salvador Allende earlier with great fanfare and Third World solidarity appeals.

It is also during the Echeverría sexenio that Mexico discovered heretofore unknown petroleum reserves. This exciting promise, coupled with President Echeverría's own penchant for stature as a world leader (Echeverría let it be known that he was "available" for the secretary generalship of the United Nations once his presidential term ended) led Mexico to proffer itself as a spokesman for Third World nations. The 1981–82 collapse of Mexico's oil-based claim to economic greatness dimmed its Third World leadership hopes. Yet Mexico was still able to assert itself as a moderator in the Central American conflict of the 1980s. Part of this role consisted in providing assistance (including oil products) to the Nicaraguan government after the United States reduced its role in the early years of the decade. Moreover Mexico took a leadership role when it sought to persuade Cuba against drastic provocations that might generalize the conflict throughout Central America.

Understandably, Mexico sided with the Sandinistas in Nicaragua against the United States. The Sandinistas came to power after a grim and messy civil war against an odious dictatorship (the Somoza dynasty) just as Mexico itself had emerged from a bitter revolutionary war after 1910 against the tyranny of Porfirio Díaz. If Mexico had not supported revolutionary Nicaragua in the 1980s it might have called into question its own revolutionary credentials. Mexico also shares with all Latin American countries a common historical distrust of the United States; thus it could not approve U.S. military involvement in Central America any more than it could back British military adventures in the Falklands war of 1982 against Argentina. In addition Mexico believes that time is no doubt on the side of the Central American rebels, with whom it will likely have to coexist some day. Should these countries fall under the aegis of Marxist regimes, Mexico hopes to have a distinct advantage over the United States in dealing with them both politically and economically. Central America is a good potential market for Mexican goods. Mexico does not accept any version of a domino theory vis a vis Central America. It believes that by supporting Cuba and Nicaragua those nations will not later seek to undermine Mexico via guerrilla insurgency from within, even if all Central America falls into the Marxist camp.

Such a foreign policy stance works well for Mexico in the short run. However there are certain risks inherent in it. Not the least of these is that while Mexico applauds the struggle against elites who perpetuate socioeconomic injustice in Central America, there are similar, although perhaps less visible, elites in Mexico doing much the same thing. Moreover, it is hard to welcome refugees, denounce dictatorships, and condemn social injustice in other countries while remaining impervious to it at home.[59] The Mexican government can hardly expect to be a champion of liberation in the Third World indefinitely without this pledge drawing notice from domestic forces for radical social change.

Although Central American conflicts in the early 1980s caught many headlines that concerned the international relations of Mexico this may not be its most important policy area in a continuing context. Mexico's economic dependency on the United States is a longer-range issue and is a major international constraint on the former's domestic growth. Much of Mexico's predicted prosperity in the late 1970s was based upon the expected sale of petroleum and natural gas to the United States. Mexico decided to build a *gasoducto* (pipeline) in 1977 that would carry natural gas to the U.S. border near McAllen, Texas. This decision was apparently taken before all financing was completed and before the United States had agreed on the price to be paid for the natural gas. A major international dispute broke out between the two countries that left bad feelings on both sides and delayed the project until 1979 when agreement on terms was finally reached. Thus Mexican development in one specific area was retarded by attitudes north of the border.

The matter of borders and migration is another major, continuing international problem of vital importance to Mexico. Since Chapter Seven is dedicated to this theme I will not linger on it here except to point out one peculiar aspect of migration (both legal and clandestine) as an international force or constraint. Quite simply Mexico does not want to do anything to provoke the United States into effectively closing the northern border for potential loss of remittances. In the words of one scholar:

> The Mexican government has a considerable stake in keeping its northern border relatively open. At least two-thirds of the migrants remit money to Mexico. For most of the Mexican households that send migrants, these remittances are their primary source of income. The value of remittances, though very difficult to estimate, may exceed Mexican net income from tourism. Moreover, even though overt unemployment is not the main reason for migration, migration reduces pressures on employment within Mexico.[60]

Mexico in the 1980s maintains considerable reliance on U.S. private banking institutions for the financing of much of its estimated $80 billion external debt. Severe concern was expressed by major U.S. lending institutions (like the Chase Manhattan Bank) when it was thought in 1982 that Mexico might default. Combine this with potential defaults at the same time by Argentina and Brazil (as was possible) and it can be seen that the financial plight of Mexico is very much a matter of American concern. Flight of capital out of Mexico bothered policy makers most severely after the oil crisis of 1981 and 1982. The government imposed heretofore un-heard of controls on the convertibility of the peso with severe penalties for Mexicans exporting or even possessing dollars without official permits. This, of course, led to a vigorous clandestine traffic in such official per-mits along with a flourishing black market in dollars, similar to many other Latin American countries. But though Mexico may try to control the flight of dollars out of the country it has a more difficult task inviting them back in. Mexico's recent industrial development plan, its national development plan, and its experiment with a national food production and distribution system, all presupposed financial help from the world price of its exported petroleum. This was expected to increase at an an-nual rate of between 5 and 7 percent until the year 2000 and perhaps beyond.[61] This, as we have previously observed, simply did not happen. The vicissitudes of the international marketplace threw Mexico headlong into recession and economic chaos. Mexico's leaders probably could not have foreseen the world price decline in petroleum. Mexico's heavy de-pendence on the export of petroleum, agricultural, and a few manufac-tured products, leaves it vulnerable to the international marketplace. That undermined the Mexican economic miracle of this decade.

No attempt will be made here to survey the complete range of other international forces that impinge on Mexico's political economy. To the above sampling could be added a number of dynamics involving foreign continents. For instance, in 1975, when Mexico voted in the United Na-tions to condemn Israel (more accurately, international Zionism) as racist, a tourism boycott was organized in the United States causing an estimated loss of 25 percent of Mexico's tourist revenue for that year. International business is an influential force in Mexico, even though foreign firms are usually excluded by Mexican law from involvement in petroleum, bank-ing (with exceptions), insurance, railroads, agriculture (with many excep-tions), and subsoil resources generally. But many multinational corpora-tions (automotive and pharmaceutical for example) import the bulk of their required materials from the home country. Japanese firms have im-ported as much as 94 percent of their requirements.[62] This obviously af-fects Mexico's import-export balance of payments situation.

When Mexico (or any Third World country) seeks to persuade its foreign creditors to grant debt moratoriums there is frequently greater flexibility in dealing with state banks or governments than with private banks. Mexico's heavy reliance on private bank financing from foreign nations means it has less freedom in maneuvering when it cannot service its foreign debt, just as happened in 1982. Of course being indebted to private banks may mean that less diplomatic pressure is exerted upon the debtor country than would be the case when the debts are primarily owed to state banks or as government loans. Mexico has also borrowed from the

International Monetary Fund (IMF) and this also requires surrendering a considerable amount of fiscal and monetary flexibility in exchange for loans. In the case of U.S. loans, during the Echeverría administration "the Mexican government had no choice but to enter into an agreement with the U.S. Federal Reserve System to manage the relationship between the peso and the dollar. The majority of the external public debt with foreign private banks was with U.S. banks."[63] Thus international finance is a major external constraint on the Mexican political economy.

The U.S.–Mexican border region is still another critical focus of relationships between the two countries. The clandestine migration of workers is only one point of contention. For years Mexico has protested the high saline content of water coming from U.S. watersheds into Mexico. This has been most acute in the case of the Colorado River, whose water carries salt and chemical drainage from Arizona and California into Mexico. Severe problems have also surrounded discharge of water and regulation of water supply from the Rio Grande. A system of dams and filtering devices on the U.S. side and on the border has only partially satisfied the Mexican complaints. Another critical border issue involves the smuggling of narcotics to the north and the smuggling of U.S. contraband merchandise to the south.

Still a further problem is international pollution. This involves both surface and atmospheric contamination. President Reagan signed an agreement with President de la Madrid in August 1983 aimed at combating environmental pollution along the 2000 mile border. One target of this accord was air pollution. Between the cities of El Paso, Texas, and Ciudad Juárez, Chihuahua, there has been for years a "sharing" of international smog that alarms health authorities on both sides. In Arizona environmentalists have more recently become enraged over the development of a copper smelter in Cananea, Sonora, that would contribute significantly to the pollution of the air in southern Arizona. Copper companies in Arizona, already hurting from poor market conditions that idled their plants, and forced by U.S. environmental legislation to clean up their facilities, have joined in the environmentalists' battle to stop the smelter development in northwestern Mexico. To make the matter even more bitter for the Americans the Cananea development was financed largely by the Export-Import Bank and the World Bank in which U.S. funds play vital roles. Here one begins to see the complexity of international forces and constraints in the dynamics of this smog controversy. Congressional opponents of the Cananea loans might block them but Mexico indicated its intention to finance the project elsewhere.[64] Just as in the case of saline Colorado River water, the international smog problem is instructive as to how the many different issues and actors are unexpectedly intertwined and how constraints to protect the atmosphere on one side of the border may collide with development plans on the other.

The environmental pact signed by Presidents Reagan and de la Madrid would be a first step toward cooperative resolution of serious quality of life threats in the border region. Certainly both presidents were sincere. Generally their antismog agreement was accepted in that spirit in Mexico and the United States. But in one of Mexico's most prominent newspapers that was not the case. Renato Leduc, a writer of longtime popular following in Mexico and with solid anti-American credentials, wrote that the 1983 accord would not prevent the Yankees from continuing to contaminate the atmosphere just as they had done for years, when "children of Ciudad Juárez died constantly from the poisonous gases spouting from the chimneys of the American Smelting installation in El Paso, Texas."[65] He did not bother to mention the smog-producing facility on the Mexican side that would pollute the Arizona skies, nor did he cite smog control efforts then in effect in the El Paso–Ciudad Juárez area. Such reporting rendered a disservice to the efforts of both presidents, but it shows how news presentation itself can become an international force acting on public opinion.

A final consideration in this survey of the international forces impinging on Mexico relates to that nation as a receiving zone for displaced populations from internal strife and war in Central America. Since 1979 large streams of refugees have begun concentrating in Mexico's southern states, especially in Chiapas. In the early 1980s there were estimates running into the high thousands for such refugees, especially those coming from Guatemala and El Salvador. From March 1982 to March 1983 some 17,000 Guatemalans, mostly Indians who registered themselves as refugees, were recorded as having entered Chiapas alone.[66] Many more than that are believed to have come from war-torn El Salvador. The Guatemalan refugees were escaping the genocidal repression of the Lucas García and Rios Montt dictatorships.

At this time it is not clear whether the Mexican government knows just how many Central American refugees it has. A good number of them appear to be making their way to the northern border and are crossing into the United States where many have met with disasters in the desert while many others have been apprehended. A U.S. Border Patrol officer in McAllen, Texas, said that "May (1983) is the third month in a row in which we have apprehended more than 100,000 aliens per month."[67] He said a monthly record for the Border Patrol was set in March, when 107,997 aliens nationally were apprehended. This pressure was attributed to Mexico's economic crisis and the turmoil in Central America. With thousands of Central Americans successfully reaching the United States, the Mexican government may never be able to develop accurate statistics on how many were inside its borders.

To be sure the refugees have an impact on Mexico. If their number is in the hundreds of thousands as some estimates put it then it would be to Mexico's immediate advantage to use its good offices toward ending Central American hostilities, hence ending the flood of refugees. There is rugged jungle and rain forest terrain covering much of Mexico's southern border with Guatemala. Many, if not most, of the Guatemalan refugees do not speak Spanish as their native tongue. The task of interdicting them, and then caring for them, must be monumental. Some of that responsibility has been taken over by religious missionaries and private humanitarian groups that work independently but with at least the tacit blessing of the Mexican government. The United Nations also has a program of refugee assistance that works through the Mexican government. Rumors have it that some of the U.N. aid has been wasted through the corruption of Mexican administrators.

One religious organization that enjoys the tacit blessing of the Mexican government is the Coordinadora de Ayuda a Refugiados Guatemaltecos, CARG (the Aid Coordinating Group for Guatemalan Refugees) that is sponsored by the Catholic church and has an office in Mexico City. An American priest, the Reverend Louis Michael Colonnese, wrote about his work, and that of others in the church, on behalf of the refugees coming into southern Mexico. He stated that the policy of the Mexican government, and specifically its secretariat known as *Gobernación* (roughly a mixture of the U.S. departments of Justice and Interior), is humanitarian on the surface and that the Mexican government has generally cooperated with church missionaries. The government has created a special "intersecretariat" to oversee refugee problems. "In the beginning there was little if any help. Then a year ago when the problem of malaria and measles became so acute as to be a threat to the Mexicans in the area, there were campaigns to vaccinate everyone. That helped."[68] One of the principal movers in the campaign to assist the refugees is Bishop Samuel Ruiz García of San Cristobal de las Casas, Chiapas. He has helped buffer the church people in the field from the irritation of some government people who resent priests, especially foreign priests from the United States, delving into Mexico's internal problems. Refugees, of course, are not strictly an internal problem.

The missionaries have suffered some harassment from judicial agents of Mexican state and federal agencies who often charge that renegade priests are using the refugees to foment land invasions in southern Mexico. "We know historically that land invasions have been occurring in Chiapas for many years . . . long before the arrival of any refugees. The presence of the refugees in Chiapas is a problem for the Mexican government without question. There is a lot of unrest in the area to begin with. Some say there is guerrilla activity. Others say that the Guatemalan guerrillas seek refuge in Mexican territory . . . where the Mexican campesinos assist them. The caciques and gangsters use the refugees as cover-ups for their own nefarious acts against the poor."[69]

Salvadoran refugees are persecuted as they pass north through Guatemala, hoping to get into Mexico and eventually farther north. Both they and the Guatemalans seek to escape the violence of their countries: this is their immediate migratory goal. The concentration of so many thousands of these refugees in Mexico's southern border area alarms the Mexican government, which announced in May of 1984 that it was converting a strip along the southern border into a virtual militarized zone. Some 46,000 Guatemalan refugees in Chiapas would either be repatriated or go into special concentration camps farther north. Secretary of *Gobernación* Manuel Bartlett said he doubted that most of the refugees were political but rather were seeking economic betterment.[70] This was the same rhetoric used by U.S. officials about their refugee problem in the north.

GOVERNMENT AND POLITICS:
BARRIERS TO PROGRESS

Palliatives too often typify the governmental response in Mexico insofar as solutions to domestic and international problems are concerned. At the international level it is easy for Mexican heads of state to lecture Presidents Carter and Reagan about U.S. involvement in Central America, claiming it is nefarious and immoral;[71] but when the Mexican financial house is in disorder those same heads of state are quite eager to refinance debts owed the United States and solicit new loans abroad. It is easy for Mexican intellectuals to excoriate American materialism while themselves depending on a state budget whose largesse is shared according to some of the most materialistic norms of pure greed that one can envision.

Writing in 1981 a U.S.-based scholar observed that President López Portillo had asked Mexico's poor to forgive the state for not lifting them out of their misery, yet at the same time he asked them to have confidence that he would, in fact, lift them out of it.[72] We have already seen that López Portillo probably did more to enrich himself than anybody else. A central theme of this book is the political corruption which defeats whatever quest there may be in Mexico for concrete governmental reform. If the governmental and political processes are riddled with corruption, the policy outputs are likely to be sullied and distorted. The author just quoted also observes "nobody in Mexico doubts that there is corruption . . . [it] pervades Mexican society. There are those who defend it as an integral part of an imperfect system, because poverty and greed loosen scruples. And in Mexico, nepotism has always been practiced, from presidents to street cleaners."[73] An imperfect system it is and one in which there may be grave risks in saying so publicly. That is the frightening thing about modern authoritarian states and tyrannies, that they readily label criticism of the state as sedition.[74]

A study published at the same time about Mexico's recent major electoral reform in 1977 dealt with the high degree of personalism in the Mexican bureaucracy, with the infighting that occurs among cliques or camarillas, and with the time wasted while bureaucrats try to protect their jobs from one camarilla to another.[75] Some of this occurs within U.S. bureaucracies as well; but a consensus of the testimony to the present author is that the camarilla system (to be dealt with more in Chapter Six) is so highly nepotistic and wasteful as to derail thoroughly most of the progressive public policy decisions and programs that emanate from the congress or executive branch of government. Thus, the inefficiency and corruption in Mexico's governmental system explain why little has been done about the horrendous smog problem in the capital city, for example, while other comparable cities around the world have made notable atmospheric improvements. The same can be said for Mexico's failure to professionalize its police and fire services, as the case of Arturo Durazo Moreno (discussed in Chapter Eight) painfully demonstrates. Urban zoning, pollution control, professionalized public administration—all of these reform goals are possible and known about in Mexico. But the politics of kleptocracy (where public figures are expected to steal from each other and the public) prevents their coming to fruition. Such governmental trends emerged from the norms of adventure lust implanted during Mexico's independence period that were resurrected with the Great Revolution of 1910–17.

Mexico needs reforms from within, by Mexican leaders of probity. But in the past when reforms were decreed, like wage and salary increases and expanding popular food services by CONASUPO under the Echeverría administration, the effects usually did not convince the Mexican people that their situation in life had really been improved. Thus much reform in Mexico has been what Coleman and Davis term preemptive reform. They argue that if reforms are "preemptive in nature, designed to do what seems necessary to avert the threat of uncontrolled mobilization, they will probably stop short of producing sufficient change to induce gratitude among intended beneficiaries."[76] This process has, in Mexico, contributed to a legacy of political mistrust especially among the proletarian classes. If political reforms were genuinely substantive, enough so as to please the workers, the custodians of power within the PRI establishment would be threatened.[77] Preemptive reform, essentially, is intended to deceive the workers and protect the dominant elites;

surely it is intended to avoid popular antiregime uprisings as occurred in 1968 and as could occur in the aftermath of the PEMEX scandal in the 1980s. Preemptive reform in the wake of the PEMEX affair would be used to keep opposition forces from mobilizing to make other embarrassing investigations of Mexican officialdom. The tactic of preemptive reform reflects a fundamental contradiction in Mexico's political economy that can be expected to generate future political stress and alienation.[78] .

The PEMEX scandal of the 1980s shows, however, that the Mexican political system is having a hard time containing the greed of its own members in the face of scarce budgetary resources. That affair also indicates that being blessed with a wealth of natural resources (throwing oil or money at a problem) will not solve the problems of a society if the norms that guide its governmental and political processes are programmed to sacrifice the public good in favor of private or "family" goods. And the ruling PRI is still a giant family or dominant class that gives up its perks with only the greatest resistance and reluctance. Again, to underscore a central theme of this book, political and administrative corruption (moral corruption, plus the blind and inculcated notion that "what's good for me and my family is good for the nation as a whole") can undermine the most rationally conceived state.

The Brazilian journalist cited earlier in this chapter wrote that corruption dominates all of Mexican life and that in 1981, during the last days of the oil boom largesse, some 244 members of Mexico City's transit police signed a statement that their superiors extorted money from them to, in turn, be able to extort the public. The police officers had to pay their superiors a daily fee to use motorcycles, uniforms, ticket books, and service revolvers, just to have the chance to go out and extort that much plus more from the public.[79] Such behavior, and its counterpart at the cabinet level is what President de la Madrid will have to terminate if the governmental process in Mexico is to have truly public goals. The president's order in early 1983 prohibiting nepotism in hiring was an encouraging, albeit precarious, start.

Some social scientists have hinted that corruption is a natural part of the developmental process.[80] We view that as a semantic mirage, an exercise in obfuscation and deceptive jargon, posed against the hard reality of mass misery in a country enjoying adequate brains and resources to generate change. Corruption does not hasten development in the Third World; it stifles progress, as Mexico's history well testifies. Here let us turn to an overview of some five centuries of that background.

NOTES

1. Enrique Krauze, "The Intellectuals and Society," in *Democracy and Dictatorship in Latin America,* Irving Howe, ed. (New York: Foundation for Study of Independent Social Ideas, 1982), p. 49.
2. Ibid., p. 48.
3. Raúl F. Cárdenas, *Proceso,* April 25, 1983, pp. 12–13.
4. Donald Mabry to Kenneth Johnson, August 5, 1983.
5. Cárdenas, *Proceso,* pp. 12–13.
6. Ibid.
7. Juan Rulfo, *The Burning Plain* (Austin: University of Texas Press, 1967), p. 14.
8. Ibid., p. 56.
9. Ibid., pp. 74–75.
10. Ibid., p. 87.
11. Ibid., pp. 112–113.
12. *Proceso,* July 18, 1983, p. 23.
13. *Proceso,* July 11, 1983, p. 8.
14. *Proceso,* July 18, 1983, p. 22. New population centers created around petroleum development have generated new concentrations of urban misery, like the port of Coatzacoalcos, where both "material and moral corruption" abound. See the editorial in *Excelsior,* September 9, 1983.
15. *Proceso,* July 18, 1983, p. 23.
16. Ibid.
17. Ibid.
18. Ibid.
19. Ibid., p. 22.
20. Peter Stalker, "La elección de los emigrantes," *Boletín informativo sobre asuntos migratorios y fronterizos,* December, 1982, p. 7.
21. *Proceso,* May 16, 1983, p. 22.
22. Ibid.
23. Ibid., p. 23.
24. Ibid.
25. William Weber Johnson, *Heroic Mexico,* (New York: Doubleday, 1968), p. 85.
26. *Proceso,* May 16, 1983, p. 24.
27. Ibid.
28. *Proceso,* May 9, 1983, p. 14.
29. Ibid., p. 15.
30. Ibid., p. 17. As seen in President de la Madrid's annual state of the nation message for 1983 the government's ability to address urban problems is often overcome and burdened by demands of the Federal District. See coverage in *Excelsior,* September 2, 1983.
31. *Pueblo* (Mexico City), Año VI, Número Especial 100, 1983 *passim.*
32. Kenneth F. Johnson, *Mexican Democracy: A Critical View* (New York: Praeger, 1978), p. 135.
33. Flavio Tavares, "The Shame of Mexico: Corruption and Mismanagement Amid a Sea of Oil," *World Press Review* 30 (1983): p. 26.
34. *Proceso,* July 25, 1983, p. 10.
35. Mauricio González de la Garza, *Última llamada* (Mexico: Editores Asociados Mexicanos, 1981), p. 315.
36. Ibid., p. 320.
37. Ibid.
38. Ibid., p. 332.

39. Octavio Paz, "Latin America and Democracy," in *Democracy and Dictatorship in Latin America,* Irving Howe, ed. (New York: Foundation for Study of Independent Ideas, 1982), p. 8.
40. Steven E. Sanderson, *Agrarian Populism and the Mexican State* (Berkeley: University of California Press, 1981), p. 55.
41. Ibid., p. 142.
42. Heberto Castillo, *Proceso,* May 30, 1983, p. 37.
43. Ibid.
44. Ibid.
45. *Proceso,* June 13, 1983, p. 6.
46. David Mares, "Agricultural Trade: Domestic Interests and Transnational Relations," in *Mexico's Political Economy,* Jorge Domínguez, ed. (Beverly Hills: Sage Publications, 1982), pp. 79–132.
47. Castillo, *Proceso,* May 30, 1983, p. 38.
48. John J. Bailey, "Agrarian Reform in Mexico: The Quest for Self-Sufficiency," *Current History* 80 (1981): 357-60.
49. As carried by the *St. Louis Post-Dispatch,* August 7, 1983.
50. FAIR, *Immigration Report* (Washington, D.C.), Vol. IV, No. 11, 1983.
51. Kenneth F. Johnson and Miles W. Williams, *Illegal Aliens in the Western Hemisphere* (New York: Praeger, 1981), p. 73.
52. Ibid.
53. Ibid.
54. Robert Shafer and Donald Mabry, *Neighbors: Mexico and the United States* (Chicago: Nelson-Hall, 1981), p. 102.
55. Ibid., p. 71.
56. Ibid., p. 82.
57. Ibid., p. 83.
58. Flavio Tavares, "The Shame of Mexico," p. 27.
59. In the past when a Mexican president, that is Echeverría, assumed leadership roles vis a vis other Third World nations, his posture drew criticism in the Latin American press. It was noted by *La Prensa* of Buenos Aires (May 12, 1976) that while Mexican embassies around the world were places of refuge for the politically persecuted, and for terrorists, at home in Mexico any criticism of the regime might be castigated severely.
60. Jorge Domínguez, "International Reverberations of a Dynamic Political Economy," in *Mexico's Political Economy,* p. 194.
61. Ibid., p. 188.
62. Ibid.
63. Ibid., p. 178.
64. See Stephen Mumme's a. ticle "Importing Air Pollution" in *The New York Times,* July 23, 1983.
65. *Excelsior,* August 20, 1983.
66. *Noticias de Guatemala,* Año 5, No. 92, May 15, 1983, pp. 7–8.
67. *The Monitor* (McAllen, Texas), June 2, 1983.
68. Mike Colonnese to Kenneth Johnson, August 7, 1983.
69. Ibid. On the career of Fr. Mike Colonnese see Gerald M. Costello, *Mission to Latin America,* Maryknoll, N.Y., Orbis Books, 1979, *passim.*
70. *Proceso,* No. 393, May 14, 1984, pp. 6-9.
71. See coverage in *El Día* and *Excelsior,* both on August 15, 1983.
72. Salvatore Bizzarro, "Mexico's Poor," *Current History* 80 (November 1981): p. 370. See also *Excelsior,* August 8, front page story.
73. Ibid., p. 371.
74. Cf. Christian Bay, *The Structure of Freedom* (New York: Atheneum, 1968), pp. 7, 59, and 115.

75. Cf. Merilee S. Grindle, *Bureaucrats, Politicians, and Peasants in Mexico* (Berkeley: University of California Press, 1977), especially pp. 88–89.
76. Kenneth M. Coleman and Charles L. Davis, "Preemptive Reform and the Mexican Working Class," *Latin American Research Review* XVIII (1983): p. 22.
77. Ibid., p. 24.
78. Ibid.
79. Flavio Tavares, "The Shame of Mexico," p. 27.
80. Corruption is the illegal use of public power and resources to serve private ends. Political modernization may contribute to corruption by creating new sources of wealth and by making the acquisition of wealth tantamount to acquiring power. It has been argued that in some cultures corruption may be most acute during the more intense phases of modernization. See Samuel Huntington, *Political Order in Changing Societies* (New Haven, Connecticut: Yale University Press, 1968), p. 59.

Two

The Aztec Legacy and Independence

GENESIS OF THE MEXICAN NATION

Anáhuac was the original name of the land of the Aztecs. The Spanish captain Hernán Cortés, who in the early 1500s was claiming for Spain the island now known as Cuba and other islands in the West Indies chain, heard convincing rumors of great cities to the west with gold, silver, and agricultural riches. Cortés sent an expedition to the Yucatán peninsula in 1517 which returned with two native prisoners. Using interpreters Cortés was able to verify (so he thought) these fables. In 1519 the Spanish fleet left Cuba and landed on the island of Cozumel just off the coast of the Yucatán. There Cortés found a Spaniard named Aguilar who had remained a captive of the Indians since an exploratory expedition some years before. This Aguilar proved highly valuable to Cortés as an interpreter, especially after the Spanish cavalry routed the Indians in a battle during which the natives saw horses for the first time in their lives. The Indians must have concluded that the Spaniards possessed powerful spirits and decided to yield rather than fight. Cortés's mission was further helped by a native woman of high social standing in the Indian society who came to be known as Doña Marina and ultimately became Cortés's woman. She knew both the Aztec and Maya languages and her skills combined with those of Aguilar greatly facilitated the Spaniards' march on the Aztec capital city known as Tenochtitlán.

Had it not been for the persistence of an Aztec myth Cortés might never have conquered the Aztecs and today's Mexico might never have come to exist as it appears to us now. The myth in question surrounds the serpent-god Quetzalcóatl, a phoenix that was to return from the east in precisely the year in which Cortés arrived and sent out emissaries to the Aztec emperor Moctezuma. There are various stories of how Cortés persuaded (tricked?) Moctezuma to surrender his Aztec empire. Was Cortés with his men on horseback the personification of Quetzalcóatl? Had he come to retake the Aztec throne? Cortés arrived at what is now the port of

Veracruz. He ordered his own ships burned to prevent disillusioned sailors from trying to return to their base in Cuba and began the march inland toward Tenochtitlán. Learning of this, Moctezuma sent messengers to negotiate with the Spaniards. Using Aguilar and Doña Marina (now called La Malinche) as intermediaries Cortés received the emissaries of the Aztec emperor who brought presents on the premise that the Spaniard might in fact be Quetzalcóatl. Unwisely one of the gifts was a golden sculptured disc which inspired Cortés to believe even more strongly in the "cities of gold" myths. Although Moctezuma doubted that Cortés was Quetzalcóatl, yet not being entirely sure, he decided to receive him.

To strengthen his hand Cortés made an alliance with the Tlaxcalan Indians, after defeating them in battle. The Tlaxcalans were perpetually at war with the Aztecs. They, several thousand strong, joined Cortés, who had only 400 men and 16 horses, in August 1519 when the march toward Tenochtitlán began. En route the woman Malinche discovered an ambush that had been set near the city of Cholula by Aztecs bent upon wiping out Cortés before he could negotiate further with Moctezuma. The Spaniards and the Tlaxcalan allies conquered Cholula and in so doing slaughtered thousands of that city's defenders. They then entered the city of Tenochtitlán, which was built on an island in the middle of Lake Texcoco, and were met by the emperor himself. Through trickery Cortés and his men took Moctezuma as their prisoner and persuaded him to command obedience from his Aztec citizens, who could have easily overcome the Spaniards had Moctezuma ordered them to do so. Wishing to avoid bloodshed, the Aztec chieftain chose instead to swear allegiance to the king of Spain. Cortés then declared himself ruler of Anáhuac even though his action was in defiance of his superiors in the chain of command. When a contingent of Spaniards under Panfilo de Narváez was sent to castigate the rebellious Cortés the latter used gifts of gold trinkets to bribe away the allegiance of many of the soldiers. With this done, and following a night attack in which Narváez himself was taken prisoner, Cortés took over the Spanish military contingent, adding several hundred soldiers, weapons, and dozens of horses to his independent colonial force.

Now the Aztecs rose up in defiance against the Spaniards in Tenochtitlán. Cortés had erred by releasing Moctezuma's relative Cuitláhuac, who headed the insurrection. Moctezuma appeared in public urging his countrymen to lay down their arms and practice nonviolence. He was stoned by a mob of angry Aztecs who were tired of being dominated by a relative handful of foreigners; shortly thereafter Moctezuma died. Having lost their primary hostage the Spaniards had no alternative but to abandon the city. They did this on the night of June 30, 1520, and lost more than half of their men and horses trying to cross from the island to the outer shore of Lake Texcoco. Many of the Spaniards sank to the bottom from the weight of the loot they carried; others were sacrificed to the Aztec gods. Cortés's losses on this night, called *La Noche Triste,* were a low point in his career. He took refuge in Tlaxcala where his Indian allies agreed to help organize a new army to conquer Tenochtitlán. Shipments of arms and new soldiers arrived from Spain at Veracruz which Cortés rapidly appropriated to his cause. Allies and enemies alike were riddled by an epidemic of plague but the Spaniards and Tlaxcalans survived this and within a year after *La Noche Triste* they once again marched on Tenochtitlán.

This time they took with them a squadron of portable boats that could be dismantled on land and reassembled on the edge of Lake Texcoco. These boats carried Cortés's army of Indians and Spaniards in a final assault on the island city in May of 1521. The siege of Mexico was costly in human carnage, with estimates that some 100,000 perished of battle, starvation, and disease. Much of the original city of Mexico (Tenochtitlán) was destroyed because the Aztecs under the leadership of Cuauhtémoc (the Fallen Eagle) defended the city on a house-to-house basis. Having neither the Spaniards' cannon, nor crossbows, nor modern swords, and fighting mainly with arrows, stones, and spears, the Aztecs ultimately yielded to the Spanish–Tlaxcalan power. Some say that was the moment of birth for today's Mexico. If one visits the Plaza of the Three Cultures today in Mexico City it is possible to miss a small monument honoring the last defenders of Tenochtitlán. The original name of that plaza was Tlatelolco. The engraving on the monument translates as follows: "On August 15, 1521, heroically defended by Cuauhtémoc, Tlatelolco fell to the power of Hernán Cortés. This was neither triumph nor defeat, but the painful birth of the mestizo people who form today's Mexico."[1]

The conquering Spaniards set about rebuilding the city and setting up a Spanish-dominated municipal government. Missions were sent out to establish towns and the more sympathetic native chieftains were given land grants to coopt them into the Spanish colonial plan. Cortés's own officers were allowed to set up plantations and were given Indians under forced labor obligations to work the confiscated land. These land grants and the virtual slavery of the Indians became known as the *encomienda* system. In October 1522 the king of Spain, Carlos I, had recognized Cortés as governor general of New Spain, being mightily impressed by the stories (mostly exaggerated) of great wealth to be had in what is now Mexico. Cortés, in turn, enforced those decrees of the king which he found convenient but maintained his own colonial autonomy otherwise.

Spaniards receiving an encomienda with Indian workers were obliged to pay taxes, maintain horses and arms to defend the colony, and were expected to convert the Indians to Christianity. The king sent over

several officials to watch the development of New Spain and to collect tribute to help support the mother country. In 1524 Franciscan friars were
sent to Mexico to begin the task of replacing the pagan Aztec priests. The
Spaniards set an example for their Indian wards by paying great deference to these Franciscans, who were later joined by the Dominicans. Religious conversion was slow but abolition of human sacrifice was one early
achievement of these missionaries, at least in the immediate area under
the control of Cortés. But Cortés became embroiled in a colonizing adventure to the south in what is now Guatemala and in his absence insurrections took place against his authority. In 1528 Cortés took his case directly
to the king of Spain. As a result several investigative councils called *audiencias* were appointed to oversee the colonial affairs of New Spain and
in 1535 the first viceroy was sent from Spain to govern the region. By this
time Cortés had become disillusioned; he returned to live in Spain, and
later fought in Algiers.

The first viceroy, Antonio de Mendoza, was fiercely loyal to the
Spanish crown and devoted his skills to putting down further adventures
and insurrections by ambitious officers in the colony. During Mendoza's
administration Francisco Vásquez de Coronado in the 1540s explored
northward into what is now the Great Plains area of the United States.
The discovery of silver also encouraged the northward expansion of New
Spain. Juan Rodríguez Cabrillo explored and mapped the Pacific coastal
region extending up to what is now California.

The so-called New Laws, originally promulgated in 1542, would have
freed the Indians from their obligations to the colonists who held the encomiendas. Viceroy Mendoza postponed enforcement of these laws while
an appeal was made to the king but ultimately the Indians were granted
their freedom, at least on paper. The more able of them, especially the
Tlaxcalans and Aztecs, were given colonizing rights as incentives for helping to expand the colonial frontier. Under other viceroys during the sixteenth century, New Spain earned fame for its riches as the silver mines of
Zacatecas and Guanajuato began producing. Creoles, those Spaniards
born in the New World, began to acquire wealth making it possible for
them to pressure the *peninsulares* (immigrant Spaniards) into modest
sharing of administrative power, although politically the creole remained
inferior as a class. Many creoles of newly acquired wealth settled in Mexico
City and an intelligentsia began to form around the new university that
was established in 1553. They also came to be represented in the new secular clergy that was formed outside the orders (such as the Franciscans)
which jealously guarded their established privileges. Often the poorer
creole colonists, Indians, and secular clergy joined forces against the
friars and the peninsulares. Friction also grew between some creole ad-

ministrators and the clergy laying a basis for political cleavage that would last until the independence movements of the early nineteenth century.

Indian communities remained fairly autonomous after the conquest, producing most of their own food and contributing labor to the Spaniards and local native caciques through a *repartimiento* system of forced labor assignment. Gradually the Indian communities grew weaker and isolated owing to abuses by the Spaniards and to epidemics of disease. The Council of the Indies in Spain ordered that Indian populations be civilized through transfer into towns where they could also more easily be Christianized. This effort created serious social upheaval; the Indians were to be given communal lands for pasture and planting that were supposed to be theirs forever. This foreshadowed the ejido system later to be instituted as part of Mexico's postrevolutionary agrarian reform. The planned Indian communities were off limits to other ethnic groups such as blacks, mestizos, mulattoes, or Spaniards. This laid a basis for segregation of pure Indians (those who did not intermarry with Spaniards) that would last in some parts of Mexico to the present day. It contributed to the long-range deterioration of Indians as a separate ethnic community; the transplanted Indians' lands were often seized by adventurers and the political system never defended Indian rights to the extent that it protected others.

The Spaniards could not as easily subdue the northern Indians in what came to be known as New Mexico as it had those to the south. The Apaches, Navahos, and Comanches had both sedentary and nomadic capabilities and their communities delineated the northern frontier of Spanish expansion as the sixteenth century drew to a close. Extensive missionary activity and explorer expeditions had placed an unmistakable Spanish imprint on the area, however, and the miscegenation of these influences would produce the unique culture of the American southwest today. The overall decline in the Indian population in New Spain created a labor shortage which further hampered the Spanish dreams of northern expansion. In Mexico a new mestizo civilization was being created in the land Cortés had conquered and it would take on a distinctive personality that eventually would separate it from the Spanish crown.

Some contemporary intellectuals have seen the roots of contemporary patterns of social and political behavior in the conquest of the Aztecs. The Aztecs appear to have been an intelligent people, industrious, inventive, and enjoying a well-ordered and complex social structure that should not be overlooked in the horror one finds today in such otherwise barbaric practices as human sacrifices to please the gods. Were the Spaniards, or at least the group led by Cortés, a chosen elite predestined by some divine blessing to subdue and miscegenate with the Aztec nation so as to produce a new and superior race of people? Would this be the start of a "cosmic race" of which José Vasconcelos was later to write?[2] Was Cortés, with a relative handful of men and horses, really able to trick Moctezuma into reluctant surrender, or were other psychic forces at work?

Such questions can hardly be addressed via the contemporary scientific method. But they can be addressed "unscientifically," employing historiography and philosophic insight as epistemological approaches. They may also be handled ideologically.[3] Such inquiries may yield propositions that eventually could be subjected to scientific scrutiny, for example, via clinical psychology or political anthropology.[4] How peoples differ on the basis of their comparative abilities to handle revenge, for instance, can be studied systematically. That is not the goal of this book, but uncovering propositions for such study is well within its province. When the Spaniards mixed with the Aztecs, Tarascans, Tlaxcalans, and other Indians a special kind of psyche may have been created that could explain why Mexico today has a unique political system perhaps found in no other part of Latin America even though the Spaniards may also have miscegenated there profusely.

NEW SPAIN AND THE COLONIAL HERITAGE

At the beginning of the seventeenth century New Spain was divided into two administrative units called audiencias, one named Mexico, to the east, and Nueva Galicia to the west. These, in turn, were subdivided into provinces, captaincies-general, and local governments called *alcaldías* and *corregimientos.* New Mexico was the farthest province northward marking Spanish expansion and exploration and had great value because of its silver mines. New Mexico had to be maintained by the Spanish against the westward movement of European colonists from the Atlantic coast of North America. Winning over the New Mexico territory was left to religious missionaries, since a major military effort would have been a bloody task given the fierce resistance of the Indians living there. In the remainder of New Spain the viceroys sought to replenish the king's treasury in Spain and the Indians were often used as slave labor in this process.

A mestizo class continued to grow in central Mexico and it began to share in some of the affluence which the creoles had earlier begun to enjoy. The mestizos were the basis of the predominant and most characteristic ethnic group that is associated with Mexican nationhood today. A degenerate class of idle rich, often from among the creoles, began to develop at much the same time. Immigrants from Spain, the peninsulares, had distinct advantages in acquiring social place and political power. Mexico City came to be the center of national administrative power and of the ecclesiastical hierarchy. It still occupied the island in the middle of Lake Texcoco which Cortés had taken one century before. Some ten thousand Spaniards dominated the city whose other inhabitants included a mix of some 125,000 Indians, blacks, mestizos, and mulattoes. Mexico City was the center for most commerce both domestic and international; the city boasted its now greatly expanded university, hospitals, and a range of religious and charitable institutions. There were limited opportunities for children of the poor to receive higher education. A mint for silver coins was developed along with harsh penalties for counterfeiters.

As regional economic centers grew, based on wool, foreign trade, and mining, regional politics also developed. Clashes were frequent between civil and ecclesiastical authorities. In Mexico City a problem developed with numerous idle clerics who wished to be supported by society but rejected the task of setting up new parishes where they were needed out in the countryside. Some clerics had begun to amass small fortunes and the church generally was considered wealthy. Moral corruption within the clergy led to clashes between church and state and often detracted from the appeal of Christianity to the Indians.

Religion in the seventeenth century came to be a blend of orthodox and pagan influences. It was important to the Indians and the mestizos that they find something to make the conquest understandable and that they have some way of interpreting the subsequent miscegenation of races which took place and created a new blood base for Mexican nationhood. This is a critical theme to which we shall return in a theory of contemporary political life later in this chapter, but it is important to stress here that the paganization of Catholicism may be central to understanding the Mexican mind. Inescapably the acceptance of the Virgin of Guadalupe and her identification with pagan deities in the seventeenth century created a nexus between the Indians' other (their Aztec) culture of the previous century and the new or mestizo culture that was fast creating a Mexican people of the future. Religious transformation was central to this process.

The Virgin of Guadalupe is said to have appeared in 1531 following the conquest of Tenochtitlán by Cortés:

> According to tradition, a newly converted Indian by the name of Juan Diego beheld a vision of the Virgin, who commanded him to have a temple built in her honor. Juan Diego's experience was seen as all the more miraculous because the Virgin was dark skinned, and so had a special meaning to the conquered peoples. Moreover, the apparition appeared on the hill of Tepeyac, just north of the capital, where Indians had always worshipped Tonantzin, mother of gods. A shrine was built to this Virgin of Guadalupe, and it is still of utmost importance to religious pilgrims.[5]

A complementary version of the same story told by Willa Cather is that the virgin provided Juan Diego with a "sign" to convince his bishop by making roses appear out of season and by performing a healing miracle. The result was that Mexicans regarded the Virgin of Guadalupe as "the one absolutely authenticated appearance of the Blessed Virgin in the New World, and a witness of her affection for Her Church on this continent."[6] Guadalupe was accepted as patroness Christian saint of the creoles, mestizos, and Indians in Mexico during the seventeenth century. Again, we shall return to this paganization of Christianity and its potential meaning for today's Mexican political psyche, at the conclusion of this chapter.[7]

Also during the seventeenth century Mexico developed a tradition of great landed estates or latifundios that often were accumulated by seizure of lands originally granted to the Indians. Exploitative agricultural practices began pushing small landholders toward subsistence farming and led to resentment against elites throughout New Spain. Forced Indian labor was one of the more nefarious practices as was imprisonment for debt. The practice, so common in today's Mexico, of paying for justice began during the seventeenth century as well. Some criminals were pressed into conscription for service in frontier military garrisons. This helped to spread moral corruption about Mexico in the form of escaped and released prisoners who later became regional caciques and acquired political power. It was common for the powerful, including the king's emissaries, to become corrupt and exploit the poor with threats of violence or by economic sanctions.

Conflict also grew between the creoles and the peninsulares, the latters' loyalty to the crown being not the least of sources for resentment. The viceroys in Mexico City had ineffective means of enforcing control over warring factions. Racism entered the picture, with black slaves in Veracruz rebelling against their servitude at various times throughout the century. Indian renegades, deprived of their original lifestyles by the conquest, often became highwaymen and thieves. Food monopolies caused the hungry to riot and caused class-based fear in Mexico City. One viceroy, the Marquis of Gelves, appointed in 1621, earned the wrath of upper classes for his campaign to enforce the law and to castigate corruption. Even the high clergy turned against him so close did his campaign come to infringing on their privileges. There was no efficient army or police, and it was relatively easy to unseat the viceroy in 1624; the tradition of depending on popular militias to keep the peace in cities may have spawned the tradition of police weakness so common in contemporary Mexico. Again in 1692 a food shortage generated mob action and the burning of government buildings. When the viceroy's loyal troops did restore order it was only through great brutality with the cost of lingering popular resentment.

A flood threatened to inundate Mexico City in 1629 and plans were laid to move the city. In 1634 several earthquakes caused the waters to subside. This was a miracle which the Indians attributed to their patroness saint, the Virgin of Guadalupe, and which the Spaniards credited to theirs, the Virgin of los Remedios. Other issues of contention in the seventeenth century were management and distribution of New Spains' customs collections, sharing of revenues with the alcaldías in the interior, ecclesiastical disputes over the conspicuous wealth of religious orders (the Jesuits in particular owned profitable businesses), and protection against European pirates who raided the ports and ships of New Spain. In 1683 Veracruz was occupied and looted by pirates. In 1680 the Pueblo Indians in the New Mexico province revolted against the Spanish colonists there. European wars in this period frustrated trade with the continent. New Spain remained very much a wild and volatile land, but new and distinct cultural traditions were taking root.

The early eighteenth century saw Mexico under colonial rule and struggling with the joint problems of chaos and corruption. Some headway was made, especially in reducing the threat of pirates and highwaymen. Colonial politics generated renewed clashes between creoles, Spaniards, clerics, Indians, and others who were consumed by the adventurous euphoria of the frontier. Spanish authority and religious missionaries moved northward into the Texas territory. Treasure sent to Spain continued to be a high priority of the colonial authorities but great local self-enrichment occurred in the process. Indians and poor mestizos now formed a majority exploited class out of whose sacrifices elites were formed.

The crown sent José de Gálvez to New Spain in 1765 with authority to replace the viceroy and to bring order to the administration of the colony. He established an intendancy system that more clearly defined administrative responsibility, improved administrative salaries, and appointed new figures charged with ending corruption. This meant replacing many creole and mestizo officials at the regional and local levels, who, it was believed, had often acted for personal enrichment and in detriment to the crown. Gálvez seemed also to be concerned with bettering the living status of the Indians who had been cheated just as often as had the royal treasury. Later, as minister for the Indies, Gálvez watched over implementation of his reforms toward the end of the eighteenth century. From then on New Spain was permitted to trade freely with other parts of the Spanish empire. This change, along with tariff reform, stimulated commerce in the colony impressively. A system of *presidios* or outposts was established from the Gulf of California northward along the Pacific coast of California and the establishment of San Francisco in 1776 (as the American Revolution was getting under way to the east) brought the Spanish near to contact with the southern point of British exploration that was proceeding from the Canadian north.

Native Americans, Indians, were recruited wherever possible to man the military outposts under the direction of creole or mestizo officers. Other able viceroys followed and notable progress was reported in rationalizing the enforcement of revenue collection and in remittances to the Spanish homeland. At the same time popular support was generated for many of these reform viceroys. The death of one viceroy, Antonio María Bucareli, in 1779 produced great popular sadness. If the seventeenth century had been a period of hatred for the emissaries of the crown it seemed as if the eighteenth century became a period of at least sympathy for, if not a sense of oneness with, the new colonial administrators. One is led to speculate whether a continuation of this popular sympathy, and its extension to local levels of government, might not have affected the course of the Mexican independence movement which subsequently emerged. In 1789 the Count of Revillagigedo became viceroy and succeeded in strengthening a sense of belonging between the colony and Spain which had seldom before existed. Political troubles erupting on the Spanish homefront also afforded the viceroy a maximum of independence which had seldom been enjoyed by his predecessors.

As New Spain prepared to enter the nineteenth century the quality of life left much to be desired in comparison with the mother country. Medical care was generally available only to the wealthy in both places. Physical security in New Spain still lagged behind owing to the absence of adequate police protection. Those who wanted security built walls with crushed glass on top around their homes, a practice that lingers on in much of Latin America today. The masses of people, however, were left to defend themselves. In New Spain it was expected that every man would go about armed in some fashion. New Spain's economy was characterized by textile mills, silver mines, and animal-drawn transportation systems for the output of these enterprises and for agriculture. Conditions in the workplace, however, were generally poor and unhealthy. Some of the old monopolies had been broken by the reform viceroys and this served to spread out some of the colonial wealth. It also inspired ambitions for revolutionary change in those who could see a potentially better life not far down the road.

Mexico's rugged topography created serious transportation problems. Little of its land was really suitable for agriculture. But there was as yet no overpopulation problem and a shortage of labor existed to work the silver mines of Guanajuato, San Luis Potosí, and Zacatecas. Thousands of people were employed in these mines and by the end of the eighteenth century New Spain produced about half the world's supply of silver. The colonial government had established a school of mines in Mexico City for training future administrators and engineers as knowledge about mining grew. A certain degree of prosperity flowed from this activity, but unfortunately it did not trickle down to most of the Indians and peasants. Wealth based on mining created food demands which stimulated agriculture both for domestic consumption and for export. In this way New Spain approached economic self-sufficiency, an important factor in its eventual drive for political independence.

Industries had grown up in the colonies that began to replace the Spanish mercantile system of raw goods exchanged for manufactured goods. Spain also lagged behind several of her European neighbors in industrialization which gave further impetus to the colonies for economic independence. It was foolish, for instance, to import wool, cloth, and leather goods from Spain when they could be more cheaply made at home. Trade flourished throughout the Caribbean region as Spain was gradually forced to relinquish the controls that had kept the colonies from trading with each other and with other nations.

Political power in New Spain continued to be dominated by Spaniards. But below them was a sizeable corpus of creole and mestizo bureaucrats, clerics, and businessmen whose pressure for a share in administrative decision-making was increasingly felt. This still left a great mass of poor Indians, peasants, and urban workers whose living conditions had changed hardly at all during the eighteenth century. It was these people who suffered most when drought hit the land as it occasionally did. Some of the worst abuses of the Indians had ended, however, especially those associated with the encomiendas and the repartimiento, which were phased out by the reform viceroys. Efforts had also been made to curb the Indian abuses perpetrated by local caciques. Debt peonage, however, still continued to plague the Indians as the colony neared the independence epoch. An important legacy of the eighteenth century was the series of missions to the north begun by Fathers Kino and Salvatierra in Arizona and Sonora around the beginning of the century, and carried on by Fray Antonio Olivares and Fray Junipero Serra in Texas and California. The missions they founded laid a basis for further settlement of the northern reaches of New Spain as well as for the spread of Christianity and literacy in those areas.

The economic and administrative reforms benefitted the colony as a whole. Trade was liberalized and more people were able to share in the wealth. Yet the crown also took for itself certain exclusive rights which hurt broad sections of the populace, like the government monopolies on tobacco and *pulque* which put many small merchants and farmers out of business. Spaniards still dominated the other major businesses and industries whose scope of trade had been liberalized. The imposition of intendants on administrative subdivisions ended corruption at some levels but displaced competent creoles and created resentment. Poor salaries at lower bureaucratic levels still left a built-in motive for financial corruption. Thus, there was reason to be dissatisfied with Spanish colonial rule as the nineteenth century dawned. The bulk of Mexicans were victims, not beneficiaries, of the colonial system. A change of monarch in Spain following the death of Charles III, and the outbreak of the French Revolution at nearly the same time (1789), communicated to colonial minds the message that monarchs could be deposed and dispensed with. As Meyer and Sherman have put it "it has historically been true that rising expectations of an aroused populace are not easily checked."[8] And so it was to be in Mexico.

HIDALGO, ALLENDE, MORELOS, AND THE INDEPENDENCE MOVEMENT

As the era of movements for independence grew near there was a visibly stratified society in New Spain. A small but powerful aristocracy of peninsulares existed with economic roots in land and mining. By and large this aristocracy was supported by the military and the church hierarchy. There was also the class of New World Spaniards (creoles) and a mestizo elite, both of whom aspired to the same political power and in many cases became antagonists. The Indians, mulattoes where they existed, and mestizo poor constituted the masses and represented well above 80 percent of the total population. Their illiteracy and extreme poverty was so patent that by the end of the eighteenth century even the viceroy took limited measures to aid them. But few among the elite were seriously concerned about the need for social reform. Those who recognized the need were too few and their voices were raised too late.

But the story of today's independent Mexico begins in Europe with the early nineteenth-century Napoleonic incursions into the Iberian Peninsula. Napoleon's attempt to dominate the throne of Spain weakened the mother countries' (Spain, Portugal, and France) efforts to hold onto their colonies in the New World. Haiti was the first to break away (from France) in 1804, thereby giving inspiration to others who sought to balance out the structure of power between themselves and the *gachupines.* As news spread of the fall of the Bourbon crown in Spain, young generations of New World Spaniards increasingly saw in this an opportunity to separate politically and to create locally managed sovereign states throughout what is now Latin America.

In Mexico the governing council of the capital city cajoled the vain José de Iturrigaray, the viceroy of Mexico City, into convening a special junta whose purpose would be to create a provisional government and ultimately declare independence from Spain. The creole ambition to displace the colonists was thinly veiled as was the ingenious sympathy of Iturrigaray for the idea of establishing himself as the ruler of an independent

Mexico. The Spanish loyalists responded with a coup that unseated the junta and replaced the viceroy with an infirm old man, Pedro de Garibay, who proved ineffective in suppressing the creole unrest; this did little to bridge the widening abyss between Mexico City and the artificial regime of the French-imposed Joseph Bonaparte in Madrid. The beginning of an indigenous Mexico was at hand. All it needed was a catalyst and a spark of life.

The catalyst was found in the Querétaro Club of 1810, a social and literary circle whose membership included Ignacio Allende, a creole officer of the local militia, and Father Miguel Hidalgo, a creole priest who shared visions of an indigenous Mexicanism while resenting all the while his diminished ecclesiastical status because he lacked true Spanish birth. Father Hidalgo undertook to recruit clerics to the cause of independence while Ignacio Allende and his companion, Juan Aldama, organized military support for an eventual uprising. But the activities of the Querétaro Club became too overt for the Spanish loyalists to continue to ignore. On the evening of September 13, 1810, the army seized a number of secret arms caches and arrested a small group of followers of Hidalgo. Aldama, learning of the arrests, carried word to the small village of Dolores where Father Hidalgo's parish was located. Before dawn on September 16, Father Hidalgo had assembled at his church what would become the nucleus of revolutionary anarchy. Instead of offering sacraments he called upon his parishioners to support him in a march for independence that would be directed against Querétaro. The gullible and downtrodden peasants responded, believing that God had sanctioned the displacement of their foreign oppressors. They marched on Querétaro voicing the famous "cry of Dolores" which in essence meant death to the colonialists.

Hidalgo, Allende, and Aldama had unleashed a massive wave of human violence which they were helpless to control. Disaster followed in late September in Guanajuato where Spanish loyalist bullets slaughtered some 2,000 of Hidalgo's fold. With news of this tragedy many enraged poor of the land sprang forth from their slums, spreading blood and hate in all directions about the geographical center of Mexico. Clearly outnumbering the colonists in most of their encounters, the revolutionary army (which at times is thought to have numbered close to 100,000) fell before the withering fire and cavalry tactics of the disciplined loyalist soldiers. Hidalgo's hordes retaliated in a fashion that historians do not easily vindicate. Nearly everyone not openly sympathetic to the revolutionary cause was put to the sword or torch. Multitudes thus perished, most of them innocent, in what clearly had become a fanatic uprising of the Indian and mestizo poor against the dominant upper classes. But the Hidalgo revolt was short-lived. On January 17, 1811, the volunteer army faced a highly skilled force of vastly lesser numbers near Río Lerma. The loyalist army under the superior direction of General Félix María Calleja, himself possessed by a blind fury of revenge against the insurrectionists, ordered wholesale massacres of the revolutionaries who in turn fled Guadalajara, leaving Hidalgo and his immediate staff as victims of imminent capture.

Hidalgo was defrocked, disgraced, and executed by the Spanish authorities. Thereafter the charge passed to the more able and temperate hands of another priest, José María Morelos, who earlier had been commissioned by Hidalgo to undertake responsibility for an uprising in the south. Morelos's superiority to his mentor was both tactical and intellectual. He did not attempt to control more men than was humanly possible and his well-disciplined insurgent units seldom were guilty of wantonness, terror, or outright atrocities. Ideologically, Morelos did not urge vengeance generally upon the nonmestizo. This, in part, had been Hidalgo's error, for in creating an unbridgeable gulf between the Indian–mestizo masses and the creole colonists, he had failed in his opportunity to unite many creoles to his cause. Morelos tried to cajole the creoles but failed beneath the stigma of horror he had inherited.

Morelos called for abolition of religious privileges, for division of land, and, most important of all, he launched a positive appeal for Mexican independence as a general cause; thus Morelos fought for a free Mexico and not merely against Spain. In 1813 he convened a revolutionary convention at Chilpancingo representing the various southern territories still under his control. Out of this meeting emerged Mexico's first revolutionary constitution, which was promulgated at Apatzingán in 1814. Morelos and his supporters carried the haunting specter of Hidalgo's ignominious defeat within their hearts until December 1815. Pursued by the same General Calleja who had ruined Hidalgo, the Morelos movement was gradually driven into the clandestine reaches of the forests and back streets. Forces led by Agustín de Iturbide ultimately captured the rebel priest and later defrocked him. But he could not be made to recant as had Hidalgo. Morelos gave his life as the first real cornerstone of independence, one which could be embraced symbolically and revered without the stigma of treasonable disgrace.

By the year 1819 only two of Morelos's regional chieftains still operated in defiance of the loyalists. One of them, Guadalupe Victoria, more popularly known as Félix Fernández, was driven to living as a mountain cave–dwelling recluse, later to become the object of a considerable folklore. The other, the stubborn and ingenious Vicente Guerrero, continued to fight alone. His guerrillas took a toll of loyalist troops which shocked the viceroy and made it increasingly difficult to maintain publicly that the revolution unleashed by the mad priest of Dolores had come to naught. However, if the Querétaro Club of 1810 had provided a catalyst for revolution, the insurgent wrath of Vicente Guerrero one decade later gave it a final spark. Lamentably, when the spark produced independence it was hardly of the variety envisioned by Hidalgo, Allende, Aldama, and Morelos.

Early in 1820 the government of Spain fell into the control of those who said they favored government by constitution rather than by monarch. The loyalists in Mexico feared that news of this turn would initiate a new wave of independence-minded terrorism by the small remaining patriot forces. The menace of Vicente Guerrero lived on and with it the figures of Hidalgo and others continued to tower menacingly from the past. Viceroy Apodaca commissioned the man who had overcome Morelos, Agustín de Iturbide, to exterminate Vicente Guerrero. He tried and failed. Indeed, he tried many times, to the extent of proving that Guerrero was unquestionably the better of the two men on the field of battle. Then, after stealing money from the loyalists who had paid him to eliminate Guerrero, Iturbide launched the Mexican people upon a narrow ideological course whose norm is still a lingering pestilence to this very day: he became a traitor and sold out compatriots and friends. At his headquarters in Iguala, Iturbide invited Vicente Guerrero to the conference table; this was decidedly not the latter's preferred field of battle. When Guerrero agreed to the Plan de Iguala on February 24, 1821, he sincerely thought he had won a victory; in fact, all Mexico had lost.

Incredibly, the Iturbide–Guerrero accord won support of most of the remaining Morelos chieftains: even Guadalupe Victoria came out of hiding to champion the cause of independence. Creoles too joined the ground swell and on September 27, 1821, Agustín de Iturbide marched confidently into the capital city flanked by Vicente Guerrero and Guadalupe Victoria. A change in government had taken place to be sure, but it was not accompanied by the social and economic reforms envisioned by Morelos. The man who was to rule Mexico briefly as emperor was motivated primarily by personal greed. After all, it was Iturbide who, as military commandant of the agriculturally rich Valle del Bajío, had profited by the insidious practice of monopolizing the sale of grain (and thereby multiplied the numbers of ill-fed and starving in the very midst of plenty). He undertook to govern the new nation in much the same fashion, naturally to the chagrin of Guadalupe Victoria and Vicente Guerrero. When his congress refused to approve financial measures needed to support his military establishment, Iturbide simply suspended the legislature and ruled openly as a dictator. Putting an army into the field, Iturbide succeeded temporarily in declaring an extension of his empire as far south as what is now the northern half of El Salvador, but he was forced to withdraw in the face of republican opposition throughout what later became known as the United Provinces of Central America. The short-lived empire netted only the southern territory known as Chiapas, a matter still in dispute by Guatemala although it was incorporated as a piece of Mexico at that time.

Iturbide proved to be a traitor in every sense, even to the point of neglecting his military. Unpaid, and seething with discontent, factions of the military united behind the commander of Veracruz to depose him. Iturbide's final act was fully as treacherous as had been his first. He accepted payment and agreed to leave the country forever. That was the epitome of *vendepatria,* selling out one's nation.

BITTER YEARS OF THE YOUNG REPUBLIC

In February 1823, Mexico entered upon the disastrous era marked by Antonio López de Santa Anna who had learned his style well under Iturbide, and who saw to it that his mentor was promptly executed when he attempted to return to Mexican soil in violation of the agreement under which Iturbide had been exiled. From his estate in Veracruz, known as Manga de Clavo, Santa Anna ruled his nation for virtually 30 years. The era was punctuated by numerous rebellions, interim presidents, and frequent exiles of Santa Anna himself, but until the traumatic end it was a bitter epoch which bore the stamp of a single ruthless hand. Santa Anna left Mexico with the stigma of vendepatria.

But it was Guadalupe Victoria and not Santa Anna who became Mexico's first president. He sought to rule under an absurd constitution, patterned after that of the United States, which assumed degrees of political socialization and responsibility nonexistent among the then untutored population. Victoria was opposed by the Scottish-rite Masons as well as by the York-rite Masons. The latter, deeply involved in political intrigues with U.S. Ambassador Joel Poinsett, caused the first republican government of Mexico to be rendered financially impotent.[9] In 1828 when the conservative Scottish-rite Masons succeeded in electing General Manuel Gómez Pedraza to the presidency, Vicente Guerrero rose in arms against the regime. Santa Anna pronounced in favor of Guerrero and thus in 1829 Victoria turned the reins of government over to his former revolutionary partner. The turmoil, and the atrophy of drives toward needed reforms, surrounding these and succeeding events have filled many historical treatises. Their outcome was, unhappily, not one of social progress.

Throughout these events Santa Anna remained in the background. He was soon to emerge as a hero in defending Mexico against an abortive Spanish effort to regain its lost colony and then subsequently came out in defense of President Guerrero, who was overthrown in a military coup in 1830 by Anastasio Bustamante, a mere puppet for conservative boss

Lucas Alamán. The latter was a survivor of the massacre of Guanajuato and personified the oligarchic reaction against what Hidalgo and all subsequent revolutionaries had stood for. After two years of military dictatorship and unrest, Santa Anna was finally named president; but he cleverly chose to allow his vice-president, Valentín Gómez Farías, to rule in his stead. Not proving sufficiently reactionary to satisfy the military and the clergy, Gómez Farías was ousted with the treasonable assent of Santa Anna, who had placed him in power. Santa Anna wanted to be cajoled into office so as to more easily justify assumption of absolute dictatorial powers. Nevertheless, he continued to allow the actual governance of Mexico to be handled by lesser figures, all the while remaining skillfully in defensive isolation at his Veracruz estate.

The first great challenge to Santa Anna's cunning began to emerge in 1830 when the question of American settlers in the northern Texas territory generated concern among Mexican nationalists. U.S. Ambassador Poinsett had explored the possibility of purchasing the territory. To unsettle matters further, Stephen Austin was temporarily jailed in Mexico City after attempting to secure independent statehood for Texas—but as a Mexican state—from a hostile Mexican congress. In 1836 Santa Anna led an army north to reaffirm Mexican sovereignty over the territory. After overcoming the dramatic stand of a handful of Texas settlers at the San Antonio mission known as the Alamo, Santa Anna's ill-trained forces were routed near San Jacinto by well-trained American volunteers under Sam Houston. Spared the ignominy of imprisonment upon his capture, Santa Anna was taken to Washington to confer with President Andrew Jackson and made to guarantee the safety of the Texas settlers in return for an American promise not to annex the territory. By returning Santa Anna to Mexico the United States had committed the first in a series of unpardonable acts against her southern neighbor.

By 1845 the attitude of the U.S. government had changed from one of hands off Texas (originally dictated by the fear of a new slave state) to one of annexation under the mantle of Manifest Destiny, in competition with gestures of acquisition on the part of Great Britain. A mission headed by the American diplomat John Slidell, which can best be described as an attempt at international bribery, was sent by President Polk to Mexico City and was rejected promptly by the proudly nationalistic President José Joaquín de Herrera. The Mexicans then began massing troops in the north to defend their territory, and in April 1846 the United States declared war. The design of President Polk was more the conquest of California than Texas but one could not be had without the other. Border incidents used to justify the war declaration are considered by some historians to be of questionable authenticity. When the war ended, Santa Anna was exiled to Jamaica, thousands of Mexicans had perished, the Mexican treasury had been paid $15 million for the loss of Texas, and Mexico had for all practical purposes lost the most valuable half of its national territory. This was formalized on March 10, 1848, by the Treaty of Guadalupe Hidalgo. The irony of this document is that its American negotiator, Nicholas Trist, had previously been fired by Washington for incompetence and at the time of the agreement he was acting without portfolio. The U.S. Congress swallowed its pride and ratified the treaty.

In most nations peopled by proud human beings, the defeat at the hands of the United States would most surely have been the end of a dictator such as Santa Anna. That it was not testifies to the deplorable status of political democracy in Mexico in the mid-nineteenth century. The presidency fell into the hands of a succession of political adventurers, and, however shocking, it is not surprising that the old dictator, now boasting a wooden leg, should be called once again from exile in 1853 to try to impose order upon the resulting chaos. When shortly thereafter Lucas Alamán died, Santa Anna saw no reason to honor the trust of the conservatives who had returned him to power and proceeded to loot the treasury mercilessly. He climaxed the era that bears his name with the epitome of treacherous acts: he sold a piece of Mexico's territory to the United States. The Gadsden Purchase of 1853 gave the United States a right of way along the southern Arizona border for railroad construction and it gave Santa Anna funds with which to sustain his caprice for another two years. By that time the remnants of the Morelos movement had regrouped into a truly liberal opposition determined not only to get rid of Santa Anna but also to wipe out the landed and clerical oligarchy once and for all. The liberals proclaimed their Plan de Ayutla in 1854 and the following year Santa Anna left for South America. His era of rapine had ended. But the norm of treason, vendepatria, unfortunately survived and to a large extent would plague Mexico into the twentieth century.

WARS AND HOPES OF *LA REFORMA*

The liberal forces under Juan Alvarez, which occupied the capital city following the exit of Santa Anna, brought with them Melchor Ocampo, Miguel Lerdo de Tejada, and, most prominently, the Indian leader from Oaxaca, Benito Juárez. The liberals were unable to hold the capital permanently and provisional governments were established in the regional centers of Michoacán and Veracruz. The famous liberal constitution promulgated in 1857 gave official impetus to the War of Reform. It soon became a religious war against the church and its legion of socioeconomic privileges.

The constitution embraced the earlier Ley Juárez and Ley Lerdo whose joint effect was to deny the church all but its purely ecclesiastical functions within a very narrow definition. Marriage was made a civil function, monasteries and other church properties were confiscated, priests and nuns were proscribed from wearing their habits in public and denied the right to engage in public education. Juárez acquiesced when his followers murdered priests and desecrated altars, but he never allowed the carnage to grow totally out of control as it had in the years following 1810. He occupied the important port of Veracruz and began wearing the conservative forces down by denying them foreign commerce and customs revenues. With the help of an able general, Porfirio Díaz, the conservative armies in the south crumbled as had those in the north earlier, and on New Year's Day, 1861, Juárez's army seized Mexico City. The war had been won but the reforms had yet to be institutionalized.

To Mexico, the combined costs of the age of Santa Anna and the Reform were enormous. Although the United States had favored Juárez with guns and financial aid, the European nations and Great Britain now demanded reparation payments for losses incurred by their nationals. Both liberals and conservatives had appropriated to their pocketbooks the valuables of foreigners, and to make matters worse, the Civil War in the United States made it impossible for Abraham Lincoln to continue to bolster Juárez logistically. Then in the early part of 1862 England, France, and Spain threatened the port of Veracruz in an effort to collect their losses by force. When it became apparent that France, then under Napoleon III, really intended to establish an empire in the Western Hemisphere, the British and Spanish withdrew, leaving Veracruz in French military possession.

The invaders were temporarily routed at Puebla on May 5, 1862, making this date into a contemporary patriotic symbol of Mexicans defeating a superior foreign army. Nevertheless, the French invasion continued and President Juárez was forced to move his capital north to Monterrey. Mexican clericals and conservative oligarchs returned from their Paris exile hoping to carry on in the tradition of Lucas Alamán, but they were shocked to find the French busily taking over lands under provisions of the Lerdo law and the Constitution of 1857; and to make the pill yet more bitter to swallow, Napoleon had in the spring of 1864 imposed the Austrian archduke Maximilian and the Belgian princess Carlotta on the Mexican throne. Their blindness was twice that of Napoleon III, who knew the Mexicans would not love their new royalty but hoped to maintain them by force of arms while the quest went on for the treasures of the Guanajuato silver, gold, and diamond mines. These mines, largely ruined and abandoned by 50 years of plunder and abuse, proved to be almost worthless. Maximilian and Carlotta believed that the people would love them and that great treasures were to be uncovered. When both proved to be false hopes, the French withdrew, leaving Maximilian to face a firing squad of Juárez's army, on a hill overlooking, appropriately, Querétaro where the drive for independence had begun in 1810. Carlotta was abandoned to a European exile and eventually to insanity.

Seldom had two cultures met in so irreconcilable a clash. When Juárez reentered the capital city in 1867, the power of the clerics and landed oligarchs appeared broken and aid from the United States again began to trickle in, but he ruled a nation bled of its human and material wealth. It is hard to imagine how so much misfortune could be continually visited upon the same nation, and that it should still exist.

Desperately lacking in financial resources, Juárez commenced at once to rebuild his ravaged nation. He constructed schools, encouraged railroad development, and sought credits abroad. He was reelected twice to office and seemed to enjoy the confidence of the masses. Notwithstanding, former soldiers-turned-bandits plagued the nation and often intruded into the political arena via attempted coups against state and municipal governments. Increasingly the people looked for a leader, other than Benito Juárez, to bring security to the troubled land. In the elections of 1871 attention turned to one of Juárez's most valuable field commanders in the War of Reform and in the campaign against the French occupation, General Porfirio Díaz. Since no candidate received a majority of votes, the congress returned Juárez to office over the objections of Díaz, who had campaigned on the pledge of "effective suffrage and no reelection." Tragically for Mexico, Juárez died in 1872 before his new term had hardly begun. Congress replaced him with Sebastián Lerdo de Tejada, who could not quell growing unrest and who fell ultimately to a military coup led by Porfirio Díaz in 1876. At that point, Latin America's longest single dictatorship began.

TOWARD A THEORY OF THE MEXICAN POLITICAL PSYCHE

We have seen in the foregoing pages how Mexico's foundation began with a pagan authoritarian tradition, that of the Aztecs. It was then interbred with the Christian authoritarianism of the Spaniards under Cortés. The sixteenth century saw the beginnings of creole and mestizo classes, which would come in the seventeenth and eighteenth centuries to desire shares of the political and administrative power of the Spaniards, the gachupines or peninsulares. Despite the efforts of the reform viceroys, a tradition of moral and political corruption was passed on to the independence era. Corruption occurred when private motives were placed above those of the society or state, or when colonial administrators enriched themselves via the deprivation and suffering of other human beings. The Indians and mestizos were most frequently victims in this process.

To the degree that the Indians (through their relatively few able spokesmen), the creoles, and mestizos were able to experience in common the ongoing thrust of their history they found they needed an explanation for what had happened to them with the conquest. Between the beginning of the sixteenth and the end of the eighteenth century, the Aztec and other Indian nations had disappeared as entities and a new nation, Mexico, stood in their place. At some point all the atomized parts of former units began coming together in a coalescence of minds, lifestyles, and public values. Yet well into the nineteenth century the conflict between those who would champion private goals at the expense of public ones was still in progress. Suspicion and resentment prevailed among ethnic groupings. Law and morality, as bases for a benevolent social order, were as yet elusive.

The quest to unite diverse parts and to reconcile incompatible motives was implanted in the nineteenth century Reform Era, albeit attended by considerable public violence and human carnage. Much of Mexico's quest for unity has had to do with uniting or reconciling the incompatible. A part of this quest may be found in the felt need, conscious or not, to build a bridge between the Aztec past and the creole–mestizo future that will somehow assuage even temporarily the sense of wandering about lost. Do Mexicans follow messianic extremists like Hidalgo, who offer unrealistic panaceas, because their truncated ethnic identity means they are innately lost in a flow of events they cannot understand? Can any benevolent viceroy or governor win their hearts with only superficial kindness for that reason? Are revolutions in Mexico the mere result of exploiting emotion-laden but spurious claims?

Perhaps Mexicans have never shaken off their colonial yoke; perhaps no social synthesis ever occurred leaving them with little more than a latent but controlling pagan identity. Perhaps the political violence and social turmoil of Mexico, even to the present day, is the compulsive self-flagellation of those wishing to be released from the chains of their colonial past so that somehow they may be reunited with their Aztec past. Then one could view interpersonal violence, political corruption, and mass uprising as products of psychic frustration over the failed symbiosis of Spanish and Aztec cultures.

Looking back with certain historians into the labyrinthine depths of Aztec legend an important theme emerges. Sixteenth-century Mexican intellectuals and their conquerors felt it necessary to create for themselves a past that would lend the appearance of continuity with the future they were determined to erect. It has been argued that Mexico is a case in point of colonialism interfering with the creation of an authentic national self-image among the colonized people. Both the colonized Aztecs and the creoles needed a common historical bond. This was even more important for their successors, the mestizos who resulted from the miscegenation of Aztecs and Spaniards and who were, in the spirit of 1521, the first Mexicans.

The Mexicans needed to separate themselves from the loyalist Spaniards. All Spaniards who intended to remain in New Spain, their creole progeny, the Indians, and the resultant mestizos, needed instinctively to explain why the conquest had succeeded. Cortés led relatively few men against the entire Aztec nation; he also had the help of some warring nations who opposed Moctezuma's central authority. Cortés's victory in such circumstances required a credible explanation couched in terms that would generate a feeling of national consciousness which future Mexican generations could inherit. Accomplishing this seems to have been done by practicing (acquiescing in) a convenient historical sleight-of-hand, that is, the deliberate fabrication of a myth. (The use of such myths has become a constant in Mexican political life.) Recent scholarship has revealed that "spurious elements in a spurious history [were] predetermined by inherited assumptions and expectations . . . and that . . . the script writers [were] themselves unaware participants in a drama they [did] not fully control."[10]

Or to put this another way, it is alleged that Hernán Cortés sat down with his emperor, Charles V, and explained his famous encounter with Moctezuma during 1519 which resulted in the latter's surrender of the Aztec nation. It seems Aztec legend held that a plumed serpent-god, a phoenix named Quetzalcóatl, would return from the east in precisely that very year. Moctezuma feigned belief that Cortés was the serpent-god returned. Cortés apparently encouraged Moctezuma in that belief, or so he is supposed to have told his king. And Moctezuma is said to have reciprocated by pretending to invest Cortés with a messianic role. (The professing of messianic roles has become a standard political skill in Mexico.)

This historical entrepreneurship generated a cultural illusion of continuity. The Judeo-Christian messianic presence, embodied by Cortés, was made compatible with the pagan Aztec phoenix newly returned as a symbol of immortality. This act of creating (fabricating?) a doctrine of historical continuity was not only useful in long-term nation building, but in the short run it allowed Moctezuma to save face while he surrendered to a Spanish force of inferior numbers, notwithstanding the subsequent decision of Cuauhtémoc to fight to the death to save the Aztec empire. This also enabled the Spaniards to pretend that their arrival was the natural denouement of an Aztec prophecy, a psychological advantage in legitimizing their later control over the colonial population and in trying to win allegiance from the subject people by telling them that they were all acting out the Creator's grand design. Thus, it is argued, Quetzalcóatl–Cortés became one symbiotic person, the forerunner of a great society to be built, a vital connecting link between the ruptured past and a yet uncomprehended present.[11] But the two were really incompatible, or so we suspect, thus symbiosis never occurred.

However, the maze of fantasy and fact continues. Through additional machinations of the intellect one is asked to believe that the identification of the Aztec plumed serpent-god with Cortés was tantamount to including Saint Thomas in the equation. Saint Thomas is spuriously alleged to have conducted missionary work throughout Central America and perhaps parts of Mexico. Moreover, there was a professed and certified apparition in 1531 (ten years after the fall of Cuauhtémoc at Tlatelolco and the birth of the mestizo nation) which turned out to be the Virgin Mary come to the Aztec capital and available to be metamorphosed into a brown-skinned Mexican saint, the Virgin of Guadalupe. She became for the Indians and mestizos the protectress saint against floods, earthquakes, and other natural disasters. (Today the figure of Guadalupe protects Mexican taxi drivers and politicians alike from each other.)

Later, Guadalupe was adopted by the creole population in the seventeenth century as the official patroness saint of New Spain. Here was a spiritual metamorphosis, a tie with the past, yet one which was unique to the New World. Guadalupe became the principal giver of succor and protection for all Mexicans, and since she prefigured the early church in New Spain she gave seventeenth-century Mexico its own separate spiritual identity, not of direct European derivation, but distinct from the Quetzalcóatl–Cortés–Saint Thomas compound. This, then, gave to creoles, Indians, and mestizos a special sense of belonging to a common past and the ability to experience mutually the thrust of an ongoing history. They thought they had roots. It ended the Christian–pagan dichotomy of the conquest era at least in theory if not entirely in practice.

Surely, most of New Spain's inhabitants were not aware of this identity-forming process in any sophisticated sort of way. But they did welcome the protection afforded by the newly-metamorphosed saints and protectors. Had they been left alone spiritually in the New World these transplanted Spaniards and their progeny could have gone mad. Some believe that today's Mexicans are suffering spiritual atrophy, frustration, and aggression, because their political system denies them the protection they once felt they had enjoyed via Guadalupe and others. That might partially explain the urban *jacquerie* at Tlatelolco in 1968 to be discussed presently.

Out of this miscegenation of races and mystiques emerged a new and powerful dichotomy that would rend Mexico, which was the dichotomy between mestizo-Mexican and creole-Spaniard. This laid the basis for conflict leading to the independence movement in the early nineteenth century: and out of that would emerge a certain fusion as "creole, mestizo, and Indian were brought closer together (at least in theory) as common heirs to a mystical past."[12] The association of pagan gods with those of the Judeo-Christian tradition laid a spiritual basis for declaring a new Mexican nation to exist and this, at least intellectually, was essential to achieving independence in the 1820s.

As we have already stressed, Cortés besieged and conquered Tenochtitlán and defeated Cuauhtémoc in the battle of Tlatelolco of 1521. This was where the Mexican nation was really born. That is what today's Mexican officialdom asks us to believe. The last sacrificial priest (*tlatoani*) to lead the Aztec resistance was Cuauhtémoc. He is of great symbolic importance for he sought to undo the betrayal of Tenochtitlán to the foreigners. He tried to atone for the treason of Moctezuma and La Malinche. Cuauhtémoc symbolically is anathema to the concepts of vendepatria and malinchismo. Cuauhtémoc was Mexico's first martyr, but by no means its last. As will be noted, Mexico needs its martyrs. Cuauhtémoc, now a name often adopted by patriotic contemporary Mexicans, is venerated along with Guadalupe as a symbol of resistance vis-a-vis a hostile external environment. But emotionally it is really Guadalupe who purports to bridge the gap between the Spaniards, the creoles, the Indians, and the mestizos. Her brown color is no accident. She accomplished what Cuauhtémoc could not do. Guadalupe supposedly belongs to everyone.[13]

Part of the illusoriness of Mexico's authoritarian political system lies in its symbolic capability to deceive. A mystical presence such as the Virgin of Guadalupe lends itself to a facade of stability. The Virgin was the protective symbol of those who fought with Hidalgo and Morelos following 1810 in the beginning of the independence movement. Guadalupe is celebrated as a national cult of worship on December 12, a major spiritual ritual for many Mexicans; she adorns the interiors of most public transportation vehicles which pass through Mexico. Guadalupe is the answer to the dilemma of fixing one's origins, and it has been argued that she has a critical dual role, that of the violated woman who is victimized by a wicked outside world, and at once the source of morality and tenderness with which to cement family life. Whether she appears as the mother–victim or as the protectress saint, it is Guadalupe who will steer the believing Mexican to heaven, if not before that to the temporal good life as well. Guadalupe is ubiquitous; so is her duality. Guadalupe is an important part of Mexico's symbolic capability, a spiritual basis for cohesion and allegiance to the nation and she is at once a source of refuge from a threatening political system. Guadalupe is Mexico!

It is very much like the account given by an *Excelsior* reporter concerning today's Otomí Indians. He met a woman who could have been the incarnation of Guadalupe in her dual role of victim and giver of succor. Along with a young girl this woman bore a heavy load of cactus to be sold. The little girl held an axe that her mother used as a basic tool:

> poorly dressed they all looked at us with terror, as if we were going to strike them. The woman maintained a certain beauty but all that she could tell me I knew in advance. Her breasts rose under the ancient worn shirt that she got from a religious charity agency. She was mother earth, the giver of life and at once a beast of burden. Her primitive force and the natural beauty that she gave to her children was sullied by her tatters and rags, her bare feet to which decomposed sandals still clung.[14]

This is the sad duality of Guadalupe in Mexico's phenomenal world of today. The decline of the Otomí woman to tatters and rags may symbolize the social and political atrophy of Mexico as well. And to the extent that the Guadalupes of the real world are also mestizos the implication may be critical.

For the Mexican nation to emerge, the mestizo, who formed the great power base of the independence drive, had to be elevated out of his ambiguous role of an expendable pariah. Octavio Paz writes that the mestizo was not always able to avail himself of the creole's religious and historical syncretism as a way of capturing identity, and

> socially the mestizo is a marginal being, rejected by Indians, Spaniards, and creoles; historically he is the incarnation of the creole dream. His situation vis-a-vis the Indians reflects the same ambivalence; he is their hangman and their avenger. In New Spain he is a bandit and a policeman, in the twentieth century a banker and trade union leader. In Mexican history his ascent signifies the sway of violence; his silhouette embodies endemic civil war.[15]

Tired of exploitation by foreign-dominated elites, the mestizos exploded into civil war early in the nineteenth century and later between 1910 and 1917. Today's revolutionary Mexico was born. The mestizo is the new Mexican of the 1980s and beyond; the mestizo stamp is patent in the political life of Mexico. Thus the mestizo is in a very real sense the embodiment of contemporary Mexico's diverse heritage of two cultures, the Spanish and the Aztec. The mestizo provides the third culture, and thus Tlatelolco, the ancient site of human sacrifice rituals where the Mexican nation was born in 1521, was renamed the Plaza of the Three Cultures, today's site of more tragic rituals which seem to be a self-fulfilling prophecy thrusting onward into the twentieth century.

Octavio Paz also wrote that under the Spanish crown New Spain knew a great deal of abundance and stability; not that all the viceroys were good, but the system had a built-in balance of powers with state authority limited by the church and the viceroy's power balanced by the audiencias of the crown. This division of powers made it necessary for the government to seek some level of public consensus from even the masses. "In this sense, the system of New Spain was more flexible than the present presidential regime [of the 1970s and 1980s]. Under the mask of democracy, our presidents are constitutional dictators in the Roman style. The only difference is that the Roman dictatorship lasted six months, while ours lasts six years."[16]

It could be theorized, then, that psychic frustration resulting from imperfectly fused cultures leaves Mexicans perpetually in search of benevolent authoritarian political regimes under messianic leadership. This would be a combination of the eighteenth-century reform viceroys and Cuauhtémoc. Guadalupe provides only an imperfect symbiosis of the two. Today's ruling PRI, and the messianic president it elects to a dictatorial role every six years, are also imperfect synthetic achievements; they represent the Spanish and Aztec cultures that were ineffectively merged. Today's Mexican, thus, is instinctively distrustful and resentful of the state and, at once, afraid to know himself as an entity within it.[17] He is therefore psychically unable to defend himself against corruption and abuse; all he can do is tolerate repression, and eventually explode violently against it.

One has to assume, then, that an effective cultural symbiosis did occur in the process of colonizing Canada and the United States and that this explains much of the difference in political norms and institutions that developed (although some will say the different experience stems from the fact that little miscegenation with the Indians was attempted). Whether or not one agrees that the above cited cultural schizophrenia is key to understanding the development of the Mexican political psyche it is, nevertheless, essential to an understanding of the basic events of the nineteenth and twentieth century political history to which we turn in the following chapter.

NOTES

1. As photographed in Mexico City's Plaza of the Three Cultures by this author.
2. He argued: "thus we have the four stages and the four racial types: the black, the Indian, the Mongol, and the white. This last, after organizing itself in Europe, has become the invader of the world and has proclaimed itself the master of all peoples as did previous races each at the height of its power." From José Vasconcelos, *La raza cósmica* (Mexico: Austral, 1948), p. 16.

3. See Willard A. Mullins, "On the Concept of Ideology in Political Science," *American Political Science Review* (June 1972), especially p. 508.

4. For instance note the approach to studying the supernatural basis of consensual power that political anthropologists have developed and its possible application to our own discussion of the Mexican political psyche. Cf. Marc Swartz, Victor Turner, and Arthur Tuden, *Political Anthropology* (Chicago: Aldine, 1966), *passim*.

5. Michael C. Meyer and William L. Sherman, *The Course of Mexican History* (New York: Oxford University Press, 1979), p. 186.

6. Willa Cather, *Death Comes for the Archbishop* (New York: Vintage Books, 1971), pp. 46–49 (originally published 1927).

7. In an often utopian-sounding account of Indian life in Mexico one study captures, nevertheless, the synthesis of pagan and Christian influences in saying "the Maya, who number around 30,000, are among the most deeply religious of all Indian peoples. Spanish Catholicism has merged so completely with their ancient beliefs that it is difficult to separate pagan rites from Catholic ritual." From Ana Gyles and Chloe Sayer, *Of Gods and Men: The Heritage of Ancient Mexico* (New York: Harper & Row, 1980), p. 171.

8. Meyer and Sherman, *Mexican History*, p. 262.

9. The involvement of Masonic lodges in Mexican politics apparently began around 1815 when the Hidalgo insurrection was seen as particularly threatening to the United States. Scottish-rite Masons and York-rite Masons soon became enemies in Mexico's ongoing power struggle. There were no Mexican political parties at that time and the lodges formed the basis for political parties eventually to emerge. The Scottish-rite tended to represent the monied classes and enjoyed close contacts with Spain. The York-rite favored political independence and more democratic political participation. In 1825 Mexican federalists favoring an independent republic organized the York-rite lodges with the help of Joel Poinsett who was then U.S. minister to Mexico. Cf. Jan Bazant, *A Concise History of Mexico* (Cambridge: Cambridge University Press, 1977), p. 38.

10. J.H. Elliott, "The Triumph of the Virgin of Guadalupe." *New York Review of Books,* May 26, 1977, p. 28.

11. Ibid., p. 29.

12. Ibid., p. 30. See also Enrique Maza, "Guadalupanismo que libere." *Proceso,* December 11, 1976, p. 19.

13. Elliott, *op. cit.* p. 29. A bold claim for the cult of Guadalupe is made by Jacques Lafaye in that "it is the central theme of the history of creole consciousness or Mexican patriotism. Every study of that subject must inevitably lead to that cult or take it as its point of departure." From his *Quetzalcóatl and Guadalupe: The Formation of Mexican National Consciousness, 1531–1813* (Chicago: University of Chicago Press, 1976). Also, according to this analysis, Mexican creoles had sinful souls and were unsure of their national origins. Identification of Quetzalcóatl with Saint Thomas and, from there, metamorphosing the Virgin Mary into the cult of Guadalupe gave these creoles a passport to respectability, both spiritually and politically. Without these sources of dignity and respect the creoles were doomed to be branded infidels. Lafaye argues that the aspiration to secure dignity was not just a Mexican phenomenon but became a constant that could be identified in other Hispanic-American societies, like Argentina (see Lafaye p. 303). He argues further that the image a society has of its past may be more revealing of its present state of consciousness than any utopian future vision (p. 306). Mexicans thought they saw the hand of Quetzalcóatl behind Madero's victory in the great revolution of 1910–17. They saw him again in Lázaro Cárdenas, the populist messiah-president of the

1930s. No sooner, says Lafaye, does one messiah disappear than another is ready for reincarnation. And as Mexicans pass through the hazardous throes of this process they are watched over protectively by Guadalupe, over whom no elitist political group (not even the PRI) has exclusive control. But who controls Quetzalcóatl? Does any dominant class in Mexico today have an exclusive franchise over his wrath? That poses several elusive hypotheses that could be examined within the context of modern Mexico's political life, e.g., does corruption mean that the spirit of Quetzalcóatl has been honored or betrayed? And Guadalupe?

14. From *Excelsior*, July 9, 1972.
15. From Octavio Paz's introduction to Lafaye, *Mexican National Consciousness*, p. xvi.
16. Ibid., p. xviii.
17. A Mexican writer has recently characterized his people as fearful of everything that embodies authority, an atavistic experience dating to the times of the Aztecs which instinctively tells the Mexican that authority is always bad and unjust. Cf. Juan Miguel de Mora, *Mexico país del miedo* (Mexico: Anaya Editores, 1981), p. 56.

Three

Emerging Nationhood and the Great Revolution

THE *PAX PORFIRIANA:* DEVELOPMENT AND DICTATORSHIP

General Porfirio Díaz sought to be the builder of modern Mexico. He did so during what became Latin America's longest dictatorship until then, and some would say its bloodiest as well. Today, in the 1980s, only the South American dictatorship of Alfredo Stroessner in Paraguay seriously threatens to surpass in length what came to be known as the Pax Porfiriana. Díaz, in many ways a vain man, tried to cover up his Mixtec Indian blood by feigning European ways even to the point of trying to lighten the pigmentation of his skin. It was Díaz's goal to build a modern Mexico and live to see it celebrate the centennial of its independence movement in 1910. But the road to that centennial from Díaz's assumption of power in 1876 was troubled. Some argue that Díaz was Mexico's most ruthless president, others that he was also its most economically creative.

For all the monuments, parks, and plazas he left behind he is scarcely honored today. Díaz installed honorific shrines to his former enemy Benito Juárez and is rumored to have wept at the dedication ceremonies. Yet Díaz's public life was directed against most of what Juárez stood for. Díaz governed for 34 years, occasionally stepping out of office to allow a puppet to take over out of deference to his campaign pledge. He cleaned up the violence in the countryside via a commissioned militia of mercenary rogues called *rurales* who tried and shot criminals summarily and guaranteed the security of the vast legion of foreign investments that now poured into Mexico. In this way Díaz built a gigantic railroad and highway system, providing the basic infrastructure the country so badly needed to industrialize. This is the great Díaz legacy to twentieth-century Mexico. As might have been expected, it was accomplished with a full measure of blood and brutality, and at the almost total expense of political freedoms and individual guarantees for the masses.

Porfirio Díaz was labeled the inventor of concentration camps for the numbers of countryfolk he displaced from their land in order to create latifundios, of which many went to foreigners. Under Díaz's orders some 5 million Mexicans were dispossessed and condemned to debt peonage and slavery. Many large parcels of land went to U.S. companies and magnates like the newspaper tycoon William Randolph Hearst. Many European and U.S. industrialists were attracted as well. While mass exploitation was the order of the day, Mexico was, nonetheless, receiving infrastructure investments that would be important to its economic development. The discovery of Mexican petroleum corresponded temporarily with the development of the internal combustion engine; thus the combination of oil and motors made Mexico attractive for foreign investment. Díaz guaranteed the safety of these investors.

The Porfirian regime tried to advance Mexico to an industrial economy based on agricultural growth, but that very growth depended upon circumstances that were anathema to each other: semifeudal socioeconomic relations, repression, racism, slavery, and favoritism toward autocratic social castes. As foreigners exploited Mexico's subsoil wealth and cheap labor the socially disadvantaged masses rose to support various cries for liberation. Indeed, Díaz himself, on September 15, 1910, shouted out to the populace crowded into the Zócalo at the height of the centennial celebration "death to the hated Spaniards from whom we have won independence" and "down with bad government." But Díaz was seen as a brutal dictator. He was not revered as a statesman and educator as Juárez had been. Thus it was that across the traumatic sweep of nineteenth-century Mexico a collectivity of forces had gathered that would oppose Díaz just as they had fought Iturbide, Santa Anna, and the interim conservative oligarchs. Among the most dedicated foes of the Díaz regime was the Liberal Constitutionalist Party, a regrouping of previous reformist movements now under the leadership of Ricardo Flores Magón. Toward the end of the Pax Porfiriana, Flores Magón's publication *Regeneración* had become a troublesome thorn in the side of the Díaz oligarchy. In 1906 the Liberal party, largely forced into exile in various cities of the United States, issued a program that was directed against a legion of abuses committed by the Díaz government. The Liberals demanded that Díaz honor his commitment to no reelection, the abolition of military conscription, restoration of freedom of the press, increased budgetary outlays for education and school construction, enforcement of the anticlerical provisions of the Constitution of 1857, radical land reforms, and, generally, the disestablishment of the wealthy oligarchy. Not unexpectedly, such entreaties fell on deaf ears in the national government. Although Flores Magón pretended to be heir to the liberal tradition of Juárez, he was much more radical than the Zapotec Indian from

Oaxaca; Flores was bent upon the total destruction of Mexico's socioeconomic fabric, in the fervent belief that a new ideological consensus would somehow be forthcoming. Violent strikes against a U.S.-owned copper company at Cananea and the famous Río Blanco strike of January 1907 brought federal troops into play against the liberal insurgents and revealed the butchery of which Porfirio Díaz was capable when he felt pressed.[1] Ricardo Flores Magón, at first exiled in Los Angeles, California, then in other U.S. cities, imprisoned while in exile, hounded by the American "yellow" and "jingo" press of William Randolph Hearst (himself the owner of valuable property in Mexico), ultimately became a dedicated anarchist. Flores Magón's writings breathed a spirit of beauty into the violence which he came to worship as a goal of life, whereas formerly it had only been a means to secure justice.

Irony was a lingering trait of Mexican political development. So it was that when true revolution came (not a resignation of cabinet or president, or even a widespread insurgency of national proportions, but rather an uprising that produced lasting and profound socioeconomic change) it was fronted by a meek little man who did not drink or violate women, seldom ate meat, and was not as virile (macho) as most leaders of the Mexican stripe were expected to be. It was not Flores Magón who visited revolution upon his populace but the innocuous aristocrat from Coahuila, Francisco Ignacio Madero. Madero's timid manner belied many of his great skills, but the art of politics was not among them. He had been an early contributor to the Flores Magón movement but broke this tie when it became certain that the Liberals sought carnage first and democracy last. Madero was first and foremost a champion of democracy, as he indicated in his mild-sounding treatise, *The Presidential Succession of 1910,* in which he suggested that Mexicans ought to be free to choose their own leaders.

Interestingly, Madero did not write this treatise via the spontaneous outpouring of his soul as Flores Magón had done. Rather he wrote it after being prodded by an influence from the United States: the publication in March 1908 of an interview by James Creelman held weeks earlier with Porfirio Díaz, in which the aging dictator allegedly stated that he would welcome the rise of an opposition (loyal) political movement in Mexico as a measure of the nation's growing political maturity. With this apparent invitation, numerous factions (including Madero's and the followers of Flores Magón) began to declare their candidacies for the approaching elections. Díaz and his brain trust (the "scientists" led by José Yves Limantour) felt uncomfortable. Theirs was a natural reaction. Following publication of the Creelman interview in the Mexican press, a somewhat embellished version to be sure, Francisco Madero announced formation of his Anti-Reelectionist Party whose motto also became "effective suffrage and no reelection." Madero demanded that the choice of his party's candidate be made in an open convention and made a speaking tour of the country in which he emphasized that he did not seek to impose himself on the people.

Not only did Madero win his party's nomination, he attracted enough of a following so that in June 1910 a threatened Díaz government had him arrested on false charges of sedition. Later that month the election results were declared to have been overwhelmingly in favor of returning Díaz to the presidency. Madero's family arranged a bribe to free him from prison under his agreement to remain out of the capital city. He honored this pledge, while all the time gathering evidence (it was abundant) that Díaz's election had been fraudulent. On October 25, 1910, Madero and his swelling ranks of supporters issued the famous Plan de San Luis Potosí, which was effectively a declaration of war against the Díaz regime: on Sunday, November 20, 1910, all Mexicans were urged to rebel. Madero by this time was enjoying unofficial sympathy from Washington, and logistic support for his uprising began to cross the Río Grande. The United States was infuriated with Díaz's apparent favoritism toward European oil concessionaires and annoyed by his aid to José Santos Zelaya, the Yankee-baiting president of Nicaragua.

From exile in Texas, Madero sought to mold U.S. public opinion while also attempting to lend direction to the now incipient revolution which was bursting forth in Chihuahua and Coahuila under the leadership of such guerrilla fighters as Doroteo Arango (better known as Francisco "Pancho" Villa) and Pascual Orozco. In February 1911, Madero crossed the Río Grande and shortly thereafter made his famous assault (unsuccessful) on the town of Casas Grandes. He emerged from the encounter as a man of courage if not of military talent. News came that in the state of Morelos to the south Juan Andréu Almazán and Emiliano Zapata had risen in arms in support of Madero's cause. Venustiano Carranza assumed leadership of the revolutionary forces in Madero's home state of Coahuila. In May 1911 the frontier city of Juárez fell to Madero's forces.

The federal armies, alleged to be some 40,000 strong, were in fact no larger than 15,000 due to the prevalence of the curious greed syndrome developed earlier by Iturbide: the padding of payroll budgets with fictitious names (today's *aviadores*) whose salaries went into the pockets of greedy officers. When it came to battle, the payroll list of fake soldiers was an empty resource. Shortly after occupying Juárez, Madero faced an open confrontation with Orozco and Villa, both intent upon assuming command of the revolutionary movement, and the mild-tempered vegetarian once again proved himself to be a man of courage. Thus his charisma and popular following continued to grow. City by city the country fell to the revolutionaries, and on May 21, 1911, representatives of Díaz and Madero signed a treaty at Juárez providing for the dictator's abdication.

THE GREAT REVOLUTION:
MADERO'S VICTORY AND BETRAYAL

Díaz, however, balked at resigning. Late in May, crowds that had gathered outside the national congress building in response to rumors that the dictator was about to abdicate were disappointed and moved on the Zócalo where they were charged by Díaz's palace guard. Before the melee was over several hundred Mexican citizens had been machine-gunned, enough to convince Díaz it was time to resign. By the end of May 1911 Díaz was aboard a German ship bound for Europe and his minister of foreign relations, Francisco León de la Barra, had become interim president, with the promise that he would conduct new presidential elections in the fall and that he himself would not be a candidate. Here was where Madero probably made a serious mistake, one that his country was to pay for dearly and in blood. According to one analyst of the period: "There would have been no hindrance if Madero had seen fit to declare himself President immediately. He might have saved both himself and Mexico much trouble had he done so. Taking power at the high tide of his popularity might have brought peace and stability."[2]

By insisting upon a strict adherence to constitutionality in the succession, Madero gave ample opportunity for separationists within his own ranks, like the Flores Magón group now centered in Baja California, to vie for place and power. To complicate the matter further, Madero naively expected not only de la Barra but the entire federal bureaucracy and army to become loyal to his movement overnight. Compounding the risk, Madero disbanded many of his revolutionary troops, thus denying them a greater share in the spoils of victory and disarming himself of their protection. Many of these disappointed troops became followers of Zapata who openly rebelled against Madero, charging that the process of agrarian reform was going too slowly. Old followers of Díaz like Bernardo Reyes revived their power ambitions.

With chaos threatening from all sides, interim president de la Barra turned over the reins of government to Francisco Madero several weeks early on November 6, 1911. By this time Emiliano Zapata had openly broken with Madero over the failure of the land reform program. Indeed the followers of Zapata had charged Madero with treason: "Mexican citizens: because of the cunning and bad faith of one man blood is being spilled in a scandalous manner; . . . because he is incapable of governing we will take up arms against him for he has become a traitor to the Revolution."[3]

Three major uprisings now threatened: those of Zapata in Morelos, Orozco in Chihuahua, and Félix Díaz (nephew of the exiled dictator) in Veracruz. Madero's Constitutional Progressive Party, now headed by his brother Gustavo, sought to cultivate popular loyalty and tolerance but by this time Francisco's charisma had worn thin. Francisco Madero was honest, and brave, but more than that was needed to rule Mexico. Perhaps what was needed was a skilled imposter such as Rodolfo Usigli was later to create in a brilliant play whose insight into the psychology of Mexican politics was keenly penetrating. But this was not Madero; he simply lacked the strength of his opponents. He would lie to no one; he deceived only himself. The story of Madero's demise unfolds from the fateful trust he placed in General Victoriano Huerta, one of Porfirio Díaz's trusted chieftains who had personally escorted the fleeing dictator aboard his Europe-bound vessel.

In February 1913 Huerta undertook to do battle in the center of Mexico City with the forces of Félix Díaz, now stockaded inside an old military arsenal known as the Ciudadela. Ostensibly Huerta was to smash this rebellion against the constitutional government but it is now believed that the action, known as the Tragic Ten Days, was a facade for a pact being arranged between the two men, with the fighting designed, cynically, to decimate the ranks of the government troops. The cruel barbarity of the event has been shown brilliantly by William Weber Johnson, who described the revolution's birth pains during the Tragic Ten Days.

Johnson's account stresses the gullibility of Madero's followers, especially that of his brother Gustavo, and the president's own blindness to the deception that Victoriano Huerta and others had laid in the Revolution's path. As corpses were burned in the streets and public utilities came to a virtual end, all semblance of social and political order vanished from Mexico City. When the Madero home in the Calle Liverpool was put to the torch by anarchists the president's family finally took refuge in the Japanese legation.[4]

When the slaughter ended President Madero and his brother Gustavo were prisoners. The president had tried to repeat the success of the personal confrontation he had had with the rebels Orozco and Villa who earlier sought to depose him at El Paso. This time his defiance failed; the magic of his charisma had waned. Then came the nadir of shame in the history of Mexican-U.S. relations. U.S. Ambassador Henry Lane Wilson, acting apparently without the knowledge of the president of the United States, offered the U.S. Embassy as the stage from which Huerta and Díaz (the supposed enemies to the death) could proclaim their infamous Pact of the Ciudadela. Huerta would become interim president and in exchange Díaz would be guaranteed the support of Huerta to succeed him in the next election. Nor did the odious story end there. After Madero and his vice-president, José María Pino Suárez, were forced to sign resignations, they were both murdered under mysterious circumstances while being transported in the safe custody of their military captors.

The ultraconservative U.S. ambassador, who was slavishly loyal to U.S. business interests and who viewed Madero's reformist bent with alarm, was inescapably involved in the tragic affair.[5] Mexican research contends that Madero's promises to create a "Mexico for the Mexicans" frightened powerful North American business interests. It is argued in Mexico that U.S. Ambassador Henry Lane Wilson, devoted to protecting American business interests, acted without formal orders from Washington and took it on himself to conspire with Huerta's henchmen in the cause of Madero's violent overthrow. In point of fact, President Madero and Vice President Pino Suárez were taken to a secluded site in Mexico City where a battle scene was faked. Madero and Pino Suárez were shot amidst this cover. One year after the night of the murders, February 22, 1913, an eyewitness swore to having seen these executions. Clearly the United States was shamefully involved behind the scenes via the actions of its ambassador.[6]

In the light of the foregoing those Americans who today ponder the fact that Mexican intellectuals often dislike us should review and rethink the following: no later than 1913 the United States had succeeded in taking by force the most valuable half of Mexico's terrain, purchased a collateral piece of the national patrimony, and had then sought to ingratiate itself further by presiding over the assassination of the father of Mexico's (and indeed Latin America's) first true revolution. That is a melancholy and sobering truth with which we must live and which our Mexican neighbors cannot easily forget.

The regime of Victoriano Huerta was foredoomed by the very personality of the man who headed it. Huerta was the most inept of dictators. He alienated such regional chieftains as Venustiano Carranza, Pancho Villa, and Emiliano Zapata, who now rose in arms against the Mexico City government. To make matters worse, Huerta began an exchange of insults with President Wilson, after which U.S. marines were ordered to seize Veracruz in April 1914. War between the two countries was barely averted through the good offices of the foreign ministers of Argentina, Brazil, and Chile. In 1914 Huerta resigned and fled to Europe with a generous array of loot taken from the Mexican treasury. In August of that year he was succeeded by General Carranza, who became a de facto president and was later recognized as such by President Wilson. Carranza was forced to flee the capital by an invasion of forces under Pancho Villa and Eulalio Gutiérrez, but returned safely after a major triumph by his trusted general, one of Mexico's truly great military figures, Alvaro Obregón. Carranza sought to repair the injured relations between his nation and the United States, a task made difficult by the border raids of the Mexican Robin Hood, Pancho Villa, during 1916.

Also in that year the state of Morelos (just south of the Federal District) had become a caldron of revolutionary activity. The forces of Zapata held the state in defiance of Mexico City and maintained themselves isolated from the capital. The revolutionaries (at least the Zapatistas) had an internal dilemma: "Precisely because they were sincere revolutionaries and not bandits or vandals they could not derive from the dispute [with Mexico City] alone a motive to keep themselves going."[7] There was disagreement as to whether the revolutionary movement should even continue, in addition to the controversy over goals. It was the charismatic leadership of Emiliano Zapata which, in large measure, held the Morelos revolutionaries together. And it was fortunate also that Zapata had shared power and experience with some able lieutenants, like Gildado Magaña, who were able to carry on the struggle after Zapata's passing.

This period, often referred to as "the storm," is probably the most critical point in the growth of Mexican nationhood. Her political and military leaders now grew aware that the social fabric of the country was almost in tatters. The chronicle of events which led to the month of December 1916 tells little or nothing of the apathy, the naked despair, of the people of Mexico during this horrendous six-year period. The novel *Los de abajo* by Mariano Azuela tells this story in the poignant words of a disillusioned revolutionary who was caught up in the anarchy which swept across the countryside like a plague in the aftermath of the revolution. Perhaps it was the pitiful blindness of those who fought onward to their destruction which ultimately produced a vision of lasting order and the conviction needed to make that vision real. Order was the determination of Venustiano Carranza when he called a constitutional assembly into session at Querétaro at the end of 1916. The following February the assembly promulgated a document which has provided the basic governing format of Mexico to this day.

INSTITUTION-BUILDING AND THE CARDENAS REFORMS

The Constitution of 1917 embraced most of the liberal principles of the Juárez–Ocampo–Lerdo Constitution of 1857. The four key features of the new constitution were the following: Article 3 prohibited clerics from participating in public educational instruction and severely limited the political rights of religious groups (specifically, the article proscribed the use of religious titles in the names of political parties and endorsements by religious groups of political parties); Article 27 deprived the church and foreigners of landholding and subsoil rights and provided a basis for agrarian reform throughout the republic; Article 33 opened the door for the Mexican president to expel foreign companies and person-nel from the land; and Article 123 endorsed the principle of workers' rights, laid a basis for collective bargaining, and recognized the right of workers to organize into unions and to receive compensation in case of ac-cidents. It would be an enormous understatement to say that Mexicans of 1917 were ready for such measures as these.

It should also be stressed that Article 27 (and Article 123) of the 1917 Constitution encouraged the division of great landed estates and the de-velopment of rural hamlets and villages. But it also underscores the gov-ernment's right of eminent domain which the state could use on behalf of private property–based capital formation if it so chose. It can be argued that such reform articles gave only the appearance of equality as a goal while providing a legal basis for quite the opposite. States, for instance, were allowed to fix maximum limits of landholding and to allow latifun-distas to decide what lands they would keep and which would be relin-quished in the name of agrarian reform.[8] Under such strictures lands that were rich, irrigated, and bordering highways and railroads were seldom relinquished voluntarily and only rarely expropriated. When such ex-propriation occurred the tenure of the affected parcels was more likely to pass to government bureaucrats and political figures rather than to the campesino masses.

Few emerging revolutionary governments are corruption-free, nor was the new Mexican state. President Carranza recognized the need for the reforms defined in the Constitution of 1917, but he was not eager to enforce them. His own cronies and followers partook generously of the booty that issued from the presidency, but little filtered down to the mass-es. Thus the populace again came to wonder whether the revolution had been for naught, since it resulted in merely a paper document of reform. Pancho Villa's forces in Chihuahua and those of Zapata in Morelos and Guerrero still opposed Carranza's rule. Ignominiously—and, it is be-lieved, with the blessing of Carranza—the legendary Zapata was assassi-nated in 1919, and thus a revolutionary of wide popular following became a martyr. Treachery had, from the time of Cortés and Moctezuma, be-come a constant norm in Mexico's political life. Perhaps nowhere could this better be seen than in the death of Emiliano Zapata, the populist and charismatic revolutionary leader dedicated unselfishly to the cause of agrarian reform, the man who also believed instinctively that all thrones of power should be abolished for their innate tendency to corrupt.

Like Moctezuma, Zapata was also deceived. The way it was done left no doubt in anyone's mind what President Carranza thought of those who would take Mexico's agrarian reform cause into their own hands. Car-ranza's emissary in this case was Colonel Jesús Guajardo who invited

Emiliano Zapata to lunch on April 10, 1919, ostensibly to talk peace. They were to meet at the ranch known as Chinameca in the state of Morelos.

> It was a splendid day. Nothing suggested danger. He was to see Colonel Guajardo and trusted him . . . it was 2 p.m. plus 10 minutes. Zapata ordered ten of his men to accompany him to the gates of the hacienda. He went on horseback; he went to his death . . . the colonel's guard had formed a position as if to render honors to Zapata . . . three bugle calls heralded his arrival. General Zapata reached the doorway as the last note of the bugle faded . . . then, at close range and from the position of 'present arms' the colonel's men turned and fired into the body of our unforgettable General Zapata who fell never to rise again.[9]

As a reward for handling the assassination President Carranza ordered Colonel Guajardo elevated to the rank of general.

Out of such deeds is the stuff of Mexico's political symbolism made, its history evaluated and reinterpreted. But Zapata, posthumously, may have had his own requital. The following year Carranza himself was assassinated (while attempting to flee the country) by forces loyal to Zapata. Carranza had refused to honor his 1917 pledge of "no reelection" and in April 1920 used federal troops to interfere with a Sonora strike involving Luis Morones's newly formed CROM, the Regional Confederation of Mexican Workers. With organized labor and the followers of Zapata still against him, Carranza recognized the precariousness of his situation and abdicated, only to lose his life in attempted flight.

Resistance to the Carranza government came also from General Alvaro Obregón who resented the former's selling out of the promised land reform to the hacendados and his callous attitude toward the poor masses. Obregón was proclaimed president for a four-year term in 1920. The average daily wage in Mexico was then 90 centavos, about 40 cents U.S. By 1925 the nearly 69 percent of the national population subsisting in rural areas had seen land reform measures benefitting only 0.54 percent of the rural population, again under the unfavorable tenure conditions described above.[10] Obregón enjoyed labor support through the COM or *Casa del Obrero Mundial* which had participated in a general strike against the Carranza regime in 1916. He came from a small farming background in Sonora giving him a basis to sympathize with landless campesinos, peons, and even with the northern Yaqui Indians, although Obregón was not prepared to give in to their anti-white radical demands. He was not prepared to persecute the Indians either. Obregón's military career, especially after his victory over Pancho Villa's forces at Celaya in 1915, had made him something of a warlord.

President Obregón's Ejidal law of 1920 created a maze of legalisms that gave much lip service to distribution, and did accomplish some, but still left the major rights of private property intact. That law was abrogated the following year as being unworkable. Agrarian reform movements sprang up during this period with Obregón's blessing, including Díaz Soto y Gama's PNA or National Agrarian Party. The president felt politically obliged (owing partly to the support he had received from Zapata's followers in the political battles of 1920) to attempt some concrete agrarian reforms. Obregón's famous Decree of August 2, 1923, became enshrined in Mexican folklore and is cited later in this book as a symbolic basis for contemporary political alienation in Mexico. It permitted a kind of provisional tenancy of unused national lands called *baldíos.* His government also enacted legislation providing for governmentally sponsored agricultural credit and for compensation to those whose lands had been legally expropriated.

Prevailing criticism, however, contends that of the 1.2 million hectares of land distributed during Obregón's first presidency only half were even marginally cultivable. In Sonora only 8.8 percent of the land given out under agrarian reform was marginally suitable for cultivation. The Decree of August 2, however, would become a symbolic basis later for campesinos throughout Mexico to justify invasions and occupation of idle lands. Conflict with the state and its protected elites would prove inevitable. It is noteworthy that because of the Obregón precedent in land distribution some Mexican presidents thereafter would often boast of their own land distribution figures to dramatize their fealty to the revolutionary promise, but such claims were usually diminished if one took into account the immediate agricultural utility of such land to peasants lacking capital or credit. Bureaucratic inefficiency, and corruption in the CNA or National Agrarian Commission often resulted in another frustration of the agrarian reform campaign: granting nonexistent land to petitioning campesinos.

It can be said that Obregón tried to implement the land reform promises of the constitution, as his predecessor had failed to do, and carried out an ambitious program of public education under the brilliant guidance of the philosopher José Vasconcelos. Despite an attempted coup by Adolfo de la Huerta, Obregón turned the presidency over to Plutarco Elías Calles, the constitutional president-elect, in 1924. Whereas Obregón had begun educational and land reforms pursuant to the Constitution of 1917, Calles considered as his special province the implementation of the anticlerical provisions of the constitution. To this end he confiscated church lands, abolished religious instruction in public schools, deported priests, forbade the wearing of religious habits in public, and in general waged a Kulturkampf against religious privilege in all its protean forms. A counterrevolution of rightists and clerical fanatics, under the banner of the *cristeros,* or defenders of Christ, erupted in defiance of Calles. Despite the shock felt by foreigners over Calles's treatment of the church, Mexico's relations improved with the United States, largely because of the adept qualities of U.S. Ambassador Dwight Morrow, who sympathetically understood the Mexican dilemma and sought constructive channels to aid it.

The cristero rebellion tore deeply into Mexican political life between 1926 and 1929, pitting, as it did, landowners against rural workers, religious fanatics against the state, and some parts of the establishment church against the state as well. President Calles was branded an enemy of traditional Catholicism. Some agrarian worker groups were sponsored by reform-minded clergy, others by reactionary clergy seeking to cast secular power in heathen and atheistic garb. Most of the agrarian reform groups, like Díaz Soto y Gama's PNA, fought for the government against the reactionary clergy but often with mixed feelings. These *agraristas* favored land tenure under the fledgling ejido system and urged more expropriations. The cristeros opposed this and defended private property, even though they too were for the most part campesinos. And as the cristero violence continued to rend Mexico the thorny problem of the presidential succession emerged again, but in new form.

The "Sonora Dynasty" of presidents Obregón, de la Huerta, and Calles (a celebrated clandestine agreement to rotate national power among these men) was rent by de la Huerta's rebellion of 1923, which was put down by forces loyal to Obregón. This began a new stage of Mexican political development, the professionalization of the armed forces and their subordination to postrevolutionary civilian leaders. Obregón and Calles then remained the dominant political figures and when the latter entered the presidency in 1924 it was with the strong approval of U.S. interests. He thus had ample freedom to unify the country in the aftermath of the Revolution, whose fragmented conflicts and animosities still flared out of control regionally. Calles's agrarian reform ambitions became clouded, however, as the postrevolutionary state became involved in the cleric-backed cristero insurrection that took on major proportions.

Obregón, without Calles's backing, wished to return to the presidency in open violation of Article 83 of the Constitution. He was opposed by Francisco Serrano who sought to start an uprising against the government and was assassinated, it is believed, at the behest of Obregón who then proceeded to have himself elected via elections of dubious honesty in 1928. But before Obregón could take office he too was assassinated in a public restaurant by a religious fanatic who, anachronistically, was allegedly one of the defenders of Christ now working in the employ of Calles. So vigorously did Calles denounce the affair, however, and so determined was his appeal for government by law rather than by passion, that violence of major proportions was avoided. Calles, like other contemporary leaders, was not above enriching himself at the public trough, but he exhibited moments of progressive conviction, as had Carranza and Obregón, which allowed the revolution's paper gains to inch forward toward realization.[11]

The death of Obregón may have hurt the cause of agrarian reform in Mexico, and his supporters, including the PNA, began to lose influence. Multiparty politics ended with the death of the Mexican Labor Party (PLM) at about the time of a rebellion led by General José Escobar and other military figures in 1929. That action included the massacre of several hundred agrarian reform sympathizers in Durango and Sinaloa. Congress named Emilio Portes Gil, an intimate and supporter of Obregón, to be provisional president for 14 months. During this time Calles and his group, which now included Luis Morones, formed Mexico's first revolutionary political party, the PNR, or National Revolutionary Party, which held its first convention in 1929 and nominated Pascual Ortiz Rubio to succeed Portes Gil. The latter, in his *Quince años de política mexicana,* described Ortiz Rubio's defeat of José Vasconcelos in a bitter electoral struggle which pitted the reformist thrust of the revolution squarely against the conservative forces of clerical reaction. Not only was Ortiz Rubio a puppet for Calles, he was also a poor risk. The congress challenged the president's budget, and during the ensuing controversy, Ortiz Rubio saw fit to fire several pro-Calles members of his own cabinet. To this gesture of contempt, Calles, the great cacique, retaliated and forced Ortiz Rubio's resignation, replacing him with a wealthy militarist and landowner from Baja California. Abelardo Rodríguez finished the term faithfully in service to his chief.

Indeed, the trio of Portes Gil, Ortiz Rubio, and Abelardo Rodríguez were sometimes referred to as puppets of Calles who controlled things from behind the scenes during what is called the *Maximato* from roughly 1920 to 1934. Calles is credited with slowing up the rate of agrarian reform which Obregón had sought to accelerate. In 1930 the CNA stopped land grants and subdivisions and concentrated its efforts ostensibly on helping established small farmers to modernize their production. In that year over 80 percent of the land was still controlled by landholders with plots of over 1000 hectares. Only 6.4 million out of a total 36.4 million pesos that were loaned by the National Agrarian Credit Bank went to small local borrowers, the remainder going to larger private individual landowners. In Sonora "*latifundistas*—numbering only 919—controlled 89 percent of the land, in plots over 1,000 hectares" making Mexico the "most *latifundista* country in the world" as of 1930.[12] Agrarian reform had become a piece of an ideology, an enigmatic promise that was used more for manipulating the masses than for satisfying their needs. The world depression at the same time brought labor and peasant violence to Mexico and even former cristeros joined the agrarian reformists in denouncing the misery in which the vast majority of Mexicans had to live. Their reward from the Revolution seemed, in the early 1930s, to have been violence, hunger, and deception. During the decade of the 1930s it would be the ideological and pragmatic task of a new leader, General Lázaro Cárdenas del Río, to give substance to the promises of the Revolution and in so doing to pacify and feed the Mexican nation.

The elections of 1934 saw the left wing of the PNR erupt in disgust with a situation in which the Mexican presidency was obviously being run by Calles from his villa in Cuernavaca. The new revolutionaries were able to impose upon Calles their own favored candidate for the presidency, General Lázaro Cárdenas, who was promptly elected and assumed office. That Calles had underestimated the general as a potential puppet became swiftly obvious. Soon Calles was in exile in the United States, marveling at the socioeconomic reforms that began to sweep the republic.

With the coming of President Cárdenas in 1934, Sonora, like many Mexican states, was predominantly rural and had benefitted relatively little from agrarian reform efforts to that date. Few among the state's population held any land at all. Some 89 percent of the land, controlled by 8.8 percent of the landholders, was taken up by latifundios. Cárdenas's presidential campaign had promised, again, true substantive agrarian reform. In an ejidal census conducted in 1935 "some 48 percent of ejidal land—which represented only a fraction of total arable land—went uncultivated."[13] The PNR had not been able yet to coopt all interest groups and agrarian resentment over the "Stop Laws" (that stopped the land reform) produced clashes between campesinos and the state.

Potentially, the Cárdenas era (1934-40) was a take-off stage for the Mexican revolution during the postviolence period. Casting aside all remnants of bondage to the Calles machine, Lázaro Cárdenas distributed agrarian lands to peasants more generously than had any other previous chief executive. He did so via the usufructuary device of ejidos, or communal farms, regulated by the state. He sought political change internally by scrapping Calles's old PNR in favor of a new party, the PRM, or Mexican Revolutionary Party. At the same time the old CROM of Luis Morones was replaced with the CTM, the Mexican Confederation of Workers, which came under the new and vigorous leadership of Vicente Lombardo Toledano. With both Calles and Morones exiled to the United States, Cárdenas governed without serious opposition. His support rested squarely on a broadly-based configuration of peasantry, urban labor, and the armed forces.

Lázaro Cárdenas was popular with peasant organizations which along with other worker groups lobbied for the candidacy of the retiring general and fought with hacendados and government cronies throughout Mexico. To the peasants' and workers' organizations Cárdenas seemed genuinely committed and able to challenge those who had frustrated the agrarian reform promises of the Revolution. He took the capitalist system to task for the world depression it had visited upon the great majority of Mexicans. This meant that Cárdenas's strength came from many of the key sectors which Calles and his puppet presidents had neglected. After receiving Calles's blessing for the presidency Cárdenas used his popular following to resist manipulation by the old cacique. In 1935 when Cárdenas did open political battle with Calles the support of groups like the CCM helped the former immensely. Cárdenas's friendship with and support from Vicente Lombardo Toledano suggested that an end might be forthcoming to the corrupt labor politics that grew notorious under Luis Morones and his CROM, an integral part of the old Calles political machine. When numerous state governors loyal to Calles were successfully purged by Cárdenas during 1935 with impressive organized agrarian backing the cacique ex-president was effectively unseated from his dominant position in Mexican political life. There was a corresponding purge of senators and deputies from the state and national legislatures as well.

By the end of 1935 Cárdenas was the dominant figure in Mexican politics and he was endorsed by the newly formed CCM (Mexican Peasants Confederation). This seemed the first time that the common people felt in their hearts that they had been incorporated into the Revolution's onward march. The old PNR, renamed PRM, was reorganized under Cárdenas to include state-dominated sectoral organizations. One of these was called the CTM, or Mexican Workers Confederation, which would present a united worker front against the industrialists and bourgeoisie generally. Another sector was called the CNC or National Peasants (small farmers) Confederation to defend the interests of all peasants including sharecroppers, contract workers, and all other peasants previously excluded from agrarian reform benefits. Under inspiration of the CNC the ejido was scheduled to become the basis for establishing a new agricultural order to accompany dismembering of many latifundios. Cárdenas's plan was to offer a third alternative to capitalism and communism, a state-controlled economy allowing for capital formation and responsible private property and profit while socializing the distribution and redistribution of much of the nation's wealth so as to wipe out poverty. The state, that is, the official Cárdenas party PRM, would intervene socioeconomically for the benefit of both capitalists and workers. Undercutting the Calles political machine was only to be a political beginning. The state would take a leading role in infrastructure development and capital formation, as well as in promoting social justice.

Cárdenas's agrarian reform program goes down as one of the hallmarks of his administration and earned him a place of distinction in Mexican revolutionary tradition. The president saw the process as political, social, and economic, and all aspects had moral human goals. The central instrument for agrarian reform organization was the ejido, a variety of collective farms. Before the Revolution ejidos had often meant common land belonging to a village or pueblo under old Spanish law. Cárdenas's reform saw the ejido as both a social unit and an economic unit of production to feed the population. Codification of the agrarian reform laws in 1934 was meant to integrate the campesinos politically and economically with the state, but also with the urban workers via the nexus of the CNC and CTM, which would be the principal sectoral organizations of the official party PRM.

The 1934 and 1937 agrarian laws significantly expanded opportunities to landless peasants for acquisition of land and limited credit for development of it, and at once reduced the loopholes the latifundistas could use to exempt idle property from confiscation and redistribution. Ejidos under the Cárdenas plan were either "collective" or "cooperative", but always used usufructorally, thus remaining property of the nation in the ultimate instance. Previous ejidal concepts had awarded perpetual ownership of lands in question to a politically established unit, a qualified person or family, or a corporate group that could meet application criteria. Ejidal lands not used efficiently or honestly could be reclaimed by the state and credit depended upon the indulgence of the state's lending agencies. More was done under Cárdenas to involve campesinos in the agrarian life of their nation than under any previous presidency. Unfortunately some of this involvement would be eroded under succeeding Mexican presidencies although symbolically all would approve publicly of the achievements of the Cárdenas era. Equally unfortunate under the Cárdenas plan was the lack of protection for ejidal debtors from easy foreclosure by the agencies extending credit. To this day ejidal credit societies have lived in precarious circumstances vis a vis the financial controls of state banks.

Among Mexico's true revolutionaries—that is, leaders who were instrumental in bringing about concrete change—Lázaro Cárdenas merits a special place in his nation's quest for the benefits of socioeconomic political modernity. Not only did Cárdenas refuse to become a puppet for Calles's political machine, he was opposed to the exaggerated religious persecution that had led to the cristero crisis. Cárdenas was, to be sure, unsympathetic with fanatical clerics who sought to enslave ignorant peoples via superstition and witchcraft and he lent government support to community reformers who fought to secularize public education; but he would not be a party to extermination of the clergy. To this end he ordered an end to the dissemination of antireligious propaganda in the classroom and encouraged Mexican families to come together around a nucleus of Christian values and practices. In making a limited peace with the church, Cárdenas had done much to pacify and stabilize Mexico politically. However, this should not be taken to imply that the anticlerical reprisals of the Calles period were without justification. Organized Roman Catholics had emerged from the great Revolution clinging tenaciously to a myriad of nefarious economic practices and social evils. The dilemma facing Cárdenas was how to keep a just retribution from becoming ecclesiastical genocide.

Although Cárdenas's quelling of the church-state dilemma was only to be temporary, it was nonetheless an important achievement. He sought to accomplish an even greater step toward modernity in his attack upon the agrarian and land-use structure of Mexico. Cárdenas is said to have spent more time traveling about the country listening to the complaints of the poor and landless than he did in his capital city office. He knew the imperative need for land reform and, perhaps naively and within a somewhat Marxist intellectual framework, believed that redistribution of land would assuage the nation's ills.

Cárdenas's personal administrative style was memorable. He superintended the reform personally and often from the actual site of a given land distribution. Mexicans have never forgotten this; indeed they should not, for Cárdenas, his naive Marxism and simplistic populism notwithstanding, conquered the hearts of his people, as Madero could not do for long enough to institutionalize a stable regime. The people loved Cárdenas while the bureaucrats often hated him; he put down political roots:

> He created administrative chaos, but he distributed land. In his first three years he doubled the number of heads of family with land to work and the amount of land available to *ejidatarios*. By the end of his term he had expropriated and distributed over 17 million hectares to nearly 8,000 new villages in which over two million people lived. As a result of his efforts and those of his predecessors, by 1941 nearly 15,000 villages accounting for a quarter of the total populaton enjoyed the use of slightly less than half the crop land and about one-fifth the total land. Twenty-five years earlier almost none of these people had land they could call their own.[14]

At the end of Cárdenas's term the nation was experiencing a somewhat better distribution of wealth than that which existed at the advent of Madero's effort to front the Mexican revolution. But the large landowners, despite all of their shortcomings from an egalitarian point of view, still were able to demonstrate that private enterprise could produce more food than socialized enterprise. The distribution of the food and its financial earnings was another matter, one that Mexico still must solve. A central, and remaining, fact in this dilemma was that the government bureaucrats appointed to redistribute land, hence wealth, ultimately became a sort of special interest group in themselves, and much of the redistributed land is known to have ended up in their hands.

Another major feature of the Cárdenas era was the decision to nationalize Mexico's oil resources and production. Foreign companies, many of them U.S.-owned, had challenged a decision by Mexico's Supreme Court in 1938 requiring that workers' pay and living conditions be improved. After creation of the CTM with Cárdenas's blessing in 1936, organized labor began to make itself felt. Rumors of U.S.-sponsored intervention in Mexico spread when Cárdenas used the court's decision as a legal mandate for his expropriation decision in 1938. The U.S. was implementing its Good Neighbor Policy then, and the rise of Nazi Germany would have benefitted from siphoning off Mexico's oil in case of an American boycott. Thus the United States acquiesced in the Cárdenas nationalization and worked out a modest settlement for the expropriated property.[15]

It is important to understand that by the year 1921 Mexico produced nearly 25 percent of the world's supply of oil and, significantly, out of that part of its territory which the Americans had neglected to conquer in the 1840s. In addition, the Constitution of 1917 gave the Mexican nation exclusive rights to subsoil minerals. During the Pax Porfiriana, subsoil rights were sold profitably to foreigners. Despite the lip service given to nationalization, little concrete action had really been taken to assure that profits from subsoil exploitation would even in part be reinvested in the Mexican nation or redistributed to her nationals.

On March 18, 1938, President Lázaro Cárdenas signed a decree intended to rectify this imbalance. The overall result of his action, in long-range terms, is still a moot issue. What is clear is that before 1938 the majority of Mexico's oil production was destined for foreign consumption. Low salaries and poor living conditions aggravated the complaints of Mexican workers who were forced to labor in the employ of foreign concerns. After Cárdenas expropriated the oil, up until about 1951, the quantity of petroleum production destined for local markets almost tripled and thereafter Mexican petroleum products continued to play an important role in the domestic economy (favored, of course, by protective legislation). Politically PEMEX, under Lázaro Cárdenas, was an early domestic success. As we will see later the oil fiascos of 1981 and 1982 may have dimmed that popular image on the contemporary scene.

Lázaro Cárdenas's reform era was anathema to the forces of the Mexican oligarchy, the same powerful upper class against which all previous reformers had struggled. Wearing modern attire of the twentieth century, the oligarchs arrayed against the reforms were still essentially the same as earlier, but now they were joined by former oil companies and other commercial newcomers (such as U.S.-owned grain farms in Sonora's Yaqui Valley). In his drive for a progressive liberalism, Cárdenas entered into the lineage of Juárez, Morelos, Madero, and Zapata, probably more than any other figure. Cárdenas shaped the image of his PRM as an organized spokesman for popular distress. He instilled securely the notion of public entrepreneurship as a copartner with the private sector in his nation's development and institutionalized the psychology of being revolutionary as a credential of legitimacy (a concept to which we will return at various times throughout this book).

By 1938 a severe economic crisis gripped Mexico, brought on in part by Cárdenas's oil expropriations and fears of a peso collapse with international credit repercussions. There was a significant flight of capital out of the country and foreign investment declined. In this circumstance Cárdenas could do little more to promote his agrarian reform program given that his sexenio was approaching its end. Cárdenas's economic orientation shifted from redistribution of land to stimulation of production. This approach was more to the liking of established agriculturalists, yet the populist president was not about to sell out his Revolutionary Era commitments to the masses. His PRM now claimed alone to be the organized voice of labor and the peasants and farmers. Cárdenas toured much of Mexico during 1939, his last year in office. He gave emphasis to Sonora, dispensing gifts about the state, "the return of an old church to the faithful of Nacozari"[16] which earlier was the scene of an act of martyrdom and enshrined in the hero worship of Mexican popular folklore.[17] He even made pledges to lift the Yaquis from their poverty, but these hopes would be left to the good will of future regimes.

As he did so Mexico's reactionary conservatives were preparing their electoral game plan for 1940 and the millions of poor in whom Cárdenas's populist rhetoric had inspired hope were pressing for a continuation of the reforms he had begun. It is fair to say that Cárdenas, while a disappointment to Calles, proved to be a delight to the Mexican populace. He combined Juárez's ideological commitment to concrete change with Zapata's ability to reach the common people. He accomplished this without being deposed or exiled as was Juárez and without falling victim to his own violence as did Zapata. At the moment of this writing the late Cárdenas's mystique still inspires the Mexican people; he was, in a very real sense, the father of the contemporary Mexican political system. Yet he very well might not recognize it as the decade of the 1980s unfolds.

NOTES

1. In 1906 a workers' strike at the U.S.-owned Cananea Copper Company in Sonora was put down violently by federal troops and local strike breakers. Porfirio Díaz sent in rurales to add to the repression as well. In that year the brothers Flores Magón met with other revolutionaries in St. Louis, Missouri, and proclaimed the Mexican Liberal Party in exile. In 1907 the famous Río Blanco factory strike was again put down violently as the dictator's troops littered streets with corpses. This added currency to the antidictatorship revolutionary efforts of Flores Magón and hastened the coming of the Revolution.
2. See William Weber Johnson, *Heroic Mexico* (New York: Doubleday, 1968), p. 73.
3. Heriberto García Rivas, *Breve historia de la revolución mexicana* (Mexico: Editorial Diana, 1964), p. 112. Also see Jan Bazant, *A Concise History of Mexico* (Cambridge: Cambridge University Press, 1977), pp. 125-27.
4. Johnson, *Heroic Mexico,* p. 101.
5. Based on an account in *Hispano Americano,* No. 968, November 21, 1960, pp. vii–xxxiv and *passim.* This magazine is in the author's possession but it is no longer published under the above name.
6. Ibid.
7. John Womack, Jr. *Zapata and the Mexican Revolution* (New York: Vintage, 1969), p. 287.
8. "Practically all of the subsequent state laws allowed landlords to retain possession of their properties until expropriated; gave landowners the right to choose the land they would relinquish; and allowed them to sell excess lands or divide them voluntarily as they wished. In Chihuahua, *latifundistas* were still legally able to own 44,000 hectares after the state reform laws were put into effect." Steven E. Sanderson, *Agrarian Populism and the Mexican State* (Berkeley: University of California Press, 1981), p. 67.
9. This is an oft-quoted description of the final treason against Zapata. My translation is from Mauricio González de la Garza, *Última llamada* (Mexico: EDAMEX, 1981), p. 240, but a similar version appears in Womack, *Zapata.*
10. Sanderson, *Agrarian Populism,* p. 75.
11. A negative view of the Calles period is contained in Juan Gualberto Amaya, *Los gobiernos de Obregón, Calles, y regímenes "peleles" derivados del callismo* (Mexico: Editorial del Autor, 1947).
12. Sanderson, *Agrarian Populism,* pp. 75-78.
13. Ibid., p. 95.
14. Charles C. Cumberland, *Mexico: The Struggle for Modernity* (New York: Oxford University Press, 1968), p. 299.
15. Daniel Levy and Gabriel Székely, *Mexico: Paradoxes of Stability and Change* (Boulder, Colorado: Westview Press, 1983), p. 217.
16. Sanderson, *Agrarian Populism,* p. 125.
17. See Don Dedera and Bob Robles, *Goodbye García Adiós* (Flagstaff, Arizona: Northland Press, 1976).

Four

Decline of
the Revolutionary Axis

TRANSITIONAL REGIMES TO THE
DECADE OF THE 1960S

With the reality of World War II threatening all the Western Hemisphere President Cárdenas stepped aside gracefully and allowed a smooth transition to the presidency of General Manuel Avila Camacho. The demands of World War II improved Mexican imports to the United States and gave her migrant laborers a near-open border to cross in search of jobs. Mexico benefited by this war boom. Also in the 1940s the impact of the *Nacional Financiera,* created under Cárdenas, began to be felt in the promotion of industrial growth. The government of Avila Camacho was able to declare the export of finished manufactured products as its policy in 1945 and those leading sectors received protective treatment. At the same time protection and promotion of the ejidos declined and the government seemed to look the other way as large business interests attacked them and other socialistic reminders of the Cárdenas era. Again the official party's name was changed. The PRM was reorganized in 1946 and its military sector removed. It was renamed the PRI or Institutional Revolutionary Party, and the name and three basic sectors (labor, agrarian, popular) are maintained to the present decade of the 1980s as the basic political and governing institution of Mexico.

Avila Camacho's candidacy in 1940 was matched against the independent candidate General Juan Andréu Almazán whose support came from a number of splinter parties including PAN, the National Action Party, which foreshadowed the growth of a permanent political opposition in contemporary Mexico. The elections of 1946 and 1952 were tranquil compared to the previous Mexican experience in the twentieth century.

The newly renamed official party PRI supported the successive regimes of Miguel Alemán Valdés and Adolfo Ruíz Cortines. Alemán Valdés's rise to fame set a pattern which was soon to be repeated in Mexican political life. He rose from governor of a major state, Veracruz, to campaign manager for Avila Camacho in 1940, and from that position to secretario de gobernación in the president's cabinet. With the end of World War II, it was felt that Mexico needed a president somewhat to the political right of the Cárdenas tradition who would promote commercial and industrial development. Miguel Alemán Valdés became one of Mexico's most entrepreneurial presidents. During his regime the nation's industrial economy surged forward impressively.

The selection of Adolfo Ruíz Cortines as the PRI standardbearer in 1952 represented only a mild reaction to the conservatism of the Alemán administration. This selection is somewhat paradoxical inasmuch as Ruíz Cortines was one of the more trusted Alemán followers who had pursued exactly the same route of ascent as had his predecessor and mentor. Ruíz had always been distinguished, even within Alemán's orbit, as being impeccably honest, and Alemán is known to have assigned to Ruíz certain financial custodial tasks which Alemán did not even trust to himself. Under Ruíz Cortines, Mexico's public administration was purged of many of its former objectionable practices, and definite strides were taken to expand the state communal farm program, public welfare, and other needed social reforms.

In 1958, Adolfo López Mateos brought to the presidency a distinguished background as a labor mediator and organizer. His service as secretary of labor in the Ruíz Cortines cabinet and earlier as a troubleshooter for the Mexican treasury had attracted the admiration of ex-president Cárdenas which, coupled with López Mateos's longstanding friendship with Miguel Alemán, served ideally in fitting López for the PRI candidacy. He was unusual in that he enjoyed the unanimous support of not only the three principal emeritus figures in Mexican politics at the time, but also the unqualified support of most businessmen, of organized labor, and of the military establishment.

The election of Adolfo López Mateos in 1958 was significant in several respects. It was the first time in Mexican history that the franchise had been extended to women. Moreover, part of the PRI's campaign pledge was the institution of a sweeping program of socialized medicine, medical and dental clinics, and maternity care centers intended particularly for rural and depressed urban neighborhoods. López Mateos generally made good this pledge and thereby endeared himself to many Mexicans who otherwise might have remained apathetically on the edge of their national political life.

But in terms of overall impact the socioeconomic promises of López Mateos were too little too late. Corruption prevented many of the programmed services from reaching the people effectively. Disease prevention without birth control saw Mexico's population growth outrun its economic development. López Mateos was attacked from the right by PAN and its spokesman Luis H. Alvarez whom the president had easily defeated in 1958. At that time PAN represented a number of clerical and reactionary interests like the *sinarquistas* who saw the PRI as conducting Mexico into atheistic communism. The PAN also enjoyed support from moderate conservatives within the business and professional communities and was developing into what promised to become a significant opposition party.

A major railroad workers' strike in 1959 threatened the stability of the López Mateos sexenio as did several naval and border skirmishes between Mexico and Guatemala over fishing rights and natural resource access. There were international tensions over Mexico's refusal to break relations with the newly-installed Castro regime in Cuba. Mexico and the United States quarreled over control of salinity in the Colorado River and the matter of clandestine migration of Mexican workers. But despite its trade unionism, superficially booming economy, welfare services, and expanded educational system, López Mateos's Mexico was a nation of growing social despair. Some said the president was impervious to this fact due to his own failing health and personal drug dependency.

It is said that on the occasion of Charles De Gaulle's visit to Mexico the French president stood on the balcony of the Mexican presidential palace and asked López Mateos if the human throngs in the Zócalo below them really loved the Mexican president. López Mateos is quoted as replying in the affirmative. To this De Gaulle responded that the French people did not love him, they only needed him. López Mateos had made the mistake of other Mexican presidents, confusing public adulation for popular approval, even love.[1]

DIAZ ORDAZ AND TLATELOLCO: THE WOUNDING OF A NATION

One Mexican scholar contends that for a nation to function democratically it is absolutely essential that its masses know and respect the interdependency they share as individuals, and not act simply as a docile herd of sheep to be prodded along by a shepherd. Nonetheless, he continues, "since from the Spanish conquest Mexico has known respect only for the shepherd's commands . . . without this Mexico feels lost."[2] During the sexenio of Gustavo Díaz Ordaz (1964–70) the sheep in this metaphor felt lost, went rampant and attacked the regime, then retreated into a somber twilight of political uncertainty. Díaz Ordaz was no more loved by the Mexicans than López Mateos had been. But at least the latter was *simpático,* likeable superficially, whereas his successor Díaz Ordaz was cold, stern, not very handsome and hardly an inspiring speaker. Presumably Charles De Gaulle, if standing on a balcony overlooking the Zócalo, would not have ventured to ask Díaz Ordaz if he was loved by the Mexican people.

It is possible to make too much of a leader's personality, yet this seems to have been integral to Díaz Ordaz's inability to negotiate and compromise, thereby generating conflict. Díaz Ordaz inherited pressures of the young seeking a mobility which for most was not there. The poor and wretched were increasing in numbers and the PRI was growing into such a considerable family that the trickle down system of remuneration through graft was not satisfying nearly all its members. The regime itself placed heavy pressures on the new president and Díaz Ordaz did not communicate skillfully; nor did he easily bring conflict to a peaceful or graceful compromise. Key events during his administration speak for themselves.

Violence rent the peasant sector of the PRI. After an armed clash between members of rival factions of the CNC on August 20, 1965, which left upward of 30 workers dead, the head of the CNC, Amador Hernández, resigned under pressure from Díaz Ordaz. The conflict dramatized growing cleavage high up in the national power structure and Díaz Ordaz saw expulsion as more feasible than a negotiated compromise. The reform-minded mayor of the Federal District, Ernesto Uruchurtu, was fired in the wake of a controversy over his campaign to eliminate vice and corruption. Carlos A. Madrazo (to whose case I will return) was ousted in a direct confrontation with Díaz Ordaz over the question of democratizing local elections. Madrazo, as president of the PRI, had been in effect Mexico's second most powerful political figure. Governor Enrique D. Ceniceros of Durango was fired for his incompetent handling of a student strike against foreign mining interests. Saltiel Alatriste, director of Mexico's Social Security System, was fired in the midst of an anticorruption campaign he had launched. Ignacio Chávez, chancellor of the National Autonomous University of Mexico, was forced to resign for his excessive tolerance of student demonstrations on campus (he had been forced into resigning by what was widely believed to be government-sponsored vigilante terrorism against him).

There were other signs in the late 1960s that the PRI's revolutionary axis might be crumbling. In 1967 and 1968 student protests occurred in Yucatán and Sonora against unmasked electoral fraud. President Díaz Ordaz was inescapably tainted with indirect responsibility for these frauds and for the police repression visited upon the protesters. But the greatest evidence of the declining axis of the revolutionary family system came in August, September, and October of 1968 in a series of events that now have been conveniently packaged under the rubric of Tlatelolco. This was the most serious uprising of the Mexican people against the central government since the cristero rebellion against Calles of the 1920s and perhaps since the uprising led by Francisco Madero himself in 1910.

Tlatelolco was an urban jacquerie, a people's uprising, against a central authority perceived as cruel and uncaring vis a vis the needy masses. Organized, and sometimes armed, university students became the voices for interpreting and articulating that which the masses could not articulate for themselves. Historically, it has become a great cathartic event in contemporary Mexican political life. It is interesting to speculate what might have transpired had Mexico's president still been Adolfo López Mateos. Tragically, and perhaps ironically, ex-president López Mateos, whose skills as a compromiser might have been invoked to restore peace, had himself been removed as national chairman of the forthcoming Olympic Games; he was slowly dying in a coma with brain damage and complications following surgery when the disaster of Tlatelolco occurred in 1968. Here is the why and how of Tlatelolco.

A new sports palace was being built in Mexico City for completion during 1968. In it many of the international Olympic Games of that year would be held in the summer months. Many Mexicans could see the sports palace; few had the entrance fee to become a spectator. The majority of students at the national university UNAM and other institutions could ill afford to attend the Olympic Games. Only a tiny percentage of them could expect to find both graduation and employment. They saw the sports palace as a gigantic and arabesque symbol of the emptiness of Mexico's dominant political regime, of the moral bankruptcy with which the PRI chose its public symbols for group attachment. The students saw the sports palace and the Olympic Games as Mexico's governing regime showing off to the world while thousands starved.

The view of the PRI was quite something else. The regime needed the Olympic Games for international recognition and had sought tirelessly to convince the populace that they also shared this need. Protests against Mexico's investment in the Olympic Games grew into a major governmental headache. The mayor of the Federal District, General Alfonso Corona del Rosal, felt forced to take action in July 1968 to maintain a peaceful atmosphere in the capital city that would permit building of the sports palace to go ahead. On July 22, the principal of a privately-operated high school called for police help in handling a fight between her students and those of the nearby Vocational School No. 2. This is where a tragedy of major national proportions began.[3]

Fights that turned into small riots were not unusual given the traditional rivalries between the vocational and preparatory schools, the latter often jealously seen as stepping stones to a college education. The request for police assistance was no more than routine, yet Corona del Rosal sent

200 grenadiers to handle the students. At that point their fight could have been over games or girls. What followed strongly indicates that the grenadiers overreacted and visited brutality upon the students. A political element was thereby injected into the incident where none had existed before. Police brutality quickly inspired an atmosphere of "students vs. the state." The newspaper chain of Colonel García Valseca (e.g. *El Sol de México*), which adheres to the official government view, tried to blame the students and lauded the police,[4] but most other reports condemned the military for the reprisals taken. A psychological catharsis was beginning as the cause célèbre grew. On July 25, the National Federation of Technical Students (FNET), a dependency of the PRI, sought a permit to hold a public march, at the end of which the resignation of General Luis Cueto Ramírez, chief of the Federal District's police force, would be demanded. Here was open conflict between powerful pressure groups within the PRI.

Coincidentally, the march was planned for the following day, July 26, which is generally known as Fidel Castro Day to the youth of Latin America. Not unexpectedly, the same day had been picked by the principal youth group of the Mexican Communist Party for its celebration. This group, CNED, National Confederation of Democratic Students, merged at Mexico City's famous central square, the Zócalo, with around three thousand other students who had been invited by the FNET. Hostile acts occurred and police units were summoned to disperse the students. Immediate recriminations were taken against the Mexican Communist Party and seven employees of *La Voz de México* including Gerardo Unzueta, a member of the PCM's central committee, were jailed. Charges were traded in the press as to who was to blame, with most of the venom directed against the students. The next day, July 27, student bands appeared once again at the Zócalo and demanded release of the previous day's prisoners. They repeated their demand that Cueto Ramírez be fired and added his principal assistants to the list. By Monday, July 29, the students were claiming that hundreds of their numbers were incarcerated and that scores were missing and dead. Many such charges were exaggerated although police brutality was becoming daily fare.

The students began addressing their demands to the president. It was charged that the crisis was already of national proportions and that Díaz Ordaz was personally responsible. The downward chain of command was Díaz Ordaz, to Luis Echeverría (as Minister of the Interior) to Corona del Rosal, to the police and army commanders. By July 30, the Zócalo had been cleared of students and secured under military command. At this point a critical ideological marriage began to show itself, featuring the union of a number of groups and camarillas both within the revolutionary coalition and outside of it.

Student radicals retreated into the National University and the National Polytechnic Institute (IPN) to begin the work of creating a youth coalition against the state (it is well to keep in mind the approximate student enrollment in those days for UNAM was 90,000 and for IPN, 70,000, as a crude index to the human resource potential on which the organizers could draw). It is important to note also that Interior Secretary Echeverría, who was widely rumored to have presidential aspirations for 1970, came to be a principal target for student wrath as the new coalition was being formed.

The ideological marriage came to fruition with the declaration of the National Strike Committee CNH (*Consejo Nacional de Huelga*). It handed Echeverría a list of six basic demands: 1) the firing of the police chief and his assistants, 2) public admission of the government's responsibility for atrocities and violence, 3) freedom for all jailed students and for a loosely defined spectrum of other "political" prisoners, 4) dissolution of the grenadiers, 5) payments to families of the victims of police brutality, 6) and the abolition of Articles 145 and 145b of the Penal Code which define the Mexican version of sedition and which had been a traditional legal backstop for jailing opposition critics of the PRI. These demands were deliberately framed in language which would have made the government's accession to any one of them a major confession of guilt. It is doubtful that any of the student leaders truly expected the government to give in. Indeed, they wanted further confrontations to dramatize their grievances and to exhibit publicly the ideological gulf between them and officialdom. Demand number three was especially explosive as its refusal by the government opened the way to student oratory in favor of imprisoned labor leaders Demetrio Vallejo and Valentín Campa. The National Strike Committee was gaining symbols of unity and attachment.

Amid reports of supportive student uprisings at other universities about the country, the law student and faculty contingent of the UNAM took temporary control of the National Strike Committee on July 31, and sent out brigades of five to ten students to circulate throughout the city carrying handbills and placards to the public. They went to factories, office buildings, and slums such as Ciudad Nezahualcóyotl on the edge of Mexico City.[5] Their psychology stressed the dichotomy of people and state. The blame assigned went to the doorstep of the government and the political cabal which surrounded it. One handbill urged citizens not to be "taken in by those who through the press, radio, and television try to hide the truth about what is happening in Mexico. They never mention the hunger, the lack of freedom and the corruption in the unions, and how the government uses your *pesos* to line the pockets of a select few."[6]

On Thursday, August 1, the rector of the UNAM, Javier Barros Sierra, led an estimated 50,000 faculty and students in a demonstration against the police tactics of the government. Subsequently, all classes at UNAM were suspended. The National Strike Committee began to assemble students from other schools and nonstudent sympathizers within the walls of UNAM; at times it was estimated that as many as 40,000 persons congregated there to hear antigovernment oratory. Many of them were women and children whose presence, it was hoped, would discourage police invasion of the campus. Demands continued for capitulation by the government and these were met with silence until August 8, when the mayor, Corona del Rosal, offered to set up a commission to investigate the charges of atrocities. But he continued to trumpet the conspiracy theory, telling a gathering of sanitation department employees assembled in the Lázaro Cárdenas Park that the student behavior was part of an international communist plot.[7] The National Strike Committee (CNH) won encouraging support when on August 13 the Teachers Coalition for Democratic Liberties was formed and endorsed the six basic student demands. This is significant, for many of these teachers were also members of the CNOP via a number of subgroups.

On August 22, Minister of the Interior Echeverría made what he considered to be a concession, by agreeing to a private dialogue with the student leaders. The National Strike Committee countered that any such discussion would have to be broadcast publicly with government officials, including Echeverría, submitting to questioning. Surely, none of the student leaders expected the government to accept this challenge. Another march of protest followed on August 27 in which the National Strike Committee succeeded in assembling parents, workers, and a number of small businessmen, farm laborers, and medical students who stood out in their white uniforms. The government learned of this march and assembled its own "counter-demonstration" in the Zócalo by giving all employees the day off with encouragement to participate on behalf of the government. Here the government was hoping to draw upon a membership reserve which was an important power base for the PRI, namely, the CNOP or popular sector, generally, and on its bureaucrats union, FSTSE, in particular.

There is impressive testimony to indicate that at this point the PRI showed serious evidence of frailty: many of its popular sector personnel, released from government jobs to support the status quo counter-demonstration, actually cast their lot with the National Strike Committee. By noon August 27, nearly half a million people jammed the Zócalo. The counter-demonstration had failed and the students claimed an impressive victory. The oratory on that day stressed the "oneness" of the Mexican people against the government. One speaker, a laborer, said that if a peasant asked for better wages or tried to join an effective non-PRI union, his employer spoke to police and the man was jailed.[8] It is worth stressing that, at least during the preceeding decade, such open attacks on the government were customarily issued at opposition rallies sponsored by the PAN, the Sinarquistas, or the MLN, and were almost never made in front of the National Palace. Now they were emanating from a heterogeneous congeries of disaffected groups from both within and without the revolutionary coalition, directly in front of the National Palace.

At the climax of the demonstration, students invaded the main cathedral and set off the fireworks stored there for the Independence Day celebration on September 16. The invasion of the cathedral brought an angry reaction from the establishment press which said "Communist guerrillas . . . took control of the Cathedral converting the sacred temple into a center of agitation."[9] Students also hoisted a flag of North Vietnam on the national flagpole. Late that evening (August 27) the Zócalo was still occupied by multitudes sympathetic to the National Strike Committee. Then, between 1:00 and 2:00 A.M. on August 28, the troops moved onto the Zócalo under protection of tanks and armored cars (largely of U.S. manufacture). By dawn Wednesday the students had fled and only the troops remained.

During the night it was alleged that army elements disguised as hoodlums of the reactionary right carried out attacks on student hiding places. One of these, at Vocational School No. 7 in the housing complex Tlatelolco, gave an ominous foreshadowing of a tragedy yet to come.[10]

Traditionally presidential state of the union messages are routine affairs but on September 1, 1968, it was a special occasion. A Mexican president had been confronted with the most serious public challenge since, perhaps, the cristeros rose against Calles in the 1920s. Díaz Ordaz held his audience in uncomfortable suspense for two and a half hours. Then he touched the theme of national confrontation: "the situation has reached the point where methods of expression have been grossly abused."[11] He told the nation that he could not permit the "juridical order to deteriorate" and that any force necessary would be used to keep antisocial elements from disrupting the Olympic Games. Despite student disclaimers that they wanted to interfere with the games, Díaz Ordaz stated that foreigners whom he implied to be Cuban agents were hoping to destroy the Olympics. He said that for the first time the games were to be held "in a country that speaks Spanish, for the first time in a Latin American nation, and for the first time in a developing nation. This accomplishment should be a legitimate satisfaction for the Mexican people."[12]

Considering the more than $150 million invested by the Mexican government to promote the games, the president's concern was to be expected. He ended his address with what he considered to be concessions, one of them a promise for legislation granting more autonomy to the Polytechnic Institute and the high schools; the other, a congressional investigation of charges that the sedition laws had been abused. But the second concession was followed by a caveat. Díaz Ordaz asked "should it not be considered a crime to affect our national sovereignty, endangering the territorial integrity of the republic in compliance with the dictates of a foreign government? If it [the subversion law] is abolished, no crime will have a political character. Is that what is desired?"[13] Díaz Ordaz seemed to be forewarning his congress to disregard the second concession in order to protect its own immunity from political attack; at least, that is how the students understood it. Students, professors, and a multitude of sympathizers answered Díaz Ordaz's message on September 13 with another large demonstration. Thousands paraded in silence carrying placards of Ho Chi Minh, Fidel Castro, and Che Guevara. Public orators reiterated the demand for a dialogue with the government that would be broadcast by radio and television. Interior Minister Echeverría ignored the demand and the government maintained a determined but fragile calm.

Although the government controlled the streets of the capital city, the students and the National Strike Committee controlled the schools. Before September 18, no tanks or soldiers had entered the university or the Polytechnic Institute, but it was clear that some sort of confrontation was in the making. On September 17, Echeverría spoke. He repeated the government's determination to safeguard the Olympic Games within constitutional means and at any cost. The García Valseca newspaper chain stressed repeatedly that the National University was being used as a staging ground for direct attacks on the sports palace. An impressive effort had been made to convince the public that UNAM was a center of subversion that must be stifled.

On September 18, an estimated 10,000 troops in battle dress occupied the campus. Federal district attorney Gilberto Suárez Torres said that some 145 persons had been arrested. An American newsweekly put the figure at close to 1,000.[14] Interior minister Echeverría defended the action saying that the UNAM was public property being used illegally by persons who intended to perpetrate antisocial and criminal acts.[15] At this point the breach between the government and the National Strike Committee became complete, the latter having been branded as criminals. The action also helped to mend the traditional animosity between students of UNAM and the Polytechnic Institute, the latter bearing a stigma of social inferiority. With UNAM occupied, its students were welcomed into the IPN which remained the National Strike Committee's last operational bastion. Both politically and tactically this was a union of no small importance.

On Sunday, September 22, the UNAM rector, Javier Barros Sierra, submitted his resignation in protest against the military occupation of his campus. The UNAM's governing council unanimously rejected his resignation under the threat that if accepted, the university's 7,000 professors would also resign. It was rumored that Sierra's action was taken as a disguise for his real complicity with the government in the campus takeover, but this has never been substantiated. What is clear is that the government had taken its toll on the students, and the well-organized cadres of the National Strike Committee were falling into atrophy.

Bands of disillusioned anarchists began roaming the city pillaging and looting wantonly without the legitimizing pretense of an ideological commitment. Buses were commandeered and set afire and streets were barricaded. Such events lasted until the end of September, giving Mexico City the terrifying spectre of anarchosyndicalism gone rampant. It was clearly the worst outbreak of anomic violence and political alienation since the Great Revolution. By the end of September a lull had fallen over Mexico City. The violence subsided, and a Mothers March was staged from Insurgentes Avenue to the Chamber of Deputies in protest of the deaths of youths. On October first, Javier Barros Sierra returned to his office at UNAM as the last contingent of troops left the campus. The Olympic Games were only a few days away.

Although few realized it at that time Mexico was about to experience a national catharsis of violence that would feature the people in a spirit of armed uprising against the regime. This first part of the catharsis would much later be termed by Mauricio González de la Garza as *la primera llamada,* the first cry or call.[16] The bloody episode now known simply as Tlatelolco reached its initial climax in a way that social scientists might treat in a game theory context. Thus an analogy from game theory comes to mind, that of the shepherd who relentlessly pursued a wolf into a corner where the animal was forced to fight and succeeded in destroying the shepherd in what amounted to an unnecessary defeat. Looking back on the Mexico City violence it appears that on October 1, 1968, the point of no return was crossed. The government failed to take advantage of the temporarily improved atmosphere to seek a negotiated peace with the National Strike Committee. Instead, a decision was made to pursue the students like wolves and drive them into a corner from which there was no escape. The name of that corner was Tlatelolco, site of the Aztec's last stand, a major apartment complex housing an estimated 75,000 persons of middle class status. It was popularly alleged that most of the residents of Tlatelolco were then permitted to live there because they were loyal supporters of the revolutionary coalition. If this was true it was little in evidence in the early days of October, 1968 when the National Strike Committee resolved to make a final public effort to regroup its ranks and to mobilize additional public support behind its challenge of the government.

A well-circulated public rumor carried news of a gigantic rally to be held at the Plaza of the Three Cultures, Tlatelolco. In the early morning hours of October 1, police agents discovered the hiding place of two Guatemalan terrorists in one of the giant buildings that adjoins the Tlatelolco complex. Anachronistically, the name of this building was Miguel Alemán, the former president and financial boss, whose son had been busy during the summer telling the press optimistic tales about Mexico's progressive youth.[17] The terrorists were said by police to have been well stocked with weapons. Their names were given as Carlos Ruelas and Leopoldo Ernesto Zepeda who, along with a Mexican accomplice named Luis Sánchez Cordero, were taken into custody and offered as evidence that Mexico was the victim of an international plot. From interrogations the police claimed to have learned that other violence-prone student groups had rented apartments in the area which were being used as bases for planned insurgency. Their strategy appeared to be provocation of conflict in zones of great population density where riot police would be least effective and where it was hoped that a great amount of public support (or at least sympathy) for the students would be found.

Rumors spread of police invasions of the Tlatelolco apartments. In order to protest these police actions and to reiterate earlier demands, the National Strike Committee announced that it would hold a demonstration march to begin at Tlatelolco and to end at the Casco de Santo Tomás, which had recently been occupied by troops.[18] At the last minute, according to the account given by Gilberto Balam, the National Strike Committee called off the march thinking it would provoke troop reprisals.[19] If this is correct, then a slim possibility for dialogue still remained. Instead of the march the committee called for a public meeting to be held at Tlatelolco in the Plaza of the Three Cultures. The purpose was ostensibly to articulate grievances. Around four thousand persons gathered (not a huge group compared with previous meetings) and a large number of these were women and children. Speakers cajoled the audience to believe that the government had shut off all discourse on the six demands and urged the throng to "unite and take the city."

This occurred at approximately 6:30 on the afternoon of Wednesday, October 2, 1968.[20] At that moment the army and police appeared and surrounded much of the area with tanks and armored cars. The speakers on the platform tried to calm the people: "*no se muevan compañeros! Permanezcan tranquilos ante las provocaciones de la tropa y la policía!*"[21] Using a bullhorn, an officer ordered the people to abandon the area. When they did not obey, white-gloved riot police moved into the crowd swinging clubs and chains against the people. This was the signal that converted the spectator–participant crowd into a mob.[22] The police were attacked furiously by the citizens. When police opened fire they were greeted by rifle shots from the upper floors of the building, Chihuahua, that had also served as a frequent meeting place for leaders of the National Strike Committee. It was clear now that elements were present who either wanted a violent confrontation or at least had become convinced, however reluctantly, of its necessity. The police retired and called for troops. The army then responded with mortars and armored cars, and a helicopter began dropping green flares about the area and into the crowd.[23] General José Hernández Toledo, Commander of the First Batallion of Paratroopers, attempted to speak to the crowd via a portable loudspeaker. As he did so snipers opened fire from the building Chihuahua and the general fell seriously wounded to the pavement.

This was approximately at 7:00 P.M. A firefight then ensued with incredible ferocity until nearly 4:00 A.M. the next morning. Thousands of Mexicans were caught in the murderous crossfire. Mob behavior was mixed with crowd panic. People ran in terror from the nearby Tlatelolco movie theater, and many of them were slugged and wounded without provocation. Backed up by armored vehicles firing tracer bullets from high calibre machine guns the soldiers are said to have fired at nearly anyone who moved. Automatic weapons swept building ledges where some youngsters had climbed to safety. Many innocent people were killed and many more injured. The Italian journalist, Oriana Fallaci, herself a veteran of Vietnam reporting, was seriously injured.[24] When the holocaust was over, the army was in command of Tlatelolco and the Plaza of the Three Cultures. Sniper nests were discovered in the buildings Chihuahua, Molino del Rey, General Anaya, Xicoténcatl, and also (ironically) in a nearby building which houses the service organization of the CNOP's favored bureaucrats union (FSTSE) known as the Institute of Social Services for Workers of the State (ISSSTE). Several dead snipers were identified as of Cuban and Guatemalan origin. The death toll of Tlatelolco will never be known. Gilberto Balam places it in the upper hundreds, and official estimates claimed around two hundred. Defense Minister General Marcelino García Barragán said that his orders were to crush the uprising at any cost,[25] even (apparently) at the cost of first having to create the conflict.

It would be inaccurate to blame the government for the entire disaster, for it is clear that the students were armed and had brought in experienced guerrillas to help them. This came, however, after it appeared certain that a dialogue with the government would never be allowed. The students had also been encouraged by various sectors of the press and clergy. Alejandro Aviles (a former PAN militant) wrote sympathetic articles in *Excelsior.* Thirty priests of the diocese of Cuernavaca signed a document sympathetic to the student cause and support came from Enrique Maza and Ramón de Ertze Garamendi, priests who lauded the students for their bravery. There is at least one other melancholy truth underlying the holocaust: many of the students who (with and without arms) attacked police had first inebriated themselves into a hideous pitch of revelry by consuming a mixture of tequila, rum, and a drug known as "cyclopal" whose effect is to make one reckless and impervious in the face of certain death. Many students "liberated" themselves in this suicidal fashion.

By exploding in open defiance against the repressive state and its exclusionary single-party rule the Mexican students and their supporters at Tlatelolco staged a partial fulfillment of one of Emiliano Zapata's dreams: the burning of power thrones. The great agrarian revolutionary had urged that thrones which become institutionalized and bureaucratized can be undone only with great sacrifice and pain. The pain felt at Tlatelolco became a national catharsis for Mexico; at the popular level Mexico's people had symbolically dethroned the regime by this unequivocal public dramatization of their contempt for authority. The student protest movement shattered certain political traditions like reverence for the president while he remains in office. The political system was held up openly as unjust, unrepresentative, corrupt, wasteful, and uncaring.

How the protest became an urban jacquerie that reached so monumental a national stature will need historical study in a comparative context vis a vis the cristero revolt of the 1920s, the Madero revolution of 1910, popular support for the War of Reform in the mid-nineteenth century, and Father Hidalgo's independence uprising of 1810. Why the Mexican people lend themselves periodically to such violent outpourings merits similar systematic study. It is tempting, although not scientific, to attribute events such as Tlatelolco to a latent death-wish innate to the Mexican psyche. Several of Mexico's finest literary and philosophic minds have lent their talents to such interpretation (it is well to add that a rigorous application of the scientific method is not assumed here to be the only fruitful avenue to truth).

One of these is Octavio Paz who viewed the student uprising of 1968 as a phenomenon of *enajenación juvenil,* youth alienation that mirrored deeply felt and widespread sociopolitical atrophy. Paz referred to a predetermined extension of an Aztec death ritual that has been operative throughout Mexican history since the conquest.[26] His analysis exhibits nuances of a Hegelian dialectic, a march of uncontrollable spiritual forces across the earth. When President Díaz Ordaz and Secretary of Interior Luis Echeverría took the decision to risk the massacre of hundreds of citizens at Tlatelolco, and to injure thousands of others, the government was, in Paz's view, regressing to the behavior of premodern, that is, Aztec, times. Aggression is a synonym for regression. The massacre of Tlatelolco revealed the prevalence of a violent potential for destruction that had been latent in the Mexican people since the death rituals of the Aztecs. In ancient times such death rituals had indeed been conducted at Tlatelolco, a coincidence we noted earlier.

It is significant that Octavio Paz, in order to write *Posdata* both in protest against, and in analysis of, the meaning of Tlatelolco, had to resign his prestigious position as Mexico's ambassador to India. And it is perhaps equally significant that President Díaz Ordaz felt compelled to speak out on national television against both Paz's act and his book. Octavio Paz was too renowned as an intellectual to be sacrificed like the students. Nor could the novelist Carlos Fuentes be ignored. He summed up the message of Paz's challenge in a way that is unmistakably clear:

> The official repression, too, was inevitable. Unaccustomed to dissent, the regime panicked; it had no political answers to political challenges. . . . The ritual bloodletting once more took place, ordered from the top of the pyramid by the Tlatoani in power, President Gustavo Díaz Ordaz, in the name of a perversion of nationalist and revolutionary theology. The hidden subconscious mechanisms of power probed by Paz were once more in operation.[27]

Paz saw the universities and the new bourgeois middle class as fertile sources of rebellion against Mexico's official party, PRI, which he viewed as an unnatural political monopoly whose path toward dictatorship was then being strewn with insurrection and anarchy. PRI was created as a recourse against military intervention in the political arena, a phenomenon intimately involved in the political alienation that one finds in many other Latin American nations. One of the ways in which the Mexican military was disestablished politically was through the enshrinement of the presidency along with it. The revolutionary Emiliano Zapata, before his death in 1919, had viewed the presidential chair with horror, urging that power should be dispersed among the people. Zapata was murdered for his heresy. Exactly 50 years later another would-be reformer, former PRI president Carlos A. Madrazo, also sought to redistribute power to the localities and died under what many consider to be mysterious circumstances.[28] Paz says that Zapata was right: all thrones should be burned. But are there regular predetermined time-cycles for such events?

Looking backward still, Paz argues "for the Spaniards the conquest was an exploit [*hazaña*] but for the Indians it was a ritual [*rito*] . . . between the two extremes of exploit and ritual the Mexican sensibility and imagination has always oscillated."[29] Tlatelolco was a conquest or exploit for the regime; for the students it was a sacrificial ritual (this is my interpretation of Paz). The Aztec cult required a sacrifice in human blood to reify its omnipotence and to deify the onward phenomenal thrust of the universe that the Aztec rulers pretended to embody. The imperative was for Aztec domination of all other cults and groups, domination by force if necessary.

Modern-day Mexicans institutionalized Aztec domination in a unique way according to Paz: the Aztec capital's pre-Hispanic name Mexico-Tenochtitlán, shortened to Mexico, was given to the entire country. This symbolizes, yet personifies, the domination of all Mexico by the capital.[30] The capital, in turn, centered about the ancient Aztec Zócalo that dominates all of Mexico today through the government and the PRI, the official party, which itself is a pyramid of power with the National Palace and Zócalo at its apex.

Mexico's enshrined presidency is the modern-day high priest of the Aztecs, the tlatoani, who represents the extended and perpetual domination of the Aztec mystique and ritual over a submissive Mexican populace. Every six years another high priest is elected. He is invested with a mission; it is not personal power but a continuity with the Aztec past. And along the way he may have to perform sacrificial rituals, like that of Tlatelolco, if the Aztec mystique is to be saved from those who would threaten its perpetuation. The Plaza de las Tres Culturas, today's official name for the ancient square of Tlatelolco, is a counterpoise to the Zócalo which symbolized the perpetuation of Aztec power via the PRI. The massacre of Tlatelolco on October 2, 1968, was a sort of denouement, through blood and carnage, that revealed the historic petrification of the PRI.[31]

If a line is drawn on a map of contemporary Mexico City from the Zócalo to Tlatelolco, then in order to form an Aztec pyramid a final point is needed. This is provided by the national Museum of Anthropology, which has been transformed into a functioning temple for worship and adoration of the ancient grandeur of Mexico-Tenochtitlán. It is filled with symbols of death. The museum completes the pyramid. Paz asks why the Mexicans should hold up such a mirror of reverence to their past. His reply is that the true inheritors of the legacy of those who massacred the pre-Hispanic (Aztec) world are not the creole Spaniards of today but the mestizo Mexicans and the remaining Indians. There is a causal bridge connecting past and present. The Museum of Anthropology and the plaza still known as Tlatelolco form the base of the power pyramid. This is an image, but, says Paz, all images suffer the fatal tendency of petrification, and only with the acid of verbal criticism can such images as Mexico's living-power triangle be dissolved. Progressive thought can break the power pyramid and then Mexicans will be free.

There are a number of ironies in the fact of the Tlatelolco massacre. The Plaza of the Three Cultures is supposed to symbolize the unity of Spaniards, Indians, and mestizo descendents of the conquest. Tlatelolco should be symbolic of Mexico's unity with its past. Today the Ministry of

Foreign Relations conducts people's diplomacy from a towering building at Tlatelolco. It is also the site of a major housing project, reflecting the alleged progressive urban policies of the single-party dominant political system. Tlatelolco seems always to have been a mystical place, just as in the ancient days of religious human sacrifice. Inescapably, one encounters in Mexico's writers a fascination with the political and spiritual symbolism of Tlatelolco.[32]

When troops turned their guns on the student demonstrators at Tlatelolco it enraged many persons who previously had little to do with the protest movement. Infuriated beyond control at the horrors of military repression, they grabbed hidden weapons and attacked the army.[33] An anomic rebellion erupted at the mystical site. There were more illusory phantasms; Tlatelolco was an urban jacquerie chock full of human variables which scientific rigor will be hard put to explain. Such is the political life of Mexico: it generates new martyrs; its revolutionary mystique is claimed to be endless. In Mexico, "time hungers for incarnation," says Carlos Fuentes.[34] It may be the central truth of today's Mexican political psyche that the nation has fallen schizophrenic, maddened from the quest to know its very self.

President Díaz Ordaz stepped aside in 1970 as tradition and the constitution required. He left his office sullied, the aftermath of Tlatelolco. The regime's legitimacy was still bolstered by symbols of attachment and allegiance out of the past. Some of them had also been sullied yet the popular mind was expected to honor them mechanically. Díaz Ordaz had been conservative, bourgeois, even reactionary. He governed in the pro-business style of former president Miguel Alemán. When Díaz Ordaz left office Mexico's peso still was worth its customary 12.50 to the U.S. dollar, tourism was good, and the Mexican economy showed signs of growth. Foreign investors still considered Mexico a good risk. The issue of whether the student insurgents at Tlatelolco had acted out an ancient Aztec death wish had not yet been placed before the public eye, not even for philosophers to muse or for scientists to reject. Díaz Ordaz's own minister of the interior, Luis Echeverría Alvarez, the man who had given the orders leading to the massacre, was to become Mexico's next president at the end of 1970. Perhaps the succession of tlatoanis was complete, or else it was time for Mexican politics to make a quixotic swing to the populist left.

ECHEVERRIA AND LOPEZ PORTILLO: THE ATROPHY OF CONFIDENCE

Whereas the government of Díaz Ordaz had been conservative in its public pronouncements the administration of Luis Echeverría Alvarez beginning in 1970 was often likened to that of Lázaro Cárdenas for its prolabor and propeasant rhetorical style. The new president's personal demeanor touched on populist demogoguery; his ability to convey an intensely felt sense of personal mission gave Echeverría an enigmatic yet media-sensitive charismatic appeal. Echeverría's shirtsleeve approach to popular contact, known as *guayabera* politics, was a psychological trick that got him short-run emotive results from the simple people. This was widely exploited by the popular media. Mexico's economy in 1970 was, however, facing a decline and the balance of payments was worsening. The long-stable peso, it was rumored, might have to be devalued unless inflationary pressures could be restrained. Import substitution programs were calling for more and more public investment. Economic growth had not kept up with Mexico's birth rate and expanding labor force, more and more of whom were being forced to search out employment illegally north of the border. The Echeverría development program addressed this circumstance with promises of poor relief, regional development, revitalization of agriculture, housing and educational reform, and much more. Echeverría's rhetoric placed him on the side of the working classes against the commercial and industrial class. This perceived class conflict lasted throughout his sexenio.

Echeverría's fiscal reform initiative included an advisory commission which recommended measures to increase tax collection from the business sector and assure income tax collection from delinquent sectors of the society generally. Most of this initiative died under pressure from COPARMEX, the Mexican Employers Confederation, which represented conservative and antilabor interests generally. Also rejected by the business community was a labor-sponsored initiative in 1972 to control prices against inflation. When Echeverría called for limits on profits as well the bourgeois classes branded him a virtual "fellow traveller." He tried to persuade businessmen that their future depended on raising the acquisitive capacity of the workers and peasants.[35]

At the height of the controversy over Echeverría's populism in late 1973 the murder of Eugenio Garza Sada, a wealthy Monterrey industrialist, occurred. This potentially explosive act is still shrouded in considerable mystery. President Echeverría was blamed by the right wing for coddling the leftists accused of the murder. This event seemed to polarize the commercial-industrial classes away from Echeverría who then turned to labor and peasantry, and to some extent the military, for political support. In this context the president set about to reform Agrarian Code features that dated back to 1942 and before. It was proclaimed that central to this reform was the breakup of the new concentration of once redistributed lands in the hands of a few, that is, Echeverría attacked the creation of new latifundios by use of *prestanombres* (fake or borrowed names) and

other clandestine methods of hiding the concentration of large landholdings. Stronger credit guarantees were to be accorded the ejidatarios. The
government's movement to strengthen ejido collectivization was accompanied by water distribution reforms as well. There is general consensus
that Echeverría promised more than he achieved with his entire reform
package, but he had at least ideologically aligned himself on the side of the
working and dispossessed classes. That made the president a symbolic
threat to Mexico's entrenched right wing. The year 1973 was proclaimed
the year of the *campesino* and land grants, more credit, and improved irrigation started reaching the small farmers.

During Echeverría's term the agricultural bourgeoisie, with considerable support from industrialists within the Monterrey Group and elsewhere, became effective and well organized politically. Peasant groups
countered with extra-official organizations that rivaled the CNC and
nominally coopted CCI and UGOCM which meant that the state with its
official PRI-sanctioned organizations effectively lost some power in the
agrarian reform dynamics. It was Echeverría's strategy to play
bourgeoisie and campesinos off against each other. This manipulative
process generated sporadic political unrest and violence. Corruption in
the SRA's agrarian reform program, like giving preferred credit to cash
crop and export producers in exchange for kickbacks to bureaucrats,
made Echeverría's promises appear cynical. Rural workers often fought
their brothers, the ejidatarios, keeping both groups easily at the mercy of
state and bourgeois manipulation. These displaced regular agricultural
workers who could not be absorbed by Mexico's cities and kept the migrant streams going north into the United States.

The quest for a stronger campesino sector brought about other conflicts in the countryside. The ejidatarios were encouraged through
FONAFE (National Fund for Ejido Development) to collaborate in a mul-
titude of enterprises including tourism. This underlay the scheme in
Nayarit to develop the ill-fated Bay of Flags (*Bahía de Banderas*) area as a
tourist attraction. In that scheme seven ejidos were coerced into giving up
their lands to the tourism developers. Inflation, foreign debt, an artificially high value of the peso, and waste through corruption slowed the
real growth of the GDP to 2.2 percent in 1976 and hampered the ability of
the state to invest in genuine agrarian reform.[36] The populist rhetoric of
the Echeverría government also took its economic toll by dampening the
willingness of foreign investors to risk their capital in a country whose
president openly courted international socialist and communist figures
including Fidel Castro. By Echeverría's last year in office the flight of capital had seriously undermined the Mexican peso and weakened the government's foreign borrowing strength. The agrarian reform program,
even at the rhetorical level, contributed to this economic weakening for it

seemed to foreign investors that the Mexican state was making a direct attack on private property no matter how ineffectively that attack was carried out. Similar bourgeois reactions took place as the state reasserted its established right to control public education.

Land invasions had continued to erupt in Sonora and at least five other states. With this unsettling background President Echeverría did final battle in November 1976 with the politico-economic right wing. He announced some 250,000 acres in land confiscations and ejidal grants to over 10,000 peasants, focusing in Sonora on latifundio families whose control was maintained by registering land parcels in the names of young children, even infants. The newly created ejidos were to get rapid credit through the Ejidal Bank. More production stoppages were staged by the agriculturalists. PRI spokesmen on the left accused the Monterrey Group and its instruments like COPARMEX of fabricating destabilizing political rumors against Echeverría and of organizing the deliberate flight of capital into United States banks to weaken the peso and embarrass the president. More FCI and Pact of Ocampo[37] land invasions occurred touching even such classic Sonoran families as that of former president Calles. Subsequently the uprisings spread south into Sinaloa. When Luis Echeverría was succeeded by José López Portillo on December 1, 1976, the bourgeois interests of Mexico hoped the agrarian reform and anti-industrial populist fever would have reached its end.

In retrospect the Echeverría sexenio exhibited considerable instability insofar as turnover in prominent political actors was concerned. Echeverría inevitably clashed with a number of regional power figures in his effort to shed the stigma he bore from 1968 (he was often disparaged as the hyena of Tlatelolco). He alienated many conservatives in his drive to make himself into a leading spokesman for Third World nations. Indeed it is widely believed that Echeverría's personal goal was to win the secretary generalship of the United Nations after his sexenio ended in 1976. The president also had a near mania for consolidation of personal power. In one way or another he alienated powerful governors in the states of Guerrero, Nuevo León, Puebla, Hidalgo, and Sonora, all of whom he eventually removed. Instability also occurred in the presidential cabinet including several attorneys general in 1971 and the secretary of finance and treasury in 1973 (the man who resigned was Hugo Margain, who became Mexico's ambassador to Washington in 1977 and his replacement at finance and treasury was José López Portillo who later succeeded to the presidency following Echeverría).

Echeverría's term was marked by several clashes with popular protesters and drew its own measure of moral turpitude as public scandals unfolded. One of these involved the government's use of clandestine paramilitary squads to put down public condemnation of the regime. The

public spectre of official terrorism also gave Echeverría a pretext to remove the mayor (*regente*) of Mexico's Federal District, Alfonso Martínez
Domínguez. This event, discussed in Chapter Five as the *Jueves de Corpus* affair, exemplifies the role of political violence in contemporary Mexican politics. It also relates to the processes of camarilla-building and re-
juvenation of deviant or "burned" charisma.

The sexenio of Luis Echeverría is noteworthy economically for the
new promise of economic power held out by the oil reserves that were
known to exist and which received great attention in the later 1970s. In
October 1974 there had been numerous press reports of large oil reserves
that could be suitable for exploitation in Chiapas and Tabasco in southern
Mexico. After June 1974 Mexico achieved self-sufficiency in oil, thus
enabling it to suspend imports from Venezuela. In 1974 Mexico achieved
a production level of 240,000 barrels per day compared with 71,000 at the
start of that year. Unofficial prediction floated internationally regarding
Mexico's potential petroleum reserves. In May of 1975 President
Echeverría announced publicly that Mexico would join OPEC, the Organization of Petroleum Exporting Countries, if it were invited to do so.
This announcement contradicted statements by Francisco Javier Alejo,
Secretary of Natural Resources, but it took place just as Mexico was announcing that its daily oil production had ascended to 700,000 barrels
daily. Echeverría's OPEC statement reflected his desire to project an international image of power; this propensity often clashed with the domestic political and economic realities of his country.

Late in 1975 Echeverría's foreign minister Emilo Rabasa resigned, an
example of the cabinet instability cited earlier. The resignation was attributed to Rabasa's disagreement with President Echeverría over Mexican
votes in the United Nations that were anti-Zionist. In November 1975
Mexico had voted for a resolution branding international Zionism as racist and it supported another UN resolution categorizing international
Zionism as colonialist and detrimental to the progress of women. This
provoked a tourist boycott in the United States by outspoken Jewish organizations. There was widespread belief, not proof, that Echeverría personally ordered these votes, over the objections of his United Nations
team in the hope of gaining Arab nation support for his candidacy to succeed Kurt Waldheim as secretary general of the United Nations.

Significant achievements during the Echeverría sexenio included
signing an agreement with the United States in 1973 for the construction
of a desalinization plant to remove salt from Colorado River water moving
southward for Mexican agricultural usage. Two new states were also
created out of former federal territories in 1974; the addition of Quin-
tana Roo and Baja California Sur as fully accredited states made Mexico
into a federal republic of 31 states plus the Federal District (comprising

the heart of Mexico City). During his term President Echeverría toured many Third World countries including Egypt, Tanzania, and Cuba. The president made strong appeals for solidarity among the developing nations and proferred Mexico (and himself) for potential leadership roles wherever he could. In March of 1976 President Echeverría announced his amnesty decree for some 250 persons still imprisoned as a result of the Tlatelolco uprising in 1968. The president's term was drawing to an end and he sought to resolve this unpleasant business before his successor took office.

The final months and weeks of President Echeverría's administration revealed Mexico's unsettled economic and political condition. Since 1954 Mexico's peso had maintained its value at 12.50 to the U.S. dollar. In August 1976 the Echeverría government allowed the peso to float, meaning it would devalue itself on the open market. Its value dropped 39 percent to 20.50 pesos to the dollar and in October it dropped to 26.50. Before leaving office Echeverría imposed selective wage and price increases and suspended the conversion of the peso into foreign currency to stem the flow of dollars out of the country. It was widely rumored that many high government officials changed millions of pesos into dollars before the devaluations, thereby taking advantage of their inside knowledge of planned monetary policy. Imposing further taxes on Mexican exports to enrich the national treasury began to damage the Mexican economy. Inflation and recession abroad also began to have deleterious effects on Mexico.

José López Portillo, the finance secretary, had earlier been chosen the PRI's official candidate to succeed Luis Echeverría and he resigned his cabinet position in September of 1975. López Portillo had been a lifelong personal friend of the outgoing president. He was replaced in the cabinet by Mario Ramón Beteta. It was believed that the choice of López Portillo was made personally by President Echeverría and to the not inconsiderable displeasure of the principal organizational-sectoral leadership elements within the PRI, who felt they had been bypassed in the presidential succession. This theme figures prominently in an understanding of Mexican political power and I will return to it in the chapter to follow.

National elections were held on July 4, 1976, for the presidency and state and local offices. José López Portillo won 94 percent of the vote over several minor candidates including Valentín Campa of the Mexican Communist Party. The principal opposition, PAN, had earlier declined to run a party-sponsored candidate but an independent unofficial PAN candidacy was put forth by Pablo Emilio Madero. The ruling PRI also captured all but one of 64 Senate seats and took 194 seats out of a total of 250 in the Chamber of Deputies. López Portillo assumed the presidency on December 1, 1976. He had been under secretary of the presidency under

Díaz Ordaz and secretary of finance under Echeverría. Otherwise López Portillo had little political experience via the electoral process.

Soon after taking office the new government announced it would tolerate no more *paracaidismo,* land invasions, by peasants as had occurred late in the previous administration. Troops and police were used almost immediately to dislodge squatter peasants who had seized land illegally in Sonora and Sinaloa. Well-known Mexican jurist Ignacio Burgoa won a federal judicial decision declaring the Sonora land seizures illegal but his clients, all wealthy landowners, expressed willingness to negotiate a settlement with peasants and thereby avoid violence as had been threatened by the UGOCM. More land invasions then occurred in the northern state of Coahuila.

President López Portillo announced in his inaugural speech that the treasury would begin to mint silver peso coins again in the hope of creating a "strong peso" via real silver against the ongoing inflationary process. He promised free convertibility of the peso and stressed his government's full support for the business community both domestic and foreign. There would be a special (lower) peso conversion rate to enable companies to pay off dollar debts incurred during the recent peso devaluations under the preceeding administration.

The first year of the López Portillo government saw a great amount of political violence throughout Mexico, the subject of part of the chapter to follow. When time came for the new president's first state of the nation address on September 1, 1977, the PRI-dominated regime must have decided that the time was at hand for major political reform. López Portillo announced a complex new electoral law that would allow more political parties to participate, including the communists, and which would remove many of the existing obstacles to getting such parties on the ballot. This also meant that the size of the Chamber of Deputies would be increased from 250 to 400, with 300 of these chosen from individual constituencies and 100 to be divided up according to a complicated formula of proportional representation. These electoral reforms would go into effect with the state and local elections of 1979.

Mexico's economic growth rate in 1977 was under 3 percent, the same as the previous year, and the population growth rate was estimated at 3.7 percent. The best response López Portillo could make to these unfavorable conditions was to appeal to both workers and employers for cooperation with wage limits and price freezes for the remainder of 1977. Emphasis would be placed on government aid to new businesses, on import substitution, and on promotion of exports to earn foreign exchange. In the first half of 1977 the inflation rate had dropped to 1.8 percent from 4 percent during the previous six months. The president expressed confidence in Mexico's ability to rebound from recession conditions based on the growth of Mexico's continually reevaluated oil wealth. He declared an "alliance for production" as a positive approach to economic reform.

An effort was made by López Portillo personally to smooth over existing bad feelings within the U.S. Jewish community resulting from the 1975 anti-Zionist Mexican vote in the United Nations. While visiting President Carter in Washington during February 1977 he conveyed Mexico's regret for the incident. The ongoing Jewish tourism boycott was subsequently lifted. López Portillo also stressed in a speech to the U.S. Congress his nation's concern about American pressures against Cuba concurrent with toleration of human rights violations in Chile. He also blamed illegal Mexican migration and drug traffic on economic distress caused by U.S. trade restrictions against Mexican products. Both presidents reiterated their commitment to nonintervention in the internal affairs of the hemisphere's sovereign states. President Carter also thanked President López Portillo for his sincere concern over the cultivation of narcotics for export in Mexico and announced a binational plan to attack this problem.

University unrest plagued Mexico during 1977 as the newly-formed employees and academics union (STUNAM) at the National University staged sit-ins and strikes at the Mexico City campus with support from similar groups at other universities about the country. The strike became so troublesome that the National University rector ordered lectures to be broadcast over the radio during June. Earlier in March an academic strike at the state university in Oaxaca had led to the removal of that state's governor by decree from Mexico City. Peasant groups in Yucatán charged that government agents had murdered more than 50 of their members and that some 300 had been illegally detained. President López Portillo also agreed during 1977 to pay reparations to the dispossessed landowners in Sonora, reiterating that the land invasions and the previous distribution of land by his predecessor had been illegal; but he bowed to political reality in the interest of avoiding continued violence. The new administration proceeded against former officials of the Echeverría government charging financial dishonesty and corruption; these were Augusto Gómez Villanueva and Felix Barra García (former secretaries of agrarian reform) and Alberto Ríos Camarena who had been detained in Miami for his complicity in the Bay of Flags scandal.

Throughout 1978 and 1979 euphoria grew in Mexico over the constantly expanding claims of oil wealth. Several cabinet positions experienced turnover owing to budget disputes and Mexico continued its indebtedness to the International Monetary Fund (IMF) and to foreign banks. Mexico also entered into a natural gas dispute with the United States that is touched on in Chapter Six. Illegal Mexican aliens in the United States continued to be a point of diplomatic irritation between the two countries. In February 1979 President Giscard d'Estaing of France vi-

sited Mexico and ratified a binational agreement for major French purchases of crude oil beginning in 1980. France also agreed to aid Mexico in
the construction of nuclear energy plants. Other agreements were also
signed with Canada and Japan. The technology of these countries was
welcomed by the Mexican president in developing Mexico's uranium
supplies, most of which lay in Chihuahua to the north.

In his state of the nation address of September 1, 1978, President
López Portillo linked future political reforms to new legislation granting
freedom of information to the public and allowing the Senate to replace
any state governor where the constitutional order had been "suspended."
He also suggested that some powers should be returned to the state governments to enable them better to cope with local needs (previously some
45 percent of state revenues had been from federal subventions with the
remainder depending on local taxes and loans). Several gestures were also
made toward pacification via amnesty grants to political offenders. This
was a partial response to domestic and international pressure from
human rights groups protesting the disappearances of allegedly "subver-
sive" persons in Mexico. The Mexican government also gave a partial accounting for a number of missing persons who had perished.

Elections held for state and local offices took place on July 1, 1979,
(see Chapter Five) and produced a greater representation for opposition
political parties, as López Portillo had promised at the time of the electoral
reforms in 1977. The state's liberal image was further enhanced by the release of more political prisoners under the government's continuing amnesty program. This followed a brief occupation of the Swiss embassy in
Mexico City during 1979 by human rights protesters demanding more
comprehensive amnesty grants. Finally a gas agreement was signed with
the United States in September of 1979 ending two years of often acrimonious negotiations. Discussions continued on extending a gasoduct
from inside Mexico to the U.S. border near McAllen, Texas. López Portillo visited Washington in September and gained President Carter's support for a world-wide energy conservation plan which the Mexican president presented to the United Nations. Some viewers felt that the Mexican
proposal was a counterpoise to world criticism of Mexican petroleum
management following the disastrous 1979 blowout of the offshore oil
well Ixtoc I near the Campeche coast on the Caribbean. This was called
the worst such oil spill in recorded history. It caused extensive damage to
U.S. beaches, especially along the Texas coast. Mexico had been roundly
criticized internationally.

Other international issues surfaced during the López Portillo administration. In 1980 the president visited Cuba and pledged Mexico's support in Cuba's struggle to regain control of Guantánamo, a long-standing
point of contention with the United States which maintained a naval base

there. He stated Mexico's support for Cuban independence, criticized the growing U.S. involvement in Central America, and condemned a recent military coup in Bolivia against a civilian government. Much of this was obviously not the kind of thing the Mexican president had said publicly on his last visit to Washington. López Portillo and Castro promised to exchange oil and sugar as demands would dictate. They also worked out an extensive plan for subsidized exchanges of tourists. In the same year Mexico reached an agreement to supply oil to the new revolutionary government of Nicaragua. It declared that fines would be levied against U.S. and other fishing boats that came within Mexico's 200 mile limit for tuna. Earlier arrests of American tuna boats resulted in a U.S. ban on the importation of tuna, which affected about one-third of Mexico's total sales at that time. The United States still insisted on a 12 mile limit for the catching of tuna, a position that had brought it into conflict with Canada, Costa Rica, and Peru. Mexico also signed agreements in 1980 with Venezuela for petroleum exploration and with Brazil for oil sales.

According to tradition the announcement of Mexico's next president (the PRI's candidate) is made about one year before the election. In September of 1981 the government announced that its standard bearer in the July 1982 presidential election would be Miguel de la Madrid Hurtado. He had served as budget secretary in the López Portillo cabinet since May of 1979. The following month the PRI's national convention endorsed de la Madrid as candidate. It was thought that he would be an excellent choice given his background in international finance and a business management degree from the United States, and he was well-versed in the finances of an oil-based economy. De la Madrid, like López Portillo, had little political experience via the electoral process.

The López Portillo presidency included visits with President Ronald Reagan, the first in June of 1981. The two presidents had met previously on the border at Ciudad Juárez in Mexico. In October they met again at a special summit hosted by López Portillo in Cancún, in southern Mexico, once it had been agreed that Fidel Castro of Cuba would not be present (owing to pressure from the Reagan White House). Reagan and López Portillo had obvious differences over American involvement in Central America but the Mexican head of state said that for the first time he felt totally comfortable with an American president. Mexico's obligations to Cuba had been discharged at a previously arranged special meeting between Castro and López Portillo at Cozumel where the two leaders acknowledged Cuba's right to be present at Cancún and Cuba gracefully agreed to the exclusion in the interest of hemispheric well-being.

Because the legacy of López Portillo's sexenio is critical for understanding Mexican politics and policy issues in the remainder of the 1980s it is appropriate here to draw up a partial balance sheet for that administration. When the president assumed office Mexico's inflation rate was running near 30 percent and the country's foreign debt was surpassing 20 billion. But oil discoveries during this period led to estimates that Mexico could rival Saudi Arabia and by 1981 Mexico was earning over $14 billion annually from the sale of petroleum products. With this wealth expected to continue indefinitely López Portillo undertook a number of expensive development projects including improved infrastructure to support agriculture and nuclear power plants. With oil as collateral foreign banks loaned Mexico nearly all the money it needed to start these developments. This infusion of hard money created serious inflation; it also spawned gross corruption that was highlighted by the president's own lavish personal lifestyle and by the beginning of the PEMEX scandals which produced the resignation of its director Jorge Díaz Serrano in June 1981 (ostensibly over his decision to lower the price of Mexico's export oil in view of a growing world recession and a glutted oil market). López Portillo's government, it is now generally recognized, should have stopped borrowing in 1981 when the world oil glut became obvious. That he did not explains why his successor inherited a major recession of crisis proportions.

As Mexicans lost confidence in their economy a rush to convert pesos into dollars occurred. Dollars were leaving the country for U.S. banks. In February 1982, the peso was again allowed to float resulting in a devaluation from 25 to 50 to the dollar. A second devaluation occurred in August and a third in December (under de la Madrid). This left Mexico's peso worth over 80 percent less at the end of 1982 than at the beginning of that year. President López Portillo responded to the flight of capital by the extreme step of nationalizing some 33 private banks having over 4000 branches and 140,000 employees around the country.[38] The government imposed fines for purchasing dollars without a permit. The president publicly accused his erstwhile friends in the business sector of plundering Mexico and of practicing the technique of *sacadólares* or sneaking their dollars out of the country. However, it is widely believed that López Portillo and his family were doing the very same thing. There was obvious resentment in the business community, which had begun the sexenio on honeymoon terms with López Portillo. Like Echeverría, the president climaxed his term by taking some unpopular actions which probably were necessary, albeit mixed with some hypocrisy, and thereby left a clean slate for his successor. The long-term ramifications of corruption during the López Portillo government could not, however, be disgused nor wiped away.

Presidential elections were held on Juy 4, 1982. The PRI's candidate Miguel de la Madrid Hurtado won easily with 74.4 percent of the total vote, yet this was 20 percentage points down from the victory of his predecessor in 1976. New parties and candidates had entered the political arena via the electoral reform of 1977 (which applied to a presidential election in 1982 for the first time). Miguel de la Madrid's prospects are discussed in the final chapter to this book. Suffice it to say that he inherited a nation near economic bankruptcy although with notably expanded political participation. The new president's tone, if taken at face value, was positive and reformist. He imposed austerity during his first year which temporarily ended Mexico's trade deficit. This, of course, intensified recession conditions and idled more workers. At the same time he moved to aid businesses that were hurt by curbs on imports. De la Madrid took concrete action through legal reform to punish corrupt public officials. He even pushed through the Chamber of Deputies the needed clearance to deprive Jorge Díaz Serrano of his senatorial immunity so that he could be prosecuted for corruption as director of PEMEX under the previous administration. Whether Díaz Serrano *really is punished* along with other high officials could be the moment of truth for de la Madrid's administrative reform. His slogan was "moral renovation." The president also ordered an end to nepotism in public employment, a revolutionary decree to be sure if genuinely carried out.

Two of de la Madrid's greatest challenges will be in expanding the political reforms begun by his predecessor to make Mexico more truly a democracy, and in raising the purchasing power of Mexican workers. In the latter case Mexican economists have estimated that since early 1976 the standard of living for Mexican workers dropped 20 percent and that it fell another 25 percent by late 1982.[39] That has severe implications for overall Mexican poverty as well; and perhaps poverty is the greatest challenge any Mexican president can confront. Internationally it is President de la Madrid's perhaps unwelcome task to mediate the growing conflict between the United States and the various revolutionary movements in Central America. When he met with President Reagan in La Paz during August of 1983 de la Madrid waxed optimistic saying "we will make progress in the hemisphere when we stop seeing our neighbors as problems and include them as brothers who should share in the development of solutions."[40]

NOTES

1. Mauricio González de la Garza, *Última llamada* (Mexico: EDAMEX, 1981), p. 76.
2. José Vásquez Amaral, "Democracia mexicana," *Diorama Excelsior,* May 23, 1982, p. 2.
3. Gilberto Balam, *Tlatelolco: reflexiones de un testigo* (Mexico: no publisher cited, 1969), pp. 24–26. The narrative of events to follow is based largely upon accounts previously published in the first and second editions of this book. Fifteen years after the Tlatelolco massacre the international press remembered the event saying that the outcome left these legacies: creation of the PMT or Mexican Workers Party, radicalization of a nucleus of liberal journalists, growth of an extensive leftist literature and organization of the political left generally, and the electoral reforms of the

late 1970s. This commentary went further saying "the journalist Elena Poniatowska, author of the book *La noche de Tlatelolco,* the most important historical testimony to the importance of what happened, recalled that President Díaz Ordaz ordered the massacre of students in the Plaza de las Tres Culturas in a fashion worse than war." Translated from *Diario Las Américas* (Miami), October 4, 1983.

4. *El Sol de México,* August 19, 1968.

5. *Por Qué?,* September, 1968, *passim.* This publication was closed down by the government in 1974 because it had opened its pages to guerrilla communications and frequently embarrassed the regime with revelations of corruption. Most embarrassing was probably the revelation in *Por Qué?* over the kidnapping of President Echeverría's father-in-law José Guadalupe Zuno concurrently with the kidnapping of Senator Rubén Figueroa who was the PRI's candidate for governor of Guerrero. Figueroa could not campaign for himself because he was, indeed, kidnapped by the Party of the Poor led by Lucio Cabañas. Ultimately the government said publicly that Figueroa had been liberated through the valiant efforts of the Mexican army. *Por Qué?* contended, however, that it would publish a signed statement by Figueroa acknowledging that a ransom had been paid for his release. This made Echeverría out clearly to be a liar and that is why his agents took over *Por Qué?* and smashed its presses, at least according to testimony given to me later by Roger Menéndez one of the brothers who managed the publication. See also J. Natividad Rosales, *La Muerte de Lucio Cabañas* (Mexico: Editorial Posada, 1975), p. 39 and p. 166. See also his *Quien fue Lucio Cabañas* (Mexico: Editorial Posada, 1976), pp. 94–95. In August of 1972 the present author was arrested by agents of *Gobernación* and subsequently expelled from the country over my involvement with the editors of *Por Qué?* and for having criticized U.S. aid to repressive Latin American regimes including aid to the Mexican Federal Judicial Police. Later, President Echeverría sent an emissary to assure me that he knew nothing of this affair and that he regretted what had happened. The entire episode involving *Por Qué?* including jailing and exile of its editors revealed the threshold of regime sensitivity to press criticism then prevailing in Mexico.

6. Handbill of the National Strike Committee (*Comité Nacional de Lucha,* UNAM).

7. *Por Qué?,* September, 1968, p. 43.

8. G.M. Bergman, "Flags, Tanks, and Students," *The Nation,* September 30, 1968, pp. 298–300. See also John Womack, "Unfreedom in Mexico," *The New Republic,* October 12, 1968.

9. *El Sol de México,* August 28, 1968 and *Excelsior,* August 29, 1968.

10. Balam, *Tlatelolco,* p. 77.

11. *Visión,* September 1, 1968, p. 16.

12. Ibid.

13. *Los Angeles Times,* September 29, 1968.

14. *Time,* September 27, 1968, p. 33.

15. *Visión,* October 11, 1968, p. 13.

16. De la Garza, *Última llamada;* the author González de la Garza has been criticized as an apologist for the Mexican political system but his writing in the book cited acknowledges nepotism and other nefarious practices to a degree that constitutes critical evidence if one chooses to use it. He does not whitewash the regime on the massacre of Tlatelolco. He does criticize many of the student leaders for being conveniently absent from much of the conflict they helped to orchestrate, e.g., pp. 283–84.

17. In his *Última llamada* González de la Garza adds that President Díaz Ordaz had warned the students that disorders would be met with force, that the president had no other emotional equipment than a battle mentality, and that if the students had

wanted to have their October 2 demonstration and minimize bloodshed they could have picked a place less boxed in than Tlatelolco. This account holds essentially that both the student leaders and the president wanted blood and that is what they got, unfortunately at the expense of many people who would have preferred nonviolence.

18. Balam, *Tlatelolco*, p. 96.
19. Ibid.
20. I am relying on the testimony published in previous editions of *Mexican Democracy* of persons who then wished to remain anonymous.
21. Balam, *Tlatelolco*, p. 97.
22. See Thomas C. Shelling, *The Strategy of Conflict* (New York: Oxford University Press, 1963), p. 74 and p. 90 relating to signals providing a sense of personal immunity that enable one to join in aggressive mob action.
23. Balam, *Tlatelolco*, pp. 97–98. See also *Newsweek*, October 14, 1968, p. 64, and *America*, October 19, 1968, p. 340.
24. *Los Angeles Times*, October 4, 1968.
25. *Los Angeles Times*, October 3, 1968.
26. Octavio Paz, *Posdata* (Mexico: Siglo Veintiuno Editores, 1970), *passim*.
27. Carlos Fuentes, "Mexico and its Demons," *New York Review of Books*, September 20, 1973, p. 19.
28. I spent some time with Madrazo in 1968 at which time he was trying to create a national front organization potentially to oppose the PRI. This was after he had been fired as CEN president by President Díaz Ordaz for Madrazo's efforts to democratize the PRI via local nominating primaries. Madrazo expressed to me his concern that the government kept him perpetually under scrutiny and pointed out his window to show me the cars that were posted to watch his every move. One year later he died in an airplane crash which some critics still believe was no accident. See the article in the June 25, 1969 issue of *Voz Nacional*, p. 5, which questions the official story of Madrazo's death. My own estimation of Madrazo on the basis of having known him was that he had the charismatic appeal necessary (deviant from the official PRI standpoint) to challenge seriously the regime via peaceful means. That may have made him more threatening than someone who had actually taken up arms against the regime and could easily be discredited as a terrorist. Madrazo's "peaceful terrorism" may have been harder to come to grips with, especially for Díaz Ordaz and in the wake of Tlatelolco.
29. Paz, *Posdata*, p. 114.
30. Ibid., pp. 121–22.
31. Ibid., p. 149.
32. See "an entire nation was wounded at Tlatelolco" and the remainder of novelist Luis Spota's treatment in *La plaza* (Mexico: Joaquín Mortiz, 1972), p. 165.
33. Ibid., pp. 215–16.
34. Fuentes, "Mexico and its Demons," p. 16.
35. *El Día*, August 31, 1973.
36. Steven E. Sanderson, *Agrarian Populism and the Mexican State* (Berkeley: University of California Press, 1981), p. 184.
37. The so-called Pact of Ocampo was an invention of the Echeverría government to symbolize peasant involvement in the political process and to discourage rival peasant organizations that might threaten the official CNC, the National Peasants Confederation.
38. *Diario Las Américas*, September 12, 1982.
39. *St. Louis Post-Dispatch*, August 17, 1983.
40. *Siempre*, August 24, 1983, p. 6.

Five

The Practice of
Esoteric Democracy

DEMOCRACY AND PRESIDENTIAL POWER

The Mexican political analyst Mauricio González de la Garza notes the oft-quoted dictum of Simón Bolívar that the new republics of the Americas needed kings that could be called presidents and adds that, in Mexico, these have become kings for six-year periods. He argues further that arrogance or haughtiness (*soberbia*) is one great notable sin of Mexican presidents: "If we treat them as God is it any wonder that they eventually believe they are deities who see themselves as the only ones who can think and decide for all Mexicans?"[1] How presidents are expected to behave, and how they do ultimately behave, is a revealing commentary on the degree to which the state may be considered democratic. Some Mexican presidents have been less authoritarian than others. We have seen that historically they can be arrayed on a continuum from the worst of tyrants (Santa Anna in the nineteenth century) to the most generous and benevolent (Cárdenas in the 1930s). But it is well, first, to consider some of the requisites of political democracy as bases for judging Mexican presidents.

As a phenomenon, political democracy is intimately related to people feeling that they are part of the state. As Robert Wesson observes, this feeling may be generated by propaganda for some time, but eventually the alienation of people from the state, if allowed to fester, will likely reveal itself as repression under authoritarian rule.[2] When the repression generates popular uprisings, as at Tlatelolco in 1968 or the peasant movements of 1976 and 1982, then the democratic semblance is broken. A condition of popular inequality contrasted with wealthy oligarchy is likely to accompany authoritarianism. As Wesson puts it there is some degree of inequality beyond which democratic politics simply won't work and most Latin American societies have probably seen inequality grow to such a degree that democracy will have difficulty in growing.[3] As we will see presently, the facade of pluralism may only partially compensate for the socioeconomic inequality that one finds as a built-in threat to Mexican democracy.

Although we cannot make rigid applications of judgmental criteria to the political life of any Latin American country (and expect to evaluate the status of democratic practices realistically) it is possible to list substantive criteria for political democracy and rate nations in relative terms. As I have developed the concept elsewhere, the following categories set forth characteristics that I would expect to find in strongly democratic political systems:

1. The existence of popular sovereignty under impartial rules that are applied equally to all competing interest groups and individuals.
2. There is a clear and enforced distinction between that which is public and that which is private; the state and its custodians serve the public and do not enrich themselves at public expense.
3. Free and popular elections are held for selecting leaders of the state; there is a substantive ideological choice among candidates and issues; there is free press and speech without fear of extralegal reprisal.
4. Leaders and public officials so chosen are subject to criticism, accountability, and removal by public initiative under equally applied impartial rules of a nonviolent nature.
5. The stakes in the political process are not so high as to render arbitration by popular vote impossible.
6. The state so constituted has a humanistic goal, i.e., it seeks out and promotes the popular consensus of a good life rather than repressing the populace to preserve elite privilege.[4]

Mexico in the 1980s does not rate highly on any of these criteria. Some nations, like Paraguay, can hardly be rated at all in these terms. Even when applied to the English-speaking states of North America democracy may have its culture-relative dimensions. As this discussion of esoteric democracy in Mexico proceeds one may refer to the above criteria from time to time, keeping in mind that a society like Mexico which allows for substantial political pluralism is much closer to democracy than a nation like Haiti which enjoys almost none. And, as the image-index studies[5] reveal, Mexico's democratic image compared to the spectrum of its Latin American neighbors is toward the positive (democratic) end.

Mexico claims to have a democratic political system. As a nation it claims to be the "united states of Mexico" and these states are represented in a parliamentary body which resembles, on the surface, other parliaments within the democratic tradition. At the apex of political power in Mexico is a very powerful chief executive, the president. If the Mexican president were truly the first choice in the hearts and minds of the people there would be no need of committing fraud in the process of getting him elected. In fact few observers today would argue that any of Mexico's recent presidents needed ballot fraud to get elected. But that is not true of some congressional elections where many opposition candidates, especially those of the parties PAN (National Action Party) and PPS (Popular Socialist Party), are thought to have been denied seats by fraud committed by the dominant party PRI. Fraud at the state and local level has been especially nefarious in preventing the sharing of political power in Mexico. In the 1980s that may be changing drastically, but it is necessary to review the recent past to have a feeling for the contemporary political mood.

Because of the flagrant occurrences of ballot fraud in Mexican elections around the time of the 1970 presidential succession the PAN threatened to withdraw its candidate in protest against government repression and public dishonesty. By a narrow vote in a special national assembly PAN agreed to stay in the running. Its presidential candidate, Efraín González Morfín, told me personally that he had voted to terminate his own candidacy. It is known that the PRI was severely concerned over being unmasked before the world, especially the Third World, as a single-party monopoly. Ultimately, that is exactly what happened in 1976. In that election the PAN did not even field a presidential candidate, partly because of internal disagreement but also out of recognition that the party was lending itself to the facade of democracy by even participating at the presidential level (PAN did compete for lesser seats, and lost nearly everywhere). Winning in this way, the man who assumed the presidency in 1976 was under considerable pressure to mold a popular image for himself and for the rest of Mexican officialdom.

Even before José López Portillo was elected to the sexenio 1976–82, it was possible for an opposition commentator to write in an internationally-read magazine that "only his very death could impede his becoming president."[6] And days after his triumph, the official house organ of the *Secretaría de Gobernación* (one of the most powerful cabinet-level ministries) carried on its front page the assurance that "the great electoral process of July 4 has confirmed the democratic vocation of the Mexican people."[7] Inside that edition were photos of long lines of citizens waiting patiently to register to vote beneath large patriotic slogans extolling the significance of voting. Without real opposition, lacking a genuine win, the PRI must use rhetoric to a maximum as a means of symbol manipulation in the hope that popular allegiance will follow (or at least that people will feign allegiant behavior). As one PRI sympathizer has stated in an economic context, "rhetoric neutralizes dissatisfaction."[8]

Some may ask, why even bother to have an election if the results are known in advance (the same PAN candidate cited above told me he had seen official election results on a state-by-state basis, for all federal seats, that had been printed days *before* the elections of 1970 were held). Partially the campaign is to win support for the national regime, and partially it is to ensure the victories of state and local candidates whose campaigns are supposedly helped by having the PRI's national candidate visit their districts. Many of the state and local seats are contested by other parties and it is easier to accomplish vote fraud in favor of the PRI when symbolic support is present from the national organization.

If propaganda is used to create the facade of democracy its success may end when the people feel hopelessly alienated from the state as observed earlier. Events of 1968 and thereafter had dramatized such alienation. The unopposed presidential campaign of 1976 could be taken as a visible public sign that the apex of the PRI's power was unstable, that the base of the pyramid was weakening. This could have dire emotional consequences throughout the Mexican populace, or so the PRI's thinking might go. But even though individuals, isolated as human units, may be disaffected from the regime, this must not be allowed to become a consciously shared experience at the group level, such as at Tlatelolco. That is why a vigorous presidential campaign must be held, even without opposition: to give the public impression that there does exist widespread popular adulation for the regime and its figurehead at the apex of the pyramid. What happens thereafter, the kind of image that is molded, depends greatly upon the person of the president.

Out of the Great Revolution of 1910–17 emerged a constitution in the latter year which is Mexico's legal basis for government today. The real, or functioning basis is, of course, the established party customs that have become institutionalized. The Constitution and established precedent, plus amendments, give strong governing prerogatives to the president should he choose to use them. Among other things he has the power to intervene in state and local governments, to replace their elected magistrates virtually by decree. He has strong powers of the purse over all levels of government, and although the national legislature has a veto, this power has not been exercised over a chief executive since the late 1920s. The president has the power to expel foreigners and their companies. He is invested with extensive powers to protect the internal security of the nation. Security can have various meanings, including security from verbal assault, thus giving the president de facto censorship powers over the media and press.

In addition, the president has power to carry out land distribution via the ejido program of communal farms. In recent years such grants of land took on meaning to the extent that the land had value without introducing artificial means (for example, irrigation) of giving it such value. President Lázaro Cárdenas (1934–40) is remembered for his vast distribution of naturally valuable land to many peasants. More recent presidents have made land distribution into a more symbolic gesture. President Gustavo Díaz Ordaz (1964–70) is said to have distributed land of which some 85 percent was worthless. President Luis Echeverría (1970–76) made a major grant of valuable land in the northwestern state of Sonora only three weeks before his presidency ended, thus leaving to his successor a solution of the bitter fighting that ensued between peasants and latifundistas.

Mexico's president is charged with promoting collective bargaining among workers, peasants, and private-sector ownership. Since the Mexican state is also a major owner of key industries (petroleum, railroads, and steel, for example) the existence of an official party superimposed upon the government aids labor relations between proletariat and the state. On whatever level, the collective bargaining is handled through the three sectors (labor, agrarian, and popular) of the PRI and their affiliated unions. There is, to be sure, extra-official labor organizing and this has posed a threat to the PRI's traditional hegemony in recent years.

Since Cárdenas, presidents have tried to establish themselves as unique entities, as creative revolutionaries with a capital "R." Each has sought to leave his own legacy for history to record, but without outwardly repudiating that of his predecessor as Cárdenas did. This became critical as alienation against the single-party monolith intensified during the 1970s and 1980s and as that alienation, in turn, was answered with government repression.

An oft-quoted dictum of Frank Brandenburg holds that Mexicans "avoid personal dictatorship by retiring their dictators every six years."[9] This was part of the denouement of the Revolution, no immediate reelection of the president and, in effect, no reelection at all. One president, Obregón, who sought to violate this dictum was assassinated in 1928. Presidents since Cárdenas have sought to perpetuate their influence through a unique process for choosing successors. And each president has tried to select a compatible successor just as did Cárdenas. His successor, Manuel Avila Camacho (1940–46) guided Mexico through World War II and engineered significant consolidations within the single-party system. This left the PRI with its contemporary name and its present subdivision into three basic sectors. Next, Miguel Alemán (1946–52) used a hard hand in stimulating postwar economic development, especially in collaboration with U.S. interests. In this way he undid some of the hard feelings left by the oil expropriations of the Cárdenas era. Alemán's successor, Adolfo Ruíz Cortines (1952–58) made notable efforts to professionalize the federal bureaucracy and to instill the norm of honesty into Mexican politics. He seems to have been the last Mexican president to have attempted a serious rationalization of the governing system, a task Miguel de la Madrid took on again in 1982.

By the time of the presidency of Adolfo López Mateos (1958–64), Mexico was changing from a predominantly rural to an urban nation. Population pressures were increasing on the cities. Rural discontent grew. The inability of the PRI to be all things to all people was showing itself. López Mateos inherited labor unrest. The railroad workers led by Demetrio Vallejo and Valentín Campa attempted to paralyze transportation in the spring of 1959. They were put down forcefully by the army under the president's direction. The leaders of that strike received harsh prison terms of 16 years each.[10] At this point, the image of a benevolent president was weakened while the authoritarian part of the equation was reinforced.

Undoubtedly a crucial point in the further atrophy of the presidential mystique came during the regime of Gustavo Díaz Ordaz (1964–70). It was his fate to play sacrificial priest to hundreds of students who died in the government-ordered massacre at Tlatelolco near downtown Mexico City on the night of October 2, 1968. Thousands were injured and the true death toll may never be known. It was Díaz Ordaz's own cabinet minister Luis Echeverría who shared much of the public opprobrium over the Tlatelolco disaster; and the same Echeverría succeeded to the presidency for the sexenio that ended in 1976.[11] At that point free speech had been severely curtailed in Mexico.

Echeverría proclaimed a policy of democratic openness (*apertura democrática*) which was supposed to make it easier for opposition groups to win elections. This, as we shall see, was little more than empty rhetoric. There was evidence that the regime actively fomented divisions in opposition parties and in one case, that of the Popular Socialist Party (PPS), the PRI was obliged to grant a national senatorial seat to an opposition candidate (the first such victory in decades) in exchange for his admission that he had earlier lost the race for governor of Nayarit. In his campaign for popular support, Echeverría embraced socialist-sounding doctrines and branded his critics as "emissaries of the past," a posture which put him on a collision course with strong vested interests in the private sector. This conflict was sharpened by Echeverría's pronouncements during visits to a plethora of Third World countries, many of which had socialist or communist governments. Especially notable were his close ties with the socialist regime of Salvador Allende of Chile, his subsequent welcoming of Chilean exiles, and his breaking of diplomatic relations with the Pinochet regime.

Echeverría sought to heal the wounds of the private sector by granting fiscal concessions and growth subsidies in areas calculated to win allegiance. At the same time, he took a repressive stand against independent union efforts to break with official syndicates and confront management with tough demands. Despite his promise of democratic openness,

Echeverría came to the rescue of the private sector when threatened by labor. This was conspicuously true of the regime's repressive tactics against SUTERM, an electrical workers's syndicate that broke with officialdom. At the same time Echeverría sought to bolster support within the official unions with worker housing programs such as INFONAVIT.

Instability in the regime was further evidenced by violence in the countryside and the wave of kidnappings and bombings in cities. Echeverría ordered the army to suppress the guerrillas, a task which it came close to accomplishing, but not before great damage had been done to the regime. Even the PRI's candidate for the governorship of Guerrero, Rubén Figueroa, could not make an acceptance speech in person because he had been kidnapped by a band of guerillas. Later, when the opposition journal *Por Qué?* sought to publish a decidedly antigovernment version of the episode, the government shut down the publication and jailed its editors. Peasant alienation toward the regime grew and Mexican democracy seemed to be going through a low period.

Echeverría's authoritarian image was patent in his creation of the new Military University for the armed forces and the inclusion of military personnel in traditionally civilian governmental roles. This led to speculation about an elite corps of hopeful military administrators referred to colloquially as *los penecilinos,* the name derived from the notion that their special training had equipped them with a unique variety of "penicillin" which could be a useful antibiotic for an infected civilian government in an emergency. Out of these rumors emerged much speculation about renascent militarism in Mexican politics and the possibility of a coup toward the end of the Echeverría sexenio. Concern for controlling the opposition was also evidenced in the regime's decree of strict gun control following the June 10th affair.[12]

It is a revealing irony of Echeverría's increasingly paranoid style that, as his presidency drew to a close, he was consistently preoccupied with authoritarian conspiracies against him, and with authoritarianism (fascism) of one sort or another about the world, while at the same time he was reacting in the most authoritarian way to critics of his own regime at home. This leads to consideration of one of the most fateful decisions of Echeverría's career, one that would leave him open to the most severe charge of authoritarianism, indeed of totalitarianism. Echeverría decided to close the newspaper *Excelsior* during July 1976. This publication was perhaps at that time the last bastion of unfettered press freedom in Mexico. It was a cooperative in which the workers owned shares. Its editors were dedicated to open critical journalism. *Excelsior* was easily one of the three best newspapers printed in the Spanish language (in all probability it was *the* best). During most of the Echeverría sexenio the pages of *Excelsior* were filled with stories of popular uprisings against corrupt government officials throughout the country, and penetrating investigative reporting on a number of sensitive themes including intra-PRI power struggles, corruption generally, and poverty. It was difficult for Echeverría to continue to promote himself as a leader of the Third World, who merited the secretary-generalship of the United Nations, when he presided over a country with some 40 percent of its work force unemployed and over 70 percent of that work force earning less than $80 per month, a nation in the humiliating position of solving its surplus labor problem by encouraging millions to undertake illegal migration to the United States (and then accusing the United States of racism for expelling the wetbacks).[13]

Echeverría's paranoid style contradicted the image he sought to project to the outside world: he proclaimed Mexico to be the land of *apertura democrática* and also of *autocrítica* (a form of self-criticism). He denonced U.S. racism and great-power hegemony over the Third World economies. He condemned Israel for its Zionist imperialism. He paid tribute to the populism of Juan Perón and then self-righteously condemned the Argentine generals who overthrew the Peronist regime when it degenerated hopelessly into government by sheer terror after having produced the world's worst rate of inflation in 1976.[14] Echeverría condemned a group of Mexican student critics in March of 1976 as fascists working for the U.S. Central Intelligence Agency (the president himself had previously collaborated with the CIA as will be cited later). Finally he closed *Excelsior* and replaced it with a puppet newspaper published irreverently under the same name.[15] Echeverría came to power using the slogan *arriba y adelante,* up and forward. But that pledge was not fulfilled in Mexico in any meaningful sense.

Mexican presidents have the power to be undemocratic. They have the power to be inconsistent. They can break public promises with nearly complete immunity. There is no effective impeachment process in Mexico. The practice of the military coup, so common throughout Latin America, has no Mexican counterpart as of this writing. The power of Mexico's president, thus, is awesome.

TRANSFERRING PRESIDENTIAL POWER AND THE LIMITS OF CRITICISM

The incumbent president makes his selection of successor fairly early during his term and hides it as best he can until he is ultimately forced by pressures from within the PRI to declare himself.[16] Were he to announce his successor before the final year of his term, the incumbent president might progressively lose power and thereby impair his ability to carry out any programs intended to carve for him a distinct place in Mexico's political history.

The president has an intriguing procedure for testing his power structure's reaction to a potential successor. There is a political folklore in Mexico about "veiled ones" (*tapados*) who are suspected to be the president's chosen successor. But there is only one real (*verdadero*) tapado, and he is unveiled formally at the official party's national nominating convention. In point of fact, however, the unveiling may occur in other and quite informal ways. For instance, the name of the tapado may be leaked to the government-controlled press while the president and his advisors await a reaction from within the PRI. But there is also the external reaction to be considered, that is, that of the United States. Because of the close interdependency of the Mexican and U.S. economies the Mexican presidential succession becomes a matter of importance north of the Rio Grande. The CIA, as a special "policeman" who protects U.S. interests abroad (as Philip Agee put it), will also be interested in the new Mexican president.[17]

Early in his book *La sucesión presidencial,* Daniel Cosío Villegas treats the works of several U.S. scholars who found the selection of PRI candidates to follow certain logical rules explained by pendulum theories or by schemes of requisites of a personal and professional nature in which the final selection is someone capable of balancing opposing forces. Cosío finds it interesting that these scholars see the Mexican process so rationally and clearly when the Mexican insiders themselves do not see it that way at all. He specifically questions what he sees as a general unwillingness among U.S. observers to admit that the Mexican presidential succession is resolved "arbitrarily and capriciously," thereby leading those analysts into the error of creating elaborate schemes of kingmakers and power theories to explain the selection process.[18]

But there is more to the Cosío thesis. He argues carefully that the legendary Lázaro Cárdenas saw to it that his successor was a man like Avila Camacho who would rectify whatever shortcomings might remain in the outgoing president's legacy, but who would do so slowly and quietly; therefore, the rectification would not bear the stamp of condemnation and Cárdenas's image in history would be preserved as truly revolutionary.[19] Cosío Villegas was one of the best-informed scholars of the Mexican presidency and his wisdom is to be taken seriously. He is saying in effect that the outgoing president follows the tradition set by Cárdenas of controlling the selection process so as to guarantee that he will not be repudiated by his successor; yet, he must choose a successor who will allow residual powers to be retained by the outgoing president and, at once, attend realistically to the glaring needs of the nation. He must make the choice early and then test it informally via the ritual of the tapados.

During 1976 a Mexican journalist from the capital city confirmed to me much of the Cosío Villegas thesis and threw additional light on the antecedents of that year's presidential succession. The story (and I have a-greed to respect the confidence of the source) is one that can rather easily be verified or rejected by most any biographical scholar of the outgoing president, Luis Echeverría.[20] Throughout Mexico great surprise was felt when it was learned that José López Portillo of the treasury department, not Mario Moya Palencia of gobernación, would be the next president.[21] Most observers believed that Moya was to be the next president. It seems, however, that Echeverría and López Portillo were close college companions who, sometime in the 1940s, took an ocean cruise to Chile for study purposes. Furthermore, it is alleged that the only nonfamily person invited to Echeverría's wedding was José López Portillo. It is said that the most intimate of personal relationships existed between the two during the Echeverría sexenio and that López Portillo was Echeverría's principal behind-the-scenes advisor and the president's secret choice as successor all along, even while publicly an attempt was made to give the impression that Moya Palencia was the chief mover in the president's cabinet.

It is natural to find observers expecting the secretary of gobernación to succeed to the presidency as occurred in 1964 and 1970. Moya was a major power figure. His ministry has great legally built-in and informal ascriptive powers. Gobernación, after all, has control over the Mexican equivalents of the U.S. FBI and CIA (although nearly every Mexican governmental department has its own secret police of one ilk or another). Gobernación has the most complete and effective intelligence operation in the Mexican government; hence, it is the head of that department who de facto becomes one of Mexico's most feared men, and on very much the same basis that J. Edgar Hoover was feared in the United States. It is gobernación that has the files on everyone. If it is necessary to leak something unfavorable to the government-controlled press to diminish a certain power contender within or outside the official PRI, it is almost surely gobernación that will be called upon to do the leaking. As mentioned above, Presidents Echeverría and Díaz were both former secretaries of gobernación.

What is significant is the fact that all Mexicans with expert knowledge whom I interviewed in the months following the unveiling (*destape*) on September 22, 1975, confessed that the matter was a mystery. Moreover, Cosío Villegas produced a book following the destape in which he also admits that the matter was then a mystery to him.[22] My Mexican informants told me that "when Cosío Villegas does not know (or is not saying) that in itself is significant." It tends to confirm, of course, the earlier-cited Cosío contention that the selection may very well be made arbitrarily and capriciously. In his last book, *La sucesión: desenlace y perspectivas,* Cosío related the surprising story of how the unveiling of López Portillo occurred. It was done quite informally and in almost bizarre circumstances (Cosío prefers to call the 1975 announcement *el corcholatazo,* or the uncorking, which conveys better the element of mystery and surprise.

He says that late in the afternoon of September 22, Moya Palencia and some colleagues were lunching in an unspecified place to which reporters apparently had access. Their meal was interrupted by newspapermen carrying copies of *Últimas Noticias de Excelsior* announcing the unveiling of López Portillo. Apparently they were all surprised that the news was out, but confirmed it while a shocked Moya Palencia tried to maintain his composure. Cosío relates further the rumor (which he then discredits) that Echeverría in fact had arranged to have the announcement emerge as a surprise and that he had selected the weakest of the potential tapados to keep him indebted after the transfer of power in 1976 (note that while Cosío discredits this rumor, he nevertheless repeats it).[23]

It was believed that almost all the governors of the states and the key leaders of the PRI's sectoral organizations had endorsed Moya Palencia's informal candidacy to become the verdadero tapado. So Echeverría clearly dumped Moya. It is rumored that a power struggle had developed between Moya and Echeverría and that this fight became open during 1975. The most patent aspects of the struggle concerned governorships. In April 1975, Echeverría's handpicked governor of the state of Hidalgo, Otoniel Miranda, was deposed by the state legislature after only 29 days in office.[24] My informants claim that the fall of the Hidalgo governor was the indirect work of Moya Palencia, who may then have been fearing that someone other than himself could become the verdadero tapado and therefore sought a confrontation with President Echeverría to force the issue publicly.

This did not happen but the gubernatorial arena later yielded a more clearly defined confrontation in Sonora during October 1975. There, under orders from Echeverría, and with the helpless acquiescence of Moya Palencia (who by then had been passed over for the presidency), Governor Carlos Armando Biebrich was deposed by the state legislature and replaced with Sonora's incumbent senator, Alejandro Carrillo Marcor. It was the first time since 1935 that Mexico City had so intruded upon Sonora's state government.[25]

The case of Governor Biebrich has been treated elsewhere.[26] Suffice it to say here that Biebrich and much of the Sonora PRI were sullied by scandals involving arms trafficking and narcotics. In addition, in the fall of 1975 Biebrich ordered the assassination of a number of peasant squatters and pretended he had approval from President Echeverría and Moya

Palencia (which he did not).[27] Biebrich had been a protégé of Moya and it was rumored that should Moya become president Biebrich would be elevated to the cabinet post of gobernación, just a step away from the presidency. The Biebrich scandals, and Moya's continuing efforts to protect him, may have figured prominently in Echeverría's decision to drop Moya, if in fact he was ever seriously considered. There is evidence in the extradition indictments eventually brought against Biebrich that his abuse of public office had been going on for most of the time (three years) that he had been Sonora's governor.[28] It is not likely that Moya was unaware of this, given the number of public protests against Biebrich emanating from Sonora. If these considerations entered into President Echeverría's decision not to unveil Moya as the next president, one may surmise that he acted in the best interest of Mexico. Of course we will never know for sure as long as expresidents maintain the fiction that the PRI's National Assembly decided the presidential succession, and that tapados do not exist.

In considering the transfer of presidential power in Mexico one must be aware that the tradition of not attacking the person of the president while he is in office still lingers, at least early in his term. Obviously, the outgroups and satellite parties are not bound by all the PRI may consider to be traditional, but at least until 1968 there had been a general national taboo against venomous personal attacks on the incumbent chief executive. That was abandoned in 1968 when the protesting students demanded the death of President Díaz Ordaz and his minister Luis Echeverría. When Echeverría, as president, was denounced in 1971 and assaulted in 1975 it became obvious that both the man and the institution of the presidency had fallen into disrepute vis-a-vis the young intelligentsia. Loss of face before this sector must have wounded a determined power-seeker like Echeverría badly and some of his extreme reactions to criticism as his term came to a close (like taking over *Excelsior*) may have stemmed from the cumulative psychological impact of his clashes with students (in 1968, 1971, and finally 1975). The case is revealing.

Echeverría's sensitivity to criticism, and his vulnerability to attack, came to light during March 1975. He had accepted an invitation to speak at the opening of classes at the National University on March 14, and he hoped to enter into a dialogue with students. The meeting was to be held in the medical faculty's auditorium, named after the late Salvador Allende of Chile. The rector Guillermo Soberón tried to introduce the president. He was interrupted with insults and charges that "LEA [acronym for the president's name] is a fascist." The president wanted to speak. There were more insults. The student-body president tried to speak and said something about the need in Mexico for a congressional investigation of CIA activities as recently disclosed by the Philip Agee book. He was shouted down as a traitor and more verbal disparagement was hurled at the president of the republic. Then the violence became physical with gunfire. Bottles and rocks were thrown. One of these wounded President Echeverría in the forehead. Shortly before this the president had shouted that the insurgent students were "pro-fascists, manipulated by the CIA, who emulate the youth corps of Hitler and Mussolini."[29] The student leader Joel Ortega replied that it was Echeverría who was propagating fascism by sending police agents into the university and by allowing labor bosses to impede development of a free labor movement in Mexico.[30]

What is significant in this is that, despite the merits of the various charges hurled back and forth, the president had been forced into a position of retreat from dialogue with the students, and this was covered in the national press. The fact that *Excelsior* criticized the student behavior editorially did not make up for its having printed their words and points of view. *Excelsior* also opened its pages to paid notices by radical student groups who denounced Echeverría and the PRI. Undoubtedly, this contributed to the president's determination to close the publication the following year.

As a general proposition, then, we may say that one of the key power roots of the Mexican presidency is its formal image. It matters less if everyone knows that the president sends police agents to harass students, maintains paramilitary squads to beat up them and the press corps, and presides over a regime in which corrupt labor bosses enslave the workers in conspiracy with management. What does matter is the formal image that the public communications media can forge. Perhaps the classic statement of this principle came from former PRI president Carlos Madrazo, who was deposed by President Díaz Ordaz in 1965 after the former's proposal to democratize the PRI via a scheme of local primaries to nominate candidates. Just as the fateful holocaust of Tlatelolco in 1968 was building up, Madrazo told a capital-city reporter, "Do you know what one of Díaz Ordaz's ministers told me the other day? He said the people didn't count. What does count is the impression we create with our newspers."[31] In other words, it may be that the "emperor has no clothes," just don't print it publicly, or your press may be closed down. Although Echeverría's successor López Portillo was not attacked physically in public confrontations he was subjected to vehement criticism from opposition politicians, much of which got into the press. The tradition of presidential immunity to verbal attack seemed to have ended.

SINGLE PARTY OR CASTE RULE
AND THE PRESIDENCY

Both the dominant or official party PRI and the presidency have been studied intensively by Mexican scholars José C. Valadés and Daniel Cosío Villegas. There are two critical facts that must be understood about the PRI and the presidency according to Valadés. One is that the PRI is a political bureau at the service of the president and that serving him is its primary task. The second is that the PRI is not really a party because, except in its early years, it has lacked a program of concretely definable policies. For this reason, the PRI is reluctant to allow genuine competition from a real political party with a clearly defined program. The PRI is a vast elite class, surrounding an authoritarian president, but the class holds many dissimilar and often contradictory elements.[32] The class may also appear as a kind of army without arms but which employs various mafias (army, secret police, paramilitary squads, and so on) to control others and protect itself. Thus, the undemocratic practices of choosing presidents by *dedazo* and *tapadismo* (personal designation via the secret tapado process) is perpetuated so as to keep the president's authority immune from public accountability, to make it unnecessary for him to enter into public dialogue except at his convenience. Thus the president is responsible only to a handful of kingmakers and camarillas who help him to ignore the needs of society while, as before, pretending to do otherwise.[33]

What Mexico needed in the presidency of 1970, said Valadés, was a leader who met two criteria: that he not be picked by the outgoing president but by a national convention, and that the new president not be indebted to the outgoing president but he forced to win popular support on his own merits.[34] This was easier proposed than achieved given established PRI tradition. But Valadés saw the nation exhausted with presidential successions and the continued use of the PRI as a personal power bureau for the president. The public disgust was visible in popular contempt for the electoral process as a sham, a widespread disheartened feeling of abandon vis-a-vis politics, disdain of deputies and senators and the general helplessness and uselessness of the national congress.[35] Where, he asked, was the legislation that would regulate those who make life wretched for the masses, both rural and urban? The revitalization of the congress is imperative if Mexican presidents are going to return to the people those prerogatives which were originally promised as theirs. The congress, as it is, is a rubber stamp, a part of the president's political bureau.[36] "It is no exaggeration to say that in only a very few countries do presidents have at their grasp the power which Mexico's president personally enjoys."[37]

Valadés pointed to the personal designation of a successor as one of the chief evils in the system which could and must eventually lead to a grave and erroneous designation of a president who will damage the nation severely. (Some would say the López Portillo sexenio ending in 1982 was, indeed, such a damaging regime). As he analyzed the presidential succession of 1970 he saw the people asking, "Why even vote if only the official candidate can win?" Later in 1975 and 1976 this came to preoccupy high officials of the PRI greatly as the legitimacy of the regime was being called into question by the abstention of voters and other forms of repudiation that were cited earlier. Ultimately, as we have seen, the PRI was the only party on the ballot in 1976.[38]

Finally, Valadés clarified that it is not the PRI which is invincible (because the PRI lacks popular grass roots support, what he calls *engranaje propio*) but rather it is the president who is invincible because he controls the PRI. This must continue to be true as long as the president is selected by a handful of men or perhaps by his predecessor alone; that is, the PRI will never become a true party until it has been democratized. This, then, was a plea directly to the new president-to-be in 1970 to democratize the party system. Published in 1969, the work does not refer to Luis Echeverría by name. But the image depicted is clearly one of a dominant class, calling itself a party, which is really the government in disguise, and of a decidedly authoritarian president who *could* reform things if he wanted to. Valadés saw popular resistance efforts, however justified they might be, as doomed to the failure of disorganized anarchy which could not triumph over the dominant class which made up the PRI in 1970.

Let us now skip to the ambience of the 1976 presidential succession in Mexico. Here are some propositions made in light of Cosío Villegas's key work on the Echeverría presidency, *El estilo personal de gobernar,* and related to other works and evidence.

Is it the Mexican presidency per se, or is it the entire regime, that is inherently authoritarian? Valadés seems to say that the presidency is authoritarian and this, in turn, makes the regime conform to his image. In this regard, the U.S. scholar Evelyn P. Stevens argues that Mexico's political system is not oriented toward the "formulation and modification of goals through pluralistic participation in the decision-making process. Instead, we see repression of authentic interest groups and encouragement of spurious groups that can be relied on not to speak out of turn. The regime deals with bona fide groups almost as if they were enemy nations."[39] The question, then, is does this characteristic behavior originate in the regime, or in the presidency? Valadés says the presidency, Cosío Villegas seems to be saying the regime, and this writer's personal experience tends to confirm Cosío. Yet there is no doubt about the president's practically limitless power.

What has been the recent thrust of the Mexican presidency vis-a-vis the state's capability for generating and distributing wealth? According to Cosío's analysis, President Cárdenas sought to push the entire nation toward existing wealth, thereby to achieve a more equitable distribution. But since the presidency of Miguel Alemán (1946–52), emphasis has been on creating centers of abundant wealth and hoping that some of this wealth would rub off on the population. The result, of course, has been the underlying motive of the student rebellion of 1968, repudiation of a situation in which 10 percent of the privileged families control 50 percent of the national income.[40] Valadés shares the spirit of this judgment.[41]

What impact has the Mexican presidency had on the myth or reality of governmental federalism? Like his successors, Echeverría extended central authority at the expense of local initiative and autonomy. He even allowed the Sonora legislature to modify the state constitution in 24 hours, thereby lowering the governor's required age to 30 to allow the election of Biebrich who was imposed from Mexico City with the president's acquiescence.[42] This, as we have seen, Echeverría was later to regret because of the implications the Biebrich scandal had for the presidential succession. It further dramatizes what is perhaps the Achilles heel of the Mexican system, that is, the flaunting of federal prerogatives at the expense of local autonomy where critical social problems await solution. Evidence during recent years shows a high incidence of popular, anomic, and violent uprisings and protests against corrupt local governments (especially as reported by *Excelsior* during 1975–76).

Can major errors in long-range policy conduct be attributed directly to Echeverría? To give one example, Cosío Villegas argues that Echeverría was at fault in urging agrarian reform as a way to greater industrial prosperity, rather than having championed the betterment of the rural ejidatarios as an end in itself.[43] He blames Echeverría for acquiescing in a scheme to dispossess hundreds of peasant ejidatarios in Nayarit to permit building of a vacation center for military personnel and a facility for tourists.[44] Here, development was sought at the expense of those who needed it most.

Is the authoritarianism of the Mexican president to be explained principally in terms of a combination of historical thrust and personal psychic qualities? Translating from Cosío's conclusion, the demand by presidents like Díaz Ordaz and Echeverría for popular veneration stems from psychic and historical factors to be sure, but "it is due also to our political system, whose principal characteristic is a president invested with unlimited faculties and resources. This has converted him fatally into the Great Dispenser of Goods and Favors, even of miracles."[45] Valadés would seem to concur. Note Cosío's use of the qualifier "fatally." This resembles the Tlatoani analogy presented in Chapter Two.

What are the implications of the foregoing discussion of the Echeverría presidency for the conventional wisdom, that is, the established literature on Mexican politics by U.S. scholars? Space will not permit a full review of that literature here, but surely one of the best known of the U.S. writers in this regard is L.V. Padgett. The second edition of his widely used text says, "The president is semidivine father figure to the people, inherently good in caring for his children. He is never directly challenged, as for example in the press, because that would shake the very basis of secular government."[46] Clearly, Padgett's vision is extreme in light of the evidence presented earlier in this study. Yet it is correct to say that the president may *try* to appear to be what Padgett says he is.

Each sexenio is prefaced with an extensive campaign in which the president-to-be tours every state in the country and uses surrogates to reach out to the villages. The conventional wisdom is that the president-elect can probe public sentiment on key issues during his campaign tours and better equip himself to reflect his nation's desires in the policy-formation process he will later direct. True, as Valadés says, the president could do so if he wanted to. Moreover, Cosío pointed to Echeverría's use of the watchword "autocrítica" as a pretense of turning self-criticism into a public function; but as Cosío also noted, Echeverría's use of the term was inappropriate because the people were never really invited to criticize anything of substance.[47] Thus, the conventional wisdom about testing public sentiment via a grass-roots campaign (especially when no real opposition is able to express itself) needs to be rethought.

Another piece of conventional wisdom is that the president must take an intermediate position between the official party's left and right wings and that he can do so because there exists a "core consensus of Revolutionary values" throughout all of the PRI.[48] This is probably still sound, albeit tenuous. To be sure, Echeverría clashed frequently with the powerful right-wing Monterrey Group in the area of national security policy and over the question of the government's expanding role in the economy. The Marxist review *Punto Crítico* referred to the Monterrey Group as the principal source of Mexican fascism and cited the conflicts that had grown during the Echeverría sexenio between the group's powerful families and the federal government over monopolistic control of the steel industry.[49] But the same source also pointed out the impressive amounts of state capital that had been loaned on favorable terms to the Monterrey Group as an appeasement device and reaffirmed that for the group's political influence to be effective it was imperative that it operate within the PRI, not as in 1940 when certain members of the group supported the opposition candidate Almazán against the PRI's official candidate Avila Camacho.[50] So it appears that barring a complete rupture between the Monterrey

Group and the PRI the group will remain a somewhat disaffected right wing but well within the PRI's penumbra. Selection of treasury secretary López Portillo to succeed to the presidency in 1976 may have done something to appease the PRI's political right. This would support the conventional wisdom's claim that there is a core value consensus of sorts within the PRI. But it is questionable how far this applies to the disaffected left, for example, growing alienation against the PRI's labor magnate Fidel Velásquez and similar alienation against the agrarian sector of the PRI.

It has been argued that the institutionalization of the presidency is such as to put a premium on "moderation and mildness in the political style" of the president as he seeks to balance competing interests and pressures.[51] Echeverría's forcing his attorney general and others to resign following the San Cosme scandal, his repeated but unfulfilled promises to disclose the true origin of the Falcons, his conflicts with the Monterrey Group and with the students of the National University, his intervention in Sonora over the Biebrich affair (for which the president was partially responsible), and his subsequent takeover of *Excelsior,* all suggest that Echeverría found moderation difficult, especially when he was challenged personally. The San Cosme affair was an especially bitter pill to take since even the establishment press of the capital city, normally loyal to the government in any dispute, criticized the PRI and laid photographic evidence at Echeverría's feet demanding that he solve the problem of official terrorism (which, of course, he could not do in any real sense without losing face). It may be that the selection of López Portillo reflected a perceived need to bring into the presidency an actor more prone to the moderate style that has lent stability to the institution in the past. Presidents beginning with Miguel Alemán in 1946 had been able to moderate conflict before it broke into open disorder, a skill that was less characteristic of Díaz Ordaz and even less so of Echeverría.

Institutionally speaking, there is less need to modify the conventional wisdom. For instance, at the beginning of this study it was noted that much of the constitutionalism surrounding the presidency is mere formalism given the near-absolute decision-making power which has accrued to the president. That is because his formal duties are sufficiently flexible to allow for wide interpretation, hence the accretion of power. The president has a wide variety of ceremonial functions which he can use for symbolic purposes as he chooses. He is commander-in-chief of the armed forces (although in his final two years some of Echeverría's public admonitions suggested that his confidence in his own control over the military might have been weakened). Additionally, most legislation is initiated by the president, and the congress has been little more than a rubber stamp. That circumstance may be changing in the 1980s.

Insofar as justice is concerned, the Mexican president has considerable power to influence decisions of the judiciary via appointment of judges and by initiating removal proceedings through the congress. The president has enormous financial powers over the states and localities via his control of grants-in-aid and because the central government has preempted most taxation prerogatives to itself. In the field of foreign affairs, it is the president alone who decides, although normally his foreign minister will be consulted. Resignation of the foreign minister following the international reaction to Mexico's 1975 anti-Zionist vote in the United Nations makes one question whether Echeverría had undertaken to consult him or not. The same question may be raised with respect to the breaking of diplomatic relations with Chile in 1974, an abandonment of Mexico's traditional commitment (the Estrada Doctrine) to recognizing new governments de facto or de jure.

Probably the best way to summarize the importance, and complexity, of the president's power role is to depict him as the nerve center of many demands by interest groups, regional political caciques, the three sectors of his party and their subsidiary organizations, the alienated satellite parties and outgroups, the registered opposition parties, and a number of foreign influences (principally from the United States). As a nerve center, then, the president must moderate conflict and dispense a maximum number of streams of satisfactions in the hope of balancing competing interests so that the revolutionary coalition will not fall apart. Compared to his predecessors, Echeverría may have had less capability in this role, and the revolutionary coalition was, to be sure, threatened with atrophy during his regime. Yet, in all fairness to Echeverría, it may be that most any other president could have fallen victim to the same dilemmas. With population pressure far outrunning economic expansion, and with less escape-valve potential for desperate laborers north of the border, the pressures on the presidency are likely to grow. And one must underscore the fact that the constellation of alienated groups beyond the penumbra of the PRI is growing because the party is unable to spread its largesse effectively due to increased demands. Defection is inevitable.

The future of the Mexican presidency may depend upon resolution of a key dilemma or paradox. This has been put well by Padgett; that is, the incumbent is supposed to accept responsibility for all that occurs within the system even though it is not humanly possible that he can oversee it all. Thus Echeverría was sullied by the Biebrich scandal in Sonora (the president had helped to facilitate placement of a governor who later fell into disgrace and had to be removed with federal intervention). His left-leaning toward Salvador Allende of Chile made Echeverría a target of attack by the Monterrey Group for his having contributed to an atmosphere favorable to terrorism. The protesting students in March of 1975 saw the president as the personification of Mexican fascism and he accused them of the same thing. The list goes on ad infinitum. Padgett states the presidential paradox as follows:

> He is supposed to be a benevolent father. Whatever he does for the masses, he does for them personally—he endows them or gives them public structures, satniation plants, schools, and roads. By the same token, if he fails to provide these things, he has failed in his vital fatherly role. *It is paternal government, but it is only legitimate if it is benevolent paternal government.*[52]

The López Portillo sexenio was sullied by Mexico's financial collapse and by the PEMEX scandal which reached out to touch the president himself in 1982 after he had left office. Revelations of illicit enrichment by the president and his cohorts probably disqualify him from the benevolent paternal image as correctly stated by Padgett. The regime of Miguel de la Madrid now has time to clarify and resolve some of these issues. But the bottom line, however, is still a Mexican political system that has been unresponsive to critical social needs while elites enriched themselves in a political atmosphere of distrust, suspicion, and official espionage against the regime's critics. But expansion of the political system to include major opposition groups could signal the beginning of accountability in public office, enforced through political pluralism. This possibility makes the 1980s critical for the cause of Mexican political change. In this light, then, we must examine Mexico's current political spectrum.

THE SPECTRUM OF MEXICAN POLITICAL PARTIES AND OUTGROUPS

There are such conflicting and ambiguous claims as to the membership size of Mexico's political parties that no attempt is made here to clarify that. Instead the respective importance of the parties will be gauged in terms of their percentage of the national vote in recent elections and by their winning of seats in the Chamber of Deputies.

The PRI (Institutional Revolutionary Party)

Under one name or other this dominant class, which is organized as a party, has held power in Mexico since 1929. The PRI is divided up into three sectors: labor, agrarian, and popular. The PRI has a president who is accountable to the president of the republic. Immediately beneath the PRI's president is the National Executive Committee known as the CEN (*Comité Ejecutivo Nacional*). Beneath the CEN is the National Assembly.

In formal terms the National Assembly is the most authoritative collective organ of the party. Its primary function is the selection of candidates for national president. The National Assembly is charged with creating rules for membership and party conduct and has a lesser function of ratifying occasional policy stands that the party wishes to express outside of the congress.

Also, the National Assembly ratifies the party president who presides over the CEN. A second national organ of the PRI is its National Council or Grand Commission. This body is intended to represent the party organizations of the 31 states and gives representation to special delegates selected from each of PRI's basic membership sectors—labor, agrarian, and popular. The National Council differs from the National Assembly in that it represents regional and functional groups while the latter is meant to represent the people, albeit on a state-by-state basis. The PRI's National Executive Committee, along with the National Council, is expected to perform a sort of watchdog function on an interim basis between meetings of the National Assembly. The CEN exercises influence in state party affairs via the National Council and it is this nexus that often gives the PRI the appearance of a tightly knit monolith.

The CEN is clearly the most powerful of the three national organs of the PRI and is instrumental in the overall party control exercised by the president of the republic. The CEN convokes meetings of the National Assembly and controls the admission of delegates to such meetings. Great power comes from the following CEN prerogatives: party discipline on a personal and group basis; special investigations; control over state and municipal party-nominating conventions; power to intervene in the affairs of state and municipal party organizations, including the power to remove members of these organizations (the power to remove elected state and local officials belongs formally to the president of the republic); and responsibility for propaganda and recruitment to expand PRI ranks and socialize the people politically into PRI participation. In the above-mentioned list of powers, the control over the municipal party organizations became critical in 1965 when CEN president Carlos A. Madrazo campaigned to create local party primaries in which the choice of party delegates and candidates for public office would be democratized and not dictated from above as had been traditional. Madrazo, in effect, sought to weaken the powerful CEN over which he presided. He was fired for this by President Díaz Ordaz late in 1965.

All three PRI sectors operate through an informal system of camarillas or political cliques. This is central to understanding the creation, maintenance, and transfer of power within the various sectors of Mexico's PRI. As seen above, there is a formal power structure in terms of those who have the ability to allocate values, influence events, and bring to bear a near monopoly of coercive pressure upon those who *appear* to be violating formal dicta for political behavior. The formal structure operates, or breaks down, according to the functioning of the political cliques that lie at the heart of Mexico's esoteric democracy. In Mexico the informal structures are likely to take priority over legal ones. Throughout the development of the contemporary Mexican political system, the creation of pressure groups of one sort or another has been crucial to the exercise of power. Whether we refer to them in English as cliques or brotherhoods is unimportant if it is understood that we refer to tightly knit nuclei of loyalty and influence, usually founded around the power of a given individual whose ability to control behavior and allocate rewards makes that person the catalyst who gives the group a singularity of purpose and an informal loyalty web that could be termed a latent structure. The camarillas are subcircles of influence that can expand or retract as the winds of fortune change. The members are held together by friendship but, significantly, by a common desire to better their station in life (at the expense of other camarillas if need be) via the rewards that come from support of the next echelon upward. Surrounding them is a penumbra of anomic and diverse groups which can hardly be called brotherhoods. They are the aspiring satellite groups which seek to become cliques; their membership is fluid as is the changing pattern of their ideologies.

The historical development of the PRI has been covered in Chapters Three and Four. It is this party which claims to be the true heir of Mexico's revolutionary tradition. Although the PRI certainly has a right wing and a left wing, it is probably more accurate to describe it as a centrist conservative party dedicated to preserving a mixed capitalist/socialist economy, with a major leading role reserved for state initiative. The latest outgoing PRI leader, López Portillo, began his presidential term as a champion of business and industrial expansion and as a moderating force to counterbalance the land reform push he had inherited. But he ended his term nationalizing the banks and calling bourgeois interests traitors to the Mexican nation. Miguel de la Madrid sought to undo some of this damage by paying restitution to the expropriated bankers but nevertheless left the national monetary and banking systems in state hands. Thus the PRI believes that it, superimposed over the government, ought to take the lead in solving Mexico's problems and in promoting its development. It argues that the left would wipe out the entire private sector and charges that the right would debilitate the state to the benefit of capitalists.

In the 1982 elections for president PRI won approximately 70 percent of the total vote as opposed to 16 percent for its nearest rival (PAN) and approximately 12 percent for all others combined. Historically the PRI has always won by more than 70 percent of the presidential vote. In the voting nationally for the Chamber of Deputies in 1976, the PRI won nearly 85 percent of the vote, but this figure dropped to about 69 percent in 1979 reflecting the new proportional representation electoral reform that had gone into effect the first time that year. The PRI maintained roughly this same congressional percentage in the 1982 elections although the principal challenger PAN increased its percentage at the expense, ostensibly, of the socialist left. Let us, then, place the PRI at the middle of Mexico's political spectrum. We reiterate that its ideological address is centrist/conservative, when conservative is understood to mean preservation of the status quo.

The PSUM and the Mexican Communist Party

To the far left of the PRI is the Mexican Communist Party or PCM as it was known until 1981. In November of that year the PCM's national party assembly voted to dissolve itself and join in a new coalition of the socialist left to contest the coming elections of 1982. The new grouping is now known as the PSUM or Unified Mexican Socialist Party. Its leader in 1982 and as of this writing is Arnoldo Martínez Verdugo, former head of the PCM, and presidential candidate of the PSUM in 1982. The PCM is said to be the oldest party in Mexico, having been founded in 1919. It has recently been one of several independent parties of the communist world, similar to those parties in Italy and France that are often critical of the Soviet Union's posture in world affairs. The PCM (now merged into the PSUM) was historically important in Mexico's political development. In 1924 it fostered the first national peasant league (LNC); in 1935 it supported Lázaro Cárdenas; and in 1936 it supported the creation of the CTM that was headed initially by Vicente Lombardo Toledano, Fidel Velásquez, and Jesus Yurén. As of 1983 Fidel Velásquez, an octogenarian, still runs the CTM, part of the official PRI. He is easily one of the ten most powerful men in Mexico. It is significant that his rise to power had roots in early collaboration with Mexican communists. Many today fear that the death of Fidel Velásquez will result in major defections from the CTM and that this could mortally weaken the PRI's labor sector.

Other notable figures in the Mexican Communist Party were Valentín Campa, a labor and student organizer, and the internationally famous painter David Alfaro Siqueiros, both of whom served time in prison for their defiance of the state. The PCM suffered troublesome internal divisions over the years, thereby reducing its effectiveness. It also suffered considerable governmental repression. In 1961 the PCM participated in forming the MLN, National Liberation Movement and subsequently the CCI, Independent Peasant Central and the FEP, Popular Electoral Front. The latter groups sponsored the presidential candidacy of Roman Danzós Palomino in 1964 against Díaz Ordaz but without official registration the

FEP did not appear on the presidential ballot. After 1971 the PCM worked through the FSI, Independent Syndicate Front. In 1978 the PCM received official registration from the Secretariá de Gobernación under the recent electoral reform law.

Acting through the PSUM after 1981 the Mexican Communist Party's ideological address was characterized by a commitment to being a "democratic opposition against the antipopular policies of the regime."[53] Because the PSUM (PCM) has no immediate opportunity to superimpose itself on the Mexican government no effort will be made here to outline its internal structure as was done for the PRI (nor will that be done for any of the other opposition parties discussed herein). Its second national congress held in 1983 revealed an internal heterogeneity and considerable division. Valentín Campa, the old Marxist fighter, spoke to the point that Lenin's concept of a proletarian dictatorship does not carry implicit in it the Stalinist aberration of tyranny.[54] He added that worker solidarity must come before the niceties of whether one has the proper recognition in the form of official government registry of the party. The national congress also generated strong opposition, amid controversy, to the involvement of clerics in political life. This was explicitly related to the alleged use by the party PAN of church support in recent electoral victories in Chihuahua.[55] Also rejected were proposals for setting up working relationships with official PRI labor unions and for adoption of a strong womens rights plank, an issue which drew acrimonious charges of machismo from among the PSUM delegates.

The PSUM is still in the throes of its organizational birth as of this writing. The Central Committee of the PSUM is dominated by members of the old PCM, the most famous of whom are Ramon Danzós Palomino, Valentín Campa, and Arnoldo Martínez Verdugo, the current party chairman.[56] A major task of the PSUM is to integrate and accommodate all the smaller factions of which it was composed, national front style, in 1982 and to work out a coherent national program within the Marxian socialist context. Martínez Verdugo expressed a general conviction among his PSUM colleagues that the center/rightist PAN is converting itself into a supporting faction of the PRI by endorsing the government's promotion of big business and its denationalization of state-owned enterprises (such as the automotive industry) in favor of private capital.[57] The socialist left generally favors greater state control of the economy coupled with greater social democratic control over the state itself.

The PSUM and affiliated leftist groups have come into serious conflict with the PRI at the state level. Prominent in the foreground of such cases is the state of Oaxaca in south central Mexico. In the municipal elections of 1980 the PRI lost control in Oaxaca of most of the state's important municipalities. Winners were opposition parties of both the left and right. In Juchitán the municipal government was won by the COCEI which had close working relationships with the PSUM. COCEI (*Coalición Obrero-Campesina-Estudiantil del Istmo*) is the Coalition of Workers, Peasants, and Students of the Isthmus, a Marxist-leaning regional organization. There was something special about this win because "it is the only municipality in the country where peasants and workers, the majority Zapotec Indians, really have power. This is what bothers the PRI the most."[58] The governor of Oaxaca, Pedro Vázquez Colmenares, proceeded to recoup his party's (the PRI's) losses by deposing 45 mayors who had been elected in Oaxaca. This was prefaced in most cases by the state's withholding of funds for the municipal budget to prevent the new governments from providing public services. When the municipalities fell into financial distress, as they inevitably did, the governor accused their administrations of misuse of local funds. The governor also used organized cadres from the CNOP to threaten and discredit the local authorities. In some instances PRI-controlled electric power from the Federal Electrical Commission was cut off to communities by the governor's order and this was blamed on the local opposition mayors.[59]

Vázquez Colmenares also began a project to gerrymander the state by reducing the number of municipalities. Early in 1983 the governor unwisely chose to confront some of the opposition mayors at a public meeting and he was shouted down and driven away by an angry populace. In July of 1983 the mayor of Juchitán, Leopoldo de Gyves, and several other persons were injured in what they described as a government-sponsored attack. Later that month another violent encounter between COCEI demonstrators and PRI elements left two persons dead and numerous others injured. This was toward the close of a state campaign for local deputies. The PRI told the international press that its members had been attacked by the COCEI and this was faithfully carried over the UPI news wire.[60] It did not tell the news service, apparently, that the PRI regime in Oaxaca had militarized the state with troops which had provoked the population through repressive enforcement of curfews and by breaking up political meetings under the pretext that "guerrillas from Nicaragua" were helping the COCEI to plan violence.[61]

On August 1, at the governor's request, the state legislature voted to suspend the powers of Mayor de Gyves and declare his local government to have "disappeared." What is significant, perhaps, is that not only the PRI deputies supported this vote but the PAN and PPS deputies supported it also. This contributed to subsequent charges from the PSUM and other groups on the left that PAN and PPS had become adjuncts of the PRI. Mayor de Gyves had predicted in July that the PRI in Oaxaca was planning a violent confrontation that would be used as an excuse to depose his local government. His own 15-member municipal police force had been disarmed by the state government as part of the preparation.[62] The mayor, supported by PSUM leaders and his own COCEI followers, offered to abandon the municipal palace quietly in early August so as to avoid further bloodshed. His supporters, some 25,000 strong, held a mass referendum in the municipal square casting votes into boxes in support of the deposed municipal government. A threat made by the governor to PSUM leader Arnoldo Martínez Verdugo of violence against the particip-ants in the mock referendum was ignored and never materialized.[63] This reaction by the PRI to challenge in Oaxaca can only partly be credited to the paranoid style of the governor. At nearly the same time the governor of San Luis Potosí was repressing an independent municipal government there (see epilogue). In the 1980s the PRI definitely sees an independent challenge from the left as threatening.

The PMT or Mexican Workers Party

This Marxist party is perhaps to the left of the PSUM. It did not par-ticipate in the elections of 1979 and 1982, making estimation of its strength difficult. The PMT was denied registration in 1981 and has charged that the new electoral reform law is undemocratic. Its leading spokesperson is the well-known journalist and engineering professor from the National University, Heberto Castillo. His most recent fame has come from his revelations of fraud and inaccuracy in the government's management of Mexico's oil reserve. Castillo writes regular weekly col-umns for the magazine *Proceso*. Major support for the PMT comes from the Federal District but it has a following in a handful of other states. Con-sidering that it is a relatively small party its voice at the national level, via Castillo's ongoing polemic with the government, has been considerable. The PMT grew out of three Mexican protest movements of recent years, the railroad strike of 1958, the teacher and student protests of 1961, and the student massacre of Tlatelolco in 1968. Political critics and actors from those events, including Demetrio Vallejo, Octavio Paz, Luis Villoro, Car-los Fuentes, and Heberto Castillo formed the National Committee for Hearings and Consultation, CNAC (*Comité Nacional de Auscultación y Consulta*) which generated a number of fragmented socialist action groups. These came together in 1974 as the PMT which since then has sought to expand its base of membership via ties with extraofficial labor movements.[64] Many factions within the PSUM believe that the PMT be-longs with them and are working to achieve that end. The PMT leader-ship resists this pressure claiming that participation under a PRI-granted electoral registry would lend a vote of legitimacy of the dominant regime. gime.

Other Parties on the Left

The PST or Socialist Workers Party split from the previously cited CNAC in 1973. It began as basically a party of students, peasants, and homesteaders with little organized worker participation. Roberto Jaramillo, who sought to lead several splinter groups, finally declared the PST to be a "governmental leftist" grouping which would give qualified support to the PRI while maintaining a separate identity. It gained only 2 percent of the vote in 1982 and is thought to be little more than a replica of the PPS or Popular Socialist Party. The latter party was formed by Vicente Lombardo Toledano in 1948 and has grown into practically a left wing appendage of the PRI. In the 1982 elections it received barely 2 percent of the total vote. In 1979 a PPS candidate became the first opposition member of the Mexican Senate, a gesture widely believed to have been a PRI gratuity for the good behavior of PPS as the PRI's loyal opposition on the left. There is also in Mexico a PSR or Socialist Revolutionary Party. This was formed in 1976 by Roberto Jaramillo who had left the PST. It seeks to unify the Marxist-Leninist left outside the PSUM and without the Trotskyites. The Trotskyites are represented in Mexico by the PRT or Revolutionary Workers Party. Belonging to the Fourth International, the PRT came together when several smaller groups merged in 1976 and in 1978 it was officially registered as a party. The PRT claims a following among various skilled workers, some doctors, students, teachers, and a few peasants. It is definitely a minor party as of this writing. Another leftist splinter is the PPN or Mexican Peoples Party that was formed in 1977 out of splits occurring in the PPS over that party's being granted the first "opposition" seat in the Mexican Senate. None of the above leftist parties seem to have any chance at acquiring real power on their own as of this writing nor are they heard as major national voices for the socialist left.

Parties to the Right of Center

Of those which merit discussion here probably the PDM or Mexican Democratic Party is the most right wing on the overall spectrum. This is a political instrument of the fascist-looking *sinarquistas* or UNS (*Unión Nacional Sinarquista*) that was treated as a separate entity in previous editions of this book. Now in the guise of the PDM the sinarquistas have achieved electoral participation via official registration because their party is no longer formally an ecclesiastical entity, a fact which in the past prevented their formal registration as a party. The new electoral law of 1977 also made it easier for this minor party to participate. Roots of the sinarquista movement lie in the cristero rebellion of 1929 that was discussed in Chapter Three. More recently it has been supported by middle-class elements and conservative Catholic sectors including the organization *Acción Católica Mexicana* (Mexican Catholic Action). Several attempts were made to form a theocracy-oriented party out of the UNS but not until 1977 was party organization formalized as occurred under the PDM label. The following year the PDM received official registration.

Miguel Basáñez believes that the PDM is growing rapidly due to its simple populist appeal which conceals its right wing commitment to an authoritarian state with strong church involvement. Many peasants and small businessmen, artisans and workers are attracted to its ranks. The PDM competes with the PAN for votes and membership allegiance claiming that PAN is preponderantly upper and middle class while the PDM cares and works for marginally employed and the poor.[65] The PDM is a reservoir of restorationist conservative sentiment within the lower- and middle-class Catholic sectors of Mexican society. Given the staying power of its parent organization, the UNS, one might reasonably expect PDM to continue to have political relevance in Mexico. Indeed, a study as far back as 1965 argued this case for the sinarquista organization[66] and found it then competing with the PAN for the allegiance of many of the same people. The epilogue to this book treats the recent opposition role in San Luis Potosí of both PDM and PAN within an independent front context.

The PAN or National Action Party

There is some dispute in the 1980s as to whether this party is to the right of the PRI or is becoming an appendage of it. Regardless, the PAN seems to be the most significant opposition to the PRI in the Mexican political spectrum. Its recent electoral wins of Chamber of Deputies seats and important municipal races testify adequately to this. Because the PAN is not foreseeably in the position of being able to superimpose itself over the government as the PRI has done there is no point here in going into detail about the PAN's internal structure for decision-making or its unique folkways. Some detail about its growth and development are in order as PAN is ostensibly the most serious national challenger to the PRI and may be on the verge of power-sharing that is national in scope.

Recent scholarship has traced the roots of Mexico's PAN, the principal legal opposition party, to the Christian movement which supported Madero's revolution. PAN has been linked to the cristeros who fought Calles during the 1920s and to the campaign for the presidency of José Vasconcelos in 1929. It has been pointed out that the Vasconcelos movement died out because it failed to move out of the limitations of personalism and to create an institutionalized and lasting political movement with a definable program and ideology.[67] This was also a failing of Madero as we have seen in the historical sketch of Mexico's political development. The early founders of the PAN sought in 1939 (the year in which the party was formally launched) to create a more lasting political entity. It is noteworthy that the PAN's founding coincided with the end of the Lázaro Cárdenas presidency. Many early members of the PAN reacted to the anticlericalism of both Cárdenas and Calles before him. Much of their reaction was toward the official prohibition against religious teaching in the public schools and the formal endorsement given during the Cárdenas years to socialism as a fundamental part of public education in Mexico. Many conservative Catholics feared that Cárdenas was leading the nation down the road to communism.

The struggle between socialists and Christians during this epoch pitted the socialist leader Vicente Lombardo Toledano (who enjoyed the sympathy of President Cárdenas) against Manuel Gómez Morín, founder of the PAN. In 1933 Gómez Morín was elected rector of the National Autonomous University of Mexico. He demonstrated that the university could be run by nonsocialists, without constantly increasing government subsidies, and without forcing socialist teaching on students. When the PAN achieved formal government registry in 1940 it was the first time since the PCN (National Catholic Party) of Madero's era that the conservative Christian right had a political organism with which to identify (it should be noted that the Constitution of 1917 prohibited use of religious words in the title of a political party).

The PAN, despite its early conservative trappings, was essentially pledged to support most of the revolutionary program of Madero, just as much as any other group was, thus the PRI has no unique basis in historical fact for claiming that it alone is the true heir to Madero's legacy. Also noteworthy was the relative absence, during most of PAN's development, of personalistic camarillas such as are found to dominate the PRI. As we shall see later, however, personalism did have an adverse effect on the internal unity of the PAN in the years 1975 and 1976. Both von Sauer and Mabry have provided historical sketches of the PAN,[68] and this material need not be repeated here except to point out that there is some disagreement among scholars as to whether the PAN today is a Catholic, conservative, and reactionary party or if indeed it is a truly popular and reformist party vis-a-vis the PRI's monopoly. It is von Sauer's argument that the PAN's founders faced a situation of political monopoly in 1939 that was analogous to that which Madero had confronted in 1911. He contends that the PAN's true goals have been those of political pluralism via civic organization, responsible education, and the creation of legitimate and accountable institutions. This requires that the single-party system allow a loyal opposition to become effective, that is, that it have a share in the making of public policy and have the capacity to hold governmental officials accountable. This, today, the PAN does not have although its influence is increasing.

PAN also seeks to restore to the church the rights of religious education and political participation which were taken away from it by the Constitution of 1917. In fact, most of these rights have been de facto restored through increasing toleration by the official regime. There are those within the PAN who have seen Catholic religious unity in Mexico as a major goal, especially when confronted with protestant infiltration of the country. Such pronouncements were more characteristic of *panistas* during the 1940s and 1950s than is the case today. That the PAN is a version of what in other countries is called Christian Democracy seems to be a reasonable assessment, although formally it remains nonconfessional. PAN leaders frequently cite Madero's historic belief that the state should not interfere in one's private religious life. But they also hold the conviction that the church can and should play a revolutionary role in the development of the Mexican state. Most of Madero's supporters were not, of course, in agreement that the Church could be revolutionary and most of them opposed its continued role in political life.

Since 1952 the PAN has normally competed with the PRI for national and regional elective offices and has usually fielded a presidential candidate. The PAN's presidential candidate in 1970, Efraín González Morfín, told me he had voted to withdraw his own candidacy in a special national assembly due to the repression that officialdom was visiting upon various of that party's state and congressional candidates. By a narrow margin the convention voted to continue the race. Even José González Torres, the 1964 PAN standard bearer, also told me he had voted to withdraw from the race, leaving the PRI unopposed. In the 1976 campaign this is exactly what happened. PAN has stressed publicly and repeatedly the open nature of its internal procedures for candidate selection. Reputedly there is no tapadismo or back-room nominating of candidates in the PAN; all is done openly and the party is wont to remind the public of this fact so as to cast the official regime in an unfavorable light by comparison.

Many U.S. scholars (including myself) have been led to believe that the PAN is and has been a distinctly reactionary or right-wing party. Some of the anticommunist pronouncements of PAN candidate Luis H. Alvarez in 1958 and those of José González Torres in 1964 did give the outward appearance of Mexican John Birchism. But during the early 1970s when I got to know González Torres personally I found him to be quite progressive, even to the point of defending the integrity of the pro-Marxist journalist Mario Menéndez Rodríguez who was then being persecuted by the government. González Torres's anticommunism seems to come more from his profound religious dedication. He expressed affinity toward Christian Democratic movements about the hemisphere. Quite rightfully, therefore, von Sauer called me to task for having once equated González Torres ideologically with Barry Goldwater in the United States.[69]

Von Sauer gives thorough treatment to the various instances of electoral fraud that have been committed against the PAN, just as I did in the first edition of *Mexican Democracy*. In particular, von Sauer was disturbed by the PAN decision not to participate in the 1973 elections in Baja California, given that state's past history as a PAN stronghold. Indeed, he argues that just because the majority of voters abstain from voting for the PRI doesn't mean a de facto vote of confidence in the PAN. This may, in fact, be evidence of overall Mexican disillusionment with the political system generally. Speaking of the 1973 elections, he raises these questions:

> How does one explain that 16.5 percent of Mexicans chose to censure PRI by voting for PAN in 1973? What about the 38.4 percent of the electorate which showed preference for PAN over PRI in the Federal District? Or, more significantly, what about those 10,840,814 alienated voters that chose to remain home rather than vote without a voice?[70]

This should be considered against the fact that, on the basis of my own investigation, the majority of PAN leaders at the national level believed that PAN had really won in the Federal District and that the PRI allowed publication of such a large losing percentage only because the real overwhelming vote against it rendered a more lopsided figure unbelievable. The prevalence of electoral fraud throughout Mexico, and the awarding of a handful of deputies-at-large (*diputados de partido*) to PAN and to a couple of minor parties that are attached to the PRI for use as a democratic facade, was behind some of the disillusionment which ultimately led PAN to abstain from the presidential contest of 1976. It may be, however, as von Sauer concludes, that the PAN would be best advised to concentrate its forces at the municipal level in the hope of building a national organization from the grass roots on up. "Today the free, competitive *municipio* offers Mexico the most immediate prospects for an effective multiparty system."[71] Without this base, higher levels of competition will merely serve to reinforce the PRI's democratic image. And building such a base will depend importantly upon PAN ideology, its ability to communicate its interpretation of political life to the populace, and on the PRI's being forced to relinquish its hold on the localities. That process seems well under way as municipal elections in the 1980s suggest.

The reader is recommended to the works of Mabry and von Sauer as cited herein for the historical and ideological development of the PAN. My impression in the second edition of *Mexican Democracy* was that Mabry had essentially taken the position that PAN had been intended to evolve, and in fact was evolving, into an ipso facto Catholic party (that claim was still being made by PAN's detractors in Mexico following the municipal elections of 1982 and 1983). But Mabry informs me that I misread him, that PAN is essentially a secular party in which some elements, because of their extreme Catholicism, have treated the party as if its mission were to protect the church thereby lending credence to the image of PAN as a confessional party.[72] Von Sauer and Mabry thus have argued that PAN was never intended to be a confessional party but that it could very well fit within the contemporary context of Christian Democracy (if this were legal and politically viable in Mexico) such as practiced today in Venezuela, for instance. Mabry also agrees that the PAN's version of political humanism would make it highly compatible with Christian Democracy. But proclaiming itself as such in today's Mexico would probably lead to loss of political registry and PAN is sensitive to charges, especially from left wing opposition parties, that it is a stalking horse for the Catholic church.

A good deal of testimony has been accumulated by Mabry, and in my own earlier research, linking PAN and the definitely religious UNS in various local campaigns throughout Mexico. But on the other hand there is evidence of PAN's having declared its sympathy even for causes embraced by communists (but never communism itself) such as the plight of the railway strikers in 1958.[73] Yet there is no avoiding the fervent anti-communism of PAN leaders like Adolfo Christlieb and José González Torres. Acting to moderate the PAN's extreme right wing have been Christian socialists like Luis Calderón Vega and Efraín González Morfín, the latter serving as PAN's presidential candidate in 1970. Adolfo Christlieb, PAN's president during the 1960s, tried to please the several factions within his party while not running a direct collision course with the Mexican government. As Mabry puts it, "although PAN also quietly maintained relations with Christian Democratic parties, particularly in Latin America, Christlieb repudiated the Christian Democratic label because Mexicans would always believe that such a party was really an instrument of ecclesiastical power. To him, religious parties led to totalitarianism, and the Church should stay out of politics. . . ."[74] But still, according to Mabry, PAN remained close to the Christian Democratic label. Christlieb, notes Mabry, was a friend of the progressive bishop of Cuernavaca, Sergio Méndez Arceo, and without formally using a church label other panistas have adhered to this progressive, reform-oriented sector of the church.

PAN's official doctrine or ideology is called political humanism. It focuses upon bettering the life style of the individual in his total cultural context and rejects the narrow concept of man as an atomized being.[75] Man is seen as having been created in God's image and has inviolable and inalienable rights to life and liberty, to control his own destiny, and to be free of repression. Man must also respect the rights of others; he must, in effect, live the good Christian life. Political life exists to enhance mankind's self-fulfillment, not to subordinate the individual to the state or class as in fascism or Marxism. The local community is seen as the foundation of the good life and forms a basic part of the nation. But the nation and the governmental apparatus are not one and the same nor should they be. Thus since the PRI's apparatus and the nation are treated by officialdom as practically synonymous, the PAN and the official party are seriously at odds. Any regime which puts the good of an elite before the good of the individual is rejected. The PAN defends the right of private property so long as it serves a useful social function and is not achieved by leaving others in economic misery.[76] Political participation, for the PAN, is a moral duty. As we shall see, that dictum is easier proclaimed than achieved.

Mabry suggests an ironic analogy between the PRI and the church, both espousing official truths and both decrying as heretics those who challenge that truth. The irony, according to Mabry, is that today "a Catholic-oriented party has had to compete against an anticlerical, secular government which uses the techniques of the Catholic Church to maintain itself in power."[77] The central dilemma for the PAN is that by accepting a participant role as the PRI's key opposition it contributes to the very facade of democracy which the PRI wishes to perpetuate. When PAN accepts deputy-at-large seats as "gifts," it most assuredly contributes to the facade of democracy. The PRI, of course, has been afraid to give the PAN those seats it genuinely won on a district-by-district basis. That would contribute to strengthening PAN at the grassroots constituency level and undermine the PRI. However, the elections of 1983 in Chihuahua did bring single district victories to PAN as noted below. If the PAN refuses the gift deputies, it then leaves Mexico with virtually no legal alternative to the PRI. And there is also a risky probability that the PRI chooses to recognize as elected those PAN deputies whom the PRI feels it can most successfully manipulate, thus giving more basis to the charge that PAN is a "kept" party.

My own field investigation supports those of von Sauer and Mabry, that is, that the PAN is not "kept" financially or otherwise by anyone and that it seriously aspires to become a loyal and progressive opposition in Mexico. The works cited above plus my own earlier published investigations tell the story of the electoral frauds and other repressions which the official regime has perpetrated against the PAN. The intensity of such repression, especially in the campaigns for governorships and mayoral races, has progressively demoralized the PAN. This raised, as noted earlier, the possibility in 1970 and the actuality in 1976, of PAN's not contesting the national presidency so as to deprive the PRI of its desired international image as a popular and revolutionary party that repeatedly won sweeping electoral victories against the "emissaries of the past." One great unknown was the impact of such national abstention on the PAN's state and municipal roots.

In the 1979 federal elections to the Chamber of Deputies (under the new proportional representation electoral law) the PAN won 4 seats in simple majority districts and 39 others at large under proportional representation. That was more than twice the seats won by PAN's nearest rival among the opposition parties, the PCM, which won 18 proportional representation seats. PAN, thus, had some 11 percent of the total national vote. In the 1982 general election PAN won 50 proportional representation seats. PAN candidate Pablo Emilio Madero received about 17 percent of the presidential vote in 1982 with a national total of nearly 4 million votes against 16 million cast for the PRI's Miguel de la Madrid. Third in the 1982 presidential balloting was the PSUM candidate Arnoldo Martínez Verdugo whose 1 million-plus votes amounted to about 4 percent of the total vote.

PAN publicity during 1982 had focused on the party as a naturally structured party, contrasting the PRI as bureaucratically structured. It stressed PAN's dependence on volunteer workers as opposed to officially (government) paid cadres of the official coalition.[78] Referring to some two million votes for PAN officially recognized in unspecified recent elections the party urged that this figure could be multiplied by ten in the coming elections should the vote count be honest. It specified also two false determinisms, the Marxist and the *priista* (that of the PRI) alleging that history moves inevitably toward either of them. Mexico, PAN urges, should practice the true federalism espoused in the constitution and not the political and economic centralism of the PRI which stifles local and regional growth and freedom thereby damaging the overall development of the Mexican nation.[79] Mexicans were urged to deposit in a fixed bank account number at any branch of a given chain throughout the country anything they could afford to support Pablo Emilio Madero's presidential campaign. Madero claimed to be a descendant of Francisco I. Madero though the presidential candidate of 1982 was probably not the revolutionary figure, comparatively speaking, that his forebear had been.

Several observers have commented, as noted earlier, on PAN's need to build from the grass roots up. The advice seems to have been taken. Elections held in July 1983 for state and local offices caused the PRI to admit the losses of 13 mayoraltys and five state deputies in the states of Durango and Chihuahua. In Chihuahua the candidates of Acción Nacional were declared victorious in the mayoralty contests of Ciudad Juárez, Camargo, Delicias, Nuevo Casas Grandes, Parral, Casas Grandes, Meoqui, Saucillo, and the capital city, Chihuahua. The five state deputy positions were also won in Chihuahua by a majority. Several parties to the left of the spectrum won three other mayoraltys. The PAN also won the mayoralty race in Durango, capital city of that state. This brought to five the state capitals then under opposition mayors: Hermosillo, Sonora (PAN); San Luis Potosí, S.L.P. (PAN–PDM–Frente Cívico Potosino); Guanajuato, Gto. (PDM); Chihuahua, Chih. (PAN); and Durango, Dgo. (PAN).[80] This gave at least the appearance of PAN as an aggressive second party seriously building at the grass roots. While PAN federal deputy Gerardo Medina publicly thanked the president of the republic and the respective governors for their fairness in recognizing these wins a former president of the PRI Alfonso Corona del Rosal stated that if the PRI did not return to its roots it would keep on getting weaker.[81] Never before had PAN or any other opposition party won so many local seats with national significance. Added to the PAN's federal representation in the Chamber of Deputies these victories seemed considerable.

In Chihuahua and elsewhere the PAN employed the communications media extensively for its electoral propaganda including allegedly "subliminal" tactics involving ads placed by businesses urging people to vote (without citing a party preference) but printed using the PAN colors, blue and white. Both the Catholic Church and some nonprotestant Christian sects were credited with having supported the PAN both by suggestive sermons and by allowing PAN materials to be passed out in front of temples of worship. Food shortages along the northern border, radio and television from the United States, women's organizations, and neglect by PRI labor unions of workers in the border factories (*maquiladoras*) were also credited as factors behind the PAN victories.[82] Luis H. Alvarez became the new PAN mayor of Chihuahua, a long road to power since his national presidential candidacy of 1958. In 1983 Alvarez was talking not of "creeping socialism" but of inadequate municipal services and corruption of justice at the local level. In Chihuahua the PAN's total vote was 81,940 compared with 51,354 for the PRI with 157,086 abstentions out of a registered electorate of 292,343.[83]

PAN's national president Abel Vicencio Tovar said that with the exception of his party's abstention from the presidential race in 1976 (which hurt, he admitted), the fortunes of the PAN have gone upward at the expense of the PRI. He assured that the funds to support the expensive campaign in Chihuahua came from sympathetic Mexicans who contributed personally and not from government subsidies. The winning PAN mayor of Ciudad Juárez, Francisco Barrio, said the people were tired of lies, deception, and all the economic problems.[84] But the president of PAN's principal rival to the left of the spectrum, Arnoldo Martínez Verdugo of the PSUM, reiterated the charge that PAN's victory was "demogogic and fragile," and added that PAN and PRI are both leading the country in the same direction. Before the present crisis is over, he asserted, the people will know that the only viable and concrete solution is from the left.[85] His charge from the left was accompanied by other press speculation that the PAN had help from the U.S. embassy, international Christian Democracy, Opus Dei, and that the 1983 PAN victories in Chihuahua and elsewhere were PRI-orchestrated experiments in "bipartisan politics" with the clear intent to close the door to future meaningful participation by the left wing of the political spectrum. Such claims, of course, are too new to be evaluated here and must be considered against the thrust of Mexican politics during the remainder of the de la Madrid sexenio. That will include the PAN's ability to rectify the serious socioeconomic problems and municipal administrative failures it has so often decried.

ECONOMIC INTERESTS AND POLITICAL POWER IN MEXICO

Writing just before the presidential elections of 1982 the Mexican political analyst Raúl González Schmal contended that the LOPPE (Spanish acronym for the new electoral law) was another ploy to create the appearance of genuinely competitive political democracy in Mexico. The regime would yield congressional seats in a controlled way that would not threaten its power. He also argued that except at election time most of the opposition parties in Mexico had little organized internal strength and that the majority of those voting for an opposition party would not attend a political rally during the remainder of the year. The truth, he claimed, was that "the forces that really influence political power in Mexico *do not* act through political parties. One well organized national workers syndicate is more important than ten political parties; one economic group, for example the Monterrey Group, has more power than all the opposition parties together."[86] He added that it sounds at best sarcastic for the PRI's presidential candidate to pretend to "moralize" Mexico's financial administration and create an egalitarian society in a country in which the political and economic oligarchy has always been "more equal" than the rest of the Mexican people.[87] This assertion means, in effect, that parliamentarianism in Mexico is of much less political relevance than the private and state-owned economic groups that may act either through key congressional figures or through the president of the republic and his cabinet officers.

Private groups (outside the sectoral organizations of the PRI but with ties therein) lie within an informal hierarchy, at the top of which is the allegedly "mythical" CMHN or Mexican Businessmen's Council.[88] Beneath this is a CCE or Business Coordinating Council which ties together a network of chambers of commerce and economic associations. "Business powers appear to have their most important operative force in Monterrey (economically) and in *Televisa* (ideologically); their organizational representation is headed by the CCE and their leadership representation presided over by the CMHN. Foreign investors appear to have their operative force distributed between Mexican affiliates and transnational corporations with their primary representation being in the CAMCO or American Chamber of Commerce."[89] Based on the foregoing, Basáñez divides the principal economic interests of Mexico into four sectors which do not constitute an exhaustive nor exclusive listing. These are 1) the Monterrey Group, 2) transnational corporations, 3) the CMHN, and 4) Televisa.[90] Each of these sectors, of course, is divided into multiple interest groups often corresponding to a given industry in a specific place. A listing of these would be quite outside the scope of this book, but examples include a brewery and a steel complex in Monterrey plus several financial institutions for that particular sector. In this case the steel-making wing of the Monterrey Group is known as the Alpha Group.

Before the Mexican oil boom collapsed in 1982 the Monterrey Group expressed concern over the government's petroleum-based economic power which might present unwanted competition within the established order. Under the category of transnational corporations, in the 1970s it was estimated that there were nearly 800 North American companies with some 2,500 affiliated companies operating in Mexico giving a notion of the potential importance of that sector whose political influence can be exercised via CAMCO. This becomes especially critical in view of the recent history of transnational corporations and their influence in the political life of host countries as more sadly exemplified by the case of Chile in 1973 and the Watergate revelations about international political influence of American companies.[91]

The sector under the rubric of CMHN, Mexican Businessmen's Council, is composed of 30 members who are usually the heads of the most important economic groups in Mexico. These include confederations representing 54 percent of the total major private enterprises in Mexico.[92] An oversimplified picture is created by grouping them under six major nationwide confederations: 1) CONCANACO (Confederation of National Chambers of Commerce), 2) CONCAMIN (Confederation of Industrial Chambers of Commerce), 3) COPARMEX (Confederation of Mexican Employers, 4) ABM (Mexican Bankers Association), 5) AMS (Mexican Insurance Association), 6) CCE (Business Coordinating Council). The above listing of associations is grouped under the aegis of the CMHN. Outside this pyramid are two related but nonmember associations, the CNG (National Cattlemen's Association) and CNPP (National Confederation of Small Property Owners). A complicated listing of subgroups or dependencies can be developed for each of the above confederations (for instance the National Chamber for Industrial Transformation, CANACINTRA belongs to CONCAMIN cited above).[93]

Although the sector labeled Televisa is a member of CMHN it is the most powerful mass communication organ in Mexico and consists of a conglomerate of 45 companies which operate radio, television, and press media. A clear picture of how this syndicated entity evolved since a modest beginning in 1946 is presented by Basáñez and it is notable that key figures in Televisa overlap into other sectors and associations cited previously. Televisa had been criticized by *Excelsior* for lending itself as a tool of the government and for alleged involvement with international espionage, including the CIA and Mexico's own gobernación. The conflict between *Excelsior* and Televisa contributed to the former's being victimized by the Echeverría government as noted earlier. Because of the amount of information Televisa can manipulate and control, and its relationship to the economic fortunes of numerous enterprises, Televisa is considered by Basáñez to be a major economic sector in and of itself, having top political importance.[94] The organization enjoys intimate access to government and to many industries. It is kind of a "big brother" information system operating throughout the republic, upon which people depend and whose mass influence is considerable.

If one could study a range of critical public policy issues to be resolved at high levels of political power in Mexico one might find that the economic influence sectors outlined above have greater relevance than any political party for the pressures they can apply to the presidency and bureaucracy. Should it ever become possible to study the handling of the PEMEX scandal (1980s) prosecutions, currently underway as of this writing, a great deal of light would be shed on real political power in Mexico. The private sector, acting through the congeries of organizations cited above, exert their influence in certain ideological directions. According to Basáñez these are: 1) emphasize economic growth before distribution of wealth, 2) tie rapid economic growth to dependency on private rather than state enterprise, 3) financial stability through controlled wages but free pricing, 4) reduce political interference in the economy, 5) reduce the severity of constitutional strictures against the church and deemphasize agrarian reform; 6) control population growth, 7) restrict rural-to-urban migration in the hope of preserving urban services, 8) accept social stratification with limited mobility from birth, 9) preference for white people over brown, 10) prejudice toward religions other than Catholicism and toward Marxism; 11) resistance against value change either religious or ideological.[95]

Not all groups in the private sector embrace all these notions, or do so equally. Small enterprises seem more willing to have governmental intervention to protect them against foreign competition than do those already involved in transnational commerce. Religious and outright political prejudices are not always manifested publicly. Pressure for influencing power in Mexico is exercised in subtle and often concealed forms, rendering it difficult to study, and casting doubt upon the overall relevance of the political party spectrum vis a vis socioeconomic change in Mexico. Many of these economic groupings have in the recent past seen themselves as beneficiaries of the political status quo, a circumstance that may change in the aftermath of the early 1980s and Mexico's petroleum-related economic collapse. Parliamentarianism, then, may not be the most thorough route to understanding political power in Mexico nor the best hope for political change.

A bulletin of the PAN some years ago described the PRI deputies in the congress as *levantadedos* (finger-raising yes-men) who approved automatically everything coming from the president of the republic.[96] And what comes from the president is probably more the result of pressure and input from the dominant economic formations in Mexico than the result of parliamentary debate. Yet one asks what will transpire if the surge of opposition party victories in Mexico does give these groups even a plurality voice in Congress. Will the parliament acquire power ascriptively to counterbalance the economic interests? A foreshadowing of this eventuality might be seen in the resolution to the PEMEX scandal, i.e. whether it will continue to be treated as a scandal at all! Both political figures and economic interests are intimately and painfully involved.

The Mexican political analyst Raúl González Schmal cited earlier collected some figures on the sharing of parliamentary power (to the degree that it is real power) in Mexico over the last half century. From 1929 to 1976 there were nine presidential elections which the PRI (or its forebears) won by majorities ranging from 80 to 98.19 percent. Nor did the PRI lose a single gubernatorial contest in some 265 elections during that period. The PRI also won 540 elections for senators even counting the PPS victory of Jorge Cruikshank in 1979 which was a self-serving PRI gift. Out of the 3192 elections for seats of federal deputies the PRI won 98 percent of the time. And between 1929 and 1981 there were 41,500-plus contests for mayors in which the PRI won 99 percent of the time.[97] Regardless of this the PRI, says Gozález Schmal, has tried to mask its political dictatorship by creating places for opposition parties in the Chamber of Deputies where they have not even a fragment of real power but contribute to the image of political pluralism.[98] The plural member districts and proportional representation scheme of the new electoral law creates a democratic facade without requiring the PRI to yield real power. And if the opposition parties refuse to participate, as did the PAN in 1976, they now lose their party registry. Thus the PRI is always guaranteed an opposition but the cost to those opponents is that they must abdicate their right *not to participate.* If voting is a natural right, so is abstention![99] And it is perhaps more than coincidental that the new electoral law was passed the year immediately after the PAN abstained and left the PRI in the ostensibly undemocratic position of having no registered opposition.

But the equities and fortunes of the electoral process tell only part of the story of how the actors who decide the quality of life policies are recruited in Mexico. Apart from electoral politics is the broad and complicated spectrum of public administration and administrative power and politics. This is touched on in the chapter to follow. It should be noted as a general proposition, however, that the official PRI is only one channel through which political figures arrive at key administrative positions where they can at least potentially influence the quality of life. In fact impressive work has been done by Professor Roderic A. Camp suggesting convincingly that the PRI is not the most important route for attaining top-level Mexican administrative positions. Rather the element of personal contact and trust developed within the public universities and particularly the National Autonomous University, UNAM, in Mexico City seem to have been the constant background factors in top level politico-administrative recruitment during much of this century. Camp puts it this way in his own book:

> The reader, who doubts the major thesis of this book—that the public universities are the location for most political recruitment in Mexico— need only ask why not one graduate from the prestigious Ibero-American University (an institution graduating many PAN leaders) or Monterrey Institute of Higher Studies (financed by the powerful Monterrey industrial group) has never succeeded in reaching the top.[100]

The potential problem for Mexico, argues Camp, is that public sector recruitment is relatively closed to progeny of the private sector. This is the reverse of the situation prevailing in the United States where doors to top-echelon government roles are traditionally open to those educated in the private sector. Mexican political leaders tend to become prominent in business only after holding high political office, but not before. Private sector recruitment from the public sector, but not vice versa, leads to the risk that the sort of tensions and antagonisms roused by President Echeverría toward the private sector may become permanent in terms of conflict. Such tensions were exacerbated by President López Portillo again toward the end of his term in office.

If the principal route for getting into top level government in Mexico is via the public universities, and particularly the UNAM with its pervading hostility toward capitalistic private enterprise, then cleavage between government and business may grow to system-threatening proportions. Since also, as we have seen, the Mexican government is committed to keeping the private sector alive via subsidies, investment incentives and tariff protection, then the above-mentioned cleavage could threaten the stability of the state if hostilities should ever lead to severe curtailment of state-provided business protection. We would conclude, then, on the basis of Camp's analysis, that personal trust and ideological relationships formed within the state educational system may rival the PRI as a formal recruitment mechanism in upper level Mexican politics and government. One sees developing a dangerous four-part cleavage between government, private sector, opposition political groups, and the marginal society which constitutes the great majority of Mexicans. In this case government is understood to include the three sectors of the PRI and their legion of subsidiaries.

It may be, then, that studying Mexican democracy realistically at the moment requires only cursory treatment of parties and parliaments. As far as concrete conditions of human existence are concerned, it is necessary to examine public management in Mexico and the socioeconomic needs that are its province. It is crucial as well to understand Mexico's resources, both natural and man-made, as well as the constraints which limit the effectiveness of their use. As we consider this in the following chapter one should remember that, the realities of power politics notwithstanding, Mexico is a federal republic with representatives chosen to represent the people in a parliament. The people have been told that through these representatives they can demand policy changes and remedy their grievances. The Mexican parliament can be a sounding board for popular discontent, as can the extralegal routes and arenas that desperate people may use when their requirements go unmet. In Mexico, it must be remembered, the linkage between political and administrative arenas is close. And it is not unrealistic to see the PRI, as many still do, as the government disguised as a political party.

NOTES

1. Mauricio González de la Garza, *Última llamada* (Mexico: Edamex, 1981), p. 77.
2. Robert Wesson, *Democracy in Latin America: Promise and Problems* (New York: Praeger, 1982), p. 89.
3. Ibid., p. 131.
4. Derived from Kenneth F. Johnson and Miles W. Williams, *Power, Democracy, and Intervention in Latin American Political Life* (Arizona State University: Center for Latin American Studies, 1978), *passim*.
5. Surveyed in Johnson and Williams, *Power, Democracy, and Intervention*.
6. Ignacio González Gollaz, "La posibilidad de JLP," *Visión*, June 1, 1976, p. 48.

7. *Gobernación,* July, 1976.

8. José Luis Reyna and Richard S. Weinert, eds., *Authoritarianism in Mexico* (Philadelphia: Institute for the Study of Human Issues, 1977), p. 160.

9. Frank Brandenburg, *The Making of Modern Mexico* (Englewood Cliffs, N.J.: Prentice-Hall, 1964), p. 141.

10. Evelyn P. Stevens, *Protest and Response in Mexico* (Cambridge, Mass.: MIT Press, 1974), p. 126.

11. Following the Tlatelolco disaster a clandestine book without author entitled *El móndrigo* circulated in Mexico City. It tended to blame persons in the presidential entourage including Luis Echeverría, and also blamed the CIA. There was speculation that Díaz Ordaz had privately commissioned the book to shed blame on others.

12. On June 10, 1971, another student protest movement was put down violently by the government in the San Cosme neighborhood of Mexico City. Elsewhere I have published evidence that the government knew about the paramilitary group known as the Falcons or *Los Halcones.* This produced a major confrontation between President Echeverría and even the establishment press and resulted in the removal of Alfonso Martínez Domínguez as mayor of Mexico City. The June 10 affair is still a blight on the record of esoteric democracy in Mexico and was especially damaging to the incumbent president. After the "burning" of Martínez Domínguez following the San Cosme affair he was "resuscitated" and elevated to the governorship of Nuevo León. See my Chapter Four in the previous edition of *Mexican Democracy.*

13. See the *Arizona Daily Star,* May 15, 1977.

14. Kenneth F. Johnson, *Guerrilla Politics in Argentina* (London: Institute for the Study of Conflict, 1975).

15. See the *New York Times* editorial on July 13, 1976. See also Enrique Krauze, "The Intellectuals and Society," in Irving Howe, ed. *Democracy and Dictatorship in Latin America* (New York: Foundation for the Study of Independent Social Ideas, 1982), p. 48.

16. Daniel Cosío Villegas, *La sucesión presidencial* (Mexico: Cuadernos de Joaquín Mortiz, 1975), p. 144.

17. Philip Agee, *Inside the Company: CIA Diary* (London: Penguin Books, 1975), p. 509.

18. Cosío Villegas, *La sucesión presidential,* p. 18.

19. Ibid., p. 145.

20. Interviews in Mexico during 1972 and 1976 by this author.

21. Gastón Rivanuva R. (pseudonym), *El PRI: el gran mito mexicano* (Mexico: Editorial Tradición, 1974), p. 79.

22. Daniel Cosío Villegas, *La sucesión: desenlace y perspectivas* (Mexico: Cuadernos de Joaquín Mortiz, 1975), *passim.*

23. Ibid., pp. 94 and 103.

24. *La Batalla,* May 1975.

25. *El Imparcial* (Sonora), October 26, 1975.

26. See the previous edition of *Mexican Democracy,* especially Chapter Seven.

27. Based on this author's interviews in Sonora during 1976 and also an account given by *Onda* (Sinaloa), November 12, 1975, which links both Biebrich and Moya Palencia to the international narcotics traffic.

28. A document in this writer's possession designated *consignación* and dated January 20, 1976. It is a legal indictment against Biebrich, then fugitive in the United States by the Sonora government's attorney general.

29. *Excelsior,* March 15, 1975. See especially the testimony on p. 12-A, and also the article by Jean-Claude Buhrer reproduced from *Le Monde Diplomatique* (Paris) by *Excelsior* on September 17, 1972.

30. *Excelsior,* March 15, 1975.

31. As quoted in the first edition of *Mexican Democracy* (1972) p. 164.
32. José C. Valadés, *El presidente de México en 1970* (Mexico: Editores Mexicanos Unidos, 1970), pp. 82–83.
33. Ibid., pp. 100–102.
34. Ibid., p. 125.
35. Ibid., p. 148.
36. Some renovation of the congress occurred as a result of the electoral reform of 1977. The previous year the first opposition senator was admitted to the senate, but that was seen widely as a self-serving token gesture by the PRI.
37. Valadés, *El presidente de México en 1970*, p. 150.
38. This was attributable in part to the internal crisis suffered by the opposition PAN in 1976.
39. Stevens, *Protest and Response in Mexico*, p. 259.
40. Cosío Villegas, *El estilo personal*, pp. 49–50.
41. It is only fair to cite examples of attempts during the Echeverría years to deal with social needs such as the INFONAVIT housing program.
42. Cosío Villegas, *El estilo personal*, p. 57.
43. Ibid., p. 58.
44. Ibid., pp. 60–62. I treated this in the previous edition of *Mexican Democracy* as the Day of Flags scandal.
45. Ibid., p. 128.
46. L.V. Padgett, *The Mexican Political System* (Boston: Houghton Mifflin, 1976), p. 187.
47. Cosío Villegas, *El estilo personal*, pp. 112–14.
48. Padgett, *The Mexican Political System*, p. 196.
49. *Punto Crítico*, July, 1976, p. 18.
50. Ibid.
51. Padgett, *The Mexican Political System*, p. 197.
52. Ibid., p. 214 (emphasis added).
53. *Proceso*, No. 355, August 22, 1983, p. 16.
54. Ibid., p. 17.
55. Ibid., p. 20.
56. *Proceso*, No. 353, August 8, 1983, p. 30.
57. *Proceso*, No. 349, July 11, 1983, p. 18.
58. Ibid., p. 21.
59. *Proceso*, No. 353, August 8, 1983, p. 8.
60. *Diario Las Américas* (Miami), August 2, 1983.
61. *Proceso*, No. 349, July 11, 1983, p. 23.
62. *Proceso*, No. 351, July 25, 1983, pp. 31–32.
63. *Excelsior*, August 8, 1983.
64. Miguel Basañez, *La lucha por la hegemonía en México: 1968–1980* (Mexico: Siglo Veintiuno Editores, 1982), pp. 119–20.
65. Basañez, *La lucha por la hegemonía*, pp. 118–19.
66. Kenneth F. Johnson, "Ideological Correlates of Right Wing Political Alienation in Mexico, *The American Political Science Review*, September 1965.
67. Franz A. von Sauer, *The Alienated "Loyal" Opposition* (Albuquerque: University of New Mexico Press, 1974), p. 31.
68. In addition to von Sauer's book cited above see Donald J. Mabry, *Mexico's Acción Nacional: A Catholic Alternative to Revolution* (Syracuse University Press: 1973).
69. Von Sauer, *The Alienated "Loyal" Opposition*, p. 125.
70. Ibid., p. 138.
71. Ibid., p. 148.
72. Mabry to Johnson, August 5, 1983.

73. Mabry, *Mexico's Acción Nacional,* p. 59.
74. Ibid., p. 74.
75. Ibid., p. 99.
76. Ibid., p. 101.
77. Ibid., p. 189.
78. *Panismo,* No. 4, February 1, 1982.
79. Ibid.
80. *Proceso,* No. 350, July 18, 1983, p. 14.
81. Ibid., p. 15.
82. Ibid., pp. 16–17.
83. Ibid., p. 18.
84. *Proceso,* No. 349, July 11, 1983, pp. 16–17.
85. Ibid., p. 18.
86. Raúl González Schmal, "Las elecciones y la crisis del sistema," a paper presented at the reunion of SOLIDARISMO on June 12, 1982, mimeographed, pp. 9–10.
87. Ibid., pp. 11–12.
88. Basáñez, *La lucha por la hegemonía,* p. 81.
89. Ibid., pp. 82–83.
90. Ibid., p. 87.
91. Ibid., p. 94.
92. Ibid., p. 98.
93. See the various writings of Susan Kaufman Purcell including *Mexico–United States Relations,* Proceedings of the Academy of Political Science 34, No. 1, New York, Academy of Political Science, (1981), for additional valuable insights and a more thorough treatment of Mexican private sector politics.
94. Basáñez, *La lucha por la hegemonía,* pp. 104–105.
95. Ibid., p. 108.
96. PAN, *Información* de Prensa, August 25, 1977.
97. González Schmal, "Los elecciones y la crisis," p. 4.
98. Ibid.
99. Ibid., p. 5 (my italics).
100. Roderic A. Camp, *Mexico's Leaders: Their Education and Recruitment* (Tucson: University of Arizona Press, 1980), p. 63.

Six

Management of Mexico's Public Resources and Public Policy

PROBLEMS OF PUBLIC ADMINISTRATION: AN OVERVIEW

It has been suggested that Mexico needs "less politics and more administration," a slogan which Juan Miguel de Mora attributes to an act of circus clowns going back into the nineteenth century.[1] The matter of separating political action from public administration in Mexico is at once challenging and threatening to the system, given superimposition of the PRI over the government bureaucracy. The PRI's popular sector, with its CNOP and bureaucrats' organizations like the FSTSE, are intimately wed to the governing bureaucracy. This gives rise to an oft-heard opposition charge cited in the previous chapter, namely that the PRI is little more than the government disguised as a political party. This has some rather serious consequences for the ability of the state to serve the needs of its populace via the administration of public policy.

A classic work by Fred Riggs on public administration in developing countries treats many cause and effect relations involving bureaucracies that do not accomplish what they were created to do. Often times the self-interest of bureaucrats (in keeping their organization going) gets in the way of what they are supposed to achieve; he gives an example of flood control bureaucrats in one country who allowed their physical plant to deteriorate deliberately so as to justify more appropriations in the succeeding budget year. In Mexico he cited poor maintenance of railroads in the same context.[2] Other problems noted by Riggs having contemporary Mexican counterparts are overly-centralized bureaucracies (as in federal education) resulting in neglect of needs throughout the countryside. Also it is difficult to enforce Mexico's minimum labor legislation partly because it does not apply to everyone and partly because of political involvement in the enforcement of those provisions that are applicable to given cases. Sometimes employees will be dismissed without severance pay and in other cases not, depending on the politics of union and management; the same goes for hourly pay. The political element may adversely affect economic development when management sees itself forced to pay tribute to corrupt union bosses or obliged to pay excessive employee benefits as a penalty for not coming to an agreement with the unions (note the case of PEMEX later in this chapter). Unequal enforcement of wage and salary laws, as with tax and profit repatriation controls, can also have an adverse effect on overall economic development.

Riggs found a tendency in developing nations for the state to assume a major entrepreneurial role. In this chapter we will consider several cases of the state's leading role in Mexico's economic development. Faulty management of state enterprises has, in recent years, taken a serious toll in Mexico. Administrative inefficiency results from poor personnel administration, the underutilization of personnel, appointment of unqualified persons, spending of fake bureaucrats or aviadores, and unclear mandates from the executive and/or legislative branches of government. Low morale and the substitution of personal goals for public ones may also be cited. Use of inappropriate technology (as in the case of PEMEX) also weakens goal achievement. Much of the above can, quite obviously, be grouped under the rubric of corruption. It may be financial corruption, or nonmaterial corruption in cases in which prestige is acquired with the holding of a title even with little or no pay. Vacant titles of this sort may do little to promote the goals of a public service and if corruption is rife then additional investments may need to be made in watching and auditing the performance of the bureaucrats. This becomes a wasteful and morale-shattering enterprise. It may mean, as is often the case in Mexico, that the costs of tax collection outdistance the tax that is ultimately collected. Having inspectors to watch the tax collectors and supervisors to watch the inspectors may deplete taxation as a governmental resource.

In some developing countries the excessive concentration of decision making in the capital city makes a bureaucracy unresponsive to the regions and localities it is supposed to serve. This is a common complaint against Mexico's SARH (Secretariat of Agriculture and Hydraulic [Water] Resources) as well as against CONASUPO, the government's staple foods distribution system. Excessive centralization of decision making also elevates local disputes to a high level, often ministerial, creating a logjam of paperwork and resultant bureaucratic inaction. In Chapter One we touched on this complaint regarding peasant applicants for idle lands under Mexico's various reform programs noting the large backlog of petitions that have waited for years without governmental action. Persons far from the scene of a problem may have little interest in or comprehension of what needs to be done and this fact in and of itself builds inefficiency into the administrative system. Other administrative waste comes from poor coordination among agencies whose functions may overlap. Riggs found that in Mexico there was an urgent need for coordination of government transportation agencies to prevent damage to existing transportation systems and to make railroads, in particular, into genuine promoters of economic growth.[3] He argued also that in American government the interplay among legislatures, parties, organized interest groups, the press, and professional societies generated compulsion on the part of administrators to work toward their organization's public goals. In developing countries, by contrast, he found bureaucracies more often oriented toward personal survival and tolerance of corruption. He described corruption as an integral part of the *sala* model, his concept of bureaucracy in many developing countries.[4]

The above observations closely parallel those of a recent Mexican writer who treats Mexico's bureaucratic malaise as a function of his nation's overall fear complex. Juan Miguel de Mora cites many cases of one bureaucracy employed to keep watch over another, beginning with the customs personnel who inspect travelers crossing Mexico's borders or entering her airports. In his words "this mechanism of creating one bureaucracy to watch over another and a third to watch over the second is one of the causes of Mexico's condition" of underdevelopment.[5] He cited various examples including the Federal Automobile Registry which he labels a "Kafkaesque" organization designed to make life more difficult for the citizenry and to create a source of bribes to be collected in return for administrative services, a characterization he applies generally to the police function throughout Mexico.[6] Fear among employees of each other, of their superiors, of "living outside the budget" as the Mexican saying goes, keeps down criticism of corruption which pervades the entire Mexican administrative system as a general rule, not as an exception. Mexican bureaucrats are amoral vis a vis corruption, and this amorality is a prime characteristic of the Mexican bureaucratic system.[7] The same fear complex extends to the majority of the press whose editors and reporters know perfectly well what can be published without reprisal from the PRI-dominated officialdom and what cannot.[8] And the government seems to fear that which is spoken over television much more than that which is printed.[9] Nepotism is an integral part of the Mexican administrative corruption, that is, of its inefficiency and waste. Each year and each sexenio new spots (*plazas*) must be created for uncles, cousins, brothers, etc., so that progressively more bureaucrats are added to the public payrolls without a corresponding output of services. When the new spots are in fact aviadores then nothing but pure drain occurs on the public resources. "It is as if the secret design of the Mexican revolution were to solve Mexico's problems by ultimately converting all Mexicans into employees of the state."[10] Such nepotism, an integral part of corruption, pervaded

Mexico's public administration to an alarming degree during the 1976–82 sexenio of José López Portillo.[11]

The Mexican state, then, is the nation's leading employer of people. Estimating the size of this public service is made difficult by the juxtaposition of political and administrative roles. It was estimated by Basáñez that the public sector in Mexico represented 18,000 elective positions and 25,000 appointive positions that could expect to be changed every six years and that beyond this there were 4 million other functionaries in the total Mexican public sector.[12] These estimates are based on other estimates and include legislative, executive, and judicial branches of government plus state and municipal governments. They also seem to include functionaries of the PRI's sectoral organizations and the state-run enterprises. One can appropriately conclude that the public sector in Mexico is ubiquitous and massive even though it may be impossible to get an accurate head count.

CAMARILLAS AND PUBLIC ADMINISTRATION: SPECIFIC APPLICATIONS AND INSTANCES

With the foregoing conditions prevailing throughout Mexico it is understandable that agencies which exist ostensibly to carry out national development goals might fail to bring these endeavors to fruition. That may explain why countries like Mexico seem to be always "developing" but somehow never really do develop. In Mexico the imposition of an official political party over the governing apparatus of the state is a key environmental condition for this process. Camarillas are power cliques within the PRI. Members of a camarilla render services and pay homage to a political figure who rewards the members with deference, status, and income. Usually the income is derived from jobs, either fake or real, that are available and/or specially created within a government bureaucracy.

Here is a true story of one Mexican who aspired to status and mobility via participation in the camarilla system.[13] I have omitted proper names for obvious reasons. Our neophyte aspires to a career in his country's political life. He is eventually awarded a specially created spot in Mexico's Secretariat of Agrarian Reform, the SRA. It is his job *formally* to aid in processing land grant applications for the creation of new ejidos. The job in question does not really need to be done, it is still another contrived "review" of applications which pass through the bureaucracy and affords its holder the chance to enrich himself by speeding up the administrative process in exchange for a monetary consideration. Hence, this post is a sinecure within the Mexican concept of aviadora. By creating this unnecessary position the review process for land grant applications is merely slowed down by requiring another signature. To that degree our neophyte is not a pure aviador who would receive a salary for doing absolutely nothing and not even making the pretense.

We must start at the beginning, however, for whereas our neophyte seeks status and mobility he lacks the family or primary group ties on which to base a rise to fame. These are the steps through which he passes en route to a sharing of socioeconomic and political power in Mexico.

1. He joins the PRI. This is indispensable.

2. He must participate in party affairs, beginning at the grass-roots level, and above all he must attach himself to the coattails of some prominent politician whose orbit of success is already firmly established. He will do this through intermediaries already having contact with the politician himself; such access has great symbolic value and is shared sparingly by those who possess it.

3. In making his attachment he has joined a camarilla. This is a point of some considerable risk, for should the camarilla fail to grow in power and wealth our young aspirant will have to seek admission to another one and this could be both embarrassing and costly. The camarillas combat each other and the young man and his colleagues must become vehement loyalists to the camarilla and its leader if they are to confront their competition. The leader's cause becomes that of the group. There is a kind of internecine warfare among competing camarillas that often leads to acrimony, something the PRI seeks to cloak from public view.

4. Once a final commitment to a camarilla is made, the young political hopeful must direct himself to carrying out a legion of mundane and highly pedestrian tasks for his group and for the PRI at large, for example, arranging youth meetings, distributing propaganda, answering correspondence, all of which can be done in his spare time and without pay. Our political neophyte has yet to be permitted to live from his politics.

5. Our candidate is intelligent, capable, and performs his tasks well, thus his immediate boss rewards him with a better spot, that of private secretary to a deputy who belongs to the same camarilla. This is a full-time low-paid job in which the neophyte learns how to resolve minor political problems and undertakes special missions about the republic in connection with electoral plans and propaganda. He will later be handed the task of writing minor political speeches; in general he becomes initiated into Mexican politics. He learns the art of covering up the mistakes of his mentors, and doing so without outwardly using the term "mistake."

6. Having shown promise in this role for several years, the young politician (probably living on a salary of around $400 per month) naturally aspires to a greater position; that, after all, was why he entered the arena in the first place. At this point he must pass successfully the tortuous throes of a crucial series of ordeals; he must keep himself on ice cautiously

and patiently; he must perform a range of trying but essential ritual functions varying from political breakfasts to greeting party dignitaries, all the while molding an image favorable to his silent candidacy for greater fame and higher place. Playing this game skillfully results in his being elevated to the role of secretary for political action within the Youth Committee of the PRI for the Federal District. This is a test of his political sensitivity and an important one. Unfortunately, this position is only honorific, not remunerative, and he must arrange another salary to sustain himself. This, he finds, can be accomplished by means of a special sinecure which is little more than a fake salary (aviadora) paid to our young politician for work he does *not do* in an office within the Secretariat of Agrarian Reform that he seldom visits. He manages, however, to collect his salary and now and then receives extra payments for speeding up someone's land grant application. Doing this free of charge can be a political favor as well, one that helps build personal alliances and power within the basic camarilla. This is not unusual, for among the ingroup of the PRI there are many persons who receive five or six phantom sinecures of this sort. In this way the PRI can subsidize its political figures with salaries from the public budget while leaving them maximum freedom to work full-time for the party. This, incidentally, is how secret paramilitary enforcement squads are often financed.

7. As secretary of political action in the Youth Committee our young man performs well and wins for his camarilla certain honors that qualify him for two more fake salaries and the promise of more to come. He now earns well over $1,000 per month, which is excellent in peso equivalents.

8. At this juncture the young politician has become somewhat seasoned and, feeling secure, he gradually begins to form his own camarilla. He enjoys having younger men look up to him with dreams of future reward. His power is limited but he has some of it nonetheless. He can, for example, recommend a young aspirant of his own camarilla for a special although minor post; he can convene special political meetings based upon his own new circle and can begin to attract a following by doing a legion of minor favors for friends and acquaintances. He is beginning to be successful in the game of politics. By this time he receives a salary of nearly $2,000 per month (thanks to his several sinecure paychecks) and has his own loyal constituency whose members obey his every command. He even offers an occasional political breakfast, the sign that one has "arrived." His supporters want him to rise, as the coattails effect of this will surely benefit them when the power and related largesse are distributed.

9. Our neophyte politician still has not taken over as head of the larger camarilla which he joined originally at the grass roots. But he remains in the good graces of the man who continues as boss and thereby it is arranged that our politician is named alternate deputy for the PRI in

the Federal District. This is a second-rank post as positions of federal power go, but it carries its privileges and credentials which enable one to jump from stone to stone in the upward spiral of trails and trials which constitute the quest for national power in the Republic of Mexico.

10. As an alternate deputy in the Federal District our aspirant welds a series of providential relationships in the upper circles of the federal government. He gains favor with the PRI's top echelon, the CEN, which in turn names him electoral delegate for the State of Guanajuato. He must travel there to represent CEN on the official team in the PRI's coming campaign for governor of the state. It becomes our man's personal charge to appoint special CEN representatives in the various electoral committees around Guanajuato for purposes of liaison with the national party organs. First and foremost in his portfolio, however, is the imperative that the PRI win in Guanajuato, preferably by legal means, but in the last analysis by any means at all. These he is free to invent. But public image and revolutionary symbolism must be preserved unsullied at all costs.

11. Here is where our politician's career is damaged by partial defeat and considerable public disgrace. PRI wins the elections in Guanajuato to be sure, but at the expense of being caught by a vocal opposition with an impressive cache of false ballots, an incident the opposition is able to inflate into proportions of national scandal. Certain organs of the national press carry the story in detail. Federal executive power is necessary to quiet the public storm via the promise of an investigation. Our political hero is blamed by the opposition press for the fraud and his own superiors chastise him for ineptitude. This is a setback and he will have to wait for an opportunity to overcome it. He has been burned.

12. As a result, not unexpectedly, of his failure in Guanajuato, our exemplary politician loses favor with his former boss and his political privileges and salaries remain frozen for a time. Nonetheless, he continues to work quietly, organizing a special student group inside the National Autonomous University and in this endeavor he makes good use of his own small camarilla which is still intact. He knows that the university will be a fertile breeding ground in which to reingratiate himself with his boss. Some accuse him of organizing *porros*, student goon squads that act in paramilitary fashion inside the university.

13. For a considerable time the name of our politician remains forgotten in the spiderwebs. Then one day in the very bosom of the university a serious conflict explodes, one which the government fears it will not be able to control. The PRI and the government are one and the same vis-a-vis a common helplessness of not knowing how to proceed. There are groups of rival porros at each other's throats. The government is already under a stigma for sending police into various universities. The president

himself seeks a way to avoid another bloody university intervention. This case is worse yet because a university employee's union is involved.

14. It is then, during these moments of crisis, that our disguised personage becomes suddenly very optimistic and ventures to tell his boss: "I can control these students by way of my movement and the extreme loyalty they feel for me. But there is a price tag. The government and the PRI will have to name me as principal candidate for federal deputy in the next elections, and assign several of my followers to positions within the Youth Committee of the PRI." Here he is placing members of his camarilla as an insurance factor.

15. This offer is quietly accepted. With government backing, our politician and his camarilla succeed in squashing the student effervescence that surely would have led to a university–government conflict. Out of such a test of strength no one could possibly win, but the PRI would be a sure loser. The conflict subsides and our man is named candidate for deputy along with new positions for his followers. His name has been cleared, the stains of the Guanajuato campaign are forgotten. He has achieved success, he is now invited to political breakfasts, and the press begins to laud him. (Its members form lines to receive their *embute,* a monthly gratuity paid to reporters in exchange for their efforts to create a favorable public image for a given person). At the top level of the PRI our man is now being discussed for assignment to the CEN. He has made it from the unknown to a high place in the PRI. He has lived within the system, he has honored the sacred dictum, "Live not in error."

"Live not in error" in effect means live within the PRI budget. Our neophyte politician's loyalty was to the PRI first and to his sinecure positions, in the SRA and elsewhere, last. In effect, it might be said that his loyalty to Mexico was also last. But the PRI loyalists believe that their party is the only legitimate heir to the revolutionary tradition of Mexico and that they, better than any competing group, can bring this mandate to fruition for the benefit of the Mexican people. Nevertheless the basic fact is that the public goal of agrarian reform which accounts for the existence of the SRA was left to its fate in the hands of a bureaucracy many of whose members were there for personal goals of enrichment and power within the official party. Working in the SRA was only a pretext to get them paid. Is it any wonder that Mexico today would have a backlog of land-grant applications within a bureaucratized program whose forward motion is sloth-like when it moves at all?

Above we viewed the process from the perspective of a politician and administrator. Here let us examine agrarian reform from the standpoint of peasants seeking land. This is a classic story that I have told before but one which my Mexican colleagues assure me continues to be valid, with only a few names needing to be changed, well into the 1980s. Article 27 of the constitution provides that idle lands may be confiscated by the state and given as grants to those who will use them profitably.[14] But there are groups of untouchables, *los intocables,* who survived the land granting years of Cárdenas and have used the political system to keep thousands of peasants dispossessed and to swindle others out of lands they have been granted. This is done not only by use of the amparo or appeal whereby landowners keep land grant applications tied up perpetually in the legal system, but also by corrupt practices in arranging for land grants to be an-nulled and the peasants evicted. Such corruption requires collusion be-tween large landholders and well-placed persons within the various sub-divisions of the SRA. Poor peasants about to be dispossessed of their land would probably not have the cash money at hand to pay a bribe (gratuity?) to our neophyte politician/administrator to see to it that their claim was not annulled. As in the present instance they would inevitably become vic-tims of both the intocables and the bureaucracy. Unhappily their tale is typical.

As the story has been told, some years ago Anastasio Rodríguez and his common law wife Manuela Domínguez occupied a poor and deserted piece of land in the wilderness of Chihuahua and created a precarious life from practically nothing. They were destined to collide with Mexico's great landowners, with the U.S. companies, and with the Department of Agrarian Affairs and Colonization (DAAC). So begins a novel based on the real life experiences of Carlos Chavira Becerra, one-time federal deputy from Chihuahua, who tells a bitter and empirically well-grounded account of the other face of Mexico and the realities of agrarian reform.[15]

A village was born in the desert rocks and mountains at a spot called Cañón de la Madera, a misnomer to be sure, for there was no wood in sight nor water to grow crops. The squatters carried in water, built misera-ble huts, and collected a few head of cattle and goats. Most of their income came from labor on nearby farms and in mines. At the onset, the squatters defended their tenancy under the legendary decree of August 2, 1923,[16] which all the rural poor knew how to invoke by saying "*Pos yo estoy posiando aquí por el Decreto del dos de agosto.*"[17] In reality no one knew how to define this decree. One day an engineer named Rivera came to survey lands near the old coal mine of Don Adolfo Orlich, a friend and benefactor of the squatters. From Rivera they learned of a way to consti-tute themselves legally as a communal farm under the Agrarian Code. The squatters designated Pedro Alvidres to go to the state capital and begin procedures for an ejido application. It was a difficult task for the il-literate Alvidres, but with help and advice from Rivera and Orlich the squatters finally received a large envelope with the national crest on it con-taining papers they could not read but which were interpreted to them as being a preliminary approval by the government's Agrarian Commission of their application for state farm status. It was a moment of great joy.

From that time on the residents of Cañón de la Madera were integrated politically into the CNC (*Confederación Nacional Campesina*) and received corresponding periodic instructions as to the intermittent formalities they must satisfy. Among these was the task of being brought like cattle in trucks to the municipal center called Manuel Benavídes to contribute their presence toward the appearance of popular adulation in favor of a PRI candidate for federal deputy. Once the candidate's presentation had ended, the squatters were herded rapidly back into the trucks and buses. Somehow no one remembered to pay them the five pesos they had been promised by CNC rural bosses for their participation.

Pedro Alvidres remembered quite seriously the lectures his village folk had received from CNC officials: if they did not go to vote on election day the reactionaries would come to power and take away their land.[18] But when they arrived to vote they were rudely cursed by the polling place attendant for even showing up, thereby causing him the extra work of putting the electoral procedures in motion. All the time he had been marking ballots and stuffing the box in favor of the PRI. The peasants learned, although they did not thoroughly understand, that "the Party of the Government" had voted for them. Their bodies were needed; their minds and souls were superfluous. They had obeyed dutifully and expected their recompense. They wanted final title to their land. But the agrarian delegate for Chihuahua sought ways to prevent the state farm from gaining final legal status. Nevertheless, friends of the squatters prevailed. On November 30, 1933, the publication *Periódico Oficial del Estado de Chihuahua* contained a decree in which the governor gave (*dotaba*) the land including the ejido Cañón de la Madera to Pedro Alvidres and his peasant neighbors. The dotation was classified as provisional. Then, silently, a curious thing occurred. A certain engineer named Martínez was removed from the Chihuahua office of the Agrarian Commission (*Comisíon Agraria Mixta*) for having disagreed with the national agrarian delegate for Chihuahua in the matter of the dotation. And thus a basis was laid whereby many years hence the land grant could be challenged by the untouchables, permanent enemies of agrarian reform, who considered Martínez's indiscretion to have been unpardonable.

The resolution of the governor was subject to final review in "second instance." Here an intricate web of power relationships unfolded. Licenciado Parrá of Chihuahua was legal council for a company of untouchables called *Compañía Ganadera del Norte* that was in the process of liquidating its lands via commercial sale but which had encountered the obstacle of several farms in "first instance" within its original terrain. The only way in which all of the original landed estates could be sold was by dissolution of these communal farms and removal of the squatter peasants. That required a signed resolution from the president of the republic. The key people were Licenciado Parrá and an obscure, but powerful, department chief in the Department of Agrarian Affairs and Colonization (DAAC) who saw to it (in return for a generous financial consideration) that when the president signed into law a number of resolutions during January of 1953 (and did so innocently and blindly) among them was a document whose effect was to dispossess the residents of nearly every communal farm in the municipality of Manuel Benavídes of the property they had cultivated and cared for during many years. This was to please the untouchables who sought to make a profit selling the land (and leasing it to North Americans) in small parcels. During these years the land values increased as the peasants had finally discovered water (via their own sweat and blood) and U.S. geological surveys indicated the presence of valuable minerals. Therefore, the poor but courageous peasants of Cañón de la Madera had to go; in this case the pretext was simple: when Pedro Alvidres and his farmers had made their initial solicitation they had presented thirty-five names as parties to the petition . . . the law only required twenty signatures; the transaction was "obviously" fraudulent,[19] at least so reasoned the key figure of the DAAC and Licenciado Parrá. Money had "oiled" the wheels of the so-called agrarian reform bureaucracy.

An order was sent from Mexico City to a rural marshal known as Castro Carrillo telling him to dislodge the thirty-five peasant families from the land they believed to be theirs. Castro Carrillo was told to use the "federal force" to the extent he considered necessary. The pitiful spectre of this eviction is described by Carlos Chavira in his book and becomes in itself something of a study in bizarre administrative psychology at the government-to-people level. The peasants were taken to the municipality of Manuel Benavídes, tried and convicted by an illiterate justice of the peace, and then abandoned to die in the disease-ridden slums of this poor village. Their captor, Castro Carrillo, told them to get out of his sight, to disappear; then he stole their livestock and left.

With the help of their old benefactor, Don Adolfo Orlich, a letter was written to the president of the republic asking for mercy and intervention. By the time a reply was received Pedro Alvidres and others were dead from disease and misfortune; but when the reply did come months later, it said only that the peasants' complaint had been turned over to the Department of Agrarian Affairs and Colonization, ironically, the very source of corruption in which the traumata of their displacement had begun. Then follows the poignant tale of the uprooted men who lacked the eight-hundred peso bribe needed to be smuggled to work in the

United States and whose already fragile health carried them to the dregs of a compassionless society and death. There is also the tale of the rural marshal Castro Carrillo whose biggest defeat was the indiscretion of getting caught accepting a bribe but who escaped punishment to retire graciously on hacienda lands he had helped to "liberate" from peasant occupation.

A balance sheet on the ejido Cañón de la Madera, otherwise known as dotation number 826 in the municipality of Manuel Benavídes, state of Chihuahua, reads as follows: a) peasants begin occupation of the land in question in 1924, b) they win provisional ejido title in 1934, c) a presidential resolution cancels their title in 1953, d) they are forcefully ejected from these lands in 1957. Carlos Chavira served as a PAN deputy in the federal Chamber of Deputies during the last years of the López Mateos regime. He tried repeatedly to secure administrative relief for peasant farm groups like those of Cañón de la Madera, and sought unsuccessfully to gain an audience with the president himself on their behalf. Pressure from the untouchables of his state made it impossible for Chavira to gain a second term in office; the peasant evictions continued, and the profitable sale of Chihuahua land continued (notably to foreign groups like Mennonites from the United States who could pay for the benefits of agrarian reform).

The tragic character in this revealing novel is Pedro Alvidres who had been proudly chosen Presidente Comisariado Ejidal for the ejido Cañón de la Madera and whose badly disfigured body was found floating in the Rio Bravo del Norte (Rio Grande) shortly before the reply to the letter sent to the president of the republic was received in his name. Pedro had become a "wetback" and crossed over into Texas to work in the melon fields in order to support his starving family; but lacking bribe money to purchase protection, he was "caught by the law" as the poor Mexicans say and was executed. Unable to pay tribute to Mexican officialdom he paid with his life. Pedro was superstitious, yet religious, and held faith in witchcraft medicines and in mysterious revelations of divine truth. But, as Chavira writes, "Alvidres believed in things even more absurd than those":

> he believed, for example, in honor, justice, in human integrity and in respect for the rights of others, in decency, in love, in labor; he believed, ultimately, in a series of utopias, he had that great faith of the miner. But his belief was a pathology in itself, he was dead serious in putting it forth, serious in respecting the law that was in force, in giving an open road to nature's vital forces; he had faith also, an immense faith, in the benevolent justice of the President of the Republic.[20]

The agrarian affairs bureaucrat who took a bribe in exchange for helping rig the expulsion of Pedro Alvidres and the others from their land in Chihuahua could have been an aviador who came to work occasionally and performed such favors in exchange for gratuities or he could have been a full-time employee on a salary so low that bribery had become a necessity of life for him; or he could have been merely a greedy figure already well paid. The common element is moral corruption. The bureaucracy feeds off the public and exploits the system for personal gain in derogation of its own goals. The principle of agrarian reform is forgotten by all except the dispossessed peasants.

Like Pedro Alvidres many simple Mexicans believe that they can depend on the president of the republic to save them from a hostile world. But these same simple Mexicans have not belonged to the camarilla system of power-sharing. When efforts were made to go around the camarilla power structure and appeal to the president directly a threatening precedent was in the making. Those making such appeals have fallen victim to harsh reprisal. Martyrs have been made as the bureaucracy defends itself. The case of Rubén Jaramillo is one of these and he remains a populist hero in Mexico's agrarian reform folklore today. About one hour by car southwest of Mexico City in the Morelos hills Rubén Jaramillo and his followers challenged the agrarian reform bureaucracy of the DAAC and President López Mateos along with it. Rubén Jaramillo has come to symbolize Mexican agrarian resistance to authority in general and to the PRI's agrarian sector in particular. Jaramillo had reputedly served with Zapata's guerrillas both for and against Madero. After the Revolution Jaramillo continued to lead squatter movements against the remaining great landowners of which there were many. During the Cárdenas land distributions, Jaramillo suspended his more militant activities although it is said he never really believed that the reformist general-president would ever be anything but a puppet for Calles who had arranged his candidacy in 1934.

The regimes of Miguel Alemán and Ruíz Cortines drove Jaramillo and his men into legendary exile where he remained, in the hills and mountains of Morelos, until President López Mateos offered him amnesty and a chance for peace following 1958. In fact, López Mateos met personally with Jaramillo in one of the century's most celebrated cases of a truce of convenience. Apparently the president promised the guerrilla chieftain many things, including considerable land for Jaramillo. But nothing happened and so Jaramillo's squatters began to occupy properties belonging to powerful friends of Morelos's governor Norberto López Avelar.

For a brief time it looked as if the DAAC might support Jaramillo's plea that the unused land be given to his people under the agrarian reform laws. Then, suddenly, the DAAC ordered Jaramillo's men to vacate the property. This coincided roughly with the announcement of plans to build a major hydroelectric project in the immediate area and on lands occupied in part by Jaramillo and his men. Here was another case in which private profits were to be made by claiming the abandoned land and by dispossessing the squatters. Apparently no offer was made to move the peasants to other lands of a comparable quality or to indemnify them for the loss that their eviction under eminent domain would produce.

There are a number of versions in the popular folklore of what happened next and of who was responsible. The crude and bizarre fact of it is, explanations notwithstanding, that Rubén Jaramillo and his entire family were taken by force and machine gunned to death. Their bodies were found a short distance from their home on May 23, 1962. The government announced an investigation of the atrocity and President López Mateos had the officialist press carry the photos taken earlier of himself and Jaramillo making "cause," as Madero and Zapata had one in nearly the same political and geographic circumstances a half century earlier. It is significant to note that Jaramillo could not be coopted, although he was certainly disposed toward a dialogue with officialdom in the interest of progress. Folklore in Morelos blames Governor López Avelar. John Gerassi has cited impressive evidence that the Jaramillos were killed on top orders from the PRI.[21] For a time, at least, the bureaucratic self-interest has been protected from the threat of populist challenge.

RECENT ECONOMIC POLICY AND GOVERNMENTAL ENTREPRENEURSHIP

The contemporary Mexican state has a major role in the nation's economic development. Those constraints and norms outlined in the foregoing pages, resulting from the imposition of an official political party over the governing bureaucracy, have an especially dire impact on achievement of Mexico's socioeconomic reform and development policy objectives. That has been clearly established and need not be detailed further. It is a broad goal of Mexico's developmental thrust to make industry function for the benefit of Mexicans. Most presidents have stressed the leading role of state-run enterprises. The incumbent regime of Miguel de la Madrid chooses to return some industries, e.g. the automotive, to private management. It is true, moreover, that a significant number of Mexican commercial enterprises are under some form of foreign control. It has often been fashionable in Mexico to blame foreigners for many of Mexico's economic woes. Politically it would make little sense for the PRI government to take the blame itself. Mexico has major areas of direct economic dependence on the United States. Tourism is one of these. Agricultural sales plus the remittances that migrant Mexican workers send back from their jobs in the United States are others. The remittances of migrant workers will be estimated in Chapter Seven, but one contemporary observer believes they may amount to as much as all the tourism dollars combined.[22]

Mexico has normally had a favorable balance of tourism situation, especially when compared with other Latin American nations.[23] Most of this is from the United States. It is quite possible that stopping American tourism into Mexico would cause that nation's economy to collapse completely and throw its political system into revolutionary turmoil. This is well understood in both Washington and Mexico City. There were times during the 1970s when political terrorists in Mexico attacked U.S. tourists hoping to undermine the Mexican government by denying tourist dollars. Closing the border by orders from Washington could similarly precipitate economic disaster. Mexican figures working for U.S.-owned companies (like Jaime Castrejón Díaz of Coca Cola in 1971) have been attacked, kidnapped, or killed. Some Mexican presidents, like Luis Echeverría, have openly consorted with Latin American personages of the far left, perhaps as a thinly veiled threat against Yankee imperialists whose extractive enterprises might get out of hand in Mexico. Recent Mexican economic policy has reserved a favorable role for government initiatives in the leading sectors. Thus government entrepreneurship has taken various forms.

In 1952 the government of Miguel Alemán set forth the Plan of Ciudad Sahagún that was carried out by subsequent administrations. Located in the state of Hidalgo some 35 miles northwest of Mexico City this experiment sought to create a satellite city for industrial growth that would attract workers away from the capital city's slums. Originally there was a mix of Japanese, private Mexican, and state capital in the founding of a series of automotive and heavy industrial plants. This was later taken over by the government via the national development bank known as Nacional Financiera. Today, some of that industry is in the process of being turned over to private management (e.g. Renault). There is considerable disagreement today as to whether Ciudad Sahagún has been a success in both social and economic terms, but the project has served as a model for development in other Latin American countries.

Much of the technology that was put to work in Ciudad Sahagún and throughout Mexico depended on patent controls held by U.S. and other foreign interests. These franchises require licensing and payments to parent firms in the respective foreign countries, a major complaint of Mexican industrialists. Some controversy has also surrounded the involvement of Mexican labor unions in the management of the industrial components of Ciudad Sahagún. A general Mexican dissatisfaction with the terms of foreign industrial investment is concerned with the imposed requirement that local subsidiaries produce only for the domestic market, i.e., that Fords made in Mexico not be sold in neighboring Guatemala. Another problem is the requirement that the local subsidiary purchase large amounts of its primary materials in the foreign home country. As cited in Chapter One this can amount to over 90 percent of primary material purchases in some cases and affects not only Mexico's balance of payments but the price of manufactured goods for the domestic market as well.

Foreign controls in one guise or another are a major feature of Mexico's political economy. Lorenzo Meyer has estimated that generally foreign capital accounts for less than 10 percent of the Mexican GNP but looking at key economic sectors only about 70 percent of total manufacturing has come from approximately 800 enterprises in which foreign capital was present. He also contends that in industries such as automobiles, capital goods, and chemicals, foreign participation is around 100 percent,[24] and that the rate of growth of foreign as compared with domestic enterprises in Mexico is an astonishing 60 percent higher or even more.[25] The vicissitudes of the oil boom of the late 1970s and its collapse in the early 1980s have undoubtedly affected the established trends in foreign participation. President Miguel de la Madrid's commitment to rejuvenating the private sector is also to be considered as an influential factor for economic change.

A frequently mentioned statistic is that some 80 percent of the patents used in Mexican industry are U.S.-owned. This is to be considered in addition to the degree to which the Mexican government has mortgaged itself to foreign lending agencies both public and private. As cited previously the 1983 estimate for such indebtedness was put at around $80 billion, about twice that of Argentina for the same year. The willingness of foreign lending institutions to renegotiate Mexico's foreign debt, especially since the peso devaluations of 1982, has been crucial in maintaining Mexico's financial system. To a real extent it is foreign lenders who have kept Mexico afloat along with salary scales that keep worker incomes low, thereby aiding Mexico in its export competition.

It is believed that government (public sector) investment in Mexico's economy accounts for about half of the total. This includes infrastructure investment such as roads and airports. Overall capital formation in Mexico went from about 8.4 percent of the GDP (gross domestic product) in the 1940s to around 19.2 percent in the 1970s. Since the 1940s less emphasis has been placed on agriculture and more has been accorded to manufacturing. In 1970 only about 33 percent of the national labor force was dedicated to agriculture. This reflected the rural-to-urban population shift which has become acute in the second half of the twentieth century. Unlike some other Latin American countries Mexico's emphasis on a public sector–supported industrial economy has not meant expanded military involvement in that industry. Mexico's military establishment is primarily concerned with national defense as contrasted, say, with Argentina where the military constitutes virtually a political party with an institutionalized bureaucracy having economic management responsibility.

In the 1970s the public sector's total expenditures as a percentage of gross domestic product approached 25 percent, an outcome of government tax and tariff incentives and subsidized services provided to the private sector. This government outlay resulted in a general impoverishment of the public sector and placed a special burden on wage earners and professionals for support of the government. As Levy and Szekely have put it:

> ... contrary to the situation prevailing in most countries at a comparable
> level of development in 1976, Mexican wage earners and professionals
> together were contributing as much of total government tax revenues as
> were all private entrepreneurs. This shows the remarkable degree of official support for private capital.[26]

This has meant heavy public sector borrowing both domestically and abroad and contributed to Mexico's $80 billion-plus foreign debt in the 1980s. The probability of a national default on the foreign debt underlay the peso crises of 1982 and 1983. A pattern since World War II of balance of trade deficits (importing more than one exports) contributed further to Mexico's overall indebtedness and financial instability. In some years during the decade of the 1970s as much as 50 percent of Mexican imports were for capital goods without tariffs. Here were direct losses to the treasury plus the lost opportunity to use protectionism in favor of developing a capital goods industry at home. This is potentially risky yet it would be congruent with Mexico's oft-stated policy of import substitution through industrialization.[27]

Importation of capital goods (heavy machinery for manufacturing, etc.) has accompanied the trend in Mexico toward capital-intensive industries and mechanization. This stems also from the increasing cost of skilled labor as private employers are required to contribute to increased worker benefits including housing and health plus end-of-year bonuses. Despite such benefits worker purchasing power overall has fallen in recent years. Figures ranging from 10 to 15 percent are frequently quoted to reflect the losses of worker purchasing power under the López Portillo government alone. There is general agreement that income distribution in Mexico is seriously skewed with the highest 20 percent of income groups receiving over 50 percent of total earned income in 1977 and the lowest 40 percent receiving under 20 percent of the total.[28] By 1982 this meant that "two-thirds of all Mexicans were undernourished."[29]

It has been argued that foreign control of 4 to 8 percent of México's total national investment has had a stultifying effect upon the remaining 90 percent. Policies of tariff protection have aided the growth of Mexican industries whether foreign or domestically controlled. In 1975 the protective tariff structure was changed with the number of tariff items reduced drastically.[30] Production intended mainly for the domestic market has hurt Mexico's balance of payments (e.g. the automotive industry) and has restricted expansion possibilities. This, in turn, has affected employment possibilities. The Mexican state controls 51 percent of mining operations (e.g. sulphur), has exclusive control over petroleum, electricity, railroads, and has major control over communications media. An investment of at least 51 percent Mexican capital has been required in firms in the areas of credit, banking, insurance, bonds and securities. But in 1982 the López Portillo government nationalized Mexico's banking system. A subsequent program of reimbursing the former bankers under de la Madrid left the banks to the province of the state. It has been required that at least 51 percent of capital be held by Mexicans in such areas as petrochemicals, rubber products, glass, fertilizer, and cement but the steps taken by the de la Madrid administration toward returning much of the economy to private hands may eventually alter this pattern. The general point to be made, however, is that past programs of Mexicanization of the economy often have not produced great benefits to the nation because of foreign controls on the use of technology and patents, overseas purchasing of prime materials, foreign repatriation of profits, and "sweetheart deals" between private sectors and government.

It has also been estimated that whereas the average investment profit earned by U.S. investors within the United States in recent decades was around 10.1 percent, the comparable profit in Mexico was three times that percentage. Mexican investment policy allowed that to happen by granting special tax privileges to firms which could show they were in the process of Mexicanization, an ambiguous and easily-detoured rule. The economist Mota Marín once estimated that foreign-owned enterprises in Mexico pay on the average no more than half the taxes they rightfully owe the state.[31] This fact, in and of itself difficult to ascertain with precision but generally believed, makes it likely (in the view of some Mexican economists) that foreign investments may be generating a profit greatly in excess of 30 percent annually and the majority of that, they maintain, is not reinvested in the nation. It is difficult to generalize at the moment of this writing about industrial profitability in Mexico due to the recession conditions of the early 1980s and the accompanying decapitalization of Mexico following the peso devaluations of 1982. Many industrial concerns have been idled indefinitely due both to market conditions and to managerial and investor decisions to "migrate" their capital into safer bank depositories in the United States.

A continuing development problem in Mexico, however, has been the reluctance of enterprises to modernize and to hide behind cheap labor (while working politically to keep it cheap, often with the collusion of union officials) and government protectionism while embracing archaic technology and primitive construction and manufacturing methods. Mexican factories often did not take advantage of economies of scale and deliberately kept prices high and production low through the creation of oligopolies. The case most often cited of this sort of large-scale diseconomy is the automotive industry.[32]

The automotive industry was still protected by a 100 percent import tariff on cars assembled abroad in 1977. Official unionism was another source of protection via sweetheart contracts between management and the PRI's official CTM. After the mid-1960s the official unions were increasingly challenged by independent automotive workers' unions that were more aggressive in their efforts to promote employees' interests both vis-a-vis management and before government arbitration and conciliation boards.[33] Occasionally this was done in conjunction with leftist political parties. The upsurge of an independent unionism in the automotive industry could encourage a similar development in other major industries as well. It was spearheaded in Mexico by the FITIM or International Industrial Metalworkers Federation which sought to protect the gains of workers in industrialized nations against the expansion to cheap labor markets, like Mexico, of transnational automobile manufacturing companies.[34] At this moment of writing it is not clear that independent unionism in Mexico has won greater salary or benefit increases than has official government unionism. A broad political implication is seen in the potential alliance of the independent unions with opposition political parties if Mexico's electoral reforms continue to allow for greater politically-relevant participation by opposition parties.

Also questionable is whether Mexico's experiment with state-run automotive industries has been successful. In 1983 the de la Madrid government sold to French capital the VAM (American Motors) and Renault concessions that had been operated by government *paraestatal* enterprises for some twenty years. In making the sale the Mexican government agreed to absorb the debts of these concerns, which had been managed by the state financial group known as SOMEX. The losses suffered by VAM and Renault had for long been blamed on their inability to penetrate the North American car market, including Canada. As a condition for the sale, it was reported, agreements had been worked out with both parent firms to allow Mexican automobiles to be sold in North America.[35] It was hoped that economies of scale would enter here allowing greater volume in automobile production and resultant lower costs for Mexican purchasers. One industrial spokesman, Miguel Angel Rivera Villaseñor, charged that in 1980 the automobile industry had been responsible for 47 percent of Mexico's commercial deficit and 58 percent of that in 1981.[36] Opposition parties criticized the sale of these automotive industries. On the left the PST and PRT charged the de la Madrid government with selling out to private enterprise. The center/right PAN lamented that the sale was to foreign purchasers rather than to Mexicans.

Poor signs for Mexico's automotive industry appeared in late 1983 when the government announced that it would close for the remainder of the year the DINA diesel engine plant at Ciudad Sahagún due to poor sales and financial problems within the industry. That plant produced public transport buses and it was announced that 75 percent of some 4500 workers would be laid off. This action followed cutbacks in automotive production at Ford and General Motors facilities that reduced by 50 percent the income of workers in those plants. An estimated 10,000 workers were idled in 1983 alone. The Mexican congress passed a law to go into effect in 1984 that would prohibit the production of 8-cylinder autos, a move to force the industry to concentrate on majority needs rather than on supplying luxuries to the upper classes.[37]

Automobiles are for the relatively well-to-do in Mexico. But everyone has to have food. In the field of food distribution an example of government entrepreneurship is the national staple food products company known as CONASUPO. The Mexican government has in recent decades held up this entity as a showcase organization. One such occasion was January 24, 1968, when the president of El Salvador, Fidel Sánchez Hernández, paid an official state visit to CONASUPO facilities. He said "we congratulate the Mexican people for achieving this level of perfection in an institution of such popular benefit."[38] There are mixed views of CONASUPO, the official one and opposition criticism. It should be noted, however, that CONASUPO continues to function into the 1980s and there is general agreement that the enterprise has served an important function in Mexico despite its shortcomings. Were the administrative norms and practices of CONASUPO reformed it might indeed become a showcase enterprise for government entrepreneurship in Third World nations.

Here is an official view of what CONASUPO (*Companía Nacional de Subsistencias Populares*) has been, and is, intended to be.[39] CONASUPO's administrative roots can be traced back to 1938 when an affiliate of the state-owned Banco Nacional de Comercio Exterior was transformed into the Comité Regulador del Mercado de las Subsistencias (Committee to Regulate the Market of Staple Goods). In 1941 this committee was converted into another organism (Nacional Distribuidora y Reguladora, S.A. de C.V.) that involved government, private sector, and organized labor (practically the same as government) participation in a joint attempt to regulate prices of staple goods throughout Mexico. This became CEIMSA (Companía Exportadora e Importadora Mexicana S.A.) in 1948. CEIMSA is well-known in recent Mexican history as a programmatic bulwark of the PRI and can be translated loosely as Mexican National Import–Export Company (colloquially it has been called the Mexican National Company for the Exploitation of Corn).[40]

By 1952 CEIMSA was subsidizing the production and sale of corn, beans, eggs, and wheat throughout Mexico and had begun its own system of distribution of staple goods to poor people in depressed neighborhoods. A part of this program was a series of mobile vans which travelled to the various neighborhoods selling staple goods at very low prices and under a rationing system. On the basis of the present author's investigations it seems certain that many poor people in Mexico were benefited by this program and a part of their enduring respect for President López Mateos is rooted in the successes of CEIMSA.

In 1961 CEIMSA was liquidated and replaced with CONASUPO S.A. (Companía Nacional de Subsistencias Populares S.A.). During June of that year the government announced a vastly expanded program of mobile units that would be managed under a subsidiary of CONASUPO called Companía Distribuidora de Subsistencias Populares S.A. and would seek to extend services to all parts of the nation. Ultimately, in 1965, the S.A. was dropped and the organism became CONASUPO, which differed from its predecessor in that it would be decentralized administratively with a headquarters in each state (prior to that time CONASUPO had functioned nationally out of a headquarters in the Federal District).

As it exists today CONASUPO has two basic functions: 1) protection of peasant and agrarian incomes generally via a system of price subsidies not unlike the U.S. system, at least in principle; 2) support for the purchasing power of the common people by means of a decentralized (and mobile) system for distribution of staple goods of high quality at the lowest feasible price. Price supports are in effect now for corn, wheat, beans, rice, sorgum, saffron, sesame, soy beans, and cotton seed. Official figures published by one of CONASUPO's dependencies called CIANO (*Centro de*

Investigaciones Agrícolas del Noroeste) located in Ciudad Obregón indicated that a high level of productivity had been achieved throughout much of Mexico under the aegis of the protective price supports.[41] CONASUPO fixes the prices which may vary among regions for the individual commodities. This is done to provide an incentive to the farmer for increasing his productive capacity.

The effect of the price supports is to guarantee that the farmer will have an immediate market for his produce and a rapid financial return despite the various economic cycles through which Mexico, like other countries, must pass. The agricultural producer, whether he be a small tract farmer, an ejidatario, or a larger producer organized into associations or credit unions, takes his products to one of the 615 authorized CONASUPO receiving centers. There the grain is recorded and stored by the agency known as *Almacenes Nacionales de Depósito S.A.* which is also a part of CONASUPO, but with a limited separate autonomy from it.[42] When the agricultural product arrives at any of the authorized CONASUPO centers, a laboratory analysis is made of the quality of the grain to determine if it can be accepted for market within the program. If his grain passes, the farmer receives a form that is labelled CM-13 which he takes to one of the official banks (Banco Agrícola, Banco Ejidal) participating in the CONASUPO program where the total value of his harvest is determined and reconciled with any credits which may have been charged to his account. The difference is then paid to the farmer in cash or in a form of his choosing. The final record of each transaction is sent to CONASUPO headquarters in Mexico City.

There is no official limit to the amount of grain that a participant farmer may sell to CONASUPO but there are fixed dates that vary from year to year for the sale of various grains. It is intended that the guaranteed market approach will prevent the growth of black markets in staple crops. In addition to price supports and unlimited sale guarantees, CONASUPO provides a subsidized fertilizer program, irrigation development subsidies, and offers controlled credit to participant farmers via one of several participating government banks.

The second basic goal of CONASUPO mentioned above, i.e., the distribution of high quality staple goods at low prices, is carried out via several dependencies that operate trucks in working class neighborhoods throughout Mexico and serve an estimated population of over two million poor people. Despite criticism of CONASUPO that will be cited presently, the mobile truck stores have done much to endear the government to Mexicans. In addition there is a chain of CONASUPO stores in poor neighborhoods where a system of rationing aids in guaranteeing a minimum diet to the poor. In rural areas there are country stores providing the same service. The Mexican government projects significant increases in the numbers of such facilities during the coming years.

In addition to the above there is a CONASUPO dependency which provides powdered milk and another specializing in corn meal and flour. These tend to set market prices although there is a free market which usually runs higher. CONASUPO claims to have special outreach personnel and programs specializing in aid to the rural poor and in helping rural people to set up new homesteads where ejido franchises or other land grants have been made. Thus the CONASUPO program is intended by the government as a major arm of both economic and social policy. It is evidence that the Mexican government has tried to reach the needs of the poor with subsidized foodstuffs and social counselling.

Criticism of CONASUPO, however, focuses on inefficiency due to administrative corruption and charges the program with being more political than socioeconomic. It has been charged that officials of the agency swindled countryfolk out of the profits from their grain harvest, artificially elevated the price of food charged to the poor, and that Mexican grain was unnecessarily sold at below cost on the international market for the enrichment of government bureaucrats.[43] Whether better administration would improve CONASUPO's performance, or whether Mexico has fallen victim to demographic growth and economic recession, it is true that in the 1970s CONASUPO became a habitual importer of foodstuffs. In fact it became second only to PEMEX as a major public sector importer of foreign goods.[44] CONASUPO holds regular sidewalk auctions at its Mexico City center for food distribution (Central de Abastos) that is fed into the independent market system but under government price guidelines, an important feature of the Mexican food supply system.[45]

Insofar as staying power is concerned one would conclude that CONASUPO has been a relatively successful entrepreneurial venture for the Mexican government. There is broad feeling in Mexico that CONASUPO is more successful at the retail sales level than at fomenting production of basic foodstuffs in the countryside. Thus, as cited earlier, CONASUPO is Mexico's second largest importer of foreign goods after the oil agency PEMEX. One more example of governmental entrepreneurship should be considered and in this instance the outcome is less positive. This involves the government's regional steel production center in Michoacán known as SICARTSA which was nearing completion in 1975.

The name SICARTSA, a Spanish acronym for Siderúrgica Lázaro Cárdenas Las Truchas S.A., makes little sense when translated literally, but it was well-described by Marvin Alisky as "the Mexican government's new complex to make the steel industry self-sufficient."[46] Launched in the early 1970s, SICARTSA had both economic development goals and those of political symbolism. Economically it was a government corporation intended to complement the private sector so as to achieve import substitution and end Mexico's dependence upon imported steel by the late 1970s. It was also meant to provide thousands of new jobs, that is, it was to be a labor-intensive industry, although this did not work out. Ultimately it was intended that the Mexican federal government would dominate Mexico's steel industry.

Politically and symbolically the project was the brainchild of a former president, the late Lázaro Cárdenas, who lobbied effectively with the Díaz Ordaz administration for location of the project in his home state of Michoacán. The location was blessed by the presence of good hydroelectric sources, rich iron ore deposits, and the availability of abundant labor. Indeed, Michoacán traditionally had been one of the principal states from which Mexicans migrated because of chronic unemployment there. Symbolically, then, SICARTSA became the aging caudillo's legacy to his home state. Cárdenas hardly needed to improve his symbolic capability, having been perhaps Mexico's most charismatic president since the great revolution of 1910–17. But the legacy of a Mexico independent in steel, and done in the name of Cárdenas, was a politically useful tool for the PRI. The coastal village where the steel complex was to be located was renamed Cárdenas City as well.

The venture captured the imagination of both governmental and private entrepreneurs, and in the case of the latter some envy and resentment. It was supposed to be functional by 1976 when President Echeverría left office. Part of SICARTSA was in fact operating, but not all of it. Plans had been for the complex to generate 10 million tons of steel annually by the end of the century, hopefully making SICARTSA the largest such complex in Latin America. But early in his presidency José López Portillo suspended some of the construction on the project. Both he and outgoing President Echeverría had inaugurated SICARTSA shortly before the transfer of power in December 1976. They announced that the equipment needed to run SICARTSA had been acquired in 13 distinct countries so as not to tie them to any one source of capital goods and replacement parts.[47] Of the SICARTSA investment, 40 percent was made by the Mexican government and the remainder was financed through international loans via Nacional Financiera. The overall investment at the end of Echeverría's term had exceeded original estimates by some 24 percent. SICARTSA might be symbolically Mexican but there was a considerable external debt underlying it. Because the foreign loans were made in dollars, the 1976 devaluation of the peso almost doubled Mexico's cash indebtedness. Eight months after its opening, SICARTSA was operating at only 30 percent of capacity, a fact which its director, Adolfo Orive Alba, explained in terms of a natural breaking-in period necessary for both men and machines. Other steel experts charged that the low output was due to incompetent management.[48]

Shortly after the opening of SICARTSA the same Orive Alba was quoted as having said, "We live today in the civilization of steel and steel is a thermometer to use for measuring the development of a people."[49] A critical analysis likened SICARTSA to a "black elephant" and called it a bureaucratic monstrosity of managers and submanagers with little to do but look important. It was argued that there were a total of 40 managerial positions at SICARTSA of which only 15 were necessary, the remainder being expensive aviadores.[50] This was in contrast to quality-of-life conditions for the proletarian classes whose labor had contributed to the building of the SICARTSA complex.

Affected were some 17,000 common laborers who came for the initial construction phase of SICARTSA and who, once it was completed, were discharged as unneeded unskilled laborers. They and their families were attracted from various parts of the country, lured by the myth of permanent opportunity. They came in such quantities as to depress salaries to the advantage of the construction contractors (who apparently passed little of this saving on to the Mexican government). The majority of the migrant workers remained in squatter settlements, slums (*asentamientos ilegales*) surrounding Cárdenas City. This was hardly in keeping with the symbolism the late president had envisaged. SICARTSA was supposed to provide poverty relief. Instead, it had created new slums, vast concentrations of poverty surrounding the steel complex, a bitter testimony to the expendability of Mexican humanity. When reporters asked the management of SICARTSA about the misery of their former employees a spokesman replied, "Anyone in Mexico is free to choose his place of residence as he pleases."[51]

The final word on SICARTSA is not necessarily in, but at the end of the López Portillo sexenio it had not yet achieved its intended goals. The theory underlying SICARTSA was that concentration on such capital goods as a major steel plant would generate supporting industries and businesses. Perhaps with efficient management that would have occurred but this would also have implied efficient and realistic credit availability for potential service industries. In 1980 the SICARTSA experiment was labelled a colossal boondoggle because of shoddy management, inadequate infrastructure, inferior quality control, soaring prices, and inattention to the social services that should have been provided the workers.[52] The recession of the early 1980s has not promoted SICARTSA. As of this writing it is uncertain whether the de la Madrid government will be able to salvage it.

PETROLEUM AND THE GREAT
PEMEX SCANDAL

The development of Mexico's nationalized petroleum was sketched in the first and third chapters of this book. Here let us focus on the contemporary operation of PEMEX as an instrument of national development and at the same time a source of political discord. From December of 1976 until June of 1981 Mexico's state-run petroleum company PEMEX was directed by Jorge Díaz Serrano. A native of Nogales, Sonora, this petroleum engineer guided Mexico's oil development during the early years of great hope and expectation that were summarized in Chapter One and which underlay Mexico's short-lived aspirations to world power and for prosperity on the domestic scene. That this did not occur was due in part to the vicissitudes of the world oil market and in part to administrative inefficiency and corruption within PEMEX. The case offers valuable insights into how corruption may stultify the development drives of a Third World nation. It demonstrates also that major national administrative breakdowns can be linked to international influences and actors. The case of Jorge Díaz Serrano and his cohorts had to be resolved if President de la Madrid's campaign pledge of "moral renovation" were to have meaning; but its resolution would place the entire Mexican political system on trial as well.

As we have seen, President de la Madrid took office in December of 1982. Before he became the PRI's candidate for president he had been the titular head of Programming and Budget, a cabinet position under President López Portillo. De la Madrid's office, it is reported, knew as early as August 1980 that grave financial irregularities were occurring in the management of PEMEX.[53] Apparently these charges were sufficiently serious to have merited penal action against the PEMEX high management. One of the prominent figures in this scenario was Jorge Díaz Serrano, director of PEMEX and intimate friend of President López Portillo. Internal studies done by Programming and Budget were made public by the Mexican critical press in May of 1981. The following month Díaz Serrano resigned from his first major public position, one which brought his name to the top of Mexico's oil development euphoria and even placed him high on the list of those frequently speculated as being the verdadero tapado who would succeed López Portillo. Instead, with the forced resignation, the "real veiled one" turned out to be de la Madrid who then headed Programming and Budget. One can find rich ground for speculation as to the cross-pressures on López Portillo during this process.

Early in July 1981 Díaz Serrano announced that Mexico would drop its international price of crude oil by $4 per barrel from $38.50 to $34.50.

He defended this action as an attempt to conserve Mexico's oil clients in a market then controlled more by buyers than sellers.[54] Mexico's buyers were pressuring for a price reduction in the light of the ongoing world oil glut fueled by Saudi Arabia's commitment to maintain its current level of production (10.3 million barrels per day) despite OPEC measures to reduce barrel per day output. But by lowering its price and continuing production Mexico contributed to the world oil glut. The decision to cut the price by $4 per barrel was apparently made by Díaz Serrano and came as a fait accompli to López Portillo and his cabinet. Díaz Serrano, and PEMEX, were becoming targets for bureaucratic envy within the official governing power structure. Foes of Díaz Serrano, like José Andrés Oteyza, the minister of Patrimony and Industrial Development, took advantage of the "precipitous" oil price cut to demand the ouster of Díaz Serrano. "Other critics complained about the bloated salaries and the egregious corruption in PEMEX, a company run as if it were the director-general's personal fiefdom."[55] The revelation of government documents implicating Díaz Serrano in fraud came at an opportune time for his enemies to stop the upward thrust of this powerseeker and his camarilla. The revealed documents and the oil price-cut decision led to Díaz Serrano's resignation on June 6, 1981. The corruption charges painted a picture of waste and chaotic financial administration in the management of Mexico's most important enterprise. They included monetary shortages and losses, programs without supervision, confused accounting practices, and some $34 million in fraud attributed directly to Díaz Serrano as director general.

One of the most flagrant cases of financial mismanagement involved the international purchase of two oil and gas transport ships.[56] A subsequent investigation of the ship purchase was made by the SCGF (Secretaría de la Controloría General de la Federación) or controller-general's office. It led to formal charges against Díaz Serrano by the PGR, Procuraduría General de la República (the Justice Department). The substance of the charges was that during 1979 and 1980 PEMEX advertised for bids on the construction of two ocean-going oil and gas tankers. One bid came from the Boelwerf Company of Belgium, but its tankers were originally judged to be inadequate for the needs of PEMEX. Subsequently PEMEX contracted to buy these same two tankers through an intermediary firm known as Navigas International of Liberia. PEMEX is said to have paid a total of $158 million to Navigas International, which was $34 million more than would have been the case had the purchase been made directly from Boelwerf.[57] But PEMEX technicians had already gone on record against that purchase. When the director general authorized the same purchase, for more money, and temporarily veiled the procedure by use of an intermediary he was apparently reflecting the pressures of other interests. One of these seems to have been President López Portillo's own sister.

As the story unfolds the anatomy of corruption stands out in bold relief. On the basis of revelations in *Excelsior* (July 7, 1983) and later in *Proceso* it appears that until January of 1980 even Díaz Serrano resisted the efforts of several Belgian promoters to sell PEMEX the two tankers from the firm Boelwerf.[58] Shortly thereafter, however, it is alleged that Alicia López Portillo, the sister and private secretary of the president, called Díaz Serrano to persuade him to purchase the two tankers which he finally did in April of 1980. In November of the same year Díaz Serrano learned that documented proof was being gathered to demonstrate the fraud that had been committed and he is said to have ordered a cover-up documentary operation. But several of his subordinates had already testified informally before congressional investigators as to what was happening and reiterated that ships clearly unsuited to the needs of PEMEX were being purchased under pressures originating in the president's office.[59] This had been done at a flagrant loss to the Mexican nation which PEMEX would have to cover by means of more international loans. Clearly the president's family was implicated. But he chose not to try to save Díaz Serrano, the man he had almost promoted into the presidency. Some Mexicans think that López Portillo was then planning his own ultimate defense and eventual flight from Mexico.

A subcommittee of the Chamber of Deputies was charged in 1983 with holding hearings to determine whether Díaz Serrano, then a federal senator imposed by López Portillo on Sonora, could be *desaforado*, that is, stripped of congressional immunity so as to permit his prosecution for the crime of fiscal mismanagement and fraud in his former role as director general of PEMEX. The purchase of the two Belgian ships was only one of several charges brought against him by the Procuraduría. The subcommittee was composed of three PRI deputies and one PAN deputy. It deliberated the entire month of July 1983 and heard testimony by Díaz Serrano and his attorneys. At the surprising conclusion of the hearings Díaz Serrano was stripped of his congressional immunity. The PAN deputy, Juan José Hinojosa, said that the former PEMEX official made no defense at all regarding the charges, he only questioned procedural technicalities and "tried to buy time." This was something of a first, priistas juding priistas and voting to condemn one of their own.

Díaz Serrano repeatedly insisted "I am a party man, a man of the system." His defense was always procedural, *desmayada* (faltering), and never went to the bottom of the problem. His pending divorce was cited as a tactic for dividing his fortune thereby saving half of it, the spectre of a once powerful man now fallen into disgrace pervaded the hearings, and observers reflected that he must have been in the service of "third parties."[60] But the accusations of the Procuraduría were devastating. The PRI deputies made no effort at cover-up. Everything was honorable, "formally impeccable." By including a PAN deputy an image of political pluralism was conveyed. The PRI regime was behaving so as to honor Miguel de la Madrid's promise of "moral renovation." This could be a first in contemporary Mexican politics, for as Juan José Hinojosa repeated, in order to judge Díaz Serrano the system would be judging itself. And he reflected on what Díaz Serrano might have been: "he could have been giving orders now from the presidential residence at Los Pinos. It would have taken a mere capricious decision from López Portillo to make him president. This is possible in the Mexican system. And frankly that is terrifying!"[61]

Apart from the tribulations of Díaz Serrano there were other administrative features of the PEMEX scandal which reflect upon Mexico's developmental potential. Contracts were given to foreign firms for assistance in discovering and developing Mexico's oil reserves. Critics urged that allowing foreigners to exploit subsoil riches violated the constitution.[62] Similar charges concerned secret negotiations held with the United States for development of a Chiapas to Tamaulipas gasoduct and for the sale of natural gas to the United States. Three PEMEX functionaries were sentenced to five-year prison terms for their negotiations with, and bribes received from, the U.S. firm Applied Process Products Overseas Inc.[63] PEMEX also was found to have granted in some years as much as 40 percent of the perforation contracts for new oil wells to the petroleum workers syndicate STPRM and had given that union's officials generous subsidies for "worker services," which funds never reached their destination.[64] Millions of dollars were overspent on foreign purchases of oil drilling equipment and much of it remained unclaimed on foreign docks costing Mexico some $38 million monthly in rental fees, according to documents and internal studies acquired from PEMEX itself.[65] One international company doing business with PEMEX listed U.S. Vice President George Bush as a former interested party but it was not claimed that Bush himself had anything to do with the PEMEX contracts.[66]

Here it should be noted that Díaz Serrano had extensive investments in the international oil business and it is reported that he had helped to found one Texas company, the Golden Lane Drilling Company in 1965. Upon accepting appointment as director general of PEMEX he said that he had severed all ties with these companies, a claim his critics never believed. It was further reported that

> companies founded by Díaz Serrano hold lucrative contracts with
> PEMEX . . . one such firm, PERMARGO, drilled the exploratory well
> Ixtoc I that poured over three million barrels of crude oil into the Gulf
> of Mexico in what scientists have called the worst oil spill in the history of
> the industry.[67]

The 1979 blowout of the offshore oil well Ixtoc I and the long delay in
controlling it was laid to administrative inefficiency within PEMEX.[68]
That enterprise was also blamed for serious ecological harm done to the
states of Campeche and Tabasco. In May 1983 PEMEX signed an agreement with the Mexican government to repair the damage and make restitution to the victims.[69]

The petroleum workers syndicate STPRM (*Sindicato de Trabajadores Petroleros de la República Mexicana*) was riddled with corruption
under the leadership of Joaquín Hernández Galicia (known as "La
Quina") and Salvador Barragán Camacho (also a federal senator); great
misappropriation of union funds was frequently documented in the critical press.[70] PEMEX officials accepted bribes from Texas businessman
Donald Crawford in return for oil development contracts. Crawford was
subsequently charged with illegal practices by the U.S. government.[71]
Those contracts were said to have included $97 million in overpayments
out of the Mexican treasury.[72] One of the worst abuses in the PEMEX
scandal involved a union-based empire that was established through
worker exploitation and abuse of community and environment. This allegedly existed with the blessing of the PEMEX management and via
sweetheart contracts with the petroleum workers union STPRM. It was
reported that from commissions on digging contracts and subventions for
social works the principal union leaders took in 100 million pesos annually.[73] This was the result of working agreements between the union and
Díaz Serrano. The syndicate leaders gained control of union pension
funds and additional worker contributions into the high millions of pesos.
Investments made with these funds included expanses of cultivable land,
clothing factories, furniture stores, movie theatres, and other enterprises
which union leaders used freely and with great personalism. Few benefits
from these investments were found to accrue to the workers.[74]

Juan Sierra, a peasant from the village of Oteapán in the state of Veracruz was once employed by PEMEX as a laborer. He had to pay 2000
pesos to a union boss to get his job, a contract which expired in 28 days.
Then he had to pay another 2000 and each month thereafter the fee
would increase. He continued to work off and on for PEMEX in the early
1980s but raised food on a plot of land he rented to be able to eat during
times when there was no work. He said that too many people have been attracted to the oil wells, more than can be employed. The official union

STPRM allows its officials to extort fees from the workers; it is a form of internal discipline. Juan Sierra also made other monthly payments: 600 pesos for taxes, 10 pesos for union dues, 10 pesos for cultural promotion, and 15 pesos to maintain the workers' casino.[75] These payments plus the under-the-table quota to keep his job and renew it left little out of Juan Sierra's monthly salary of 3500 pesos. Juan knows nothing about the social or cultural works which the union claims it provides. His case is believed to be typical. A contrasting view, however, holds that PEMEX workers are among the highest paid and that they enjoy substantial subsidies for education, medical services, housing, and recreation. That view also stresses that the union STPRM's power and cohesion is related to the nepotism it practices.[76]

Following the revocation of Díaz Serrano's legislative immunity in July 1983 he was jailed and placed under house arrest pending his trial. Two former officials of his PEMEX administration Ignacio de León and Jesús Chavarría were sought by the Procuraduría which used diplomatic channels to close their Swiss bank accounts. They, together with former Rural Bank official and former federal deputy Miguel Lerma Candelaria, became in 1983 the most wanted persons of the Mexican justice services.[77] At that point the petroleum union STPRM began a process that would give the appearance of its own house cleaning. The principal leaders Hernández Galicia and Barragán Camacho ordered the apprehension of their principal lieutenant Héctor García Hernández, known as "El Trampas." When it was found that he had taken temporary refuge in McAllen, Texas, he was abducted from there on September 8, 1983, by orders from his former colleagues and returned to Mexico in the trunk of a car.[78] Of this a veteran petroleum union former official Eulalio Ibáñez declared that all three STPRM officials were part of the same system of corruption which had served the regime well and had in the past been protected by it. He added that "fundamental political change in Mexico must come from the conscience of the masses who today are prostituted."[79]

Under Hernández Galicia ("La Quina") the STPRM could publicly claim not only to have political and economic independence but that leader declared "we can tell even presidents when they are right and wrong."[80] And there was reason to believe that "La Quina" had aspirations of succeeding to the leadership of Mexico's umbrella labor organization the CTM once the octogenarian Fidel Velásquez had passed from the scene. Labor is a major political power in Mexico. This made the "moral renovation" promises of President de la Madrid and his government's prosecution of corruption in PEMEX an essentially sensitive matter. It would be difficult to prosecute Díaz Serrano and his colleagues without touching the leadership of the petroleum workers union and that of the

CTM. As the PAN deputy quoted earlier put it, this would be, in effect, challenging the system to judge itself. That process, if painful enough, might jar loose the traditional doors of Mexican political stability; for if, in the end, Díaz Serrano were not really and truly tried then the regime's integrity would be squarely and publicly undercut.

The policy on oil followed in the 1976 to 1982 period by Díaz Serrano and López Portillo was keyed to the "ripe tomatoes" analogy which the former once used, namely that if more of the product were on hand than could be safely stored it should be sold on the open market at the best price one could get. An opposing critical point of view often expressed in Mexico was that the oil would not spoil and that it should be preserved as an economic weapon against the hegemony of the competing blocs of industrialized nations. For a basically poor nation like Mexico to sell its oil to provide debt service for the purchase of equipment needed to extract that very oil was a form of economic suicide, a view that the cases of Venezuela and Iran might be invoked to defend. Capitalist nations of the world, which consume the greatest part of Third World oil, contributed to the world oil glut of 1981 and 1982 by eliminating much waste and curbing their own consumption. Nations of the Third World, heavily indebted to the industrial powers, could not afford to store the oil. They had to sell it to service their debts. Perhaps they could have defaulted! But in Mexico's case, in order to sell the oil in sufficient quantity to pay the foreign debt more equipment and more debt was deemed necessary. Corruption in the management of Mexico's state-owned petroleum enterprise pushed that debt even farther. The government did not use its recourse to taxing its own business sector to secure the needed capital; it was committed to a policy of protecting the powerful Mexican bourgeois (as Levy and Székely have argued).[81] So the policy of selling more oil was followed even though this merely contributed to the world oil glut. Thus, in 1983 alone, estimates were that Mexico owed $35 million in foreign debt service. Exporting 1.5 million barrels daily at an average price of $28 per barrel would not meet that debt service.

In order to sell petroleum in high volume Mexico had to indebt itself also at high volume. "Thus, PEMEX, if it sells 14 billion dollars of oil in 1983 it would be required to pay 3 million of this in interest on the debt contracted for equipment needed to expand its oil production capacity accordingly."[82] But Mexico's expectation that the United States would continue buying enough of its oil to finance its debt turned out to be unfounded. In 1982 American purchases decreased. Other international factors were involved. As Iran emerged from its war with Iraq, the former increased its oil output thereby furthering the world glut. Mexico was caught dependent upon a market demand that had ceased to exist.

The official thinking of PEMEX clarifies how Mexico fell victim to unforeseen market forces. It was assumed that between 1976 and 1982 (the López Portillo sexenio) the necessary expansion of PEMEX's facilities would cost about $15 billion and that $9 billion would have to be borrowed abroad.[83] From the $15 billion, a return of $40 billion in accumulated profits to PEMEX, half in foreign currency, was anticipated. About one-third of these profits would be expected to go to foreign creditors, the remainder going to Mexico. This was expected to continue to the point that Mexico would be freed of its dependence on foreign creditors.[84] But what happened, instead, was that an oil glut occurred in 1981 and in 1982 and Mexico's income dropped due to that market force. Moreover, as we have seen, much of Mexico's revenue from foreign oil sales was lost to corruption. That is why Mexico remained seriously and perhaps hopelessly dependent on foreign creditors and markets. In October 1982 the government admitted that the petroleum exploration debt would be inherited by the coming generation. Some 30 percent of the foreign public debt of over $80 billion corresponded to PEMEX. Despite the millions of dollars collected from the foreign sale of oil the Mexican economy seemed worse off at the end of the López Portillo sexenio in 1982 than it was when he inherited it following the crisis of 1976. "In synthesis, petroleum concentrated wealth even more, broke the back of the economy, and impoverished the majority of the population."[85]

A major figure in the domestic Mexican debate over petroleum policy has been Heberto Castillo, an engineering professor and leader of the Mexican Workers Party, PMT. His criticism at times forced the government to reply to his public charges about PEMEX mismanagement and oil policy more broadly. That in itself might be called a first in contemporary Mexican politics, that is, the rise of a single critic to such prominence that the PRI-dominated government felt obliged to respond publicly and without clandestine reprisals against the critic. Castillo outlined a depressing picture in 1983. He argued that the government's effort to claim a balance of payments surplus really masked a deficit caused by foreign debt service and by the wasteful burning of up to 66 percent of Mexico's natural gas out of inept extraction and conservation techniques.[86]

Castillo denounced the burning off of uncontrolled gas as a crime against Mexico claiming that this occurred for reasons of technical incompetence and because of the unwise frenzy of PEMEX officials to exploit more oil. Natural gas is a typical by-product of Mexico's Reforma oil fields surrounding the state of Tabasco in the southeast. Gas that comes out with the oil must either be treated for use, reinjected into the earth, or burned as it is allowed to escape. Since the amount of gas pumped out by PEMEX has, in the recent past, surpassed the company's technical refinement capacity it has been flare-burned in order to keep the oil for export coming out.[87] That is the process cited by Castillo as wasting Mexico's resources, a form of burning money that could be spent on social services and food for the poor. Beyond this he foresaw that if Mexico's estimated petroleum reserves continued to be exploited for foreign exchange at the rate of 12 percent annually the country would be without oil of its own by the year 2003.[88] The country, said Castillo, was trapped economically with no way out, adding that creating an ostensible balance of payments surplus by diminishing the importation of vital staple goods only added to Mexico's store of human misery.

In the early 1980s an oft-expressed goal was for Mexico to produce some 2.25 million barrels of exportable oil daily (not including natural gas). It was widely believed that by the mid-1980s Mexico could be exporting over 3 million barrels daily to the United States alone. In the first quarter of 1983 Mexico produced (not all for export) an average 2.57 million barrels daily, an increase of 4.2 percent over the same period in 1982. Exports showed a 19.7 percent increase to 1.7 million barrels per day and it was held that this pattern would prevail throughout 1983 yielding a total revenue of about $14 billion for the year.[89] It is that same figure which domestic critics of Mexico's oil operation then claimed as inadequate to service the foreign debt. Mexico maintained price stability on oil during most of 1983 and a major Japanese purchaser committed itself to 110,000 barrels per day for an extended period provided that a per barrel price of $29 dollars was not exceeded.[90] The Mexicans would, of course, like to raise this price later in the 1980s, thereby seeing their foreign exchange earnings rise. In early 1983 Mexico enjoyed a trade surplus that could hardly be boasted; it was largely because the dearth of foreign exchange forced drastic reductions in imports regardless of how vital the needs of the masses for foodstuffs in particular may have been. This dilemma had been foreseen in 1980 by a Mexican economist. Jesús Puente Leyva foresaw Mexican agriculture taking up a rear guard position as far as investment priorities were concerned. He saw a deterioration of rural life and an increasing Mexican dependence on foreign foodstuffs and raw materials with continued rural-to-urban migration and clandestine migration northward. Further, he predicted that the increasing need to import foodstuffs would consume 35 to 50 percent of all revenue from Mexico's export of petroleum.[91]

The importation of foodstuffs brings to mind a particular irony of the Mexican petroleum story. In the southeastern states of Tabasco and Campeche the operations of PEMEX have adversely affected the environment, fishing, and agriculture. Dredges, drills and pollution have imperiled the life of renewable resources such as farms and fishing. To avoid conflict with peasants by drilling on their lands, PEMEX has set up its drilling operations in many waterways, thereby polluting entire regions and rendering the water unusable for irrigation and toxic to fish and humans. Renewable resources have been sacrificed for nonrenewable ones. Peasants forced off their land by the pollution or attracted by the lure of oil money stop producing, even for their own subsistence. Food prices near the oil fields have gone sky high. And Mexico must import all the more food.[92] Corruption allows this process to continue unrelieved. But the question of reforming the corrupt system has broader implications for all of Mexican politics, because PEMEX is a large replica (with its unions) of the broader Mexican political system and its institutional quandary. George W. Grayson posed the question well in his excellent treatment of the subject: "Why do PEMEX and other agencies acquiesce in, if not nourish, such flagrant corruption? The most cynical explanation is that malfeasance permeates the monopoly itself, and that's a 'clean-up' drive might not be limited to the union's Augean stable".[93] The corruption of PEMEX seems to permeate the entire governmental and political system. Thus being Mexico's largest state enterprise makes PEMEX an important case to study in any effort to evaluate the country's thrust toward development goals.

In summary and conclusion, Mexican petroleum inspired the euphoric belief that the nation could become a major industrial power by the year 2000. Growth rates were expected to absorb more of the working force and possibly, although not necessarily, result in a more favorable profile of national income distribution.[94] Government policy assumed the growth was inevitable if technology were provided to pump more oil. Along with the oil-based industrialization would go import substitution. This would require a "rationalization of protectionism of existing industrial plants in order to raise their efficiency and competitiveness and the aggressive development of a capital-goods industry."[95] That these developments have not occurred in part explains the continuing dilemma of Mexico's foreign indebtedness and internal financial crisis. Oil alone was not a stable basis for development. Mexico must remove itself from the status of exclusive dependence on the export of hydrocarbons because this resource will inevitably be used up, perhaps by the year 2000, and without a supplementary export capacity Mexico cannot expect to continue as an independent economic entity. At the same time its agriculture must become more self-sufficient in basic foodstuffs so as to eliminate the harmful balance of payments dilemma caused by the import of staple foods, not to mention the hardship this causes the Mexican population.

Given the administrative milieu in which Mexico's governmental entrepreneurship has operated in recent decades it is hard to be optimistic about future development goals based on state initiatives like PEMEX. Mexico's GNP in 1980 was about $80 billion, close to what its total foreign debt would soon be. By the year 2000 it hoped to increase that GNP four-fold. Clark Reynolds has characterized this hope as Mexico trying to accomplish in 20 years what the state of California alone took 30 years to achieve and in better economic circumstances to be sure.[96] And Mexico, the reverse of California, has had the problem of an oversupply of labor which must be exported to maintain socioeconomic stability. Should Mexico's oil reserves prove to be 120 billion barrels, and given a price stability above 35 dollars per barrel, the income therefrom could be over one trillion dollars or twelve-and-one-half times the 1980 GDP over coming decades.[97] This would undoubtedly mean continued inflationary pressures. But price declines, world petroleum gluts, and waste of resources due to inefficiency and corruption can undermine such predictions. Moreover, worker pressures in Mexico (where some 40 percent of the population shares around 10 percent of the national income) for a greater share in the GNP will continue if the population is not drastically controlled.

It is estimated that 20 percent of Mexican workers have at some time depended on emigration to support themselves. A large percentage of all Mexicans are impoverished and at least half the work force of some 20 million falls into that category in 1983. The work force should double by the year 2000 at its present rate of growth. Poverty in Mexico demands that a greater share of the oil wealth be devoted to social services; conditions of virtual class warfare, albeit poorly organized, already exist. For a country to see its labor force doubled in two decades without large-scale emigration is nearly unprecedented.[98] Mexico, thus, is very much at the mercy of American immigration policy in the labor facet of its economic development. Unlike some European experiences, Mexico's emigration is temporary and relatively fixed in the direction it can take.

There is need in Mexico for less capital-intensive investment and more labor-intensive development to absorb the labor surplus and avoid social pressures leading to political instability. Agricultural production, at the same time, needs to be drastically increased. One hopes it will also be labor-intensive agricultural growth. Rural and small town cottage industries need to be developed, even on a scale (and with government support) leading to international commerce for such small-scale industries. Rural-to-urban migration needs to be drastically reduced. Emigration northward to the United States must not be interrupted, from Mexico's point of view, before the year 2000 if then. And a proposal by economist Clark Reynolds for providing workers with concrete involvement in the capital stock of Mexico via a program of "workers'-bonds" could be implemented.[99] Furthermore, the Mexican government could improvise a scheme for subsidizing the investment of worker remittances from foreign labor of migrant workers.[100] All of this, however, would require honest efficient administration if it were to have salutary effects on Mexico's socioeconomic impasse. But the factors of labor force, agricultural output, export capability, and hydrocarbon dependency must all be coordinated rationally if Mexico is to avoid disaster before the end of the twentieth century.

Although the López Portillo sexenio has been widely excoriated for its corruption it is nonetheless true that administrative reforms enacted then contributed to the anticorruption drive against PEMEX that has taken broader form in President de la Madrid's "moral renovation" campaign. It is noteworthy that under the López Portillo reform a new Ministry of Planning and Budget was created as primus inter pares among other ministries and entities.[101] The basis for the charges against PEMEX came from studies done by Planning and Budget the under the directorship of Miguel de la Madrid. Planning and Budget becomes a new major actor in Mexican politics with the ascension of its director to the presidency in 1982. The web of camarilla-based power relationships will be a controlling factor in the new political establishment, and the character and drive of the incumbent president is probably still the determining element in the direction that change, if any, will take.

Oil promises to be a major factor in Mexican–U.S. relations of the future. Aside from the attention given habitually in the United States to negative factors like drugs from Mexico, illegal aliens from Mexico, oil spills from Mexico, and the Carter admnistration's dispute over the gasoduct negotiations,[102] there are several positive features of U.S.–Mexican energy relations that are to Mexico's credit and should be stressed. One is that Mexico has spent millions of dollars on the U.S.-made oil drilling equipment and plans billions of dollars of such purchases from the United States well into this decade. Also, a number of U.S. firms are under contract for specialized services, a fact not without political consequences in Mexico but having benefits for the U.S. contractors. Mexico can also guarantee the United States rapid petroleum access at lower prices and without the distance risks of dependence on the Persian Gulf countries. Moreover Mexico can give the United States something of a strategic reserve in the event that the Middle East should go up in a sequence of revolutionary explosions. For that same reason, of course, it is not in the interest of the United States to allow a Cuban or Nicaraguan style revolution to occur within its southern neighbor, at least not so long as U.S. technology is petroleum dependent.

PUBLIC HEALTH, EDUCATION, AND POVERTY

Provision of social welfare services, subsidies for education, and eradication of poverty have become hallmarks of the oil-rich countries of the Persian Gulf. This has not yet happened to Mexico. Social welfare is perhaps the most critical public need in Mexico today. Close to 80 percent of the national population is unable to provide itself with a standard of living that would be minimally acceptable by most U.S. standards. High-standard health care is available only for the small minority who can afford it. A larger middle class group receives minimal health protection. But well over half the Mexican population gets none or nearly none on a regular basis. Recourse to healers, *curanderos,* and home practitioners is the rule in Mexico. Suffering without medical attention is common.

Between 1980 and 1982 the budgetary resources assigned to the SSA, the national Secretariat of Health and Assistance increased by 132 percent; the budgetary increase for the subscription-membership IMSS, Mexican Social Security Institute, was 121 percent; and the respective figure for the ISSSTE (the federal workers' health plan, Social Service Institute for State Employees) was 61 percent.[103] But this did not allow medical services to expand adequately to keep up with the population. In global terms, in 1976 the IMSS had 1.33 beds for each 1000 qualified member-patients. By 1982 it had only 1.06 beds per 1000 and the minimum figure established by the World Health Organization is 1.8 beds per 1000 persons.[104] Considering that only those who are members of an officially recognized participating union or group can be members of the IMSS system (and it is not known for sure what the membership figure is but one 1982 estimate put it at 46.5 million persons) it means that the resources of IMSS are overtaxed and many millions of patients are left to depend on the general services of the SSA which are commonly described as poor, when available. The SSA tries to cover the poorest half of Mexican society or more than 50 million people. Here the bed-to-patient ratio is about 0.29 for each thousand persons and the doctor-to-patient ratio is about 0.31 per thousand.[105] Thus the SSA, which is charged with caring for all of Mexico's poor and marginal human beings has five times less access to resources to do this than has the IMSS which cares for the minority middle class.[106] Obviously this is one critical area in which an investment of oil profits (were there any) would be most welcome.

President Miguel de la Madrid has sought to decentralize health services in Mexico and to expand the capacity of the SSA so that all Mexicans may be covered. Under the stewardship of Guillermo Soberón Acevedo in a cabinet-rank secretaryship, problems of service duplication and ineffective resource and personnel allocation were scheduled for reform. This was to be accomplished within the broad umbrella of a National Health System, which would be accorded special funding provisions under the Secretariat of Programming and Budget. Ricardo García Sainz, director of IMSS, pointed to health care reform needs in Mexico including controlled centralized purchasing of medical supplies for the public health service and avoidance of over-installation of medical facilities in given areas at the expense of others.[107] It has been pointed out that Mexico needs its own truly national pharmaceutical industry to be run in the public interest as a paraestatal (state-run) enterprise. This would surely be opposed by the present industry, dominated largely by foreign concerns. Soberón Acevedo also has stressed Mexico's need to upgrade its professional training for medical practitioners.

Mexico's plans for major public health reform were embodied in an enabling law put before the congress in 1983 which would have radically enlarged the powers and jurisdiction of the SSA in the area of popular medicine.[108] It appeared in 1983 that Guillermo Soberón would have a major opportunity to become a pioneer in Mexico's public health reform quest. The usual questions about administrative ethics would apply here just as in the other public policy areas we have discussed. That would be especially critical in the reporting of health statistics as a basis for judging the performance of the proposed National Health System. Mexican health figures are often confusing and contradictory.

One set of mid-1983 figures contended that "officially, 15 million Mexicans have no medical services and 40 million others have incomplete services."[109] The same report held that altogether Mexico's three basic health programs (SSA, IMSS, ISSSTE) treated 99.7 million patients (Mexico's 1983 population was officially listed at around 72 million) so little comfort or certainty can be taken from the available statistics except to underscore the well-known general proposition that Mexico desperately needs health service reform. It was noted, for instance, that of some 450,000 registered deaths annually less than one percent is autopsied. This makes it difficult to determine the number of deaths due to such "new" diseases as those caused by environmental pollution and contamination.[110] But the prospects were hopeful, at least on paper, for Mexico was about to include the National Health System in the six-year development plan extending to 1988. This would also mean giving constitutional status to personal health as a basic legal right in Mexico.

Health has an impact on education. And education and nutrition are inextricably tied together. Those who are hungry can't learn and will probably abandon the effort in search of food. Mexico's National Institute for Nutrition contends that some 100,000 children die each year from diseases stemming directly from malnutrition.[111] The institute claims that malnutrition is largely to blame for the fact that the average level of achievement among school-age children is the third grade of elementary school.[112] It is further estimated by the institute that for educational purposes 60 percent of Mexicans live in social deprivation and, of them, 45 percent live in either bad or outright inhumane conditions.[113] Of the two and one-half million babies that were born in Mexico during 1979 one million and a half are expected to suffer physical and mental damage because of malnutrition and one in three would be expected to die before reaching six years of age.[114] Officials of foreign companies interviewed in Mexico (Anderson Clayton, Ralston Purina, and Nestle) pointed to Mexico's food deficiency and linked it to the related problems of reliance on the importation of grain, uncontrolled population growth, and poor transportation systems.[115] It is true also that Mexico's domestic meat production has dropped due to the unprofitability of cattle raising in the absence of tax or other incentives for production in this sector. Meat production is part of the overall dilemma of protein deficiency as a contributing factor in malnutrition. Beans are a partial answer to protein deficiency but they are now being imported and prices have risen.

Children in the schools of poor neighborhoods frequently collapse in class from nutrition-related illnesses. Teachers report that many children are unable to eat breakfast before going to school and in the poor neighborhoods (comprising perhaps as many as 60 percent of all Mexicans) most families eat only one meal daily and this typically consists of beans, tortillas, and sauce, but never eggs, meat, or milk.[116] Another problem affecting children of the poor is that their parents frequently are obliged to move about in search of seasonal contract labor. The children are always taken out of school and may not return until the following year. Added to malnutrition these absences weaken the educational process. And even should the parents go to a place where high wages are paid (like a PEMEX facility) the presence of such wages has already pushed the price of staple foodstuffs up to the point that purchasing power is restricted and poverty continues. The overall educational impact is disastrous.

The person who survives to adolescence still probably reads at a third grade level, if even that, and his chances for socioeconomic mobility are nil. The adult who emerges from this syndrome is unhappy and will procreate more unhappy and undernourished human beings. Children may be used as slave labor to help feed the parents; 60 percent of the school-age children will be underachievers if they even go to school and it is unknown how many simply give up the attempt completely. One notes the educational deficiency of Mexico's popular classes in the number of clandestine workers coming to the United States who are unable to read their nation's language and only barely can write. Undernourishment and deficient education also mean that fewer will be able to enter university training. But as we have previously observed in several contexts Mexico cannot offer employment to the majority of those who do receive a university education. The spectre of want is thus perpetuated. And it is little wonder that the universities in Mexico become revolutionary training grounds for those seeking to end the class-based injustices so rampant in Mexican society.

Charges that one-third of Mexican adults older than 15 years of age are either functionally illiterate or only "semi-instructed" are heard by the national Secretariat of Public Education (SEP) and the National Adult Education Institute (INEA).[117] These agencies admit that a high percentage of adults quit programs once started because of administrative problems, running the gamut from teaching materials to hours. The testimony also indicates that the belabored Mexican dilemma of corruption (creating fake teaching programs as devices for raking off expenditures) enters into the educational picture, at least at the adult education level. There are also labor problems involving abuses by syndicate leaders of officially recognized groups like SNTE (National Syndicate of Educational Employees). Rival independent unions have emerged to challenge the *charros* or official PRI-sponsored syndicates which are said to have grown along with the SEP itself into bureaucratic monsters.[118] This is part of the previously cited bureaucratic problem of Mexico trying to hire all its citizens as a solution to the unemployment problem (which, obviously it cannot do) and of bureaucratic self-interest completely supplanting the goals, in this case educational, for which the bureaucracy was originally created. In the struggles over how to protect one's sinecure and how to divide the spoils from the creation of "phantom associations" it is not surprising that the goals of adult education should be subverted.[119] Thus while malnutrition undermines Mexico's child education, corruption undermines its adult education. This oversimplification is surely unfair to many dedicated teachers, but it contains major elements of truth that are painfully real. Low wages paid to teachers, especially in poor urban zones and in the rural areas, discourage the best minds from entering teaching. The quality of Mexican education is further depressed.

Poverty is Mexico's most salient socioeconomic characteristic. It underlies the outrage of those who feel that only violence can redress the wrongs done to the populace by a regime that lets natural wealth slip through its grasp, wealth that could have been shared and wasn't. The impoverishment of Mexico is symbolized by the dried bed of Lake Texcoco near the Federal District and lying now mostly in the state of Mexico. The ancient Texcoco provided protection for the Aztec capital Tenochtitlán, but once crossed by Cortés (see Chapter Two) it was no longer a guarantor of national greatness. By the time of the Mexican Revolution, the area of

Lake Texcoco had become largely a dried bed of powdery soil whose high nitrate content worked against the growth of trees or shrubs. In 1929 the Mexican government allowed purchase of land in the Texcoco area for as little as 30 pesos per year payment in order to encourage settlement and to reduce the dust storms originating there which plagued the capital city a short distance away and caused many pulmonary infections. In 1946 an effort was made to halt construction of housing subdivisions in Mexico City due to overcrowding. It was then that people from around the country, drawn to the Federal District by the myth of opportunity (and occasionally by its fact, if good luck was with them) started settling the Texcoco area. There was born Ciudad Nezahualcóyotl, one of Mexico's worst slums and a showcase to its poverty.

In 1948 Ciudad Nezahualcóyotl had some 2000 inhabitants; in 1953 the figure had grown to 10,000 and in the 1970 census the area (granted municipal status in 1963) was credited with 580,436 inhabitants. In 1980 the figure had passed 2 million.[120] Of the nearly 2.5 million residents in 1983 it was judged that 72.5 percent were less than 24 years of age. In effect this meant 667,500 young people in search of work, education, food, and for some reason to have confidence in the future.[121] The reader should remember that Ciudad Nezahualcóyotl is nestled close to Mexico City, contiguous to the Federal District, and is served by the Zaragosa exit line of the subway or Metro. Men and women who have employment in the capital rise at 4 or 5 A.M. and walk through the dusty unpaved streets of the slum-colony to catch the Metro or a bus which gets them to work (either early and they are forced to wait, or late and exhausted from their long sardine-can ride amid a crush of humanity and fetid air). The sheer human pressure of Mexico City creates enormous human emotional distress. To the poor who come in from Ciudad Nezahualcóyotl it is all the worse, but only about half that municipality's residents have gainful employment at all.

It has been that way in recent years with social change arriving only in the form of the new arrivals who are displaced from somewhere else. Few would choose to live in Ciudad Nezahualcóyotl had they not been displaced elsewhere, or without some unreliable hope of finding work in the back of their minds. In 1977 the journalist Ricardo Garibay did a study of poverty in this very atmosphere. He invited his friend, an anthropologist named Margarita to accompany his group. They took a sociologist and a photographer with them to catalogue life in Nezahualcóyotl's many human "precarious zones."

The survey captured images and testimonies from people who came in from the country and brought along their own methods of survival. State and federal subventions may align the streets and pave the principal ones, those the government sells them cheaply of a grey wall-making material made of pressed sand, but they still live in mud huts with metal and cardboard tops, often no windows; inside live fathers and daughters, aunts, uncles, nephews, dogs, hens, and pigs, all scrambled up together. The area about each house is strewn with excrement, vomit, rotting garbage; cockroaches, flies, and spiders are everywhere; life inside the shacks is often one of drunkenness out of despair—men, women, children all drunk—and there is much incest. From these hovels come thousands of nighttime thieves, prostitutes, and muggers. The metropolis is surrounded by them.[122] "Don't you see," Garibay quizzes his companions, "we are surrounded by nearly half the population which lives in a way that you would not wish on your dog, and to a certain extent we who are better off owe our condition to the suffering of these poor whose services and salaries we consume."[123]

The reporter and his friends were accompanied by some women of the barrio. They said that during the presidency of Luis Echeverría and the governorship of Carlos Hank González in the state of Mexico (where the slum extends out of the Federal District) an effort was made to "varnish over" the misery of this zone and thereby hide the scandal. But they left it as it was. Echeverría went on to better things and Hank González became regenta of Mexico City where he could continue to ignore the scandal of poverty.[124] They also commented that the new president López Portillo had made a speech saying he was sorry for living conditions here and that something would be done. But he never said what would be done in any precise terms that the people could understand. The women expressed cynicism predicting that the same governmental crooks as before would siphon off any funds that could be used for welfare and deposit it in the banks of Uncle Sam to the north.

Mounds of trash and garbage build up everywhere. They are covered with disease-carrying flies and bloated rats. One of the girls accompanying Garibay asks why the public authority doesn't simply come with bulldozers and remove this fetid mess. Because, the reporter replies, it would take from many people their only way of living. Some of the trash is brought from the city and may contain things the poor can use and sell. Others simply eat the garbage, rotten though it may be. And, he adds, don't forget that the real problem is that there is little or no demand for the labor of these people.[125] The stench of the slum is overwhelming. Nausea overcomes the reporter's friends. They begin to understand, and to fear, what life in the slum must be. They speak to Pablo Romero who came to the slum five years ago from Michoacán. He is a *pepenador*, a scavenger in the trash pile, his only employment. Pablo's personal filth is such that the reporter holds a handkerchief over his nose, pretending he has a cold.

Pablo is willing to talk. There are 13 people in his family. If he has luck finding articles of value in the trash dump he earns two U.S. dollars (peso equivalent) every three days. On this and garbage scraps his family subsists. When asked if his children eat meat and eggs or drink milk he only smiles, sadly, but does not reply.[126] Pablo says he and his people are very bad off. Then he opens his shirt and displays a gangrenously infected side. The reporter becomes ill and cannot continue the interview. He leaves saying, *que mierda somos. Te aseguro que somos una mierda.*[127] Still in some of the homes he sees the national flag pasted to the wall and the image of the Virgin of Guadalupe, watching over her 5 million wretched beings.

A woman from Guanajuato tells of life in the urban slums contrasted with life in the rural slums. She says the air was much better in Guanajuato and one often had a nicer view, but there one would surely die. The rain was scarce and crops were few. Although the economic circumstances in Mexico City were bad, once in a while they sold something, they ate poorly, but they ate. She was cooking a stew made of tripe as she talked to the reporter. Her husband would carry this to a nearby street to try to sell cupfuls to passers-by. She assured the reporter that everything was clean in her kitchen and feared he might be someone from the Health Department (about which she had heard but not seen). Looking about the reporter saw pestilence everywhere, rabid dogs, diseased children, and no sign that anyone in modern Mexico knew or cared. Garibay wrote that perhaps the best one could do was to forget about these miserable people surrounding the well-to-do other half of Mexico City:

> . . . five million humans who will erupt one day, what doubt is there, even though tomorrow they will have forgotten you too; but they will erupt, or disappear in the final condition of human beings in this society: they will be erased, liquidated, to exist no more, and will become shadows beneath the splendors of rifles and clubs of the coming dictatorship which is almost inevitable.[128]

What seems also to be inevitable is the continuation of this poverty. Mexico in the late 1970s and early 1980s does not show signs of being able to absorb its excess humanity through economic growth and this will likely be a problem into the 1990s, perhaps forever.

Since Garibay's survey of Nezahualcóyotl the economics of poverty have not improved. One of the few flourishing cottage industries in the 1970s found in the area was homemade clothing. Most such sewing shops were clandestine, not regulated, paying illegally low wages, and provided no health benefits for employees as required by the national labor law.

But it was a way to make a living. Then came the financial crash of 1976 and the Echeverría devaluation. Sewing machines and parts were almost all imported but even those made in Mexico shot up in price. The cottage sewing shops of Nezahualcóyotl could not repair their machines, hence they could not keep operating.[129] Not everything went up in price, however, and CONASUPO held the price of milk firm. But this made people give more milk to their children in place of other things like beans and tortillas which did increase in price. So after the devaluations of 1982 it became necessary to wait in line at a nearby CONASUPO store serving Nezahualcóyotl from five in the morning to nine or ten just to get milk, often keeping one's children in arms and at one's side.[130]

On the bases of these precise indices alone life in the 1980s was getting worse in·Nezahualcóyotl. Then there were increases in transportation costs so that the few employed souls lost even more money. Social violence increased, fraudulent land speculation was rife, and local protective groups formed. Social services are regularly promised, but are late in coming. Instead the government has built 13 heavily fortified "bunkers" in Ciudad Nezahualcóyotl, ostensibly for public protection; but their appearance is that of defense of the regime against a social conglomeration that could erupt at any time.[131]

NOTES

1. Juan Miguel de Mora, *México: país del miedo* (Mexico: Anaya Editores, 1981), p. 161.
2. Fred W. Riggs, *Administration in Developing Countries: The Theory of Prismatic Society* (Boston: Houghton Mifflin, 1965), pp. 244–45.
3. Ibid., p. 255.
4. Ibid., p. 256 and p. 270.
5. de Mora, *México: país del miedo,* pp. 70–71.
6. Ibid.
7. Ibid., p. 77.
8. Ibid., p. 75.
9. Ibid., p. 79.
10. Ibid., p. 68.
11. Mauricio González de la Garza, *Última llamada* (Mexico: EDAMEX, 1981), pp. 47 and 327.
12. Miguel Basáñez, *La lucha por la hegemonía en México 1968-1980* (Mexico: Siglo Veintiuno Editores, 1982), p. 48.
13. This has been embellished by the author and adapted from the first edition of *Mexican Democracy.* I remain grateful to Lic. Manuel de la Isla for his counsel in its original preparation. A set of behavioral norms for aspiring political actors within the dominant official system has been set forth by Peter H. Smith in *Labyrinths of Power: Political Recruitment in Twentieth-Century Mexico* (Princeton, New Jersey: Princeton University Press, 1979, especially Chapter 9).

14. It is argued that in 1947 the government of Miguel Alemán revised Article 27 allowing greater landholdings to be considered "small" thereby diminishing Mexico's agrarian reform. See *Proceso,* June 13, 1983, pp. 6–9.

15. Carlos Chavira, *La otra cara de México* (Mexico: La Nación, 1966).

16. Issued by President Alvaro Obregón.

17. The statement in colloquial Mexican Spanish is "well, I'm living here under the Decree of August the second." This became a ritual that was handed down from father to son and became part of the peasant folklore even though it had limited legal validity beyond the presidential regime of Obregón.

18. The PRI typically attempts to convince the people (as well as foreign visitors) that there are "reactionaries" out of the past who will swoop down and annul the gains of the Revolution if people don't vote for the official regime, even in elections where the ballot boxes have been pre-(read: PRI) stuffed.

19. Chavira, *La otra cara de México,* p. 146.

20. Ibid., p. 228 (my translation).

21. John Gerassi, *The Great Fear in Latin America* (New York: Collier, 1965), p. 107. See also Rubén M. Jaramillo and Froylán C. Manjárrez, *Rubén Jaramillo, autobiografía y asesinato* (Mexico: Editorial Nuestro Tiempo, 1967).

22. Jorge Domínguez, ed., *Mexico's Political Economy* (Beverly Hills: Sage Publications, 1982), p. 194.

23. *Visión,* November 4, 1972, p. 19.

24. Lorenzo Meyer, "Historical Roots of the Authoritarian State in Mexico," in Luis Reyna and Richard S. Weinert, eds., *Authoritarianism in Mexico* (Philadelphia: Institute for the Study of Human Issues, 1977), p. 17.

25. Ibid.

26. Daniel Levy and Gabriel Székely, *Mexico: Paradoxes of Stability and Change* (Boulder, Colorado: Westview Press, 1983), p. 131.

27. Ibid., p. 138.

28. Ibid., p. 144.

29. Raúl González Schmal, "Las elecciones y la crisis del sistema," a paper presented at the reunion of SOLIDARISMO on June 12, 1982, mimeographed, p. 2.

30. René Villarreal, "The Policy of Import-Substituting Industrialization, 1929-1975," in Reyna and Weinert, *Authoritarianism in Mexico,* p. 97.

31. *Visión,* December 2, 1972, p. 12.

32. See the treatment of the automotive industry in the first edition of *Mexican Democracy* (1972) by this author, pp. 98–101.

33. See Domínguez, *Mexico's Political Economy,* p. 134.

34. Ibid., pp. 159–60.

35. *Proceso,* June 13, 1983, pp. 30–31.

36. Ibid.

37. Ibid.

38. From an official memorandum entitled *Declaración del Excmo. Señor Presidente de El Salvador Fidel Sánchez Hernández* published by CONASUPO (Mexico City), Carlos Hank González, Director General, January 24, 1968.

39. Official memorandum *Qué es la CONASUPO?,* 1968, no other identification.

40. See the first edition of *Mexican Democracy* for criticism and background on CONASUPO, especially pp. 105–7.

41. CONASUPO memorandum (1968), p. 3.

42. Ibid., p. 4.

43. Manuel de la Isla, *Porque fracasa la CONASUPO, Por Qué,* April 10, 1968, pp. 32–34.

44. Levy and Székely, *Mexico: Paradoxes of Stability and Change,* p. 141.

45. *Uno más Uno,* June 30, 1983.
46. See Alisky's monograph by the same name published by the Center for Inter-American Studies at the University of Texas at El Paso, November, 1975.
47. *Proceso,* June 20, 1977, p. 16.
48. Ibid.
49. *Proceso,* December 11, 1976, p. 46.
50. Ibid.
51. Ibid., p. 17.
52. George W. Grayson, *The Politics of Mexican Oil* (Pittsburgh: University Of Pittsburgh Press, 1981), p. 135.
53. *Proceso,* July 4, 1983, p. 9.
54. *Proceso,* January 31, 1983, p. 11.
55. George W. Grayson, "Oil and Politics in Mexico," *Current History* 81 (February, 1982), p. 381. By the same author, and same title, a newer article appears in *Current History* 82 (December, 1983). The latter is cited in Chapter 8 in the context of Mexico's anticorruption dilemma of the 1980s.
56. *Proceso,* June 25, 1983, pp. 18–19.
57. *Proceso,* July 4, 1983, pp. 6–7.
58. *Proceso,* July 11, 1983, pp. 6–10.
59. Ibid.
60. *Proceso,* August 1, 1983, pp. 6–11.
61. Ibid.
62. *Proceso,* July 25, 1983, p. 17.
63. *Proceso,* July 18, 1983, pp. 29–30.
64. Ibid., p. 12.
65. *Proceso,* July 11, 1983, pp. 11–13.
66. *Proceso,* July 4, 1983, p. 6.
67. George W. Grayson, *The Politics of Mexican Oil,* p. 73.
68. The Ixtoc I blowout seriously strained relationships with the United States and affected Mexico's relationships with the state of Texas in 1979 and thereafter. A valuable discussion of diplomatic efforts and legal liabilities is found in Robert D. Tomasek, "United States–Mexican Relations: Blowout of the Mexican Oil Well Ixtoc I," a paper presented at the 23rd Annual Conference of the Western Social Science Association, San Diego, California, April 23–25, 1981.
69. *Proceso,* June 20, 1983, p. 9.
70. *Proceso,* April 4, 1983, pp. 6–13.
71. *The Wall Street Journal,* February 23, 1983.
72. *Proceso,* February 28, 1983, p. 17.
73. *Proceso,* February 7, 1983, p. 6.
74. *Proceso,* February 7, 1983, p. 8.
75. *Proceso,* January 24, 1983, p. 22.
76. See Jerry Ladman et al., eds., *U.S.–Mexican Energy Relationships* (Lexington, Mass.: Lexington Books, 1981), p. 48.
77. *Proceso,* August 22, 1983, pp. 6–7.
78. *Proceso,* September 19, 1983, p. 7.
79. Ibid., p. 8.
80. *Proceso,* September 19, 1983, p. 16.
81. Levy and Székely, *Mexico: Paradoxes of Stability and Change,* p. 131.
82. Heberto Castillo writing in *Proceso,* September 5, 1983, p. 33.
83. Isidro Sepúlveda writing in Ladman, *U.S.–Mexican Energy Relationships,* p. 62.
84. Ibid.

85. Carlos Ramírez writing in *Proceso,* January 31, 1983, p. 12.

86. *Proceso,* September 19, 1983, pp. 33–34.

87. George W. Grayson, "Oil and Politics in Mexico," *Current History* (February, 1982), *passim,* and Grayson, *The Politics of Mexican Oil,* p. 76.

88. Heberto Castillo in *Proceso,* p. 34.

89. The Economist Intelligence Unit (London), *Quarterly Economic Review of Mexico,* No. 3, 1983, pp. 14–15.

90. Ibid.

91. In Ladman, *U.S.–Mexican Energy Relationships,* pp. 24–25.

92. Grayson, *The Politics of Mexican Oil,* p. 79.

93. Ibid., pp. 99–100. More recently Grayson has stressed the seriousness of the threat posed by corruption in PEMEX and its union STPRM to the oil monopoly and to the Mexican nation overall. He believes that the real test of President de la Madrid's anticorruption drive is whether it attacks the 120,000-member oil workers' union and its seemingly untouchable leader (de facto) Joaquín Hernández Galicia, otherwise known as "La Quina." Grayson is one of few U.S.-based scholars who seems to recognize the true enormity of corruption in Mexico and its political and economic implications. See his "Oil and Politics in Mexico," *Current History* **82** (December,

94. 1983), pp. 417–18.

95. From Ladman, *U.S.–Mexican Energy Relationships,* p. 69.

96. Ibid., p. 81.

97. Clark Reynolds writing in Ladman, *U.S.–Mexican Energy Relationships,* p. 155.

98. Ibid., p. 157.

99. Ibid., p. 160.

100. Ibid., p. 164. This proposal is developed briefly in Chapter 7 and involves the Mexican government giving financial incentives to those Mexicans who repatriate their earnings from the United States leading to small business and agricultural development at the family level in Mexico.

101. George W. Grayson, *The Politics of Mexican Oil,* p. 12.

102. Mexico apparently began constructing the gas pipeline before an agreement was reached with the United States on the price to be paid for the delivered product. This led to acrimonious exchanges between the two countries. A good treatment of this process is found in Edward Williams, *The Rebirth of the Mexican Petroleum Industry* (Lexington, Mass.: Lexington Books, 1979). In 1983 Mexico agreed to sell gas to the United States at $4.40 per thousand cubic feet (natural gas) which represented 50 cents less than Mexico had previously wanted, but in the light of its economic difficulties this was a reasonable compromise.

103. *Proceso,* December 6, 1982, p. 30.

104. Ibid.

105. Ibid.

106. Ibid.

107. *Proceso,* January 10, 1983, p. 30.

108. *Proceso,* September 5, 1983, pp. 20–23.

109. Ibid., p. 22.

110. Ibid.

111. *Proceso,* November 19, 1979, p. 12.

112. Ibid.

113. Ibid., p. 13.

114. Ibid., p. 12.

115. Ibid., p. 14.

116. Ibid.
117. *Proceso,* March 28, 1983, p. 18.
118. Ibid., pp. 20–21.
119. Ibid.
120. *Proceso,* April 18, 1983, pp. 12–13.
121. Ibid.
122. *Proceso,* August 8, 1977, p. 7.
123. Ibid., p. 8.
124. Ibid., p. 9.
125. *Proceso,* August 15, 1977, p. 14.
126. Ibid., p. 16.
127. Ibid. Translated freely this comes out "what rotten crud we are. I assure you, we're only crud."
128. *Proceso,* August 22, 1977, p. 16.
129. *Proceso,* April 18, 1983, pp. 12–13.
130. Ibid., p. 14.
131. Ibid., pp. 10–11.

Seven

Mexican Migration to the United States

BORDERLANDS: THE MEXICO–UNITED STATES INTERFACE

Migration of Mexican workers and potential citizens to the United States is one of the most explosive political issues of the 1980s for Americans. So intense are feelings about enforcement of existing immigration laws and their proposed reform that the U.S. Congress has been unable to act; many believe Congress is afraid to act! Since the issue centers largely on clandestine migration that is illegal, and since the bulk of that human traffic goes across the southern border with Mexico, it is appropriate to consider the borderlands themselves both as the interface between the United States and Mexico and as a filter for constant illegal migration. The borderlands are becoming an identifiable entity with a highly complex personality.

The importance of the borderlands achieved academic recognition in 1976 with the founding of the Association of Borderlands Scholars. Through its newsletter–journal FRONTERA, the ABS sought to bring together scholars in a variety of disciplines who study the border area from a number of cross-cultural viewpoints. Indeed, the border area is now viewed as a kind of unique hybrid culture. In recent years border study programs have appeared at several well-known universities including UCLA, New Mexico State, Pan American University, San Diego State, Texsas A & I, and the Texas state universities at Austin and El Paso.[1] These institutions have published border studies and guides to studying the border and its resources. An international consortium known as PROFMEX shares research done on Mexico and sponsors conferences. Border state governors from the U.S. and Mexico meet regularly to share ideas about common problems and joint international solutions. The border is a reality in socioeconomic and cultural terms. It is an interface or showcase to the blending of two neighboring cultures. It is partly Third World, partly industrialized world, and partly another world that befuddles and resists categorization.[2]

When Mexico imposed its currency controls in 1982, and as the peso went through successive devaluations, the reality of the border as a socioeconomic unit became painfully apparent. Mexicans lost their purchasing power and could no longer purchase goods in El Paso, for instance. This hurt American business all along the border. But El Paso residents could go with their stronger currency and buy up goods in Mexico. This further hurt El Paso businesses and also hurt the Mexican consumer who was faced with consumer good shortages on his side of the border. These conditions prevailed along the 2000 mile frontier shared by the two countries. The quest for dollars, and the collapse of the Mexican economy, also increased the migratory pressures from those going northward to seek employment clandestinely.

Mexican officials admit that the border area is a joint creation of both countries, and is integral to each of them. The U.S.-owned border twin industrial plants or *maquiladoras* (*maquilas*) which assemble goods using U.S. materials and Mexican labor benefit from the peso devaluations which keep the Mexican labor cheap. For its part the Mexican government considers the border to be one of its strategic zones of the future.[3] But the hordes of people attracted to the Mexican side looking for work far outnumber the jobs available and keep wages depressed. As Mexican inflation continues, life for these people becomes particularly difficult. As long as the border populations are fluid, i.e., residents of both sides may pass relatively freely back and forth within fixed geographic limits on either side, the socioeconomic fortunes of each will be intertwined.

That underscores a major difference between Mexican and most other non-English-speaking immigration into the United States. For the Mexicans it is easy to go between nations via the borderlands as a human filter and cultural conditioning zone.

> Because it has always been so easy to go home, many Mexicans and Mexican-Americans have displayed the classic sojourner outlook. The more total the break with the mother country, the more pressure immigrants feel to adapt; but for many immigrants from Mexico, whose kin and friends still live across the border and whose dreams center on returning in wealthy splendor to their native villages, the pressure is weak.[4]

There have been negative features to the cultural mixing: violence and ethnic hatred has been directed at both Anglos and Mexicans, discrimination and outright abuse of Hispanics has been frequent, and this includes both legal and illegal Mexican aliens as victims; the perpetrators are both private persons and public law enforcement agents in the United States. It has been all too tempting for some U.S. citizens to assume that anyone who looked "Mexican" was a wetback, and this syndrome underlies some of the fear which has impeded the U.S. Congress from passing a comprehensive immigration reform bill today.[5] Yet on the positive side marriage and intermingling among Anglos and Hispanics is considerable, so cultural miscegenation has occurred.

The border area is noted for vice: drugs, gambling, and prostitution. The topic is too extensive to be covered here. In all fairness to the Mexicans it should be said that the demand for these services originated largely with a U.S. clientele, although prostitution has been a traditional source for municipal governmental revenues in Mexico. Women from poor Mexican neighborhoods sell sexual favors on both sides of the border. Prostitutes who are U.S. citizens largely concentrate their businesses on the U.S. side. In recent years the economic crunch in both countries has brought out a new sexual phenomenon, one that has broad public health implications. This is prostitution by transvestites. It has been estimated that "two-thirds of the roughly 50 nightly prostitutes working downtown are from Juárez, most of them transvestites. Both police and prostitutes say the problem is unique to the border."[6] The phenomenon, linked to economic recession conditions as well as to social change, has contributed to the spread of venereal disease in the border area. The entire borderlands culture is spotted with vice activities of one form or another, an indication that both nations need to make socioeconomic change a higher priority item in their national development plans.

Public health crises occur regulary as a result of the dumping of trash, the spilling of sewage, flooding across the border which spreads surface contamination, and of course there is the problem of air pollution. Mexico has done little to control its smog problem, either in terms of exhaust filters on cars or filtration systems for industry. The result is that smog, like other environmental contamination, creeps about the borderlands irrespective of political boundaries. The smog problem in the El Paso–Ciudad Juárez area is a notable case in point. Copper smelters in Sonora near the Arizona border also threaten the clean air of that region.[7] Mexico still suffers the saline contamination of Colorado River water coming from the United States into Baja California, and elsewhere along the border water contamination has been a problem calling for binational action. In recent years steps in this direction have been taken.

It has been estimated that the twin plant border industries or maquiladoras generated as much as 25 percent of Mexico's manufactured exports in 1982 making them an important part of that nation's economy. Concentrated as they are on the border they are also a magnet for many job-seeking individuals who cannot be absorbed and who then become potential candidates for illegal northward migration. U.S. firms (like RCA, IBM, Samsonite, General Electric, Chrysler, etc.) set up these assembly plants to take advantage of cheap Mexican labor. But it has not always been entirely beneficial to the Mexican employees. "For example, an average worker in a Tijuana *maquiladora* earned about 11,000 pesos (US $320) during February 1982. By the end of the year, several subsequent devaluations had reduced the same income to about US $156. Although these devaluations were a hardship to workers, they have made Mexico an even more attractive setting for international companies with high product assembly costs."[8]

For those who cannot find maquiladora employment the picture is bleak but not entirely hopeless. Organizations like SOCOSEMA (an organization of trash collectors) have formed which pay their contributing workers on the basis of how much trash they collect, cans being separated for one purpose and cardboard and glass for other recycling. SOCOSEMA, thus, can pay $13 to $20 per day to the cooperating collectors and that is about four to six times the minimum wage in Mexico.[9] SECOSEMA has over 300 families as members who sort out waste materials for marketing in both the United States and Mexico. It has become a self-sustaining enterprise that has developed a housing project, a school, and plans to set up its own waste recycling plant to be operated as a worker cooperative.[10] So entrepreneurship can flourish with positive results in the borderlands. Unfortunately, it is not enough to absorb the excess population many of whom find clandestine northward migration an attractive option.

The fluidity of the working class between both sides of the immediate border area is one fact of life which makes the borderlands into a visible socioeconomic unit. This can be particularly well seen in the El Paso–Ciudad Juárez area. El Paso is ranked 283 out of 303 U.S. cities in average annual pay by the Department of Labor and Standards. Some 24,200 people or 12.2 percent of the total work force of 192,000 were collecting unemployment benefits during the first part of 1983. More than 20,000 of the 140,000 households in El Paso County earn less than the minimum U.S. poverty line income of $6,968 annually according to 1980 U.S. Census data.[11] Factors that contribute to low wages include, prominently, the availability of Mexican laborers, either with work permits or without, whose presence depresses wages. Ellwyn Stoddard of the University of Texas at El Paso believes businesses come to the area to set up manufacturing operations that depend on the cheap labor supply on both sides of the border. They then export their profits to other parts of the country leaving the border area poor in many instances.[12] El Paso is known as a low wage town and is only 10 to 15 percent unionized. Texas is a "right to work" state which also militates against the formation of unions along the border. It is general public knowledge that many employers in El Paso pay well below the minimum wage until governmental action forces them to do otherwise. Employers believe the presence of illegal aliens keeps overhead down and helps the area fo flourish by giving jobs that U.S. workers don't want to the Mexicans. It is also a frequently heard comment that too many U.S. workers would rather stay on welfare than work.[13]

To make the border survey more complete let us glance at the Sonora–Arizona portion and consider once again the implications of labor surplus and peso devaluations on the borderlands economy. The maquiladoras along the border had been exempted in the past from such requirements as the 51 percent Mexican ownership that is imposed elsewhere in the country. Thus the maquiladoras have been given preferential treatment by Mexico as an incentive to the international BIP (Border Improvement Program). That circumstance changed somewhat after the peso devaluations of 1982 and 1983. Mexico experienced an acute dollar shortage and used the maquiladoras as a way of gaining this foreign exchange so as to bolster the peso. In early 1983 an exchange rate of 148 pesos to the dollar prevailed in the Nogales, Sonora, border area (bordering Nogales, Arizona). On that basis the Mexican regional minimum wage of 455 pesos a day could have been met by spending $3.07 per employee or roughly 38 cents U.S. per hour. That would have been nearly a 30 percent cut in payroll costs for the companies without decreasing the workers' pay. That also would be an attraction factor in persuading new industries to come to the border. But the Mexican government decreed that the companies would have to purchase their pesos for payroll from the government at 115 to the dollar. That saved the companies money but it also gave the Mexican government a vital input of dollars to replenish its treasury. By continuing to pay the maquiladora employees the same minimum wage they had, in effect, suffered a 22 percent pay cut in terms of purchasing power.[14]

Women make up 75 percent of the twin plant workers in the Nogales area and the average age is 19 although some are able to begin as early as age 14. A study by professors Mitchell Seligson and Edward Williams of the University of Arizona has been quoted to the effect that 4 percent of the workers come to the border area in search of maquiladora work and that 33 percent came to the border for other reasons. They contended that about two-thirds were born on the border and that few maquiladora workers admitted migrating either legally or illegally to work in the United States.[15] But testimony given this writer all along the border is that many workers are attracted in search of maquiladora work and when they do not find it many migrate clandestinely or involve themselves in vice and smuggling activities.[16] The peso devaluations have made the imperative to feed oneself and one's family just that desperate.

Along the Arizona–Sonora border smuggling has been a way of life for years. A pattern has been well established. Mexican drugs and workers are smuggled north. U.S. manufactured goods, especially appliances and guns, are smuggled south. Just before the financial crash of 1982 the overvalued peso made it possible for Mexicans to come by droves into Arizona to purchase U.S.-made goods which they would smuggle back by bribing or simply avoiding Mexican customs inspectors. With the devaluations the Mexican pesos bought little and this affected Arizona as it did other border areas. The ubiquitous Mexican shopper was no longer ubiquitous. A Mexican customs agent in Nogales said "things have gotten so bad since the devaluation that no one can afford to smuggle anymore."[17] That cut into the bribe income from *mordidas* collected by Mexican customs inspectors for allowing goods to pass without paying duties. Moreover, additional smuggling patterns emerged in which U.S. citizens now found it attractive to buy up Mexican goods and smuggle them north, thereby creating shortages again on the Mexican side just as we observed earlier had been occurring along the Texas border. A major market opened in smuggled diesel fuel which cost 40 cents per gallon in Mexico and could be resold for a dollar-plus in the United States. The diesel smuggling was something the U.S. government turned its back on in many cases, as the ultimate benefit was to supply the United States with a scarce resource.[18]

As outlined above, the borderlands are a special hybrid cultural area generating many problems for both Mexico and the United States. The borderlands are a showcase in which the best and worst of both countries are displayed and often amalgamated. The border is also a filter through which the goods, services, values, and humanity of the two nations are shared.

ILLEGAL MEXICAN ALIENS
IN THE UNITED STATES

The mixing of humanity in the form of migrant workers is one of the most critical functions performed in the borderlands. In 1983 over one million illegal aliens were apprehended on the southern U.S. border just by the Border Patrol alone. In previous years the entire Immigration and Naturalization Service, INS (which includes the Border Patrol) had reached the one million mark occasionally but this was the first time that the Border Patrol alone had registered so many. Although most of those apprehended were Mexicans a growing percentage came from Central America by way of Mexico having fled civil war conditions in their homelands. Along the border apprehensions of illegal aliens were up 40 percent over the previous year and convictions of alien smugglers nearly tripled to 9,100. It was reported that 60 percent of all Border Patrol apprehensions occurred in the El Paso, Texas, area and around San Diego,

California. Those areas constitute only about 60 miles out of a total 2000-mile-long border.[19]

The pressure of illegal aliens coming in from Mexico is considered to have reached crisis proportions. In recent years an annual attempt has been made to put legislation through the U.S. Congress that would sharply curtail the clandestine migration. The 1983 attempt was known as the Simpson–Mazzoli Bill which passed the Senate successfully and was to be reported out of committee for a floor vote by the House of Representatives in September. On September 29, House Speaker Thomas O'Neill said he would not allow the House to vote on the bill from the floor because he feared President Reagan would veto the bill as a way of gaining support in the Hispanic community. But the Reagan administration denied this saying the president would have signed the Simpson–Mazzoli Bill. Some Hispanic spokespersons also denied they opposed the bill acknowledging that illegal Mexican migration hurt the Hispanic community as much or more than it did other minority communities. The essence of the defeated Simpson–Mazzoli Bill was to fine employers of illegal aliens, tighten the border sieve, and declare a general amnesty in several gradations for illegal aliens who had been in the United States since before January 1 of 1980.[20] There seemed to be a broad-based legislative and law enforcement consensus that passage of this bill could have dramatically stemmed the pressure from the flow of IMAs or illegal Mexican aliens. But some Hispanic groups prevailed over Speaker O'Neill with their view that making it illegal to hire illegal aliens would generate more discrimination against Hispanics, i.e. "you look like a Mexican so therefore you might be illegal and I could be fined for hiring you." It was also argued that setting up a national worker registration card would be a major step toward a police-state citizen registration system.[21] Speaker O'Neill was condemned in many sectors for hypocrisy, "a cynical effort to destroy five years of work by two presidents, a presidential commission, and two congresses."[22]

One reason why Speaker O'Neill may not have wanted to permit a floor vote on immigration reform was that it would probably have passed and perhaps he feared the stakes were too high to allow such a bill to pass. That would violate one of our major criteria for political democracy as set forth in Chapter Five. Specifically, that the stakes in a public decision not be so high as to prohibit losers from accepting a public decision. America is a land of immigrants, some of more recent generations than others. Cutting off immigration is an especially emotional issue in this country, especially where one ethnic minority seems targeted more than others. It should be noted, however, that Canada is even more visibly an immigrant nation than is the United States. Canada has in effect nearly all the provisions of the Simpson–Mazzoli Bill, especially the fines for employers and the worker ID card; and imposition of this policy did not tear Canada asunder. In 1984, the Simpson–Mazzoli Bill finally passed both houses of Congress only to be frustrated in subsequent conference committee efforts to reconcile differences.

Groups like the organization FAIR seek to fix strict limits on immigration into the United States and would ultimately end both legal and illegal immigration and achieve zero population growth overall. There are others like some "liberal" journalists and academics who would simply "let the aliens in" as one article recommended.[23] It has even been suggested that we abolish our immigration laws and lower the border fences, a proposal not taken seriously in many circles.

Computations by government agencies as to how many illegal aliens are actually in the United States are risky because it is impossible to take a census of a clandestine population. One writer points out three general mistakes that creep into statistical estimates of illegal alien populations in the United States. The first is that deportations are assumed to be indicators of the actual (latent) clandestine population. Second, there is no way of knowing how many illegal immigrants leave the country clandestinely, often within a year of their entry. Third, it is argued that since enforcement is concentrated along the Mexican border, a distorted profile may emerge showing Mexicans to constitute a greater percentage of illegal entrants than is really the case.[24] Despite these difficulties estimates from government officials and the media range between 3 to 10 million illegal aliens living in the United States. If 7 million of them were Mexicans then ten percent of Mexico's total population would be living illegally in this country. There is probably no way of checking the veracity of such a contention at this moment.

The organization FAIR cites recent survey research evidence that both Hispanics and blacks strongly supported the Simpson–Mazzoli restrictions on illegal migration, despite the formal pronouncements of some Hispanic organizations to the contrary.[25] Black columnist William Raspberry wrote in the *Washington Post* that there is widespread recognition among the lower income classes that new waves of immigrants legal or otherwise do threaten the security of those already here and that, moreover, there is just about no more room in America to comfortably and feasibly put these people.[26] An outcry has been heard from the Supreme Court case of 1982 in which it ruled that Texas school districts must provide education to the children of illegal aliens. Immigration reform and the Simpson–Mazzoli Bill were sufficiently critical to merit debate during the 1984 American electoral process. Whether it would be made into a major campaign issue could reveal the ability of the American political system to deal with a highly emotional issue, one that brings out cross-cutting alliances and lines of consensus that may defy tradition.

That is to say Hispanic leaders of groups like LULAC, League of United Latin American Citizens, may opposed Simpson–Mazzoli in public while agreeing in private that Americans can no longer absorb the people of Mexico on the same basis that has happened in the past. Perhaps immigration reform in the United States should be handled via a binding national referendum!

Probably the easiest and most effective control mechanism against illegal aliens would be severe employer sanctions that would dry up employment. Our southern border could be fortified or closed. That would undoubtedly bring about revolutionary chaos in Mexico given the interdependency of the two economies. Nor would such a measure make sense unless the northern border were also closed. The employer sanctions, thus, are clearly the most promising approach. If combined with a regulated guest-worker program perhaps much of the ill effect on Mexico could be avoided. Canada has such a guest-worker program with Mexico whereby workers are flown to Canada at harvest time and returned thereafter. Reports are that this experiment has worked well since its inception in 1974.

REPATRIATION OF EARNINGS: ALIENS AS A FINANCIAL LINK TO MEXICO

Not all illegal aliens who come to the United States want to stay. Many are just sojourners. Others have been forced to stay by circumstances beyond their control. Elsewhere I have written about the concept of "stranded" IMAs, based on research done in eastern Missouri and southern Illinois in the late 1970s and early 1980s.[27] These are people who confess they would like to return to Mexico but can't. The economic conditions treated throughout this book are, of course, an ongoing impediment to one's returning to Mexico. But I have studied cases of stranding by injuries, ill health, or other misfortune. Debts and economic dependency may have been incurred since a migrant worker began the sojourn in the United States. Others have been detained by law enforcement authorities or have become involved in civil problems involving children in school. Often the children were born in the United States and have a claim to U.S. citizenship which does not ipso facto mean that the parents get citizenship as well. There is commonly a psychological problem of personal prestige and loss of face if one returns to Mexico without having "gotten rich." And finally there is the linkage of remittance money to support families back in Mexico, a major element of dependency that often results in stranding.

The just-mentioned phenomenon of financial remittances has frequently been speculated about but little hard information exists as to the size of this link between the United States and Mexico via the stream of illegal migrant workers.[28] It has been noted in recent literature that "the money remitted by its nationals is by far the most important shortrun economic consequence for Mexico of migration to the United States."[29] Much of such remittances comes from those who are forced to work here illegally. The research for this commentary treats a micro-study group of 17 such IMAs who worked in eastern Missouri and whose lives were followed by the author, who occasionally joined them as a coworker in the fields and orchards.[30] Close personal friendships still exist and the author has often been called upon to assist in family problems, both in the United States and in Mexico. This has sometimes required action going well beyond what would normally be expected in a professional research context.

What follows has been excerpted from a larger continuing work by the author and several colleagues that examines the quality of life of IMAs residing and working in the United States. Most of the broader research undertaking is focused on selected sites about the Great Plains, Colorado, Missouri, and Illinois plus visits to Mexico. In a recent work Professor Miles Williams and I urged a hemispheric-community-of-nations concept as a collaborative approach to the solution of clandestine migration as an international and multinational problem.[31] The incumbent administration in the United States has chosen to approach the problem unilaterally with an immigration reform proposal (Simpson–Mazzoli) that would drastically restrict clandestine worker migration to the United States from Mexico as noted earlier in this chapter. That would also undermine the Mexican financial system by cutting off many remittances by IMAs. The Mexican government welcomes (not officially, of course) the dollar remittances which its clandestine migrants send home from the United States. Dependent families, many of them on the edge of starvation, see these remittances as vital.

One recent study found $7.6 million being remitted to the Mexican state of Guanajuato alone in an eleven-month period. This was about 25 percent of the total estimated remittances of $30.2 million for that same period sent to Guanajuato. It is believed that in given villages remittances from the United States constitute 50 percent of the total annual income for those rural communities. I am currently looking at the cases of El Llano and Cherán in Michoacán in this regard. It is, of course, difficult to know the remittance percentage that comes from IMAs as opposed to legal migrant aliens.

The present data involve remittances sent to the states of Querétaro and San Luis Potosí. In my migrant study group of 17 aliens only two have been able to produce bona fide legal papers to my satisfaction. The others are self-acknowledged illegal entrants. They have varying histories of work and travel north of the border. Also varied is the amount of documentation they can, or are willing to, produce to demonstrate their earnings and remittances. Three key members of this group who have an especially close working relationship with the author agreed to act as liaison with the remainder in determining financial status without transgressing the bounds and bonds of human friendship. That query has enabled me to select one IMA as typical of about half of the group of 17. He was selected on the basis of sincerity of response, trust, and availability of documentation. Specifically he made available to me his federal W-2 Wage and Tax statement forms for 1979 to 1981, along with copies of money orders sent to Mexico and journal records of cash remittances. On the basis of the inquiries made I am reliably informed that his record is typical of at least 8 out of the total of 17 workers under study here. Other workers have given me more fragmented and less complete information about their repatriation of earnings.

Manuel Becerra Ponce has a history of some 12 years of working illegally in the United States within a triangle bounded roughly by Texas, Missouri, and Florida. He has been sent back to Mexico under "voluntary departure" by the Immigration Service (INS) on two previous occasions. This man is well-liked, is considered an excellent worker, speaks only the bare essentials of English, and provides faithfully for his wife and for his son by a previous marriage. Most of the average 4000 dollars he sends home annually to San Luis Potosí (beyond food) goes into the construction and upkeep of a small rooming house adjacent to his home where transients rent beds. His wife sells miscellaneous small goods from a vending booth or *estanquillo*. Manuel spends on the average eight months away from home working. Continuous money is needed to maintain their property located in a poor neighborhood because the residents are expected to pay for and construct their own sidewalks and maintain the streets, trash, and sewage disposal services at their expense and time (Manuel says he pays municipal taxes for these services but the local bureaucrats "rip off" the money and leave the residents on their own).

Manuel's recent annual earnings varied according to his time of residence in the United States. Comparing his income to that of his other two colleagues (the selected ones with whom this author has close rapport) reveals that Manuel normally earns about 25 percent more than they for equal time peiods; but the proportion of earnings repatriated to Mexico by all three appears about the same. I have observed that among the one-half of this microstudy group of 17 who make such remittances there is a notable tendency to remain at the labor camp after working hours and not to venture out into the broader community for diversions. These "conservative workers" express continued fears that off-the-job socializing will lead to deportation. The remainder of the 17 who are more adventurous are also more frequently involved in encounters with local police agencies leading to their being turned over to INS authorities; and the adventurous ones tend to spend more money frivolously thus having less to repatriate to Mexico. So the personal character of the individual seems to be a major independent variable upon which monetary remittance to Mexico depends.

Inspection of the income tax data shows that Manuel paid no income tax via withholding. It is not required that tax be withheld from the wages of agricultural workers and, at my last check, the first $3000-plus of their income was reserved as tax-free, a special loophole intended to benefit low-income migrant families and seasonal rural workers. It does mean, however, that none of the Mexicans in my study group paid any income tax. They admit this quite openly, especially the illegals who believe that any submission of papers to the government will merely invite deportation action. But the above figures also show Manuel to have paid substantial annual stipends into Social Security (FICA tax) and this went for services he has never claimed and probably never will.

While these earnings occurred Manuel and his companions were paying the same sales taxes that were paid by everyone else. Thus it is hard to see a strong case being made that these IMAs are a welfare burden; nor did they create unpaid medical expense during the early three years of this study; that protection was covered by employer's insurance. This, admittedly, is not a universal circumstance and there are many instances on record (especially in the border areas) of illegal aliens whose medical expenses had to be borne by the U.S. public. A broader question may be raised, however, as to the impact on the already strained Social Security system if all payments into it by illegal aliens were abruptly stopped following strict immigration crackdowns via the Simpson–Mazzoli Bill, were it to pass Congress. And there is a further question implicit in the Reagan administration's new immigration reform package, especially that part granting amnesty to certain illegal aliens. Will they also be given an income tax amnesty covering the reporting years of their illegal sojourn?

But let us first consider the implications of the above microprofile of Manuel and by implication, his colleagues. Remittance money from these people goes very much for what Cross and Sandos observed in their excellent study, i.e., for immediate family survival and not for broad economic development within the receiving region of Mexico. Little of the repatriated money goes for infrastructure investment. Also many of those in my study have learned the use of sophisticated agricultural equipment and growing techniques which either are not used in Mexico or which they have no opportunity to apply in Mexico. Thus, as Cross and Sandos conclude, "the observable impact on Mexico of migration to the United States strongly suggests that the opportunity to convert earnings abroad into development at home is a challenge that still awaits a Mexican solution."[32]

Let us stress the above choice of the terms "Mexican solution." Mexico has allowed its own laws to be violated by looking the other way as clandestine emigration took socioeconomic pressure off the political system. Depending, as Mexico does, on repatriated earnings from one's clandestine emigrants is a short-term survival tactic, not a national development strategy. If Mexico's rural population were to have government subsidies to augment the foreign remittances such a development might eventually come to fruition as I will suggest presently. The few programs that do exist are so poorly and/or corruptly managed as to have minimal lasting impact. Therefore, the opportunity is lost to convert savings and skills acquired in the United States into infrastructure, food, and jobs in Mexico. Dependence upon the repatriation of clandestine migrant earnings is another of the many ways in which Mexico's governing regime shirks its responsibility for instituting long-range development. Mexico's hungry millions are the continuous losers.

Moreover, the continued flooding of the United States with migrant alien workers can only help to depress wages for the labor force already in place. In the eastern Missouri region and also on the Great Plains where my study is unfolding it is often a silent policy of agricultural management to seek out Mexicans in preference over most anyone else. This is partly because the Mexicans are superior workers (few will dispute that) but also because they almost never press for more than the minimum wage except, in my experience, those Mexicans who have achieved legal alien status or in collaboration with select native Hispanics.

Many growers in the Middle West acknowledge privately that they prefer the illegals (so long as there is no penalty for hiring them) because their precarious status makes it difficult for them to press wage demands; from this thinking comes the oft-heard expression: "Give a Mexican his papers and he'll be off to Chicago for a higher-paying job." Uttering such a remark is not always ipso facto racism; in fact, it is a true assertion in many cases that I have witnessed personally (e.g. the Mexican 19-year-old from Michoacán whose personality changed from docile to arrogant, and who soon became an intolerable employee, after he married a U.S. citizen). But so long as IMAs are available to do the work there is no need for employers to pay above minimum wage to U.S. citizens or to legal resident aliens and, thus, the salary structure for the entire agricultural job market is automatically depressed. I have not studied urban employment of

IMAs in great depth but there is evidence that IMAs do make better wages in cities, thus raising the spectre of displacement of legal residents and U.S. citizens. As it now stands rural wage structures are usually so low that many American citizens can understandably do better by remaining under some form of welfare.

Should a new immigration package like the Simpson–Mazzoli Bill become law, and should that law be strictly enforced, it could very well have disastrous economic consequences for Mexico and still not open appreciable new job fronts for the legal residents of the United States. Many vegetable producers vow they will switch to public "U-Pick" harvesting if they can no longer hire IMAs. Enough such conversions have already been made in southern Illinois to make that vow more than an idle threat. These operations need few employees and those that are needed must deal with an English-speaking public. Other growers say they will stop planting vegetables and put in soy beans or other crops requiring the services of very few manual laborers. Again, the inescapable losers are the Mexican migrants, plus the unskilled U.S. citizens, many legal resident aliens, and, of course, the U.S. consumers who will surely see vegetable and fruit prices soar if the clandestine migration of Mexican agricultural workers is drastically reduced in the months ahead.

How can the remittance figures for Manuel be extrapolated onto the broader picture of clandestine worker migration from Mexico so as to project an estimate of repatriated earnings? As stated earlier I have it on good authority that Manuel's case is representative of half of the group of 17 workers (including the two I have judged to be bona fide "legals"). So the figure of half is tempting as a base for global estimates; but it is in no way scientifically valid, even as applied to Missouri alone. Farther to the southeast in Illinois, near Carbondale, there is a concentration area for migrant Spanish-speaking workers known as the Union-Jackson Labor Camp. The bulk of the temporary residents of this camp, from about April to the end of October, have in the recent past been illegal aliens from Mexico although a number of Cuban refugees and some Central Americans with legal status have appeared recently. Social and medical services are provided these people by the Illinois Migrant Council which has a multimillion-dollar annual budget drawn from state and federal sources. The Illinois Migrant Council officials insist they do not service illegal aliens. My well-corroborated field observation is that they serve anyone and everyone who speaks Spanish without regard to the legality of his or her alienage. There are several privately-operated labor camps in that general area as well. Informed estimates hold that some 200 Spanish-speaking migrant workers have been there, around Carbondale, in any given recent summer. At least 85 percent of these, in my judgment, are IMAs.

Using the unscientific figure of half as prevailing it would be possible to estimate the annual flow of dollars from southern Illinois to Mexico in any given summer. But getting the kind of rapport I have achieved with my microstudy group in Missouri on an enlarged basis would be difficult and probably impossible in the Illinois setting, as would be any effort to gauge the sincerity of the answers on such a mass basis. A sure method of answering the question of how much is remitted to Mexico probably cannot be known as long as illegality remains the norm. Should these workers' status be legalized, which is what the Simpson–Mazzoli amnesty portends, then there might be a possibility of conducting a study of rural remittances from Illinois on a more sturdy factual base. But then the neighboring state of Missouri does not care quite so well for its IMAs, i.e., there is no true equivalent to the Illinois Migrant Council (nor does there seem to be in Kansas, but there does seem to be one in Colorado), and there are no comparable labor camps in Missouri for study that I have been able to discover. Therefore, the status of wages and remittances is more difficult to estimate even on a regional basis. Reports reach me from Arkansas and Texas of gross exploitation of IMAs and below-legal wages. Continued illegal alienage and clandestine migration will make precise estimates of financial impact difficult and probably impossible.

Cross and Sandos surveyed the various estimates of illegal Mexican aliens in the United States and concluded that there was little agreement among the estimators "except on a very broad range, i.e., two to five million Mexicans in the mid-1970s."[33] If the case of Manuel cited herein represents half of the lower figure (half of two million) then the remittances to Mexico in recent years could average some $4000 multiplied by one million persons or $4 billion. That would be a significant chunk of income relative to Mexico's recent $80 billion foreign debt. Since the figure of 2 million IMAs is probably a seriously low estimate the remittances could be much greater and more significant if taken as a fraction of Mexico's foreign debt. Much of this repatriated money surely finds its way into the Mexican government's coffers by way of taxation. But corrupt politics and administration may prevent this money from ever being used for a legitimate public purpose. That is part of the reason for the current collapse of Mexico's economy, its stringent monetary measures, and its nationalization of private banks. This also means the IMAs now have a motive to find ways to keep their funds in the United States, for once transported into Mexico all dollars must be surrendered to the government. Such a circumstance has never existed in contemporary Mexico in this writer's personal memory. It is no coincidence that some of Manuel's colleagues still working here have inquired as to setting up bank accounts along the Texas border, on this side, as a way of protecting their dollars, and of playing the dollar black market in Mexico, now rumored to be thriving.

My unscientific estimate of $4 billion in repatriated funds annually has too many defects to be considered firm. But the 1970s annual remittance figure of $200 million cited by Shafer and Mabry in an excellent recent study may also be too low.[34] Those authors have done a laudable job of presenting the picture of U.S. labor dependence upon illegal Mexican labor; they stress that whatever the remittances may be it is probably a fair price for the United States to pay for useful labor at menial jobs which most U.S. workers simply don't want.

With the possibility that some IMAs may start guarding their dollars on this side of the border, comes a new potential threat that could undermine the Mexican economy even further. In this context Shafer and Mabry cleverly explore in their book the ramifications of dividing the United States and Mexico using various kinds of "walls" including one of the Berlin type. The Mexican government, by admitting its internal financial bankruptcy via the strict monetary measures recently implanted, may have helped erect a new kind of wall, a "money wall," which that country's ruling cast did not envision. Thus, in the de la Madrid sexenio now underway, Mexico's destiny could rest more precariously than before on the repatriated earnings of its clandestine emigrants.

Repatriation of Mexican earnings from the United States could be seized upon as a starting point for solving Mexico's basic foodstuffs problem cited throughout this book. It would require daring presidential action tying foodstuffs to oil revenues. The incumbent Mexican president could drastically curtail corruption and make, perhaps, some creative reforms in the way Mexican oil money is used and in the manner in which Mexico's human resources are wasted. A proportion of the petroleum revenues (the part now being ripped off) could be placed in a special interest-drawing fund to be managed by a council of delegates taken from each of Mexico's five to seven major political parties, one delegate from each party. The fund would make available low-interest long-term loans on a matching fund basis to Mexicans who repatriated U.S. earnings to Mexico and who undertook small-scale agricultural development projects in Mexico and used their experience gained in the north for the cause of basic food production at home.

Details of administration and controls on corrupt practices should be real, verifiable, and they should be the result of an internal Mexican process; but the principal set forth would be that of rewarding those who earn abroad to invest and build infrastructure at home. That would be a sign to "fence-and-wall builders" on the United States border that Mexico does not forever want to use its northern neighbor as a human dumping ground and will reward its people for investing in Mexico.[35]

CONCLUSIONS ON CLANDESTINE MIGRATION

Elsewhere I and others have written about the human rights implications of clandestine immigration and the suffering experienced by the Mexican migrants. These problems range from parents being afraid to send their children to school lest their alien status be detected, workers living in inhumane conditions, and in extreme instances "we have had cases of women giving birth to their children on the floors of hospital waiting rooms because they were refused admittance on their immigration status" and "undocumented workers were chained to chicken coops at night to prevent their escape."[36] I have personally photographed workers being forced to sleep under citrus trees on cold nights near Phoenix, Arizona. On the other hand I have seen rather decent housing provided to illegal alien workers in southern Illinois. The immigration picture with its many impacts is a mixed bag at best.

It would probably be wisest to pass some form of the Simpson–Mazzoli Bill and then amend it as experience dictates in the interests of all concerned. Some critics believe the amnesty provisions of the bill are a trick to get undocumented workers to come out of hiding and they charge that there are so many exceptions possible to the eligibility criteria that the so-called amnesty would be meaningless to the overwhelming majority of the aliens involved. Another objection to the amnesty that is also sound, but seldom expressed, is that these people would presumably have to receive an income tax amnesty as well since the great majority did not file tax returns for the years of their illegal alienage. This would be greatly unfair to the rest of the U.S. citizens and residents who did. Another unfairness is to those law-abiding Mexicans who waited patiently outside a U.S. consulate in Mexico hoping for their turn at legal immigration. They would be pushed aside in favor of law-breakers. The amnesty carries with it the inescapable stigma of appeasing law-breakers, something that is not likely to sit well with many U.S. citizens, especially those who have been castigated for infractions of the law. If the amnesty provision were dropped and employer sanctions of sufficient severity to produce compliance were added, and an honestly and humanely managed guest-worker program instituted to fill those jobs which U.S. workers simply won't take, then the Simpson–Mazzoli Bill might be a worthy start toward U.S. immigration reform. This can be accomplished without bringing about socioeconomic and political collapse in Mexico.

And to solve the Mexican–U.S. illegal alien problem some of the reform will have to occur in Mexico. We have seen that the borderlands constitute a magnet for migration that is attached to the further socioeconomic magnet to the north. Mexico will need to create a magnet of its own to encourage its people to stay and prosper there. Wall or fence-building by either country is hardly the answer, as several scholars who studied the "Tortilla Curtain" incident in late 1978 found out.[37] From that experience in U.S. fence-building emerges this question: is it not hypocritical for the United States to build a fence to keep out the very workers whom U.S. employers deliberately recruit and legally hire considering that it is still (as of this writing) not illegal to hire an illegal alien? Moreover, are U.S. policy-makers prepared to fence off the Canadian border as well? There is evidence that considerable illegal alien traffic comes from that direction. Indeed, "a new breed of smuggler seems to have emerged in the 1980s, the north-to-south smuggler who brings illegal aliens into the United States from Canada. According to one detailed account, some of the smugglers operating out of Canada are so confident they give "money-back guarantees to their clients."[38] Many of these are from the Caribbean but, increasingly, Mexican aliens of upper status are found using this route of illegal entry into the United States.

That moral reform of the political and administrative systems of Mexico is imperative has been established in previous chapters. Such reform would assist Mexican socioeconomic development, population control, and emigration control at the source. The U.S. Congress will have to pass some form of the Simpson–Mazzoli Bill with the caveats entered above and preferably without the troublesome amnesty provisions. Charges against it of "racism" and "ethnic imperialism" cannot be dismissed lightly, but the bill could be reformed, as indeed could our immigration policy, without encouraging such nefarious results.[39] One way to do that would be to take advantage of the borderlands as a socioeconomic and mixed cultural unit for use as a laboratory to demonstrate that people of the two cultures can coexist, miscegenate, and solve problems jointly via a new binational organism.

The binational programs now existing at universities as cited earlier plus the various international commissions established for boundary control and water allocation, as well as the state-to-state diplomacy now going on in the form of governors' conferences can be drawn upon to set up, perhaps, a special international border congress. It would have representatives elected from both sides of the line and would enjoy definite policy-formation mandates from both national governments. Perhaps letting a borderlands congress set and police international policy for migration in both directions would have a chance where national congresses in Washington and Mexico City do not act.[40] In that way the United States and Mexico could participate as equal partners in the process and the eventual policy decisions would, hopefully, be seen as less punitive against any given ethnic group than apparently is the case with present legislative proposals. The short-term goal would be socioeconomic justice via dig-nified employment at an optimal level. The long-term goal is the peaceful and productive coexistence of Mexico and the United States in this hemi-sphere without a major irredenta problem of displaced population crop-ping up to provoke unhappiness and disharmony. The borderlands are evidence that Mexicans and U.S. citizens can work together successfully and fairly when the genuine desire is there.

Of course, it would also help if the United States ceased its program of aid to repressive foreign dictatorships which generate refugee aliens, many of whom arrive in the borderlands looking for asylum and thereby compound existing pressures emanating traditionally from Mexico. Re-form could also be made of the present immigration laws which allow the entry of extended family members having ties to U.S. citizens and legal resident aliens. This would, as James Fallows has suggested, favor legal immigration of independent or "seed immigrants" more likely to contrib-ute to the human enrichment of the United States than those chosen merely because they were someone's sister or uncle.[41] Additionally, the United States could create new incentives for U.S. workers to accept menial jobs by allowing them to earn a certain level of extra income with-out jeopardizing their welfare income. This would probably be cheaper than apprehending aliens and should put more money into active circula-tion, thereby increasing tax revenues. Such a "welfare proviso" would re-place the existing "Texas Proviso" which allows U.S. employers to hire il-legal aliens providing they don't harbor or abet them.[42] All of the above assumes passage of a modified version of the Simpson–Mazzoli Bill as clarified earlier in these pages. But the ultimate success of the U.S. immi-gration reform will also depend upon the outcome of Mexican President Miguel de la Madrid's "moral renovation" initiative, just as will the overall wellbeing of his nation. The borderlands are an appropriate arena for ob-serving the relative success of these reform attempts as the decade of the 1980s unfolds.

NOTES

1. FRONTERA (Borderlands Review and Newsletter) published by the Department of Geography at Northern Illinois University-De Kalb 8 (Fall, 1983), p. 1.
2. *Special Report: The Border,* by the staff of the *El Paso Herald-Post,* Summer, 1983, p. 2.
3. Ibid, p. 10.
4. James Fallows, "Immigration," *The Atlantic Monthly,* November, 1983, p. 66.
5. The Simpson–Mazzoli Bill was defeated in the House of Representatives by fiat of House Speaker O'Neill in September, 1983. Part of the pressure leading to his contro-versial action came from groups such as the Los Angeles-based National Center for Im-

migrants' Rights whose director Peter A. Schey accused the legislation of being racist and regressive. See *Washington Report on the Hemisphere* 4 (October 18, 1983), p. 2 (published by the Council on Hemispheric Affairs). The bill was frustrated in Congress again in 1984.

6. *Special Report: The Border,* p. 35.
7. Stephen Mumme, "Importing Air Pollution," *The New York Times,* July 23, 1983.
8. María Patricia Fernández Kelly, "Alternative Education for Maquiladora Workers," *Grassroots Development* 6 (Winter-Spring, 1982), p. 41.
9. *Special Report: The Border,* p. 56.
10. Fernández Kelly, "Alternative Education," p. 44.
11. *Special Report: The Border,* p. 74.
12. Ibid.
13. Ibid., p. 75.
14. Based on calculations by the *Arizona Daily Star* in its special report *Compadres in Crisis* published on May 22, 1983, p. 26.
15. Ibid.
16. An example is this account: "border town factories attract people from the interior, the overwhelming majority of whom cannot land jobs at the *maquilas.* Those without jobs either further crowd the cities, move north to the United States, or return home humiliated. As a result, border town populations have not stabilized and northward migration and joblessness have increased dramatically. . . ." From Tom Miller's *On the Border* (New York: Ace Books, 1981). See also the *Arizona Daily*
17. *Star,* March 31, 1977.
18. *Compadres in Crisis,* p. 40.
19. Ibid.
20. FAIR, *Immigration Report* IV (October, 1983), p. 1.
21. See the "Current Documents" section of *Current History* 81 (February, 1982), p.
22. 385.
23. See *Washington Report on the Hemisphere.*
    Comments by FAIR spokesman Roger Conner reported in *Immigration Report.*
    Stephen Chapman, "Let the Aliens in," *Washington Monthly* 9 (July-August, 1977).
24. This writer goes so far as to suggest that it is the "rest of us" who are a burden to the
25. aliens.
26. Sasha Lewis, *Slave Trade Today* (Boston: Beacon Press, 1979), p. 32.
27. In FAIR's *Immigration Report* IV (August, 1983 supplement).
    The Washington Post, September 16, 1983.
28. Kenneth F. Johnson and Miles W. Williams, *Illegal Aliens in the Western Hemisphere* (New York: Praeger, 1981), especially Chapter Three.
    Researcher Wayne Cornelius contends as follows: ". . . some 13.6 million Mexicans—21.3% of the total population of Mexico at present—depend to some extent upon U.S. earnings in any given year. The dependence of such a large segment of the Mexican population upon cash income earned in the U.S. is clearly undesirable as well as risky to those involved in this dependency relationship." From his *Mexican Migration to the United States: Causes, Consequences, and U.S. Responses* (Cambridge, Mass.: Massachusetts Institute of Technology, Center for International Studies, 1978), p. 51. Approaching the remittance question from a different angle the following estimate emerges: "the Mexican government has a considerable stake in keeping its northern border relatively open. At least two-thirds of the migrants remit money to Mexico. For most of the Mexican households that send migrants, these remittances are their primary source of income. The value of remittances, though very difficult to estimate, may exceed Mexican net income from tourism." Jorge I. Domínguez, ed. *Mexico's Political Economy* (Beverly Hills: Sage Publications, 1982), p. 194.

29. Harry E. Cross and James A. Sandos, *Across the Border* (Berkeley: University of California Institute of Governmental Studies, 1981), p. 114.

30. First presented in the author's "Repatriation of Earnings by Illegal Mexican Aliens," a paper presented at the Annual Convention of MALAS (Midwest Association of Latin American Studies), October 22, 1982, at the University of Kansas, Lawrence, KS.

31. Johnson and Williams, *Illegal Aliens, passim.*

32. Cross and Sandos, *Across the Border,* p. 116.

33. Ibid.

34. Robert Jones Shafer and Donald Mabry, *Neighbors: Mexico and the United States* (Chicago: Nelson-Hall, 1981), p. 104.

35. Keeping Mexican workers at home and providing them with a growing participation in the capital stock of Mexico is approached in a proposal by economist Clark Reynolds which merits serious consideration in Mexico and by foreign assistance experts interested in assisting Mexico. "A 'workers bond' program could be devised in which a capital fund would be established in the name of the working class. All workers would receive bonds as participants in the fund, in proportion to a combination of factors that would be determined to give 'labor points.' The points would be based on labor time and intensity of work effort rather than on earnings per se." Reynolds leaves details of the administration of such a program to others more familiar with Mexican institutions; certainly such a program should be planned by Mexicans, and within the spirit of President de la Madrid's "moral renovation." See Clark Reynolds's "Mexican Economic Development and the United States," in Jerry Ladman et al., eds., *U.S.-Mexican Energy Relationships* (Lexington, Mass.: Lexington Books, 1981), p. 164.

36. *Washington Report on the Hemisphere,* p. 2.

37. This involved a special fence the U.S. government was building to keep out illegal aliens. See Ellwyn R. Stoddard, Oscar J. Martínez, and Miguel Angel Martínez Lasso, *El Paso-Ciudad Juárez Relations and the "Tortilla Curtain,"* El Paso, El Paso Council on the Arts and Humanities, 1979, esp. pp. 42–43.

38. *The Washington Post,* January 16, 1980. In the last two years alien smuggling over the Canadian border has increased by 50 percent. A spokesman for INS said those coming through Canada were of a more affluent class having paid air fare from their countries to take advantage of lenient Canadian immigration and tourism policies. "We get Italians, Greeks, people from almost every nation in South America—even a few Mexicans" he said. From the *St. Louis Post-Dispatch,* September 11, 1983.

39. Chicano leader Bert Corona called the Simpson–Mazzoli Bill an attempt to legislate slavery for undocumented Mexican workers in the United States, apparently referring to the bill's amnesty provisions. *Excelsior,* December 18, 1983.

40. There is a growing literature on the border which concerns regional adjudication of international problems. See particularly Stephen Mumme, "Disputing Hidden Waters: Dimensions of Groundwater Conflict on the Border," in *Border Perspectives: A Special Issue,* **9** (1983).

41. Fallows, "Immigration," p. 106.

42. A U.S. District judge in Texas undercut the so-called "Texas Proviso" in late 1983 when he ruled that a Texas businesswoman who employed illegal aliens had violated immigration law by arranging to have illegal aliens transported to her place of business. Thus she was convicted of conspiring to transport rather than for the act of employing the illegals. The implication of this ruling is that any employer who solicits illegal alien employees will be subject to criminal penalties, but that ruling will, of course, be tested further. *The Arizona Daily Star,* editorial, December 21, 1983.

Eight

Curtain on the Twentieth Century: Mexico's Future

We have reviewed the course of Mexico's development from Aztec rule to Spanish colony, from nominally independent nation to a contemporary Third World state that is bustling with the drive for technological modernity and industrialized economic power. We have focused on the contemporary political processes by which development policy is formed and the cause of social justice pursued. In this context we have specified the prominent role of political and administrative corruption as an impediment both normative and behavioral to Mexico's ongoing quest for change.

Mexico is living through a political and economic crisis in the mid-1980s. From this comes an accelerated northward exodus of her citizens via established clandestine channels that now accommodate new refugees from a stagnant economy in the wake of the 1981 and 1982 peso and oil revenue collapses. Food self-sufficiency has been lost indefinitely. Food dependence on the United States increases Mexico's foreign debt which stood near $90 billion in 1984. Austerity measures imposed by the International Monetary Fund, as a condition for keeping Mexico afloat financially, have intensified the desperate condition of the poor. The dominant PRI now sees its governing hegemony threatened by anomic violence as a reaction to poverty conditions, by threatened defections of official (CTM) labor, and by the growing electoral reform-based competition of opposition parties (principally the PAN and PSUM) that have won impressive local victories about the countryside.

The official peasant sector (CNC-dominated) is alienated from the technocratic cabinet-oriented governmental style of President de la Madrid. Labor corruption, and government actions against it, are accompanied by an active rival unionism in Mexico. The distance that has been opened between CTM labor magnate Fidel Velázquez and de la Madrid suggests an internal crumbling of PRI power. This makes the passing of Velázquez an ominous coming event for the Mexican power structure, especially considering that de la Madrid seems disposed to court the rival CROM as a potential alternative labor base.

It is in times of major economic hardship that Mexico seems most vulnerable to political instability.[1] Public outrage over wasteful corruption during the past two sexenios has made Mexicans extremely cynical toward their political system. The commendable efforts of President de la Madrid to end the waste have won much public support and praise. They have also had unpleasant side effects, like former corrupt police officials and their gangs who now rob citizens and businesses out of uniform. Their one-time crime patron, former Federal District Police Chief Durazo, is in foreign exile with former President López Portillo. Durazo, who turned the Federal District Police into a center for extortion, homicide, and drug distribution, had *monthly* earnings into the millions of dollars from these illicit activities.[2] He will likely be tried along with former PEMEX director Díaz Serrano if Durazo is ever returned to Mexico during the de la Madrid sexenio.

But it is doubtful whether López Portillo can ever be tried. Those who would be implicated are now too powerfully entrenched. As Díaz Ordaz once said of Luis Echeverría, "remember, when you criticize the corruption, you are part of it."[3] Former presidents seem still to be immune. Yet, some castigation of high officials for wrongdoing is a step forward. The public knows of the waste, of its own penury, and of the untouchables who got away. Nor has official political repression and fraud ended in Mexico, as the ongoing traumas of Juchitán, Oaxaca, continue to reveal.[4] The Mexican public has reason to doubt revolutionary promises today more than ever before.

But there are positive features to the Mexican heritage. Unlike other Latin American nations Mexico has not in recent decades been plagued with political instability. One reason is surely that her military sector has been largely separated from politics via the institutional process itself and through generous subsidies paid to keep the military professional. Yet, as at Tlatelolco in 1968, the military is always there to back up the civilian government should there be a confrontation with the populace. The military has taken on a prominent counterinsurgency role in recent years pacifying the countryside wherever trouble erupted. As we have seen in the cases of peasant movements and popular attacks on offensive local governments, the military's pacification programs often have been heavy-handed. But Mexico is not troubled by widespread military brutality to the degree that Argentina, Chile, and Guatemala have been, just to note three prominent cases. Yet should the ongoing conflict in Central America ever threaten to touch Mexico its military establishment would undoubtedly assume a more pronounced political role. Reports of treatment accorded Central American refugees in southern Mexico suggest that the Mexican military establishment is sensitive to signs that the regional guerrilla war could spread. We can say, however, that at least as of this writing Mexico has been free of the military-rooted political instability which impedes the development of many other Latin American nations.

Moreover, contemporary Mexico has enjoyed relatively stable presidential regimes. Since the leadership turmoil of the late 1920s and early 1930s no president has resigned, been assassinated, or otherwise forced out of office. Cabinet positions have frequently experienced turnovers but a continuity of public policy has been possible. It is not as in Bolivia, for example, where in recent years one government after another was overturned by a coup or a forced resignation after only months in office and cabinets were turned out even more frequently. In that nation the formation of a continuing national development policy in recent years was nearly impossible as one group of political adventurers was replaced by another. Mexico, fortunately, has not endured that variety of instability and serious development planning has at least been possible. Add to this the rich natural resources Mexico claims, both on land and in coastal waters (Bolivia has no seacoast by way of contrast), its relatively mild climate, and its broad stratum of intelligent human resources on which to draw, and one must question why Mexico has not achieved social integration and justice and developed into a major world economic power. Certainly corruption is not the only answer. But it is a pervading norm which stultifies solution of a myriad of problems which Mexico must treat if it is to have the progress it claims to want; leadership could make the difference, and Mexico has an ostensibly reformist president residing at Los Pinos.

Toward the close of his first year in office, President de la Madrid's government admitted the country then continued in the grip of an economic crisis unknown in recent years. Recession in the United States and Mexico, the oil bust, and peso collapse lurked in the background. A Mexican study showed that those living on the interior (regional) minimum wage of 520 pesos (about 3.75 dollars U.S.) per day would have guaranteed misery since one's basic requirements could not be met for less than 2000 pesos per day. Well over half the population was in this circumstance. And in the previous ten months the price of beef and milk increased 96 percent, fruits and vegetables 119 percent, medicines over 100 percent, and clothing 60 percent. In that same time salaries rose no more than 30 percent, if at all in many cases, and over 2 million workers were laid off due to collapse of businesses alone.[5]

That was the challenge of Mexico, one that could not be solved by Miguel de la Madrid alone. His anticorruption campaign was gaining international fame (called a "moralizing broom" in the foreign press) via the newly created Federal Secretariat of the Controller General which undertook extensive audits of government development agencies, thereby renewing cries for trials of both López Portillo and Díaz Serrano, the latter then languishing in jail.[6] President de la Madrid also slowed down inflation to less than 100 percent and created a balance of payments surplus by forcing a cut of imports by some 55 percent. Payments on Mexico's foreign debt, estimated in December 1983 at $90 billion, were rescheduled and austerity terms of the International Monetary Fund had been honored. This meant reductions in social services, further peso devaluations, liquidation of unprofitable state-run industries, containment of salaries, and other measures discussed previously in this book. The foreign sector of Mexico's economy was being salvaged at the expense of Mexico's already suffering masses.[7]

The incumbent Mexican leader President Miguel de la Madrid has an educational background and practical experience that should make him the envy of most leaders of the Third World. His reputation is that of honesty, frugality, and administrative efficiency. It was his office of Programming and Budget whose audit laid the basis for the corruption charges that unfolded into the great PEMEX scandal in 1981; the same de la Madrid found himself charged with applying the principle of "moral renovation" to the cleanup of that scandal after taking office in 1982. The resolution of that affair would render a major judgment of the Mexican political system and would test the abilities of President de la Madrid against his own standard of excellence, that of "moral renovation." In this context it can also be proposed that the final character of the de la Madrid sexenio will render a judgment on both the man and the system.

De la Madrid's challenge was truly enormous: salvage the economic system, make it a viable arena for the pursuit of socioeconomic justice; at the same time he would need to continue reforming the political system, a process started by his predecessor, so as to facilitate those socioeconomic reforms. The reader will not have forgotten that President López Portillo entered his sexenio with optimistic qualifications and a positive reputation, only to terminate that period under a dark cloud. Perhaps no one person can reform the powerfully entrenched political system of Mexico, but given one of the strongest presidencies in the world, and with relatively few institutional constraints, it may be more than wishful thinking. Let us wish President de la Madrid and his entourage well!

Optimism prevails in many U.S. academic circles regarding the likelihood of social integration, economic development, and even political democracy in Mexico. That I do not share all of such sentiment need not suggest disparagement of those who do, and my own optimism occasionally peeks through just enough to compel admission of my hope that I am wrong, for the sake of Mexico. Even the most optimistic writers acknowledge the enormity of Mexico's social distress and the imperative for economic change. Not all agree that political change is also needed. My concern throughout this book has been primarily humanitarian and immediate, a concern for the millions who must suffer malnutrition and disease while waiting for the fruition of revolutionary promises. My fear is that Mexico's fate will be the continued bleak portrait of life that was conveyed in Chapter One from the works of Juan Rulfo.[8] That would be a tragic shame when the means and human abilities to achieve a happier life in Mexico are already on hand.

In a book published just before the disaster at Tlatelolco the historian James Wilkie concluded that the nation-building process in Mexico had created a climate favorable to overall development; but he stipulated that without education and public health (see my discussion in Chapter Six) social integration would lag behind economic development. Politically, he contended, "people are philosophic about the Revolutionary Family, for they have always been governed by one elite group or another. If the official party continues to sponsor national growth and cedes to the demands or desires of pressure groups, complaints will be neither loud nor effective."[9] There is reason to question some of this viewed against the recent history of petroleum mismanagement and financial collapse, the student movement and massacre of 1968, and government repression of protest movements and popular attacks on municipal and state governments in recent years. Alienation toward the regime seems to be growing, the complaints are loud, but we have yet to determine their effectiveness. Some of that judgment will be furthered by the administrative record of the new opposition municipal governments that now seem to be springing up all about Mexico despite the fact that a few, like Juchitán (see Chapter Five), have been retaken by the PRI under a cloud of repression and fraud. Also the strength of Mexico's clandestine migrant stream northward continues to reflect the inadequacy of the nation's development in socioeconomic terms.

But if Mexico is not really developing economically so as to reduce social injustice, if poverty and social margination are to extend in the indefinite future over half the populace, does this condition necessarily mean imminent political upheaval and instability for Mexico? Not necessarily so if the research findings of Wayne Cornelius on the migrant poor in Mexico City are to be believed. He found the migrant poor severely restricted in potential for challenging the political system.[10] Moreover, he found certain frankly optimistic attitudes on the part of his research population regarding their future and that of their children in Mexico. Since Cornelius's work, the fortunes of Mexico have risen abruptly and then fallen as we have seen in previous chapters. Also the electoral system has been opened thereby allowing more vehement criticism and revelation of politics and government. This has great potential for mobilization of alienated political sentiment. Unless the government assumes complete control of the press and communications media it is likely that public opposition will be increasingly shared. One source of opposition is revealed financial mismanagement in the face of a growing impoverished social stratum, and these two circumstances are getting broad opposition press coverage as of this writing. But whether the poor, or the migrant poor, can rise above despair, infirmity, and hunger to join a rebellion remains to be seen.

We have noted that Mexico's resources are not being allocated via programs that really eradicate poverty. That is the crux of the policy inequity in Mexico today. Resources are allocated disproportionately to elites and would-be elites. That is why the petroleum scandal of the early 1980s is so disillusioning to those who, like myself, wish to find cause for optimism as to Mexico's future. To date Mexico has failed to marshal oil-based wealth to attack fundamental socioeconomic problems. Edward Williams has put the case well: "Petroleos Mexicanos laid claim to the lion's share of the nation's investment capital in the 1970s, thereby diverting monies from other programs. In the case of unemployment, furthermore, the investment went to capital-intensive projects, creating few jobs. Perhaps equally cogent, the new petroleum also captured the interest of the decision makers, thereby diverting their attention away from other problems."[11] Add to this the legion of other administrative and political scandals in recent years and more reason for disillusionment appears.[12]

The question, then, comes down to the potential for political and governmental reform in Mexico to spur economic development and social integration. Is the elite that governs Mexico capable of instituting reform? It is the argument of Peter Smith that Mexico has no single power elite but basically two elites, the industrialists and the politicians. The two elites compete with and often distrust each other. They are perhaps typified by the clashes between President Echeverría and the Monterrey Group. These elites are concerned mainly with capital accumulation and popular subordination. On these two goals the elites agree while struggling with each other to control the Mexican development process. "In operation, Mexico's authoritarian regime thus reflects constant interplay between a relatively coherent state interest and a somewhat less coherent set of business interests. One consequence of this situation has been a considerable degree of flexibility for the formulation of state policy; and in its turn, the ability to play off one actor . . . against another has enhanced the stability and strength of the regime."[13] From this it seems that a complete breach between the two national elites, e.g. a drastic governmental refusal to support the private capital accumulation process, would lead to an undermining of Mexico's power truce that seems to underwrite its political stability.

Yet the state is in a quandary: its ideological heritage from the Revolution commits it to the egalitarian cause of land and wealth distribution. This runs a collision course with the goal of private capital accumulation; the masses of people are likely forgotten in the process of struggle and accommodation between the political and industrial elites. Leaders, not whole elites, must institute reform.

The overall Mexican elite, to use Roderic Camp's singular term approach, is developing faster than the political system. The political elite is losing touch with the masses of people who are manipulated, subordinated, and neglected but seldom served, as simultaneously public resources are increasingly eaten up by the elite and those aspiring to join it. The elite recruits from the middle class public universities to the exclusion of the growing mass of marginated people. The last president who really cared for the latter was Cárdenas, himself from a rural background. Camp writes that the pattern of Mexican federal budgeting is in favor of the more heavily urbanized and economically developed states lending to their magnetic quality for attracting the rural and small-town poor. Thus the social inequities continue to build. Since the public universities are prime recruiting grounds for governmental figures any rift between them and the dominant regime could have serious consequences for Mexican political instability, especially if it came in the form of a union of students at the National Autonomous University with peasants and/or labor that was directed against the PRI. This may be a major "weak link" in the system as Camp has suggested.[14] To break that link might open the road to upheaval.[15]

From the foregoing the potential fragility of Mexico's political system should be clear. Chaos could be generated by a severe rupture among competing elites, by a defection of students and intellectuals in public universities, by an alliance between public university groups with peasants and labor, or by the defection of the PRI's main peasant and labor organizations from the official party umbrella. The coming death or retirement of labor magnate Fidel Velázquez could also become the occasion for a defection of labor or its splintering; some observers believe the exit of Velázquez will create a power vacuum that could lead to internecine fighting of major proportions which would be threatening to the dominant party PRI. And all of Mexico would be threatened if U.S. tourist trade to the south or worker migration to the north were seriously interrupted. So Mexico's traditional political stability is not guaranteed as a constant any more than her petroleum boom could continue long-range without a bust. Because Mexican society and her economy are so intimately wed to the United States, despite the glaring cultural differences, a major socioeconomic or political disaster in either country would be mutually felt. Such a possibility exists in Mexico because a truly pluralistic state with a broadly participatory civil society does not exist to moderate cleavage. Reform would promote such pluralism.

Building on Steven Sanderson's argument, out of the Porfirian state no broad civil society emerged with multiple group memberships and political points of access to moderate politics and to steward economic growth. "The Porfiriato was doomed in some measure because the state undertook capitalist development as a project before the necessary classes existed as genuine social forces in civil society."[16] Out of the vacuum following the Revolution legitimately competitive political forces did not emerge. This fact has colored Mexican politics to the present day. The Mexican state became a partner in the capitalist class it had helped to create via its guarantees for private profits, property, and capital accumulation, via its generation of social overhead capital plus the creation of state-owned industries with state financing. But at the same time the state was committed to the revolutionary promise of sharing with the proletarian and peasant classes. The revolution's heritage, thus, was an obligation for the state to reconcile class conflict (over which much of the blood of the Revolution was spilled), aid the dispossessed and poor, and at the same time spawn a bourgeoisie and provide it guarantees that would aid economic development through capital accumulation. Practically, the Mexican state was charged with carrying out a Marxist and a capitalist revolution at the same time. Welfare goals were pursued notably until World War II; thereafter bourgeois goals predominated.

Mexican populism, argues Sanderson, was a rhetoric and an ideology which sought to explain how the state would behave amidst these contradictory commitments. Indeed, much of the political activism of the PRI today is ideological sleight of hand to cloak these basic contradictions which it owns. The party's task in recent years has been to keep the ideology legitimate, i.e. to make the masses believe that worker rights and social justice are still prime goals of the continuing revolutionary process while allowing for private wealth accumulation that is necessary for economic development in partnership with state capitalism. Reform and revolution must be promised to the people yet the captains of industry must still be protected. Ultimately this has meant keeping the masses poor and demobilized while telling them that the regime is saving them from a worse fate. If most Mexicans now realize that they have been deceived in this process then some catalytic event may be all that is needed to inspire an uprising, the opportunities for which I summarized above. And while that eventually is awaited it seems to befall Mexico's presidents to undertake the task of carrot-and-stick appeasement both of lumpenproletariat and bourgeoisie in the hope that neither will embark upon irrevocable rebellion.

But something in the psyche of the Mexican people must change if disaster is to be avoided. My guess is that without some profound catharsis no such change in psyche will occur. Mexico is ruled by men who see themselves as tough and intractable in the face of challenge and threat. To negotiate in the face of threat would be a feminine behavior, a sign of weakness. Men have been destroyed politically and personally in Mexico by making them look feminine or weak, or as Luis Spota puts it by depicting the political actor "as a sodomist in the country where the male cult of *machismo* is a permanent rule."[17] Herein lies a curious anomaly, and a potentially significant one. If manliness or machismo is a permanent cult in Mexico as so many authors have suggested, then why would trickery, deceit, and treason be standard political skills? Surely the more macho thing to do would be to confront one's competitors and defeat them on the battleground of skill, wit, and merit openly acknowledged. This might preclude surreptitious combat as feminine or weak, e.g. Watergate skills, passing out spurious handbills or faking damaging photographs and films. Those are political devices I dealt with in the previous edition of *Mexican Democracy* and they continue in Mexico today. True machismo would also mean the PRI defeating the COCEI in Juchitán honestly, rather than by ballot fraud.

Looking at it carefully the central Mexican political ethic may not be rooted in machismo at all. Rather it may spring from the concept of vengeful *enanismo* that was developed by me in the previous edition of this book as extracted from the writings of Oscar Monroy Rivera and my extensive interviews with him. Enanismo is dwarfishness morally and spiritually. It is cowardly weakness. That ethic says repress at Tlatelolco, don't negotiate; repress at San Cosme and Juchitán, don't bargain or compete. Violence and alienation are common outcomes. Extralegality is the broad context within which enanismo thrives. Corruption and its tolerance generate extralegality as the rule, not the exception. Instead of seriously trying to cure society's ills the custodians of the political system reap short-term profits from helping those very ills to continue, and they mask their complicity behind rituals of symbol manipulation.

Wise counsel once offered for Mexican penologists could be applied to the entire political system: "Mexican penologists need to insist that some regimentation is humane and that disregard for the law within the prison promotes a general disregard for the law in the wider society."[18] The tragedy is that for most of its people Mexico is a gigantic prison, but without enlightened penologists. Their jailer is all too often described by the corrupt Durazo prototype cited earlier. An enormous moral renovation is indeed required to topple such foes.

Like any other society if Mexico is to achieve the "good life" the basic natural right to physical and emotional inviolability must be a prime goal of the state.[19] It is incumbent upon any state in which the good life is to be a priority goal to remove barriers to human self-fulfillment and to eliminate physical and emotional repression. Scholars are far from agreement as to whether political democracy is the best form of government to achieve this. We can distinguish between political democracy (as developed in Chapter Five) and social democracy involving welfare statism that could be realized under a benevolent authoritarian (nondemocratic) regime. At this point it is not clear whether achievement of political democracy will assure social democracy. But without some rational overhaul of Mexico's governing system, either by benevolent authoritarians or benevolent democrats, it is hard to imagine social democracy and the good life coming to fruition.

Under President de la Madrid it seems possible to attack corruption, correct wrongdoings, and honor rectitude. To expect him to erase all the sins of his several predecessors within one sexenio would be unrealistic. If his government continues to open the political process to bona fide opposition groups, allows criticism to be published without reprisal, and sets an overall example of probity, it will be a major gesture toward change in Mexico's political life. Along with this we would hope to see greater effective attention paid to the vast problems of hunger, housing, and public health. That can be accomplished without creating class warfare among the bourgeoisie and the proletariat. The most sensitive class to be reckoned with, in all likelihood, is the dominant political class whose amenities are costly to Mexican society and must be placed under some rational control. Mexicans must plan a future and not suppress the future from their lives as one of their own most distinguished cultural analysts has charged.[20]

Perhaps the psychic insecurities detailed by Samuel Ramos, Octavio Paz, and others will make such rational planning for the future impossible. That would leave Mexico like a band of "amoral familists" living for the moment, for one's immediate family and friends, and depending on graft and largesse in a vicious circle of greed that can only end in a war of all against all, a scenario in which there will be only losers. Something like that was depicted by Carlos Fuentes in *Terra Nostra*. By the year 1999 Mexicans would have become hunchbacked, dwarfish, and virtual serfs of the United States, for by then the job of feeding over 100 million people will have become impossible and mass extermination will have been considered a realistic policy. As in Aztec times the public will be brainwashed into accepting this human sacrifice; apparently brainwashing never ceased to be a political skill in Mexico.

The theme of dwarfishness occasions great sensitivity among Mexicans. As noted earlier Oscar Monroy Rivera, whose life and works I am now analyzing in a separate edition, has gone far toward developing the theme of enanismo.[21] It is questionable whether either he or Carlos Fuentes truly believes that the inescapable ultimate destiny of Mexicans is hunchbacked dwarfish serfdom. Monroy for one tells me that he fears such a likelihood, but he also adds that this is by no means inescapable, at least not if normative change occurs in the way Mexico is ruled.

NOTES

1. Steven E. Sanderson, "Political Tensions in the Mexican Party System," *Current History* 82 (December, 1983), p. 402.
2. Based on public testimony given (presumably with the knowledge and protection of the de la Madrid government) by José González González, former assistant to Auturo Durazo Moreno, in his book *Lo negro del Negro Durazo* (Mexico: Editorial Posadas, 1983), passim.
3. *Proceso,* December 19, 1983, p. 17.
4. In December 1983 the government used troops to dislodge the opposition municipal government of Juchitán and imposed a PRI regime that had been elected via what was widely condemned as a fraudulent process. See *Proceso,* December 19, 1983, pp. 6–11.
5. *Diario Las Américas,* November 26, 1983.
6. *Diario Las Américas,* December 1, 1983.
7. *Diario Las Américas,* December 2, 1983.
8. In a later poem-collage published in 1980 Rulfo still sees living beings weighted down by the dead, a land without water and in search of hope. Reprinted in *Proceso,* June 27, 1983, pp. 48–49.
9. James Wilkie, *The Mexican Revolution: Federal Expenditure and Social Change Since 1910* (Berkeley: University of California Press, 1967), p. 279. A more recent income distribution study concludes urging disadvantaged groups in Mexican society to unite so as to increase their bargaining power vis a vis the government and private sectors of socioeconomic power. See Wouter van Ginneken, *Socioeconomic Groups and Income Distribution in Mexico* (New York: St. Martin's Press, 1980), pp. 146–54. This study seems to presume the existence of honest financial administration in Mexican government given the proposal it makes for more effective tax collection to reinforce federal spending programs.
10. Wayne Cornelius, *Politics and the Migrant Poor in Mexico City* (Stanford: Stanford University Press, 1975), pp. 229–30.
11. Edward Williams, *The Rebirth of the Mexican Petroleum Industry* (Lexington, Mass.: Lexington Books, 1979), p. 170.
12. In addition to the politico-administrative scandals already cited there is the yet to be explained case of Miguel Nassar Haro, former head of Mexico's Federal Judicial Police, who was implicated in an international car theft operation extending into California and who allegedly escaped prosecution in the United States because of his ties with the CIA.
13. Peter Smith, *Labyrinths of Power: Political Recruitment in Twentieth Century Mexico* (Princeton, N.J.: Princeton University Press, 1979), p. 215.
14. Roderic A. Camp, *Mexico's Leaders: Their Education and Recruitment* (Tucson: University of Arizona Press, 1980), pp. 202–8.

15. There are reports of potentially link-breaking alliances, e.g. that of COCEI students, peasants, and small rural landowners in Oaxaca. *Diario Las Américas,* November 26, 1983.

16. Steven E. Sanderson, *Agrarian Populism and the Mexican State: The Struggle for Land in Sonora* (Berkeley: University of California Press, 1981), p. 206.

17. Luis Spota, *Palabras mayores* (Mexico: Editorial Grijalbo, 1975), p. 149. Sexual perversion as a political tactic was developed in the previous edition of *Mexican Democracy,* see especially pages 195, 196, and 246. I have been told by normally reliable sources that the Mexican government is actively trying to shut down such aberrations during the de la Madrid sexenio.

18. John A. Price, *Tijuana: Urbanization in a Border Culture* (Notre Dame, Indiana: Notre Dame University Press, 1973), p. 128.

19. Christian Bay, *The Structure of Freedom* (New York: Atheneum, 1968), p. 7.

20. Samuel Ramos, *Profits of Man and Culture in Mexico* (New York: McGraw-Hill, 1962), pp. 60–65.

21. Oscar Monroy Rivera, *El mexicano enano* (Mexico: Editorial Diana, 1967) and *A la espera del día* (Mexico: Costa-Amic, 1975) plus others cited in Chapter Seven of the previous edition of *Mexican Democracy.* I am currently translating one of his best works that I will call *El Bulla: The Prophet of Silence* that will be forthcoming in a sociopolitical-biographical format.

Epilogue

Electoral Opposition in San Luis Potosí: The Case of Nava

by Robert R. Bezdek

Since the formation of the governing party in 1929, electoral opposition movements have seriously challenged the official party in only a limited number of elections at the three basic levels—presidential, gubernatorial, and mayoral. At the presidential level the only serious challenge to the governing party occurred in 1940.[1] At the gubernatorial level at least five highly competitive elections have occurred from 1956 to the present.[2] At the mayoral level electoral oppositions have officially won and ruled about seven times in state capitals from 1958 to the present.[3] There are slightly more officially recognized opposition victories at lower municipal levels than in a state capital, although these still are very rare. As has been documented, the official party, controlled by the government, will occasionally recognize an opposition victory at the local level but has never recognized an opposition victory beyond a municipal election and has always recaptured the municipality for PRI rule at the very next election.[4] This description of the pattern of official control of the electoral system is one that complements Johnson's arguments in this book.

The most unique case of electoral opposition in Mexico involves Dr. Salvador Nava (an ophthalmologist), who lives in the state capital of the state by the same name, San Luis Potosí. Nava's case is significant because he became the first officially-recognized opposition mayor of a state capital during this century (according to the best information I have been able to gather). Three years after his mayoral victory, Nava ran for governor of the state of San Luis Potosí in 1961 and won the election according even to official sources but was not recognized. He then attempted to form some regional parties in opposition to PRI, but his efforts were unsuccessful. Amazingly, after two decades of noninvolvement in the political process, Nava ran again for mayor of San Luis Potosí in 1982 after considerable encouragement from his fellow residents. President Miguel de la Madrid Hurtado recognized Nava's victory. Because of the unique nature of this case, Nava and his movement merit analysis.

I will first deal with the conditions that led to Nava's election as mayor of the capital city in 1958 and then to his decision to run for the gubernatorial position of the state. The organization that he built, the government's brutal efforts to defeat him, and their unwillingness to recognize his victory are significant elements of this case study. After the Nava or *navista* movement lay dormant for almost 20 years, one must look seriously at the factors that led to its reemergence. Certainly, this was a reflection of popular discontent with single party rule in San Luis Potosí, one that could herald the beginning of major defections from the PRI monolith.

THE MAYORAL ELECTION OF 1958

The movement grew slowly as Potosinans became increasingly aware of the economic and political stranglehold of a regional cacique, Gonzalo N. Santos. He was not only the largest landholder but also owned the most fertile lands in the Huasteca,[5] a region at a lower altitude than the rest of the state and toward the Gulf of Mexico. Along with powerful economic hegemony for more than 20 years, Santos directly controlled many politicians as well as the newspapers. According to Dr. Nava, Santos even received a monthly cut ($8,000 U.S.) of the meager budget of the state's capital city. Further, Potosinans reported that his tactics were ruthless. He frequently sent his *pistoleros* (gunmen) to prevent or put an end to attempts to thwart his activities. The specific nature of Santos's controls are not nearly as important as the Potosinans's perceptions of the cacique's almost unchecked power.

Nava reported that the anti-Santos movement actually began within the Autonomous University of San Luis Potosí. In 1956, Dr. Manuel Nava, Jr., the well-respected rector of the state university and brother of Dr. Salvador Nava, faced reelection to his position. Since he had conducted a series of reforms, Dr. Manuel Nava was highly popular with students, professors, and the state capital residents. Thus when Santos tried to impose his own candidate, the university community rallied to the support of the rector and achieved a victory over the cacique. In the process, however, Santos had provoked the ire of university professors and students and hence had stimulated the incipient stages of public opposition. Again in 1958, this pattern was repeated, as the popular rector was reelected. These first battles against Santos were important inasmuch as these successes began to encourage others to mobilize support against the cacique.

The students soon attracted national attention to their cause. During the early months of 1958, Lic. Adolfo López Mateos, the presidential candidate, visited San Luis Potosí on his nationwide tour. As López Mateos approached the university, he was greeted by students with banners, such as "Death to Santos," "Expel the Cacique," "Santos, the Assassin," and others. Similar banners greeted the presidential candidate at other stops on his tour throughout the state. Later during the campaign, in Poza Rica, Veracruz, López Mateos stated: "Los cacicazgos subsisten hasta que el pueblo los tolera."[6] ("Caciques subsist as long as the people tolerate them.") Such a statement did not go unnoticed in San Luis Potosí. In fact, my interviews strongly suggest that it was interpreted as national support for local movements against bosses and became the theme of this movement in its incipient stages.

In July 1958, a group of professionals and intellectuals in San Luis Potosí initiated a reform movement in order to: 1) join and work within the structure of the local PRI; 2) win the municipal presidency of the state capital in the 1958 elections; and 3) finally break Santos's stranglehold. They did not accomplish their first goal, although they received encouragement and support from the national PRI. To their surprise, the reformers, perhaps with the help of some emotional incidents to be described below, accomplished the third goal before the second.

As president of this group, Dr. Salvador Nava began searching for a mayoral candidate for the upcoming elections. This group wanted his brother, Dr. Manuel Nava, as the candidate because he was easily the most prestigious Potosinan and had administrative experience; but he declined for health reasons. His sudden death in August 1958, led to conflicts for the rectorship of the university. This time, however, Santos was successful in imposing one of his own candidates by manipulating the elections. Students and professors protested through a series of strikes. Consequently, anti-Santos feelings were high in the university and began pervading the community.

Since approximately 18 prestigious leaders declined the mayoral candidacy, Dr. Salvador Nava became the consensus candidate, although he lacked political ambitions and administrative experience. At this time Nava was neither as well known nor as prestigious as his brother, even though he was recognized for his social labor among workers. It should be noted that the Nava family name was well known and respected for the number of physicians who rendered their services to all sectors of the San Luis Potosí society. Specifically, Dr. Manuel Nava started his practice in this state capital city at the turn of the century. All four of his sons, Manuel (who became the university rector), Salvador, José, and Rafael, also became practicing physicians in San Luis Potosí in the 1930s and the 1940s. It is interesting to speculate on the number of Potosinans who came into contact with the Nava physicians. In any case, this situation created positive name recognition for the family as well as a fascinating network of contacts, which I did not find in the other cases of opposition at the state capital level.

On October 19, some 5,000 Potosinans attended the open convention which nominated Nava as an independent candidate of an ad hoc party called the Unión Cívica Potosiona, while, simultaneously, PRI held its convention to nominate the official candidate.[7] At its first meetings, however, the new movement did not attract as many supporters as it did when violence broke out during the last three weeks of the campaign.

As the anti-Santista movement gained momentum, Santos lost control over the press. The major newspaper, *El Sol de San Luis,* began printing cartoons lampooning Santos and his abusive political control, such as his many candidate impositions. Further, the newspaper printed pictures of students and others tearing down plaques on buildings and streets where the name "Santos" was mentioned. For example, *El Sol de San Luis* gave considerable publicity to the students who changed the name of a major avenue from "Pedro A. Santos" to Dr. Manuel Nava, Jr."[8] On other occasions it printed headlines such as "San Luis Prefers Death to the Hated Cacique System."[9] The net impact of this type of publicity was to enormously increase mass discontent, anger, and rage toward the existing system.

During the last three weeks of the campaign, violence broke out and helped assure the election of Dr. Nava. The newspaper, of course, aided by treating these incidents emotionally. While sporadic outbursts of violence began around November 15, the incident which assured massive opposition support occurred on November 20, the anniversary of the Mexican Revolution. Parades are in order on this national holiday, but the angry Potosinans had more in mind. As a group of students and others paraded in front of the governor's palace, they began tossing eggs at Governor Manuel Alvarez, who was standing on his balcony. Although Alvarez was imposed by and closely identified with Santos, it is more probable that the eggs were meant for Santos since it was rumored—apparently intentionally[10]—that he was in the palace. Rather than reacting more calmly, the understandably angered governor and his supporters immediately ordered the soldiers to counterattack. The soldiers brutally attacked and beat the students and some bystanders. In turn, the crowds were outraged and bent on revenge. Alvarez was so terrified that he left the palace under heavy guard through the back door and apparently moved to Mexico City.[11]

The soldiers' attack was a costly mistake for the regime. It was a trigger mechanism for mass outrage. Popular reaction was so widespread and intense that perhaps even the regime (or what was left of it) was afraid to tamper with the upcoming election and results. While previous navista meetings had a limited—although still large—number of supporters, now the number of active supporters appeared to include virtually the entire population of the state capital. Thus, the only remaining task for the opposition leaders was to channel this wave of outrage to victory in the December 7, 1958, elections.

On November 24, a citizens' committee presented an ultimatum to the federal minister of gobernación to the effect that if Governor Manuel Alvarez were not forced to resign, then the Potosinans would go on strike indefinitely. In order to apply pressure to their demand, the residents of San Luis Potosí closed all factories and stores at 5:00 P.M. on November 27. Meanwhile, massive demonstrations were held. Three days before the election, when violence erupted, leaving two dead and 19 injured, the government ordered a state of siege.

Against the backdrop of this tense situation, the angered Potosinans voted on Sunday, December 7, 1958. The first official results showed Nava with 26,319 to Gutiérrez's 1,683.[12] Perhaps because of this lopsided result and because of presidential guarantees to "respect the vote,"[13] the opposition leaders decided to lift the strike for five days beginning on December 9. A week after the election, the final official results gave Nava the victory by a two to one margin.[14] Shortly thereafter, the elated Potosinans dropped their demand for the governor's resignation; in any case, he resigned about a month later. The people had achieved in fact a victory of historic proportions, for this was the first opposition movement to officially defeat PRI for the mayoralty of a state capital since the formation of the official party.

THE REFORM ADMINISTRATION AND PREPARATION FOR THE GUBERNATORIAL CAMPAIGN

The reform administration in San Luis Potosí was able to accomplish some of its original goals. This movement succeeded in diminishing the political and economic stranglehold of the cacique, Gonzalo N. Santos. Moreover, although the 1958 election challenge occurred at the mayoral level in the state capital, the Potosinans still were able to take credit for the resignation of Governor Manuel Alvarez, who was identified with Santos. And, obviously, this movement did elect its candidate to the mayoral position of the state capital. The Potosinans failed, however, in their attempt to work within the PRI or to reform it.

Of course, the Nava administration had a strong impact on local policy, for even high-ranking government officials in Mexico City report that it performed more effectively than the previous PRI administrations. In one of their first reforms, Nava and his staff corrected abuses of the budget, thus increasing almost immediately the amount of money available to improve city services. Consequently, the annual municipal budget increased from $376,000 (U.S. dollars) to slightly more than $560,000 within the first year—a 49 percent increase without raising taxes. Due to this elimination of corruption and its own serious intent to reform, the new administration soon installed drainage systems, expanded electrical services and running water, paved streets, etc. In some cases where services could not be expanded due to budget constraints, Nava would meet with individuals from a particular neighborhood to work on a compromise. In one case, some residents requested running water. Nava met with them to explain the city's budgetary limitations. After a series of meetings, the mayor agreed to an arrangement whereby the residents would dig trenches for the water line and the city would provide the pipes and the technical expertise to make the system operational.

More importantly, the new administration, unlike its predecessors, was an open one. Daily, for example, the city government published its income and expenditures in front of city hall. Periodically, they also published this information in the newspaper. In addition, Nava fired one of his department heads for corruption, thus increasing his own credibility.

It is easy to understand the respect the people accorded to Nava. In fact, myths began to emerge concerning his work habits. One was that he used to take stimulants in order to work efficiently until 2:00 or 3:00 A.M. many nights.

What is not easy to understand is why President Adolfo López Mateos went out of his way to praise the accomplishments of the Nava administration. Many Potosinans welcomed the president on his visit to San Luis Potosí in August 1960. They considered him a friend since he was responsible for allowing official recognition of Nava's 1958 victory. Before addressing a large public gathering, the president had one of his aides divide a list of governmental accomplishments in this state capital according to city and to state sponsorship. Thus, when President López Mateos gave more credit to the Nava administration by reading its longer list of accomplishments, many interpreted this presidential gesture as tacit approval for Nava in the upcoming gubernatorial elections.

However, navista supporters recognized soon after winning the 1958 election that they would have to organize and publish a newspaper in order to get their message to the people. During the mayoral campaign Nava received some support from *El Sol de San Luis* and virtually none from *El Heraldo,* which had a smaller circulation than the former. But when Nava took office, both newspapers vehemently attacked his reforms.

Thus, in 1960, when around 26–28 key navistas told Nava that he had an obligation to be the gubernatorial candidate, these same core supporters decided that victory or even a strong showing was impossible without an opposition newspaper. At a high cost to these individuals and to all of his supporters, they started publication of *Tribuna* in October 1960. Starting an opposition paper in Mexico is no easy task. The initial costs of machinery and the operating costs of rent, salaries, paper, and many other items are quite high. Informants argue that along with some major contributors, there was a high number of medium and small contributors.

No one could expect *Tribuna* to be unbiased. Nava himself admits that the paper frequently overstepped the boundary of accurate reporting, for its purpose was to reinforce the antiregime attitudes of its supporters as well as to foster specific opposition activities. In addition, the newspaper editors attempted to counteract statements from the regime-controlled papers and thus engaged in a type of psychological warfare. In spite of these factors, the reporting in the opposition paper appears to have had less bias than the other two papers. In any case, many Potosinans throughout the state strongly supported the opposition paper and boycotted the other two. Informants report, for example, that *Tribuna*'s paid circulation throughout the state was at least three times that of the previously dominant newspaper, *El Sol de San Luis;* thus the former sold around 15,000 copies daily as compared with the latter's 5,000. After establishing the opposition newspaper, the Nava supporters knew that this was a key component in their effort to win the gubernatorial election. One of their next steps was to try to win the PRI nomination at this level just as they had attempted to at the local level.

THE 1961 GUBERNATORIAL CAMPAIGN

This section deals with Nava's attempt to win the PRI nomination, the campaign, the election with subsequent complaints by the opposition, and the government's repression to prevent any additional activities of the Nava movement. One can easily document that the government was taken by surprise with this movement in 1958 and thus was not prepared to suppress it. By contrast, in 1961, the government was fully prepared and was involved in well-orchestrated activities not only to deny Nava victory but also to eliminate the movement.

In order to obtain the official nomination within PRI, Nava traveled to Mexico City to solicit support from key government officials. After discussions with then Secretary of Gobernación Lic. Gustavo Díaz Ordaz (later president from 1964–70), and the president of PRI's central executive committee, General and Lic. Alfonso Corona del Rosal, Nava felt confident that he could become the PRI candidate if, as they assured him, he showed that he had a statewide, popular following. At least these two important government officials indicated that PRI was open to Nava's candidacy. In fact, Corona del Rosal told Nava to keep him informed of his activities.

Approximately two months later, after Nava had demonstrated extensive statewide support, the PRI president called him to Mexico City for a conference. According to my interviews with Nava in 1972, the gist of the conversation was as follows:

Corona del Rosal (CR): Dr. Nava, you cannot be the PRI candidate.

Nava (N): You are mistaken because the convention has not been held. If the people do not choose me, then I will bow out of the campaign.

CR: You will not be a candidate.

N: You are not the party; the people are. Besides I've already invested time and money in the campaign and have made a commitment to the people.

CR: You will not be a gubernatorial candidate. If you wish, I will make you a federal deputy. Also tell me how much you have already spent on your campaign, and I will reimburse you.

N: If the President doesn't want me for some reason, then let me talk to him. Otherwise, I will let the people decide whether I should be their candidate.

CR: If you continue, you will be sorry.

Nava did not give in to these threats. He called for a mass rally in San Luis Potosí and discussed the results of his confrontation with the chief PRI spokesman. When Nava asked the large gathering whether they wanted him as the gubernatorial candidate, they responded enthusiastically. But from this time on, it was quite clear that the regime's representatives would resort to less subtle tactics.

As mentioned previously, the state and federal governments were prepared to take whatever means were necessary to prevent an opposition victory. A case in point is the one year's residency requirement for the gubernatorial candidate, a formally-stated requisite in the state constitution. Manuel López Dávila, PRI's hand-picked opponent for Nava, obviously did not fulfill this requirement since he had spent most of his life in Chihuahua although he was born in San Luis Potosí. In fact, four months before the election, that is, at the time of his nomination as the official gubernatorial candidate of San Luis Potosí, López Dávila was still the chief administrator (*Official Mayor*) of the Ministry of Public Education in Chihuahua. Opposition complaints were ignored, but then how could the incumbents reply to this explicit violation without lending validity to it?

Other examples illustrate how widespread these tactics were. First, the busing and trucking of supporters of PRI rallies is standard procedure.[15] Second, one of Nava's campaign coordinators, Jesús Acosta, was attacked and shot by PRI workers in Tamazunchale. One suspects that his murder and perhaps even the attack on the Nava committee could have been due to high emotions, but the refusal of the regime thereafter to arrest the assassin, who was clearly identified by witnesses, suggested to many pro-Nava supporters that those who perpetrated violence against them would also be above the law.[16] Third, violence against navistas was common as some 200 opposition supporters were reportedly injured up to June 22.[17] Finally, a variety of subtle pressures were exerted against businessmen and teachers.

One event merits special attention, not because the source was absolutely accurate, but because many Mexicans and political observers know and report that public funds are used in the following manner for major PRI rallies. A PRI-sponsored rally to close the campaign occurred on June 25, 1961. A reporter from *Tribuna* estimated and spelled out the typical costs of such efforts (see Table 1). (Since all costs are expressed in Mexican pesos and the rate of exchange at that time was 12.50 pesos to one U.S. dollar, then the total estimated cost of this rally in dollars was $74,520.00.) Nava admitted that these costs were perhaps overestimated but thought that this rally would have cost the public treasury as least half that amount or roughly $37,000. Sources indicate that many peasants had to be bused in because the city of San Luis Potosí was solidly behind the opposition candidate. After the event many peasants roamed about town since PRI organizers had not paid them as promised and had not provided return transportation. Many observers have been told that PRI organizers promise money to entice peasants to attend rallies but, afterwards, pocket the money for themselves. The important point is that this is money from the public treasury spent on behalf of the official political party.

All indications were that Nava would win if his supporters were allowed to register and vote and if the government would count the votes honestly. Perhaps the best indicator of what would happen in a fair election came from a telephone operator who listened in on a conversation between the national PRI president, Corona del Rosal, and the PRI guber-

Table 1. Estimates of Typical Costs of a Major PRI Rally in 1961 in San Luis Potosí*

Gratuities to 15,000 people at $25.00 each	$375,000
Rent on 100 buses	$100,000
Rent on 50 freight cars	$124,000
Costs for the local press	$30,000
Costs for the national press including editorialists and columnists	$175,000
Radio, television, and movie advertising	$40,000
Housing, food, etc. for invited PRI guests	$25,000
Costs of entertainers from Mexico City	$35,000
Party expenses	$12,500
Other miscellaneous costs	$15,000
TOTAL	$931,500

*In Mexican pesos.
Source: *Tribuna,* June 26, 1961.

natorial candidate, López Dávila. Essentially, López Dávila stated that he wanted to resign as the official candidate because of the enormous opposition he had encountered. Corona del Rosal responded that he had to fight and could not make PRI look ridiculous.[18]

This incident was highly publicized in the opposition newspaper. Needless to say, the feelings of opposition supporters were reinforced because they knew that the PRI candidate was fearful of appearing in public. On many occasions, he was greeted by insults and chants of support for Nava.

On election day in July, many voting irregularities occurred as anticipated. The official election results showed that Nava barely won in the capital city but lost overwhelmingly in the rural areas. However, not even PRI supporters believe the election results. For example, Lic. Jesús Reyes Héroles, the president of PRI from 1972–74, told me in an interview in 1972 that Nava had won the gubernatorial election. In fact, virtually all informants, including PRI supporters, agreed that Nava had actually won this election.

After the election, when the regime had assured itself of an official victory, the government began suppressing the activities of Nava and his key followers by enormously increasing the costs of continued political participation. This time, however, the process of official suppression was accomplished by isolating the opposition leaders from their mass following and thus not provoking the ire of Potosinans through highly-visible, indiscriminate acts as had occurred in 1958.

Because many in the opposition movement were convinced that the government had stolen the elections, mass protests erupted in the state capital. But what could the opposition do? The alternatives were to protest to their "friend," President Adolfo López Mateos, who apparently had given official recognition to Nava's victory in the 1958 mayoral election; to protest to federal officials in gobernación; to stage mass protests in San Luis Potosí, perhaps including general strikes; to petition the Supreme Court in Mexico City; to engage in some violent activities; to organize an opposition party for future elections; and to recognize their powerlessness before the government and resign their efforts.

The first alternative proved futile, for the president refused to talk personally to the approximately 1,000 protestors, who made the 250 mile trip from San Luis Potosí to the National Palace; the president had one of his assistants meet with them. The second alternative similarly failed. While the opposition supporters were planning for the third alternative, mass protests, the government jailed Nava and four main organizers on "orders from the presidency," but shortly released them. On July 25, some three weeks after the election, navistas began a mass protest and reportedly stopped all commercial activity. When Nava spoke to a crowd of 60,000 protesters, violence erupted; the soldiers wounded several individuals and jailed some protesters.[19] After these incidents Nava's supporters were certain that their protests would not alter the results of the past election.

The fourth alternative was to petition the Supreme Court even though Nava knew that the president wields considerable control over the federal branch that should be the ultimate arbiter on electoral law as well as other legal matters. Some of the points made in Nava's petition were:

1. No offices were established for voter registration throughout the state. Consequently, on election day, the voter lists were arbitrarily prepared, thus eliminating the majority of voters. In the state capital, to be sure, four special voting booths were set up for voters, who had been unable to register, but the enormous vote recorded here in favor of Nava was declared null and void by the state congress.
2. The election officials in the voting booths almost always favored PRI. Opposition representatives, of course, were not allowed in the polling places. In addition, people had to vote amid threats carried out by the army, who obeyed the orders of the electoral officials.
3. With army protection, ballot boxes were carried away without an open count on the scene. This even occurred in places where numerous citizens were still waiting to cast their ballot.
4. Violation of the right of petition, that is, numerous questions directed by the Nava committee to the State Electoral Commission were ignored.[20]

As might have been expected the Supreme Court refused to investigate these claims. This refusal, perhaps more than any other official act, clearly demonstrates not only the extensive control of the regime but also *national* collusion to deny victory to the Nava movement.

According to one, highly pro-Nava informant, Nava and a very small group of supporters considered the fifth alternative, violent activities. If this was the case, then one can more easily understand the government's mass arrests of navista leaders. In any case the government attempted to pin various acts of violence on the opposition and to discover conspiracies in order to justify their own violence against the opposition as they began whipping the recalcitrant Potosinans into shape. Reportedly, in September 1961, a small group of navistas had planned to blow up a train bridge and fuel deposit of PEMEX—both of which were on the outskirts of the state capital—but changed their minds when they saw soldiers guarding these installations. Publicly, Nava definitely preached nonviolence and certainly thought opposition violence against the Mexican regime would be counterproductive. Many informants inside the government, however, argued that an appeal from Nava to his supporters for mass violence against the regime would have easily triggered a massive uprising, and probably brutal official retaliation, resulting in a bloodbath. Privately, Nava denied any knowledge of any attempts at violence within his organization. During the middle of September, the government began a massive crackdown on the opposition. Many arrests followed house to house searches for firearms. On September 15, at least 200 key leaders of the opposition were jailed. That same evening government henchmen destroyed the offices of the opposition newspaper, *Tribuna,* and warned its personnel to leave the state within 24 hours or else probably face a series of repressive acts. The government also jailed Nava but released him on October 4. When Nava returned to San Luis Potosí, large crowds welcomed him, thus signifying their willingness to continue their opposition.

By this time, however, Dr. Nava and his key organizers, many of whom had suffered from repression, decided to stop fighting the regime openly and thus curtailed their opposition activities. Many supporters told Nava that they feared further repressive acts against themselves and their families and, in addition, could not afford the high costs of such risky participation. They wanted to return to "normalcy" so that they could at least earn a living and take care of their families. Consequently, they all decided to organize an opposition party for future elections.

The *Partido Demócrata Potosino* (Democratic Potosinan Party), the. Nava party, ran Dr. Rangel[21] for mayor of San Luis Potosí in December 1961. The overwhelming majority of Potosinans, however, were dispirited and thinking that PRI would also steal this election, did not bother to vote. According to a much smaller edition of *Tribuna,* PRI falsely recorded a high turnout—some 25,000 votes. The official vote showed that at least 22,000 had voted, with the PRI candidate, Silva, receiving 17,000 votes to Rangel's 5,000. Apparently, the still active opposition members had to fight not only PRI's manipulation but also the understandable apathy of their former supporters.

For a period of time Dr. Nava traveled throughout some northern Mexican states in an attempt to start regional parties against PRI. While on many occasions he was enthusiastically received and honored by large gatherings of people, his initiatives for the development of opposition parties were by and large met with apathy and fear of opposing PRI. Even though his own attempts to form another opposition party failed, Nava never considered joining PAN or any of the other opposition parties.

The final repressive act occurred approximately a year and a half after the gubernatorial election. On February 5, 1963, Nava was once again arrested, probably on orders from the governor. As mentioned earlier, López Dávila was quite embarrassed whenever he appeared in public because crowds booed him, insulted him with whistles, and apparently succeeded in irritating him by shouting pro-Nava slogans. Perhaps, as a result, the governor decided to fabricate excuses for retaliation against Nava and attempted to put an end to Nava's support. Whatever the justification for this act, all informants reported it as highly arbitrary.

In the San Luis Potosí jail, the guards tied Nava's hands, blindfolded him, and beat him mercilessly. Nava related that he almost immediately fell unconscious some time before midnight but that when he regained consciousness around 7:00 the next morning, he realized that he had vomited considerably. When some friends, who were physicians, visited him, they were shocked by his appearance and realized that Nava needed medical attention. After the state attorney general refused their request for Nava's release, they talked to a federal judge, who demanded that Nava be freed, but the individuals in charge of the jail initially ignored the judge's legal order. Finally, the judge threatened to send in federal troops if the jailers did not release him. On February 8, 1963, Nava was taken to the hospital. From the severe beatings, Nava had a broken rib, a hemorrhage in the heart, countless bruises, and could not move his right arm.

After these acts of repression against especially Nava as well as his supporters, it is easy to understand that the government had finally achieved its objective, that is, to eliminate virtually all of the activities by the navistas. In addition, Dr. Nava himself had decided against any further involvement in politics because he felt that it was futile. One can easily identify with his sense of frustration and disappointment since he had suffered considerable harassment. Consequently, for all practical purposes, the Nava movement was dead.

Apparently, one result of Nava's movement was that PRI was more careful in choosing at least the next two gubernatorial candidates. Most sources agree that Antonio Rocha Cordero (1967–73) and Guillermo Fonseca Alvarez (1973–79) were reasonable governors and ran relatively open administrations.[22] Unfortunately, this process of acceptable governors did not continue with the next governor, Carlos Jonguitud Barrios (1979–85), who was considered the catalyst for the next Nava movement.[23] In fact, many informants referred to him as the "first navista," meaning that he was the primary factor in the reemergence of the Nava movement.

NAVA'S ELECTION AS MAYOR IN 1982

To understand Nava's election as mayor of San Luis Potosí for the second time, one must analyze several factors. First, information on the activities of Governor Carlos Jonguitud Barrios is essential. Second, a group of professionals organized a movement called the *Frente Cívico Potosino* (Potosinan Civic Front), which held a *comida de recuerdo,* a testimonial dinner, to honor Nava 20 years after the 1961 gubernatorial election. Later, the group's task was to convince Nava that he should be the mayoral candidate, help him win the election, and then at least reduce the governor's stranglehold on the capital city of San Luis Potosí. In addition, other factors, such as the national economic crisis, as detailed by Johnson in the first chapter, influenced this election. Finally, a description of what occurred during the campaign adds to our understanding of this unique movement.

Governor Carlos Jonguitud Barrios was the primary factor for the reemergence of this movement for several reasons. When Jonguitud became governor, he already had a history of leadership in the *Sindicato Nacional de Trabajadores de Educación* (SNTE) (the national union of education workers). As secretary general of teachers throughout the nation, he wielded a considerable amount of clout. Some informants indicated that Jonguitud considered himself presidential timber and was actively seeking to be the successor to President José López Portillo (1976–82). This explanation merits attention since it helps in the analysis of many of the events that occurred. Perhaps this is why he became governor of San Luis Potosí, although the traditional path to the presidency is through a federal cabinet position. Further, this may help us understand some of the complaints of the Potosinans against Governor Jonguitud. Some of the complaints were that he spent a considerable amount of time outside of the state of San Luis Potosí, that he hired many people in his administration from outside of the state, that Potosinans could not get meetings with him, and that Potosinans did not see progress in their state.

Additional complaints were that he was very authoritarian, isolated since he did not give out information on public works as did his two predecessors, and corrupt. Evidence cited by informants for corruption were items such as his allowing his director of prisons to release prisoners in return for bribes. One universal complaint that seemed to upset the Potosinans considerably was what they referred to as his vulgarity, namely, frequently getting drunk in public. This appeared to disturb the Potosinans's sense of propriety.

Consequently, for all these reasons, Potosinans from different professions began organizing the *Frente Cívico Potosino* (FCP). Their first public activity was a well publicized testimonial dinner to honor Dr. Salvador Nava in July of 1981, 20 years after his gubernatorial race. Approximately 3,000 Nava supporters attended. PRI officials criticized this dinner by arguing that those in attendance were Nava's old supporters from his movement two decades earlier, but others say this was not the case because Nava's impressive deeds had spread by word of mouth. I witnessed this positive feeling for Nava when I taught in 1973 at the School of Economics at the Autonomous University of San Luis Potosí. The directors of this school introduced me to others as the "expert" on the Nava movement with the apparent intention of attempting to gain my acceptance in this radical school of economics.

After this initial success, the leaders of the FCP approached Dr. Nava and asked him to run for mayor of San Luis Potosí. Nava, who now was 68 years old, declined saying that a younger man would be better suited for the job. As a result, the FCP leaders searched for that ideal candidate. Finally, after turning down the offer twice, Nava said he would seriously consider the candidacy. Unlike his previous races for mayor and governor, Nava knew that this time he could not run as an independent candidate because some national reforms required all candidates to run with one or more of the parties that were registered. Needless to say, this required strategy to consider which party or parties to choose to identify with as well as negotiations to receive their approval.

It is significant to point out that Nava was prepared earlier for this race than the official party. For example, in September 1982, *El Sol de San Luis* reported that Nava was considering the mayoral race. On September 9, the same newspaper notified its readers that Nava had made the decision to be an opposition candidate.[24] Having made his candidacy official, Nava, in effect, prevented the major opposition party, PAN, from fielding its own candidate because Nava and his supporters knew that the public respected him for his honesty, hard work, and accomplishments in his previous administration. A candidate from PAN—if the party leadership had been so inclined—would have splintered the opposition vote and would have allowed PRI to manipulate the election.[25] One interesting reason for PAN's support of Nava was fear that another party, such as FDM, would receive all the favorable publicity with an anticipated Nava victory if PAN had opted to stay neutral in this election. In other words, even PAN recognized that Nava's personal appeal was stronger than that of any party.[26]

In any case, *El Sol de San Luis* reported on September 20 that PAN and PDM had endorsed Nava. Nava indicated that he had had discussions with PSUM (a new leftist party) but that they could not reach an agreement. Basically, his strategy was to get several parties to endorse him because he never wanted to belong to any political party. However, he managed to receive the endorsement of only two parties. Still, this was an unusual arrangement as pointed out by Alfredo Lujambio Rafols, a PAN member, who would become the director of finance in the Nava administration.[27] PAN can endorse someone who is not a member of the party, but this is a rare phenomenon. Lujambio Rafols argued that the central issue shared by PAN, PDM, and Nava was the fight for an autonomous city, which, again, indicates the disenchantment with Governor Jonguitud and his financial stranglehold over the city.[28]

The reader will recall that in 1958 as well as in 1961 Nava attempted to gain the PRI nomination. In 1982 no such attempt was made. Strangely, however, PRI contacted Nava. José Murat Casas, the general state delegate of PRI in San Luis Potosí, visited Nava to tell him that an excellent candidate would be chosen from PRI for the mayoral position if Nava would drop out of the race. As to be expected, Nava did not drop out of the race.

In contrast to Nava's early organizational strength, PRI had considerable difficulty in getting organized, perhaps because they were well aware of the fact that their candidate would have to be the underdog against Nava in a fair election. Headlines a month later in *El Sol de San Luis* indicate that there were several possible PRI candidates.[29] Finally, the newspaper announced on October 22 that Hector González Lárraga would be the candidate. It is important to note that this choice of an official candidate occurred approximately a month and a half after Nava's announcement. According to informants González Lárraga's candidacy was not well accepted as he made several personal attacks on Nava, which added to divisions within PRI. Suddenly, about one month before the election, the newspaper reported that González Lárraga had to go to Houston for a medical checkup.[30] The next day it was reported that the official candidate had had a heart operation.[31] The following day the newspaper reported that PRI had already chosen a new candidate to challenge Nava.

He was Lic. Roberto Leyva Torres, a former rector of the University of San Luis Potosí.[32] The substitution of a candidate at this late stage of the campaign was questionable from a legal point of view, something which PDM fought unsuccessfully. More questionable, however, in the minds of many Potosinans was whether González Lárraga had a heart operation on very short notice. Further, the immediate substitution of the official candidate lent credibility to the idea that the entire process was staged.

Nava immediately condemned the whole process and argued that such dramatic changes in the official party simply meant that PRI was preparing to steal the election.[33] Interestingly, statements from government officials, such as Enrique Olivares Santana (federal secretary of gobernación) and Leyva Torres, were very defensive.[34] These officials reiterated statements such as "the election will be fair," and "we don't pay people to attend our functions." These statements lent credibility to Nava's accusations.

The "close of the campaign" on November 28, 1982, indicates the different levels of support for PRI and for the Nava movement. The close of the campaign is a typical event in Mexico that occurs one week before the election and is frequently used as a gauge of support for candidates. Both Nava and Leyva Torres chose the same central plaza for their final campaign event. After viewing some pictures as well as a videotape of both events, I would have to agree with other sources that Nava attracted approximately 40,000 people around 7:00 in the evening, whereas Leyva Torres had attracted approximately 10,000 people around 2:00 in the afternoon.[35] My interviews indicate that this was typical for both candidates throughout the campaign and that most observers agreed that Nava would win in a fair election.

Meanwhile, FCP was leading the opposition effort to train individuals to prevent fraud in the majority of precincts. Based on reports of government fraud in Nava's 1961 attempt to win the gubernatorial election, the navistas realized that they would have to train loyal supporters to challenge any illegal activities of PRI supporters in the 220 voting places. Informants indicate that this was a critical activity not only to prevent fraud but also to reinforce Nava supporters and especially to encourage these people to actually vote on election day since there was concern that violence could erupt. In fact, Nava himself attempted to reassure his supporters that trained navistas would be at 98 percent of the polling places; this statement appeared in the newspaper five days before the election.[36]

On election day, December 5, 1982, the relatively calm atmosphere appeared to surprise even some of the members of the Nava family. For example, Luis Nava, Dr. Nava's son, told me that he was approached by federal representatives of gobernación who were very friendly and simply reassured him that "they were in San Luis Potosí to make sure that no problems would occur." In addition, other informants indicated that the federal troops passing by in their vehicles would flash the "V" sign of victory to Nava groups. This atmosphere was obviously in stark contrast to what many navistas, especially the Nava family, had anticipated. For example, telephone operators supportive of the Nava movement had warned members of the Nava family even before Dr. Nava announced his candidacy that the government had their telephones tapped.

It is dubious whether the actual election results will ever be known. The day after the election, *El Heraldo,* which has a much smaller circulation than *El Sol de San Luis,* reported in its headline that Nava had won by a margin of three to one in 150 out of 220 voting places.[37] The article indicated that Nava had received 49,294 votes to Levya Torres's 17,728 or that Nava had received about 74 percent of the vote. While many navistas felt that they had clearly won the election, the important task was to receive official recognition from the federal government. This is where the Nava strategy of having key supporters in the precincts was invaluable. While the navistas were able to observe and verify the results of only 183 out of the 220 voting places, the percent of the vote received by Nava was the same as reported in *El Heraldo.*[38] The vote was 58,575 for Nava and 20,419 for Leyva Torres. Xerox copies were made of these results so that Dr. Nava could take them to Mexico City and argue that he had won the election and should be officially recognized.

Within a couple of days of the election, federal officials from gobernación called Nava to meet with them in Mexico City. One needs to remember that President Miguel de la Madrid and his cabinet had just taken office on December 1, 1982, and that the official decision on the San Luis Potosí election would be interpreted as the direction the new administration was likely to take in competitive elections. Nava went to Mexico City on Tuesday, December 7, to meet with the new secretary of gobernación, Manuel Bartlett.[39] Armed with copies of the election results from 183 out of the 220 voting places, Nava presented his argument to Bartlett. Bartlett, in turn, asked for the original voting results rather than the copies. Consequently, Nava called his family in San Luis Potosí to request the original results. Before a family member left for Mexico City with these original results, another xerox copy was made, for the Nava family believed that officials in gobernación could confiscate the original results as well as the copies Dr. Nava had, thus leaving them without any proof of victory. Meanwhile, Bartlett met in a different office with governor Carlos Jonguitud Barrios and the PRI's mayoral candidate, Roberto Leyva Torres. Nava family members who were waiting in the reception area reported that Jonguitud Barrios and Leyva Torres entered the office of gobernación in a jubilant mood and left in a somber mood. Apparently, Bartlett had told them that his office would respect the vote. Dr. Nava told me that Bartlett promised him official recognition after he evaluated the original election results. Nava, confident of official recognition, returned to San Luis Potosí.

José Murat Casas, the general state delegate of PRI in San Luis Potosí, visited Dr. Nava before the official recognition of Nava became public information. Apparently, his primary purpose was to tell Nava that PRI's votes would have to be inflated. Since Nava was assured of official recognition, the margin of his victory was not important to him. On Sunday, one week after the election, the major newspaper announced Nava's victory with extra large letters in its headline.[40] The very next day, the same newspaper reported the official results as 59,933 for Nava and 40,275 for Leyva Torres with 4,209 votes annulled.[41] Informants were virtually unanimous in reporting that Nava received 80 to 90 percent of the vote. In any case, what appears clear is that Nava won by a margin of at least three to one. Additionally, he is the first opposition leader to become the mayor of a state capital city for a second time.

CONCLUSION

This opposition movement has been built around one individual, Dr. Salvador Nava Martínez. There is no apparent successor. One would suspect, consequently, that after Nava's term expires that rule by an opposition leader would terminate. In fact, in all cases of opposition victory in the state capital city, PRI has regained control with their candidates in the next election. In the case of San Luis Potosí, however, it appears that a strong foundation for the opposition has been laid. PAN supporters, particularly, indicated that they were planning to run a mayoral candidate when Nava finished his term in office.

What will happen is subject to considerable speculation, but at least several factors are important. First, what will be the policy of the de la Madrid administration in terms of regaining control?[42] No one seriously doubts that PRI can revert to its traditional ways of winning. Second, how will Dr. Nava perform his task as mayor? One suspects that he will be as respected as he was after his 1959–61 administration. From Nava's previous administration to this administration, however, it is important to note that the population of this capital city has increased from around 200,000 to around 500,000.[43] Quite simply, this means that the need for basic services has increased very dramatically. Third, Governor Jonguitud did not give Dr. Nava's administration the financial resources it was entitled to until Nava organized a protest march to the governor's palace. As a result, the governor increased his financial support to the capital city from 9 million pesos to around 34 million pesos in May 1983; the city collects 25 million pesos on its own. The total funds available increased from 34 to 59 million pesos.[44] However, these resources are still very limited when the needs are considered, and thus one must question how much can be done with these limited resources. Finally, what will happen with the national economic crisis and how will this impact on San Luis Potosí?

In evaluating this opposition victory as well as others throughout Mexico, one needs to suggest some propositions for testing. First, some catalyzing incident occurs to lead to an opposition movement which can seriously challenge PRI. The catalyzing incident in Nava's 1958 election was the cacique, Gonzalo N. Santos, who had a stranglehold on the entire state of San Luis Potosí, while the catalyst in the 1982 election was the objectionable behavior of Governor Carlos Jonguitud Barrios. Second, official recognition of an opposition victory at the mayoral level occurs when PRI is taken by surprise as occurred in 1958 and when the margin of victory is lopsided as occurred in 1958 and 1982. Some observers suggest that the margin of victory has to be three to one, while others argue that a two to one margin would suffice. Another proposition for testing official recognition emerges from this case. As the reader will recall, Governor Jonguitud Barrios was attempting to play a more important role in national politics. Official recognition of an opposition mayor in this case, then, suggests that the president might want to reduce the power of the governor. An additional proposition for official recognition of an opposition victory would be applicable to this time period only, that is, a period in which Mexico is facing serious economic problems. Perhaps President de la Madrid's administration allows opposition victories so that opposition administrations, which are forced to rule with minimal resources, will receive some of the blame for the national economic problems.

NOTES

1. Betty Kirk, "Election Day, 1940," in James Wilkie and Albert L. Michaels (eds.) *Revolution in Mexico: Years of Upheaval, 1910–1940* (New York: Alfred A. Knopf, 1969), pp. 262–67.
2. These elections occurred in Chihuahua in 1956, Baja California Norte in 1959, San Luis Potosí in 1961, Sonora in 1967, and Yucatán in 1969.

3. These officially recognized opposition victories occurred in San Luis Potosí in 1958; Hermosillo, Sonora, in 1967; Mérida, Yucatán, in 1967; Guanajuato in 1982; Hermosillo, Sonora, in 1982; San Luis Potosí in 1982; and Chihuahua in 1983.
4. Among others, see Robert R. Bezdek, *Electoral Oppositions in Mexico: Emergence, Suppression, and Impact on Political Processes,* unpublished Ph.D. dissertation, Ohio State University, 1973. Due to some of Carlos Madrazo's attempts to reform the internal structure of PRI during the mid-1960s, opposition parties had received official recognition of their victories in 17 cities. See the article reprinted verbatim from Mexico City's *Excelsior* in the *Diario de Yucatán,* November 24, 1970. The article implies that extralegal tactics were generally used to win back all these municipalities while Alfonso Martínez Domínguez was president of PRI's national executive committee.
5. Antonio Estrada M. describes briefly the economic and political control of Santos in *La Grieta en el Yugo* (San Luis Potosí, Editorial del Autor, 1963), pp. 23–26. This book is disorganized, highly emotional, and written from a sinarchist point of view. However, it captures the highlights of the Nava movement. Dr. Nava himself stated that he began reading the book but became disgusted with its inaccuracies and thus did not continue. According to the book's inside flap, the first 5,500 copies were confiscated by the government, but subsequent copies were clandestinely printed on various presses throughout Mexico.
6. Estrada, M., *La Grieta en el Yugo,* p. 41.
7. *El Sol de San Luis,* October 20, 1958.
8. Ibid., November 25, 1958.
9. Ibid., November 23, 1958.
10. *El Sol de San Luis,* November 21, 1958.
11. Ibid.
12. *El Sol de San Luis,* December 8, 1958.
13. President Adolfo López Mateos made this promise to Dr. Nava in a meeting a few days before the election.
14. *El Sol de San Luis,* December 15, 1958.
15. *Tribuna,* June 26, 1961.
16. Ibid., May 22 and afterwards in 1961.
17. Ibid. Violent activities are reported throughout the campaign and are summarized in the opposition paper on June 23, 1961.
18. Ibid., May 10, 1961.
19. For a description of all these events, see *Tribuna* during July 1961. Nava confirmed the accuracy of these reports.
20. Estrada M., *La Grieta en el Yugo,* pp. 239–43.
21. Dr. Rangel was Nava's campaign manager during the gubernatorial campaign.
22. *Proceso,* December 6, 1982, p. 21.
23. Ibid.
24. *El Sol de San Luis,* September 9, 1982.
25. Separate interviews on August 10, 1982, with PAN members, Alfredo Lujambio Rafols and Manuel Rivera del Campo. The former became director of finance in the Nava administration, while the latter was a member of the city council.
26. Interview with Manuel Rivera del Campo.
27. Interview on August 10, 1982.
28. An autonomous city is one of the themes of the Nava campaign. See the publication of the Frente Cívico Potosino, *Democratización de la Vida Municipal.*
29. See the headlines in *El Sol de San Luis* for the first three weeks of October.
30. *El Sol de San Luis,* November 5, 1982.

31. Ibid., November 6, 1982.
32. Ibid., November 7, 1982.
33. Ibid., November 8, 1982.
34. Ibid. See the articles in this newspaper for late October and early November, especially on the following dates: October 27, November 15 and 16.
35. *Proceso,* December 6, 1982, p. 21.
36. *El Sol de San Luis,* November 30, 1982.
37. Ibid., December 6, 1982.
38. *El Sol de San Luis,* December 8, 1982, p. 40. The opposition bought an ad to show the results they had obtained from the polling places in which they had trained observers.
39. Obviously, these meetings were not reported in the press, and thus informants had difficulty remembering the exact dates of such events. Fortunately, Dr. Nava's wife kept a detailed diary of many activities, and she graciously shared the diary with me.
40. *El Sol de San Luis,* December 12, 1982.
41. Ibid., December 13, 1982.
42. Manu Dornbierer, "El Doctor Nava o como le va a un Alcalde de la Oposición," *Siempre,* June 22, 1983. The writer ends his article with questions about whether Mexican officials really care about political reform. He also indicates disgust at President Miguel de la Madrid's failure to meet with Nava to work out difficulties between Nava and Governor Jonguitud.
43. México, Dirección General de Estadística, *VIII Censo General de Población, 1960, Estado de San Luis Potosí* (México, D.F., 1963) and México, Instituto Nacional de Estadística, *X Censo General de Población y Vivienda, 1980, Estado de San Luis Potosí* (México, D.F., 1983). The exact population given for this capital city in 1980 was 406,630, but virtually everyone in the opposition administration argued that the figure was closer to 500,000 because of the small communities in the metropolitan area which were dependent on the Nava administration.
44. This information was gathered in an interview with Alfredo Lujambio Rafols, the director of finance for the opposition administration.

Selected Bibliography on Mexican Politics

BOOKS

Alba, Francisco. *The Population of Mexico: Trends, Issues and Policies.* Translated by Marjory Mattingly Urquidi. New Brunswick, N.J.: Transaction Press, 1982.

Amaya, Juan Gualberto. *Los gobiernos de Obregón, Calles, y regímenes "peleles" derivados del callismo.* Mexico: Editorial del Autor, 1947.

Ayala Anguiano, Armando. *El día que perdió el PRI.* Mexico: Editorial Contenido, 1976.

Balam, Gilberto. *Tlatelolco: reflexiones de un testigo.* Mexico: pub. unknown, 1969.

Barchfield, J.W. *Agrarian Policy and National Development in Mexico.* New Brunswick, N.J.: Rutgers University Press, Transaction Books, 1978.

Basáñez, Miguel. *La lucha por la hegemonía en Mexico, 1968–1980.* Mexico City: Siglo Veintiuno Editores, 1982.

Bazant, Jan. *A Concise History of Mexico.* Cambridge: Cambridge University Press, 1977.

Bezdek, Robert R. *Electoral Oppositions in Mexico: Emergence, Suppression, and Impact on Political Processes.* Ph.D. diss., Ohio State University, 1973.

Roderic A. Camp. *Mexico's Leaders: Their Education and Recruitment.* Tucson: University of Arizona Press, 1980.

Cather, Willa. *Death Comes for the Archbishop.* New York: Vintage Books, 1971, originally published in 1927.

Carlos, Manuel L. *Politics and Development in Rural Mexico: A Study of Socioeconomic Modernization.* New York: Praeger, 1974.

Castillo, Heberto, and Francisco Paoli Bolio. *¿Porque un nuevo partido?* Mexico: Editorial Posada, 1975.

Chavira B., Carlos. *La otra cara de México.* Mexico: La Nación, 1966.

_____. *Macario Vázquez.* Mexico: Editorial Jus, 1968.

Cockroft, James. *Intellectual Precursors of the Mexican Revolution, 1900–1913.* Austin, Tex.: University of Texas Press, 1968.

Coleman, Kenneth M. *Public Opinion in Mexico City About the Electoral System.* James Sprunt Studies in History and Political Science, no. 53. Chapel Hill, N.C.: University of North Carolina, 1972.

Consejo Nacional de Huelga. *El móndrigo.* Mexico: Editorial Alba Roja, 1968. (Note: this unauthored book is believed to have been commissioned by President Díaz Ordaz himself to help cast the blame for the Tlatelolco massacre on other members of his own regime).

Cornelius, Wayne A. *Mexican Migration to the United States: Causes, Consequences, and U.S. Responses.* Cambridge, Mass.: Massachusetts Institute of Technology Center for International Studies, 1978.

_____. *Politics and the Migrant Poor in Mexico City.* Stanford, Calif.: Stanford University Press, 1975.

Cosí Villegas, Daniel. *El estilo personal de gobernar.* Mexico: Joaquín Mortiz, 1974.

_____. *El sistema político mexicano.* Mexico: Joaquín Mortiz, 1972.

_____. *Historia moderna de México.* 8 volumes. Mexico: Editorial Hermes, 1948–65.

_____. *La sucesión: desenlace y perspectivas.* Mexico: Joaquín Mortiz, 1975.

_____. *La sucesión presidencial.* Mexico: Joaquín Mortiz, 1974.

Costello, Gerald M. *Mission to Latin America.* Maryknoll, N.Y.: Orbis Books, 1979.

Cross, Harry E. and James A. Sandos. *Across the Border.* Berkeley: University of California Institute of Governmental Studies, 1981.

Cumberland, Charles C. *Mexico: The Struggle for Modernity.* New York: Oxford University Press, 1968.

Dedera, Don and Bob Robles. *Goodbye García Adios.* Flagstaff, Ariz.: Northland Press, 1976.

Domínguez, Jorge, ed. *Mexico's Political Economy: Challenges at Home and Abroad.* Beverly Hills: Sage Publications, 1982.

Fagen, Richard R., and William S. Tuohy. *Politics and Privilege in a Mexican City.* Stanford, Calif.: Stanford University Press, 1972.

Fuentes, Carlos. *Terra Nostra.* Mexico: Joaquín Mortiz, 1975.

Fuentes Díaz, Vicente. *Los Partidos Políticos en México.* Mexico: Editorial Altiplano, 1972.

Galicia, Alejandro de. *De visita en la prisión.* 3d ed. Mexico: Costa-Amic, 1975.

García Cantú, Gastón. *El Socialismo en México, Siglo XIX.* Mexico: Era, 1969.

_____. *La Hora de los Halcones.* Puebla: Universidad Autónoma de Puebla, 1976.

García Rivas, Heriberto. *Breve historia de la revolución mexicana.* Mexico: Editorial Diana, 1964.

González Casanova, Pablo. *La democracia en México.* Mexico: Ediciones Era, 1965.

González de la Garza, Mauricio. *Última llamada.* Editores Asociados Mexicanos, 1981.

González González, José. *Lo negro del Negro Durazo.* Mexico: Editorial Posadas, 1983.

González Morfín, Efraín. *El cambio social y el PAN.* Mexico: Ediciones de Accion Nacional, 1975.

Grayson, George W. *The Politics of Mexican Oil.* Pittsburgh: University of Pittsburgh Press, 1981.

Grindle, Merilee S. *Bureaucrats, Politicians, and Peasants in Mexico: A Case Study in Public Policy.* Berkeley and Los Angeles: University of California Press, 1977.

Gyles, Ana and Chloe Sayer. *Of Gods and Men: The Heritage of Ancient Mexico.* New York: Harper & Row, 1980.

Hansen, Roger D. *The Politics of Mexican Development.* Baltimore: Johns Hopkins Press, 1971.

Hellman, Judith Adler. *Mexico in Crisis.* New York: Holmes & Meier, 1978.

Howe, Irving, ed. *Democracy and Dictatorship in Latin America.* New York: Foundation for Study of Independent Social Ideas, 1982.

Huntington, Samuel P. *Political Order in Changing Societies.* New Haven, Conn.: Yale University Press, 1968.

Johnson, Kenneth F. *Mexican Democracy: A Critical View.* Rev. ed. New York: Praeger Publishers, 1978.

Johnson, Kenneth F. and Miles W. Williams. *Illegal Aliens in the Western Hemisphere.* New York: Praeger Publishers, 1981.

Johnson, William Weber. *Heroic Mexico.* New York: Doubleday, 1968.

Kamstra, Jerry. *Weed: Adventures of a Dope Smuggler.* New York: Bantam, 1975.

Kiser, George D. and Martha Woody Kiser, eds. *Mexican Workers in the United States.* Albuquerque: University of New Mexico Press, 1979.

Ladman, Jerry R., et al. eds. *U.S.–Mexican Energy Relationships: Realities and Prospects.* Lexington, Mass.: Lexington Books, 1981.

Lafaye, Jacques. *Quetzalcóatl and Guadalupe: The Formation of Mexican National Consciousness 1531–1813.* Chicago: University of Chicago Press, 1976.

Leñero, Vicente. *Los periodistas.* Mexico City: Editorial Joaquín Mortiz, 1978.

Levinson, Jerome and Juan de Onís. *The Alliance that Lost its Way.* Chicago: Quadrangle Books, 1970.

Levy, Daniel and Gabriel Székely. *Mexico: Paradoxes of Stability and Change.* Boulder, Colo.: Westview Press, 1983.

Lewis, Oscar. *The Children of Sánchez.* New York: Random House, 1961.

López, Jaime. *10 años de guerrillas en México.* Mexico: Editorial Posada, 1974.

Mabry, Donald J. *Mexico's Accion Nacional: A Catholic Alternative to Revolution.* Syracuse, N.Y.: Syracuse University Press, 1973.

Martínez Verdugo, Arnoldo. *Crisis política y alternativa comunista.* Mexico City: Ediciones de Cultura Popular, 1979.

Medina Valdés, Gerardo. *Operación 10 de junio.* Mexico: Ediciones Universo, 1972.

Menéndez Rodríguez, Mario. *Yucatán o el genocidio.* Mexico: Fondo de Cultura Popular, 1964.

Meyer, Michael C. and William L. Sherman. *The Course of Mexican History*. New York: Oxford University Press, 1979.

Monroy Rivera, Oscar. *A la espera del día (frontera sin agua)*. Mexico: Costa-Amic, 1975.

_____. *El Mexicano enano*. Mexico: Editorial Diana, 1967.

_____. *El profeta del silencio*. Mexico: Costa-Amic, 1974; Editorial Diana, 1975.

_____. *El señor presidente de Enanonia*. Mexico: Costa-Amic, 1973.

_____. *México y su vivencia dramática en el pensamiento vasconcelista*. Mexico: Editorial Diana, 1975.

_____. *Sonora: en torno al valor de mi pueblo*. Mexico: Editorial Libros de Mexico: 1967.

Mora, Juan Miguel de. *Mexico país del miedo*. Mexico: Anaya Editores, 1981.

_____. *Por la gracia del señor presidente (México: la gran mentira)*. Mexico: Editores Asociados, 1975.

Natividad Rosales, José. *La Muerte de Lucio Cabañas*. Mexico: Editorial Posada, 1975.

_____. *¿Quién es Lucio Cabañas?* Mexico: Editorial Posada, 1974.

Needler, Martin C. *Politics and Society in Mexico*. Albuquerque, N.M.: University of New Mexico Press, 1971.

Padgett, L.V. *The Mexican Political System*. 2nd ed. Boston: Houghton Mifflin, 1976.

Padilla, Juan Ignacio. *El sinarquismo*. 2d ed. Mexico: Ediciones UNS, 1953.

Paz, Octavio. *El laberinto de la soledad*. Mexico: Fondo de Cultura Economica, 1959.

_____. *Posdata*. Mexico: Siglo Veintiuno Editores, 1970.

_____. *El arco y la lira*. Mexico: Fondo de Cultura Económica, 1972.

Pérez Chowell, José. *Requiem para un ideal: la liga 23 de septiembre*. Mexico: Editorial V Siglos, 1977.

Porfirio Miranda, José. *El cristianismo de Marx.* Mexico: Editorial del Autor, 1978.

Price, John A. *Tijuana: Urbanization in a Border Culture.* Notre Dame, Ind.: University of Notre Dame Press, 1973.

Purcell, Susan Kaufman. *The Mexican Profit-Sharing Decision: Politics in an Authoritarian Regime.* Berkeley and Los Angeles, Calif.: University of California Press, 1975.

Ramos, Samuel. *Profile of Man and Culture in Mexico.* Pan American Paperbacks Series. Austin, Tex.: University of Texas Press, 1962.

Reyna, José Luis and Richard S. Weinert, eds. *Authoritarianism in Mexico.* Philadelphia, Penn.: Institute for the Study of Human Issues, 1977.

Reynolds, Clark W. *The Mexican Economy: Twentieth-Century Structure and Growth.* New Haven, Conn.: Yale University Press, 1970.

Riggs, Fred W. *Administration in Developing Countries: The Theory of Prismatic Society.* Boston: Houghton Mifflin, 1965.

Rios-Bustamante, Antonio, ed. *Mexican Immigrant Workers in the United States.* Los Angeles: UCLA, 1981.

Rivanuva, Gastón. *El PRI: El Gran Mito Mexicano.* Mexico: Editorial Tradición, 1974.

Ronfeldt, David. *Atencingo: The Politics of Agrarian Struggle in a Mexican Ejido.* Stanford, Calif.: Stanford University Press, 1973.

Ross, Stanley, ed. *Is the Mexican Revolution Dead?* New York: Knopf, 1966.

_____, ed. *Views Across the Border: The United States and Mexico.* Albuquerque, N.M.: University of New Mexico Press, 1977.

Rulfo, Juan. *The Burning Plain.* Austin: University of Texas Press, 1967.

Samora, Julian. *Los Mojados: The Wetback Story.* Notre Dame, Ind.: University of Notre Dame Press, 1971.

Sanderson, Steven E. *Agrarian Populism and the Mexican State: The Struggle for Land in Sonora.* Berkeley: University of California Press, 1981.

Scott, Robert E. *Mexican Government in Transition.* Urbana, Ill.: University of Illinois Press, 1964.

Sepúlveda, Bernardo and Antonio Chumacero. *La Inversión Extranjera en México*. Mexico: Fondo de Cultura Económico, 1973.

Shafer, Robert and Donald Mabry. *Neighbors: Mexico and the United States*. Chicago: Nelson-Hall, 1981.

Siller Rodríguez, Rodolfo. *La crisis del Partido Revolucionario Institucional*. Mexico: Costa-Amic, 1976.

Silva Herzog, Jesús. *Breve Historia de la Revolución Mexicana*. 2d. ed. de Cultura Económico, 2 vols. Mexico: Fondo, 1972.

Smith, Peter. *Labyrinths of Power: Political Recruitment in Twentieth Century Mexico*. Princeton, N.J.: Princeton University Press, 1979.

Spota, Luis. *La plaza*. Mexico: Joaquín Mortiz, 1972.

———— *Palabras mayores*. Mexico: Editorial Grijalbo, 1975.

Stavenhagen, Rodolfo. *Sociología y Subdesarrollo*. Mexico: Nuestro Tiempo, 1972.

Stevens, Evelyn P. *Protest and Response in Mexico*. Cambridge, Mass.: MIT Press, 1974.

Stoddard, Ellwyn R., Oscar J. Martínez, and Miguel Angel Martínez Lasso. *El Paso–Ciudad Juárez Relations and the "Tortilla Curtain."* El Paso: El Paso Council on the Arts and Humanities, 1979.

Tannenbaum, Frank. *Peace by Revolution–An Interpretation of Mexico*. New York: Columbia University Press, 1933.

Usigli, Rodolfo. *El gesticulador*. 2d ed. New York: Appleton-Century-Crofts, 1963 (first edition 1937).

Valadés, José C. *El presidente de México en 1970*. Mexico: Editores Mexicanos Unidos, 1969.

Vasconcelos, José. *La raza cósmica*. Mexico: Austral, 1948.

Vaughan, Mary Kay, *The State, Education, and Social Class in Mexico, 1880–1928*. DeKalb, Ill.: Northern Illinois University Press, 1982.

Von Sauer, Franz A. *The Alienated "Loyal" Opposition*. Albuquerque, N.M.: University of New Mexico Press, 1974.

Weaver, Thomas, and Theodore Downing. *Mexican Migration*. Tucson, Ariz.: University of Arizona Press, 1976.

Wesson, Robert. *Democracy in Latin America: Promise and Problems*. New York: Praeger Publishers, 1982.

Wilkie, James W. *The Mexican Revolution: Federal Expenditure and Social Change Since 1910*. Berkeley: University of California Press, 1967.

Williams, Edward. *The Rebirth of the Mexican Petroleum Industry*. Lexington, Mass.: Lexington Books, 1979.

Womack, John, Jr. *Zapata and the Mexican Revolution*. New York: Vintage, 1969.

van Ginneken, Wouter. *Socioeconomic Groups and Income Distribution in Mexico*. New York: St. Martin's Press, 1980.

Zubirán, Salvador, et al. *La desnutrición del mexicano*. Mexico: Fondo de Cultura Económica, 1974.

SELECTED ARTICLES

Alisky, Marvin. "CONASUPO: A Mexican Agency Which Makes Low Income Workers Feel Their Government Cares." *Inter-American* Economic Affairs 27 (Winter 1973): 47–59.

_____. "Migration and Unemployment in Mexico," *Current History* 82 (December, 1983): 429–432.

Ayres, Robert L. "Development Policy and the Possibility of a 'Livable' Future for Latin America." *American Political Science Review* 69 (June 1975): 507–25.

Bailey, John J. "Agrarian Reform in Mexico: The Quest for Self-Sufficiency." *Current History* 80 (November, 1981): 357–60.

Bizzarro, Salvatore. "Mexico's Poor." *Current History* 80 (November, 1981): 370–73.

Camp, Roderic A. "A Reexamination of Political Leadership and Allocation of Federal Revenues in Mexico, 1934–73." *The Journal of Developing Areas* 10 (January, 1976): 193–211.

_____. "Losers in Mexican Politics: A Comparative Study of Official Party Pre-candidates for Gubernatorial Elections, 1970–75." In *Quantitative Latin American Studies,* edited by James W. Wilkie and Kenneth Ruddle. Los Angeles: UCLA Latin American Center, 1977.

Coleman, Kenneth M., and Charles L. Davis. "Preemptive Reform and the Mexican Working Class." *Latin American Research Review* XVIII (1983): 3–32.

_____ and John Wanant. "On Measuring Mexican Presidential Ideology Through Budgets: A Reappraisal of the Wilkie Approach." *Latin American Research Review* 10 (Spring, 1975): 77–88.

Cornelius, Wayne A. "Urbanization and Political Demand Making: Political Participation Among the Migrant Poor in Latin American Cities." *American Political Science Review* 68 (September, 1974): 1125–46.

Craig, Richard. "La Campaña Permanente: Mexico's Antidrug Campaign." *Journal of Interamerican Studies and World Affairs* 20 (1978): 107–132.

_____. "Operation Condor." *Journal of Interamerican Studies and World Affairs* 22 (1980): 345–64.

Elliott, J.H. "The Triumph of the Virgin of Guadalupe." *The New York Review of Books* (May 26, 1977): 28–30.

Fallows, James. "Immigration." *The Atlantic Monthly* Vol. 252, No. 5 (November, 1983): pp. 45-96.

Fernández Kelly, María Patricia. "Alternative Education for Maquiladora Workers." *Grassroots Development* 6 (Winter–Spring, 1982): 41–45.

Fuentes, Carlos. "Mexico and its Demons." *The New York Review of Books* (September 20, 1973): 16–21.

Garibay, Ricardo. "El hambre: un horizonte negro nos espera." *Proceso* 2 (August, 1977): A three part series.

González Gollaz, Ignacio. "La posibilidad de JLP." *Visión* (June 1, 1976): 37–41.

González Schmal, Raúl. "Las elecciones y la crisis del sistema." A paper presented at the reunion of SOLIDARISMO on June 12, 1982, mimeographed.

Grayson, George W. "Oil and Politics in Mexico." *Current History* 81 (February 1982): 379–83.

_____. "Oil and Politics in Mexico." *Current History* 82 (December, 1983): 415–19.

Grimes, C.E., and Charles E.P. Simmons. "Bureaucracy and Political Control in Mexico: Towards an Assessment." *Public Administration Review* 29 (January–February 1969): 72–79.

Hill, Kim Quaile and Patricia A. Hurley. "Freedom of the Press in Latin America: A Thirty-Year Survey." *Latin American Research Review* 15 (1980): 212–18.

Isla, Manuel de la. "Porque fracasa la CONASUPO" *Por Qué* (April 10, 1968): 6–14.

Johnson, Kenneth F. "Ideological Correlates of Right Wing Political Alienation in Mexico." *The American Political Science Review* 59 (September, 1965): 656–64.

_____. "Research Perspective on the Revised Fitzgibbon—Johnson Index of the Image of Political Democracy in Latin America, 1945–75." In *Quantitative Latin American Studies: Methods and Findings,* edited by James W. Wilkie and Kenneth Ruddle. Los Angeles: UCLA Latin American Center, 1977.

_____. "The 1980 Image-Index Survey of Latin American Political Democracy." *Latin American Research Review* 27 (1982): 193–201.

Johnson, Kenneth F. and Miles W. Williams. "Power, Democracy, and Intervention in Latin American Political Life." Tempe: Arizona State University, Center for Latin American Studies, 1978.

Koslow, Lawrence E., and Stephen P. Mumme. "The Evolution of the Mexican Political System: A Paradigmatic Analysis." In *The Future of Mexico,* edited by Lawrence Koslow. Tempe: Arizona State University Press, 1979.

_____ and Rodney R. Jones. "The Mexican-American Border Industrialization Program." *Public Affairs Bulletin* 9 (1970): 1–5. Published by Arizona State University Institute of Public Administration.

Krauze, Enrique. "The Intellectuals and Society." In *Democracy and Dictatorship in Latin America,* edited by Irving Howe. New York: Foundation for Study of Independent Social Ideas, 1982.

Lyons, Gene. "Inside the Volcano." *Harpers* 254 (June, 1977): 41–46.

Mares, David. "Agricultural Trade: Domestic Interests and Transnational Relations." In *Mexico's Political Economy,* edited by Jorge Domínguez. Beverly Hills: Sage Publications, 1982.

Mayenz Puente, Samuel. "Matices de la mordida." *Proceso* 2 (November 21, 1977): 38–39.

Maza, Enrique. "Estrangulamiento de la conciencia política." *Proceso* 2 (15 de enero de 1977): 40–41.

McCoy, Terry L. "A Paradigmatic Analysis of Mexican Population Policy." In *The Dynamics of Population Policy in Latin America,* edited by Terry L. McCoy. Cambridge, Mass.: Ballinger, 1974.

Monson, Robert A. "Political Stability in Mexico: The Changing Role of Traditional Rightists." *Journal of Politics* 35 (August, 1973): 594–614.

Mullins, Willard A. "On the Concept of Ideology in Political Science." *The American Political Science Review* 66 (June 1972): 498–510.

Mumme, Stephen. "Disputing Hidden Waters: Dimensions of Groundwater Conflict on the Border." In *Border Perspectives: A Special Issue* Vol. 9, 1984.

O'Donnell, Guillermo. "Reflections on the Patterns of Change in the Bureaucratic-Authoritarian State." *Latin American Research Review* 13 (1978): 3–38.

Paz, Octavio. "Latin America and Democracy." In *Democracy and Dictatorship in Latin America,* edited by Irving Howe. New York: Foundation for Study of Independent Social Ideas, 1982.

Poitras, Guy E. "Welfare Bureaucracy and Clientele Politics in Mexico." *Administrative Science Quarterly* 18 (March, 1973): 18–26.

Purcell, Susan Kaufman, ed. *Mexico–United States Relations.* Proceedings of the Academy of Political Science 34. New York: Academy of Political Science, 1981.

Reyna, José Luis. "Redefining the Authoritarian Regime." In *Authoritarianism in Mexico,* edited by José Luis Reyna and Richard S. Weinert. Philadelphia: Institute for the Study of Human Issues, 1977.

Sanderson, Steven E., "Political Tensions in the Mexican Party System," *Current History* 82 (December, 1983): 401–5.

Staff of *The Arizona Daily Star.* "Compadres in Crisis." Special report, May 22, 1983.

Staff of *The El Paso Herald-Post.* "Special Report: The Border." Summer, 1983.

Stalker, Peter. "La elección de los emigrantes." *Boletín informativo sobre asuntos migratorios y fronterizos.* December, 1982.

Stevens, Evelyn P. "Legality and Extra-Legality in Mexico." *Journal of Interamerican Studies and World Affairs* 12 (January 1970): 62–75.

_____. "Mexican Machismo: Politics and Value Orientations." *The Western Political Quarterly* (December, 1965): 848–57.

_____. "Protest Movements in an Authoritarian Regime: The Mexican Case." *Comparative Politics* 7 (April, 1975): 361–82.

Tavares, Flavio. "The Shame of Mexico: Corruption and Mismanagement Amid a Sea of Oil." *World Press Review* 30, no. 8 (1983): 26–28.

Tomasek, Robert D. "United States–Mexican Relations: Blowout of the Mexican Oil Well Ixtoc I." A paper presented at the 23rd Annual Conference of the Western Social Science Association, San Diego, Calif.: April 23–25, 1981.

Tuohy, William S. "Psychology in Political Analysis: the Case of Mexico." *The Western Political Quarterly* 27 (June, 1974): 289–307.

Vargas, Armando. "Coup at Excelsior." *Columbia Journalism Review* 15 (1967): 45–48.

Vázquez Amaral, José. "Democracia mexicana." *Diorama Excelsior.* May 23, 1982, p. 2.

Villarreal, René. "The Policy of Import-Substituting Industrialization, 1929–75." In *Authoritarianism in Mexico,* edited by José Luis Reyna and Richard S. Weinert. Philadelphia: Institute for the Study of Human Issues, 1977.

Wilkie, James W. "On Quantitative History: the Poverty Index for Mexico." *Latin American Research Review* 10 (Spring, 1975): 63–75.

Index

About the Author

Since receiving the doctoral degree in political science at UCLA in 1963 Kenneth F. Johnson has been known for his humanistic approach to the study of political life in Latin America. His works have appeared in the *American Political Science Review,* the *Latin American Research Review,* and other journals published in both Latin America and the United States. His field studies have included extended visits to Argentina, Bolivia, Colombia, Guatemala, Mexico, and Nicaragua. In recent years Dr. Johnson has specialized in inter-American population transfer leading to publication of *Illegal Aliens in the Western Hemisphere* (co-authored by Miles W. Williams) which appeared in 1981. For his work on clandestine migration Johnson has been recognized by the Canadian government and was named Great Plains Fellow specializing in Hispanic minorities by Emporia State University of Kansas. Currently he is on leave as Professor of Political Science at the University of Missouri-St. Louis and is visiting scholar and lecturer at Wichita State University of Kansas.